David S. Allen
1199 Lawrence St.
Lowell, MA 01852
pahson@earthlink.net

EZEKIEL

Brazos Theological Commentary on the Bible

Series Editors

R. R. Reno, General Editor
Creighton University
Omaha, Nebraska

Robert W. Jenson
Center of Theological Inquiry
Princeton, New Jersey

Robert Louis Wilken
University of Virginia
Charlottesville, Virginia

Ephraim Radner
Ascension Episcopal Church
Pueblo, Colorado

Michael Root
Lutheran Theological Southern Seminary
Columbia, South Carolina

George Sumner
Wycliffe College
Toronto, Ontario

EZEKIEL

ROBERT W. JENSON

BrazosPress

a division of Baker Publishing Group
Grand Rapids, Michigan

©2009 by Robert Jenson

Published by Brazos Press
a division of Baker Publishing Group
P.O. Box 6287, Grand Rapids, MI 49516-6287
www.brazospress.com

Printed in the United States of America

Library of Congress Cataloging-in-Publication Data
Jenson, Robert W.
    Ezekiel / Robert Jenson.
       p.   cm. — (Brazos theological commentary on the Bible)
    Includes bibliographical references (p   ) and indexes.
    ISBN 978-1-58743-166-1 (cloth)
    1. Bible. O. T. Ezekiel—Commentaries. I. Title.
BS1545.53.J46 2009
224′.407—dc22   2008054798

For all the former students whom I exhorted
to preach and teach the Old Testament

CONTENTS

Series Preface 9

Abbreviations 15

Introduction 17

1:1–3	A Double Call *31*
1:4–24	The Theophany *36*
1:25–28b	The Man on the Throne *41*
1:28c–3:15	Ordination and Commission *46*
3:16–21	The Sentinel *50*
3:22–5:4	Signs of the Siege and Fall of Jerusalem *54*
5:5–17	Jerusalem's Disaster *59*
6:1–14	You Shall Know . . . *64*
7:1–9	An End! *69*
7:10–27	The Day *73*
8:1–18	Idolatry *78*
9:1–11	The Destroyers *83*
10:1–22; 11:22–25	The Glory Departs *88*
11:1–13	The Power of the Word *92*
11:14–21	A New Heart *96*
12:1–16	Into Exile *100*
12:17–20	Desolations Again *104*
12:21–28	On Ignoring Prophecy *106*
13:1–23	Black Words and Sacraments *111*
14:1–11	The Sign of Jonah *116*
14:12–23	The Lord's Theodicy *120*

15:1–8	The Vine-Branch *124*
16:1–43	The Wayward Bride *126*
16:44–63	Sisters *132*
17:1–21	Eagles and Their Plantings *137*
17:22–24	The Lord as Eagle *141*
18:1–32	It's Not Fair! *144*
19:1–14	The Death of the House of David *150*
20:1–31	A Strange History of Salvation *154*
20:32–44	A Final Exodus *160*
20:45–21:7	The Sword, Part 1 *164*
21:8–17	The Sword, Part 2 *167*
21:18–27	The Sword, Part 3 *170*
21:28–32	The Sword, Part 4 *174*
22:1–16	The City of Blood *177*
22:17–22	The Wrathful Refiner *181*
22:23–31	After the Day *185*
23:1–27	Oholah and Oholibah *189*
23:28–49	The Sisters Again *194*
24:1–14	The Cooking Pot *198*
24:15–27	No Mourning *202*
25:1–17	Bad Neighbors *206*
26:1–21	The Fall of Tyre *210*

27:1–36   It Was Sad When the Great Ship Went Down *215*

28:1–19   The Downfall of Divine Kingship *218*

28:20–26   Farewell to the Six *223*

29:1–16   The Crocodile *227*

29:17–21   Nebuchadnezzar's Dubious Consolation *230*

30:1–19   The Day—for Egypt *233*

30:20–26   *Larva Dei* *236*

31:1–18   The Great Tree *240*

32:1–16   The Crocodile Larger than Life *244*

32:17–32   *Descendit ad Inferna* *248*

33:1–20   I Have No Pleasure in the Death of the Wicked *253*

33:21–22   Silence *256*

33:23–33   Cheap Grace *259*

34:1–31   The Good Shepherd *263*

35:1–36:15   The Mountains of Edom and Israel *269*

36:16–38   What Then? *275*

37:1–14   Can These Bones Live? *281*

37:15–28   One Holy . . . *286*

38:1–39:20   Gog *290*

39:21–29   Law and Gospel *296*

40:1–42:20   The Plan of God's House *299*

43:1–12   The Glory Returns *305*

43:13–17   The Altar *309*

44:1–3   The Locked Gate and the Prince *313*

44:4–31   Purity for the Temple *315*

45:1–8   The Holy District *320*

45:9–25   The Prince and the Offerings *323*

46:1–18   The Prince and the People *327*

46:19–24   The Holy and the Common *331*

47:1–12   The River of the Water of Life *334*

47:13–48:29   Theological Geography *338*

48:30–35   יהוה/There *343*

Bibliography *347*

Subject Index *349*

Scripture Index *359*

SERIES PREFACE

Near the beginning of his treatise against Gnostic interpretations of the Bible, *Against the Heresies*, Irenaeus observes that Scripture is like a great mosaic depicting a handsome king. It is as if we were owners of a villa in Gaul who had ordered a mosaic from Rome. It arrives, and the beautifully colored tiles need to be taken out of their packaging and put into proper order according to the plan of the artist. The difficulty, of course, is that Scripture provides us with the individual pieces, but the order and sequence of various elements are not obvious. The Bible does not come with instructions that would allow interpreters to simply place verses, episodes, images, and parables in order as a worker might follow a schematic drawing in assembling the pieces to depict the handsome king. The mosaic must be puzzled out. This is precisely the work of scriptural interpretation.

Origen has his own image to express the difficulty of working out the proper approach to reading the Bible. When preparing to offer a commentary on the Psalms he tells of a tradition handed down to him by his Hebrew teacher:

> The Hebrew said that the whole divinely inspired Scripture may be likened, because of its obscurity, to many locked rooms in our house. By each room is placed a key, but not the one that corresponds to it, so that the keys are scattered about beside the rooms, none of them matching the room by which it is placed. It is a difficult task to find the keys and match them to the rooms that they can open. We therefore know the Scriptures that are obscure only by taking the points of departure for understanding them from another place because they have their interpretive principle scattered among them.[1]

---

1. Fragment from the preface to *Commentary on Psalms 1–25*, preserved in the *Philokalia* (trans. Joseph W. Trigg; London: Routledge, 1998), 70–71.

As is the case for Irenaeus, scriptural interpretation is not purely local. The key in Genesis may best fit the door of Isaiah, which in turn opens up the meaning of Matthew. The mosaic must be put together with an eye toward the overall plan.

Irenaeus, Origen, and the great cloud of premodern biblical interpreters assumed that puzzling out the mosaic of Scripture must be a communal project. The Bible is vast, heterogeneous, full of confusing passages and obscure words, and difficult to understand. Only a fool would imagine that he or she could work out solutions alone. The way forward must rely upon a tradition of reading that Irenaeus reports has been passed on as the rule or canon of truth that functions as a confession of faith. "Anyone," he says, "who keeps unchangeable in himself the rule of truth received through baptism will recognize the names and sayings and parables of the scriptures."[2] Modern scholars debate the content of the rule on which Irenaeus relies and commends, not the least because the terms and formulations Irenaeus himself uses shift and slide. Nonetheless, Irenaeus assumes that there is a body of apostolic doctrine sustained by a tradition of teaching in the church. This doctrine provides the clarifying principles that guide exegetical judgment toward a coherent overall reading of Scripture as a unified witness. Doctrine, then, is the schematic drawing that will allow the reader to organize the vast heterogeneity of the words, images, and stories of the Bible into a readable, coherent whole. It is the rule that guides us toward the proper matching of keys to doors.

If self-consciousness about the role of history in shaping human consciousness makes modern historical-critical study critical, then what makes modern study of the Bible modern is the consensus that classical Christian doctrine distorts interpretive understanding. Benjamin Jowett, the influential nineteenth-century English classical scholar, is representative. In his programmatic essay "On the Interpretation of Scripture," he exhorts the biblical reader to disengage from doctrine and break its hold over the interpretive imagination. "The simple words of that book," writes Jowett of the modern reader, "he tries to preserve absolutely pure from the refinements or distinctions of later times." The modern interpreter wishes to "clear away the remains of dogmas, systems, controversies, which are encrusted upon" the words of Scripture. The disciplines of close philological analysis "would enable us to separate the elements of doctrine and tradition with which the meaning of Scripture is encumbered in our own day."[3] The lens of understanding must be wiped clear of the hazy and distorting film of doctrine.

Postmodernity, in turn, has encouraged us to criticize the critics. Jowett imagined that when he wiped away doctrine he would encounter the biblical text in its purity and uncover what he called "the original spirit and intention of the authors."[4] We are not now so sanguine, and the postmodern mind thinks

---

2. *Against Heresies* 9.4.

3. Benjamin Jowett, "On the Interpretation of Scripture," in *Essays and Reviews* (London: Parker, 1860), 338–39.

4. Ibid., 340.

interpretive frameworks inevitable. Nonetheless, we tend to remain modern in at least one sense. We read Athanasius and think him stage-managing the diversity of Scripture to support his positions against the Arians. We read Bernard of Clairvaux and assume that his monastic ideals structure his reading of the Song of Songs. In the wake of the Reformation, we can see how the doctrinal divisions of the time shaped biblical interpretation. Luther famously described the Epistle of James as a "strawy letter," for, as he said, "it has nothing of the nature of the Gospel about it."[5] In these and many other instances, often written in the heat of ecclesiastical controversy or out of the passion of ascetic commitment, we tend to think Jowett correct: doctrine is a distorting film on the lens of understanding.

However, is what we commonly think actually the case? Are readers naturally perceptive? Do we have an unblemished, reliable aptitude for the divine? Have we no need for disciplines of vision? Do our attention and judgment need to be trained, especially as we seek to read Scripture as the living word of God? According to Augustine, we all struggle to journey toward God, who is our rest and peace. Yet our vision is darkened and the fetters of worldly habit corrupt our judgment. We need training and instruction in order to cleanse our minds so that we might find our way toward God.[6] To this end, "the whole temporal dispensation was made by divine Providence for our salvation."[7] The covenant with Israel, the coming of Christ, the gathering of the nations into the church—all these things are gathered up into the rule of faith, and they guide the vision and form of the soul toward the end of fellowship with God. In Augustine's view, the reading of Scripture both contributes to and benefits from this divine pedagogy. With countless variations in both exegetical conclusions and theological frameworks, the same pedagogy of a doctrinally ruled reading of Scripture characterizes the broad sweep of the Christian tradition from Gregory the Great through Bernard and Bonaventure, continuing across Reformation differences in both John Calvin and Cornelius Lapide, Patrick Henry and Bishop Bossuet, and on to more recent figures such as Karl Barth and Hans Urs von Balthasar.

Is doctrine, then, not a moldering scrim of antique prejudice obscuring the Bible, but instead a clarifying agent, an enduring tradition of theological judgments that amplifies the living voice of Scripture? And what of the scholarly dispassion advocated by Jowett? Is a noncommitted reading, an interpretation unprejudiced, the way toward objectivity, or does it simply invite the languid intellectual apathy that stands aside to make room for the false truism and easy answers of the age?

This series of biblical commentaries was born out of the conviction that dogma clarifies rather than obscures. The Brazos Theological Commentary on the Bible advances upon the assumption that the Nicene tradition, in all its diversity and

5. *Luther's Works*, vol. 35 (ed. E. Theodore Bachmann; Philadelphia: Fortress, 1959), 362.
6. *On Christian Doctrine* 1.10.
7. *On Christian Doctrine* 1.35.

controversy, provides the proper basis for the interpretation of the Bible as Christian Scripture. God the Father Almighty, who sends his only begotten Son to die for us and for our salvation and who raises the crucified Son in the power of the Holy Spirit so that the baptized may be joined in one body—faith in *this* God with *this* vocation of love for the world is the lens through which to view the heterogeneity and particularity of the biblical texts. Doctrine, then, is not a moldering scrim of antique prejudice obscuring the meaning of the Bible. It is a crucial aspect of the divine pedagogy, a clarifying agent for our minds fogged by self-deceptions, a challenge to our languid intellectual apathy that will too often rest in false truisms and the easy spiritual nostrums of the present age rather than search more deeply and widely for the dispersed keys to the many doors of Scripture.

For this reason, the commentators in this series have not been chosen because of their historical or philological expertise. In the main, they are not biblical scholars in the conventional, modern sense of the term. Instead, the commentators were chosen because of their knowledge of and expertise in using the Christian doctrinal tradition. They are qualified by virtue of the doctrinal formation of their mental habits, for it is the conceit of this series of biblical commentaries that theological training in the Nicene tradition prepares one for biblical interpretation, and thus it is to theologians and not biblical scholars that we have turned. "War is too important," it has been said, "to leave to the generals."

We do hope, however, that readers do not draw the wrong impression. The Nicene tradition does not provide a set formula for the solution of exegetical problems. The great tradition of Christian doctrine was not transcribed, bound in folio, and issued in an official, critical edition. We have the Niceno-Constantinopolitan Creed, used for centuries in many traditions of Christian worship. We have ancient baptismal affirmations of faith. The Chalcedonian definition and the creeds and canons of other church councils have their places in official church documents. Yet the rule of faith cannot be limited to a specific set of words, sentences, and creeds. It is instead a pervasive habit of thought, the animating culture of the church in its intellectual aspect. As Augustine observed, commenting on Jeremiah 31:33, "The creed is learned by listening; it is written, not on stone tablets nor on any material, but on the heart."[8] This is why Irenaeus is able to appeal to the rule of faith more than a century before the first ecumenical council, and this is why we need not itemize the contents of the Nicene tradition in order to appeal to its potency and role in the work of interpretation.

Because doctrine is intrinsically fluid on the margins and most powerful as a habit of mind rather than a list of propositions, this commentary series cannot settle difficult questions of method and content at the outset. The editors of the series impose no particular method of doctrinal interpretation. We cannot say in advance how doctrine helps the Christian reader assemble the mosaic of Scripture. We have no clear answer to the question of whether exegesis guided by

8. *Sermon* 212.2.

doctrine is antithetical to or compatible with the now-old modern methods of historical-critical inquiry. Truth—historical, mathematical, or doctrinal—knows no contradiction. But method is a discipline of vision and judgment, and we cannot know in advance what aspects of historical-critical inquiry are functions of modernism that shape the soul to be at odds with Christian discipline. Still further, the editors do not hold the commentators to any particular hermeneutical theory that specifies how to define the plain sense of Scripture—or the role this plain sense should play in interpretation. Here the commentary series is tentative and exploratory.

Can we proceed in any other way? European and North American intellectual culture has been de-Christianized. The effect has not been a cessation of Christian activity. Theological work continues. Sermons are preached. Biblical scholars turn out monographs. Church leaders have meetings. But each dimension of a formerly unified Christian practice now tends to function independently. It is as if a weakened army had been fragmented, and various corps had retreated to isolated fortresses in order to survive. Theology has lost its competence in exegesis. Scripture scholars function with minimal theological training. Each decade finds new theories of preaching to cover the nakedness of seminary training that provides theology without exegesis and exegesis without theology.

Not the least of the causes of the fragmentation of Christian intellectual practice has been the divisions of the church. Since the Reformation, the role of the rule of faith in interpretation has been obscured by polemics and counterpolemics about *sola scriptura* and the necessity of a magisterial teaching authority. The Brazos Theological Commentary on the Bible series is deliberately ecumenical in scope, because the editors are convinced that early church fathers were correct: church doctrine does not compete with Scripture in a limited economy of epistemic authority. We wish to encourage unashamedly dogmatic interpretation of Scripture, confident that the concrete consequences of such a reading will cast far more light on the great divisive questions of the Reformation than either reengaging in old theological polemics or chasing the fantasy of a pure exegesis that will somehow adjudicate between competing theological positions. You shall know the truth of doctrine by its interpretive fruits, and therefore in hopes of contributing to the unity of the church, we have deliberately chosen a wide range of theologians whose commitment to doctrine will allow readers to see real interpretive consequences rather than the shadow boxing of theological concepts.

Brazos Theological Commentary on the Bible has no dog in the current translation fights, and we endorse a textual ecumenism that parallels our diversity of ecclesial backgrounds. We do not impose the thankfully modest inclusive-language agenda of the New Revised Standard Version, nor do we insist upon the glories of the Authorized Version, nor do we require our commentators to create a new translation. In our communal worship, in our private devotions, in our theological scholarship, we use a range of scriptural translations. Precisely as Scripture—a living, functioning text in the present life of faith—the Bible is not semantically fixed. Only a modernist, literalist hermeneutic could imagine that this modest fluidity is a liability. Philological precision and stability is a consequence of, not a basis for, exegesis. Judgments about the meaning of a text fix its literal sense, not the other way around. As a result, readers should expect an eclectic use of biblical translations, both across the different volumes of the series and within individual commentaries.

We cannot speak for contemporary biblical scholars, but as theologians we know that we have long been trained to defend our fortresses of theological concepts and formulations. And we have forgotten the skills of interpretation. Like stroke victims, we must rehabilitate our exegetical imaginations, and there are likely to be different strategies of recovery. Readers should expect this reconstructive—not reactionary—series to provide them with experiments in postcritical doctrinal interpretation, not commentaries written according to the settled principles of a well-functioning tradition. Some commentators will follow classical typological and allegorical readings from the premodern tradition; others will draw on contemporary historical study. Some will comment verse by verse; others will highlight passages, even single words that trigger theological analysis of Scripture. No reading strategies are proscribed, no interpretive methods foresworn. The central premise in this commentary series is that doctrine provides structure and cogency to scriptural interpretation. We trust in this premise with the hope that the Nicene tradition can guide us, however imperfectly, diversely, and haltingly, toward a reading of Scripture in which the right keys open the right doors.

R. R. Reno

ABBREVIATIONS

General

→   indicates a cross-reference to commentary on an Ezekiel passage
KJV   King James Version
NRSV   New Revised Standard Version
RSV   Revised Standard Version

Biblical

Acts	Acts	Gen.	Genesis
Amos	Amos	Hab.	Habakkuk
1 Chr.	1 Chronicles	Hag.	Haggai
2 Chr.	2 Chronicles	Heb.	Hebrews
Col.	Colossians	Hos.	Hosea
1 Cor.	1 Corinthians	Isa.	Isaiah
2 Cor.	2 Corinthians	Jas.	James
Dan.	Daniel	Jer.	Jeremiah
Deut.	Deuteronomy	Job	Job
Eccl.	Ecclesiastes	Joel	Joel
Eph.	Ephesians	John	John
Esth.	Esther	1 John	1 John
Exod.	Exodus	2 John	2 John
Ezek.	Ezekiel	3 John	3 John
Ezra	Ezra	Jonah	Jonah
Gal.	Galatians	Josh.	Joshua

Jude	Jude	Phil.	Philippians
Judg.	Judges	Phlm.	Philemon
1 Kgs.	1 Kings	Prov.	Proverbs
2 Kgs.	2 Kings	Ps.	Psalms
Lam.	Lamentations	Rev.	Revelation
Lev.	Leviticus	Rom.	Romans
Luke	Luke	Ruth	Ruth
Mal.	Malachi	1 Sam.	1 Samuel
Mark	Mark	2 Sam.	2 Samuel
Matt.	Matthew	Song	Song of Songs
Mic.	Micah	1 Thess.	1 Thessalonians
Nah.	Nahum	2 Thess.	2 Thessalonians
Neh.	Nehemiah	1 Tim.	1 Timothy
Num.	Numbers	2 Tim.	2 Timothy
Obad.	Obadiah	Titus	Titus
1 Pet.	1 Peter	Zech.	Zechariah
2 Pet.	2 Peter	Zeph.	Zephaniah

INTRODUCTION

The book of the priest and prophet Ezekiel is an astonishment. Its prophecies are either appalling or inordinately auspicious, its visions are stunning apocalyptic theater, its language is absolute, its theology leads into frightening depths, its author is an enigma.

Moreover, the book somehow contrives at once to exercise a powerful grasp on our common imagination and to be the most esoteric book in the Old Testament. What other scenes from the Old Testament are sung in such various milieus as are Ezekiel's visions of "them bones, them bones, them dry bones"[1] or of "the wheel in a wheel"? Ezekiel 33:11 is the comforting text on a Victorian edifying plate that hangs in my dining room: "As I live, saith the Lord God, I take no pleasure in the death of the wicked." Yet the old rabbis decreed that of all books of scripture, the book of Ezekiel (along with the Song of Songs) "most pollutes the hands"; that is, it teaches mysteries so deep that probing them is an exposure to deity that may unfit one for ordinary human converse.

Indeed, Ezekiel's opening vision of God's throne (1:4–24) became in Judaism the vehicle of an elite and dangerous mystical practice (for a selection of the literature, see Greenberg 1983: 206). It is said that of four notables who attempted visionary ascent to the throne revealed to Ezekiel, one died, one went mad, one apostatized, and only the famously holy Rabbi Akiba achieved the vision and survived intact (he was killed in the last Jewish revolt against Rome, in 135).

As for Ezekiel himself, he is perhaps the most intellectual of the prophets, a considerable poet, and a prose artist adept at manipulating established oral and literary genres to novel effect. Yet the behaviors the Lord mandates for him—the circumstances of his prophesying and the signs he is commanded to perform—are bizarre and humbling in the extreme. The medieval Jewish philosopher

---

1. At a break from this writing, I turned on the television and encountered a Cadillac commercial that played on "the hip bone connected to the . . . ," with the parts of an engine.

Maimonides denied that some commands that Ezekiel says were laid on him could actually have been given by God, since "God is too exalted . . . [to] turn his prophets into a laughingstock . . . by ordering them to carry out crazy actions" (cited from Greenberg 1983: 122).

Prophets

There were prophets of several sorts through the history of Israel: from the shamanistic "men of God" and/or *neviim*[2] in the time of settlement and the early monarchy, through the great preachers of the eighth, seventh, and sixth centuries, through the later authors of apocalyptic literary works, to the throwback John the Baptist. As we shall see, Ezekiel seems to incorporate the entire history. Like the other preachers, he delivered the word of God in messages that regularly began "thus says the Lord." But he also endured experiences like those of the old shamans, notably in being transported, "in vision," from place to place. And he artfully delineated dramatically stylized visions of present and future history, in the style of the apocalyptic writers to come.

Fundamental to Israel's prophets of all sorts is the claim that God has entrusted his will to them, whether as word or as vision, and has sent them to bring that will to bear in the history of his people: their message is not intended merely to inform about God's purpose but to effect it. The prophets' self-understanding is perhaps most bluntly stated in Jeremiah's account of his commissioning: "The LORD said to me, 'Now I have put my words in your mouth. See, today I appoint you over nations and over kingdoms, to pluck up and to pull down . . . , to build and to plant'" (Jer. 1:9–10).

I will in this commentary offer no general justification of the prophets' self-understanding. Theological commentary presupposes that scripture tells the truth about God in his history with us; and this supposition includes that the Holy Spirit, the living breath of God that moves all history, does this regularly "by the prophets." Apologetic theology can provide reasons to think that the prophets are not deluded, but the present volume is not of that genre.

Within their immediate times and places, the prophets met challenges to their sending that were more specific than a priori unbelief. The prophets who appear in scripture were often in contention with a crowd of officially designated[3] or self-promoted prophets.[4] For the most part, society and government recruited

2. נביא (*navi*, plural *neviim*) is the word usually translated "prophet." In some contexts this is misleading, since in its earliest uses it covers ecstatics of all sorts.

3. For a list of the advisers regarded at this time as appropriate to a royal court, see Dan. 2:27: "Daniel answered the king, 'No wise men, enchanters, magicians, or diviners can show to the king the mystery.'"

4. Amos's famous denial that he was a *navi* (Amos 7:14) was a denial that he was either a professional or a volunteer; he was, he insisted, a conscript.

prophets to speak of victory and prosperity, to put God on Israel's side, a message regularly contradicted by the prophets whose work survives in the canon.[5] In the contestation between prophets and would-be prophets or charlatans, all a prophet could do was tell of his call and commission—which Ezekiel does at length—and leave confirmation to God. By including Ezekiel's book in the canon, Judaism and the church judge that God verifies Ezekiel's calling.

I will sometimes write as if Ezekiel simply reported visions God showed him and delivered messages God mandated; and I will at other times comment on Ezekiel's style or rhetorical art or literary dependence, as if he were an ordinary preacher and author. Whether I do the one or the other will depend entirely on the sort of point to be made. This is not inconsistent. It is one of the phenomena we must get used to in dealing with the prophets: the distinction that moderns automatically make between what we are given and what we create does not apply to them, since the one who gives them a word or a vision is their Creator, in whose intention their created talents, knowledge, and historical relations in any case rest. Between revelation and authorship—even when authorship encompasses research or literary borrowing or self-correction—there is with prophets no zero-sum balance.

History

Since a prophet is sent to bring God's intentions to bear in God's history with his people, no prophet can be well understood apart from his location in that history. For our purposes, we can distinguish between Israel's history as remembered by those of Ezekiel's time and the history of Ezekiel's own time.

Given the genre of this commentary, we do not need to construct a version of Israel's earlier history; indeed, doing so would be a distraction. Thus, for example, Ezekiel's supposition that all twelve tribes of Israel emerged together out of Egypt is important for our understanding of some of his prophecies; whether it indeed happened that way is not. In this book, we therefore do not take up the latter question. Those interested in such matters in other contexts—a group that includes the present commentator—may be directed to the vast literature,[6] if with a recommendation to carry a few grains of salt against the more long-spun or "new and radical" hypotheses. Here I will without prejudice write as if the earlier history of Israel had been more or less as Ezekiel and his hearers or initial readers supposed.

---

5. Thus Jeremiah's mocking advice to self-appointed prophets: prophesy disaster, that way you'll be right more often (Jer. 28:7–9).

6. The classic studies are by German scholars of the later twentieth century. I will mention the two by which I was nurtured in these matters: Martin Noth, *Geschichte Israels* (Göttingen: Vandenhoeck & Ruprecht, 1959); and Siegfried Herrmann, *Geschichte Israels in Alttestamentlicher Zeit* (Munich: Kaiser, 1973). There is again turmoil among the specialists in Israel's early history; so far as I can make out, it does not impinge seriously on the present assignment.

On the other hand, it will be essential to have in mind a sketch of Ezekiel's more immediate historical context, the later centuries of the monarchical Israelite states. And not to leave the reader hanging, I will carry the account to the end of that history.

At the beginning of Ezekiel's book an editor tells us (1:2) that Ezekiel was called to prophesy on the fifth day of the fourth month[7] of the fifth year "of the exile of King Jehoiachin,"[8] and there seems to be no good reason to doubt this dating (see Zimmerli 1979: 9–16)—though of course some scholars have managed it. This works out in our calendar to the end of June 593 BC (Zimmerli 1979: 115). Therewith we are set within a reasonably well-documented period of history.

The Israelite monarchies—a northern kingdom usually called Israel and the southern kingdom of Judah, centered around Jerusalem—were with other states located in the region sometimes called Syria-Palestine.[9] This region forms the western arm of the Fertile Crescent, so-called because it is an arc of fertile land wrapped around the northern bulge of agriculturally inhospitable Arabia. The arch and eastern arm of the crescent are made by the Tigris and Euphrates rivers. Thus when great powers arose in the land made prosperous by these rivers—Mesopotamia, "The Land between the Rivers"—their path for feasible expansion led west[10] over the top of the arch and then south through Syria-Palestine. And since Syria-Palestine also made a bridge of welcoming land between North Africa and Asia, Egyptian expansions into Asia followed the same path in the opposite direction.[11]

The first Mesopotamian power to expand into Syria-Palestine during the time of the Israelite states, Assyria, subjugated the northern kingdom in 732. As punishment for quickly ensuing rebellion, Assyria then did away with this state in 721: her political and military institutions were disbanded, the elites were killed or scattered into exile, and foreigners were put in their places. The Israelite tribes of the north did not simply vanish because their state and elites did; the general

7. The number of the month is here carried over from 1:1, as the editor presumed readers would do.

8. Ezekiel himself, in 1:1, dates his call "in the thirtieth year." But thirtieth year from what? Either Ezekiel expects readers to know without being told—which we do not—or a piece of the text is missing. Eichrodt 1970: 52 proposes that Ezekiel's dating is from his birth, which would mean he was taken into exile when he was twenty-five, the year he should have begun actual priestly service, and builds a good bit of speculation about Ezekiel's psychological state on this disappointment.

9. Roughly embracing modern Israel, the Palestinian territories, the fertile parts of Jordan, Lebanon, and the westerly parts of present-day Syria.

10. The Mesopotamian empires regarded the territories to the east, the rugged Iranian highlands, chiefly as barbarian territories to be raided for slaves and horses—until the Medes and Persians got themselves together, and their horsemen and archers created an empire that rewrote the geopolitical map.

11. Indeed, during much of the time before the period we are describing, Syria-Palestine was under firm Egyptian control.

population seems to have absorbed the imposed overclass and still appears in the New Testament as the Samaritans.

From Assyria's appearance in Syria-Palestine until the empire's collapse in the mid-seventh century, also Judah was in varying degree subservient to Assyria. Josiah, who reigned in Jerusalem from 639 to 609, took advantage of Assyria's retreat to reassert Judah's full independence and even to reconquer much of the realm of David and Solomon. Josiah accompanied political resurgence with religious reform, aimed at eliminating polytheistic elements from the practices of the people. It could not last: first Egypt pushed northward, and then Babylon arose to replace Assyria as the great Mesopotamian power. Nebuchadnezzar defeated the Egyptians at Carchemish (in the arch of the crescent) in 605, and Babylon followed Assyria's path to become overlord of Syria-Palestine.

During Egypt's brief moment of renewed power in Syria-Palestine, Pharaoh Neco had killed Josiah, deposed Josiah's son and immediate successor, Jehoahaz, taking him captive to Egypt, and installed another of Josiah's sons, Jehoiakim, in his place. Jehoiakim pursued a foreign policy of rebellion against Babylon's overlordship and pleas to Egypt for help. An exasperated Nebuchadnezzar came in force, sacked Jerusalem, and in 598 carried much of Judah's political, military, and religious elite to exile in Babylonia. Among them was luckless King Jehoiachin, who had succeeded his father just three months before.

Babylon's policy differed from Assyria's in that she settled exiles together in Babylonia rather than scattering them and apparently treated them with some respect. Though it has been disputed, the priest Ezekiel was probably among those taken in 598 (so also Gregory 1986–90: 1.46). In any case, he was in Babylonia[12] when five years later he was called to prophesy.

Despite the prophet Jeremiah's urgent expostulations, Zedekiah, whom Nebuchadnezzar installed in Jerusalem, revolted in his turn, with the same futile appeal to Egypt. Nebuchadnezzar decided to put an end to this turbulent dependency: after a terrible siege, Jerusalem with temple and palace was in 587–586 leveled and burned, and no new king or regent was installed. Zedekiah, captured while fleeing Jerusalem, was blinded; and the remains of the Judean elite were added to the exilic community in Babylon. In Judah as earlier in Israel, most of the population remained in place, now bereft of native government, city, and temple. The Davidic monarchy was finished, as a phenomenon of what we moderns call history.

For a true historical placement of Ezekiel, the above bland recital of political events will not do by itself. Before proceeding to the commentary, readers may wish to expose themselves to something of the spiritual disaster that the exile and the agony of Jerusalem meant for Israel; I suggest reading the Lamentations of Ezekiel's near-contemporary, the Jerusalem prophet Jeremiah.

---

12. This has been disputed, by sheer lack of imagination. The book says that Ezekiel prophesied to all Israel and to Tyre, Egypt, etc., from Babylonia. That is impossible, pedants have said.

Under the next overlord of the Fertile Crescent, Persia, there was a general release (legally proclaimed in 538) and return of exiles, though the Jewish exilic community had so prospered in Babylon that many remained. Jerusalem was more or less restored, and a new temple was built. The Jews of Palestine, Babylon, and Egypt,[13] with refugees and émigrés elsewhere, emerged as an international ethnic-religious community centered on the sacrificial cult of this Second Temple—note the catalogue in Acts 2:9–11 of nations from which pilgrims had come to Jerusalem.

The further political history of this community's center at Jerusalem—within geopolitical constellations shaped in succession by Persia, Alexander of Macedon, the empires succeeding Alexander's conquests, and Rome—is extraordinarily complicated. Fortunately we may for our purposes fast-forward through the centuries to AD 70, when Rome crushed a Jewish revolt[14] and again destroyed the temple, this time leaving little prospect of rebuilding. The loss of the temple deprived international Judaism of her cultic center and compelled yet another transformation of Judaism, into the rabbinic Judaism we know today, centered on Torah rather than cult and so led by rabbis rather than priests.[15] In AD 135 Rome put down a last Jewish uprising, with terrible destruction and loss of life. On the site of Jerusalem, Rome then built a properly Roman city, Aelia Capitolina, which Jews were forbidden to enter.

A Few Points about Method

I do not belong to the guild of Old Testament scholars; my work has mostly been as a systematic theologian and analyst of culture. If this commentary were in another series, this acknowledgment might be a confession or a provocation; here it simply notes my place within the series. The preface to the series states its general aims and principles, and these need not be repeated here. Each author in the series is, however, allowed considerable latitude in achieving the series' aims.

One question left free is this: are historical-critical methods and results important for the kind of theological exegesis here to be pursued, and are they to be instanced in the commentaries? For my part, I consider that the text for theological interpretation is the canonical text presented by the church and not a putatively original or earlier text constructed by a scholar—though determining what may

13. During a period of benevolent Egyptian overlordship of postexilic Judah, an important Jewish community grew up there.

14. The Romans regarded the taking of Jerusalem as no mean feat of Roman arms; in Rome, the triumphal arch of Titus still commemorates it.

15. Second Temple Judaism had been a congeries of denominations. Those groups survived the loss of the temple who could if necessary do without it: the Judaism of the Pharisees, centered on Torah study and ritual purity, which could be pursued anywhere, and the Christian movement, which had in the sacramental body of the risen Christ a sort of ubiquitous temple (John 2:21).

be a plausibly canonical text sometimes requires considerable critical thought. I consider also that the account of events provided by the canonical text may not for theological reading be simply replaced by a scholar's construction of what "really" happened—what the relation may then be between these two sorts of history is a now much controverted question, the theoretical resolution of which is again beyond the scope of a commentary. Nor will I treat passages or editorial groupings that plainly come from other persons than Ezekiel as therefore of lesser theological interest; the providential action by which God gives his people their scripture—in most theology called "inspiration"[16]—encompasses the whole history of the canonical text's emergence.

But I also find that critical investigation of a text or of events to which a text refers is often important in understanding precisely the canonical text—and this sort of inquiry is as old as Christian biblical scholarship itself. Of such work, I am at best a dabbler. Therefore in writing this commentary I have for such matters often relied on classic historical-critical commentaries, especially the painstaking and comprehensive volumes of Walther Zimmerli, which I will frequently reference. I will nevertheless venture a few of my own critical judgments.

Ezekiel's book does indeed show unmistakable signs of additions and reworkings, and somebody of course collected Ezekiel's prophesyings and made a book of them. I am, however, skeptical about attempts to reconstruct in much detail the history by which an ancient text arrived at its present form. To make my own and readers' way through this book's often bewilderingly assembled pieces, I will need to refer to editors and interpolators; but, except with respect to a few basic structures of the book, I will not often claim knowledge of their identities or predilections, which in my judgment is usually unattainable.

The notion of "theological exegesis" derives in part from the paradigm of the church's and Judaism's premodern exegesis. A second question left free for individual authors in this series is this: in what ways are we to conform to that paradigm? I am committed to premodern Christian exegetes' aim, to read the Bible as a single dramatically coherent narrative of the coming of Christ and his kingdom.[17] But I am not necessarily committed to their exact procedures or results. To display the dramatic continuity of the biblical narrative, the church fathers and medievals, in the train of the New Testament itself, read earlier events in this narrative as "figures" of later culminating events.[18] This way of reading is rightly renewed in some volumes of this series. Discerning the way in which earlier events prefigure—as we still say—later ones is, after all, the way we naturally read

16. The early Protestant Scholastics who most carefully developed the notion did *not* mean dictation to an author.

17. For the church fathers' fundamental conviction, see Gregory the Great's comment on 40:6: "See how when we want to clarify the meaning of a passage in Ezekiel, we settle the matter at issue from one of the Gospels" (1986–90: 2.126).

18. The founding modern study of the older exegesis is Henri de Lubac, *Exègése Médiévale* (Paris: Aubier, 1959–64).

dramatically coherent narratives, especially those whose outcome we know. But with prophets, or anyway with Ezekiel, a systematic practice of figural exegesis in the fathers' own style would too much gild the lily. In primal Christian understanding, Israel's prophecy points forward christologically and ecclesially without need for specifically figural discernment: "All the prophets . . . from Samuel and those after him . . . predicted these days" (Acts 3:24).

I have recently been provided a slogan for the way in which I do then construe the christological import of prophecy:[19] I will seek to discern a "christological plain sense." On the supposition that both the biblical text and the church's trinitarian and christological teachings are *true*,[20] what must Ezekiel's text—just as he and editors and interpolators formulated it and as it appears on the page—say? What indeed is its historically "original" meaning, given the church's trinitarian and christological construal of historical reality?[21] I will not at this point further develop this hermeneutic; that will best be done by its display in the course of exegesis.

Of premodern exegesis itself, I will therefore provide samples only. Among the church fathers from whom I might have drawn, I choose the homilies of Origen of Alexandria, the third-century father of the church's scholarly biblical study, and those of the sixth-century Pope Gregory the Great.[22] Among premodern Jewish exegetes, I will regularly reference the very interesting Targum, a late-antique Aramaic[23] paraphrase for Jews with little Hebrew, that verges toward commentary—or indeed rewriting—and will sometimes cite the readings of the eleventh-century scholar commonly known as Rashi, who has a certain normative status in rabbinic Judaism.[24]

I will make no room for the supposed contributions of the various critical theories currently on offer in academia and sometimes invoked to guide biblical and other exegesis—each projected from the viewpoint of a class, a gender, a race, and so on. Critique in the relevant late-modern sense is the effort to discern what a text[25] "really" says, as against what it may to unsuspicious eyes seem to say; and a labeled critical theory (e.g., feminist theory, postcolonial theory, queer theory) is a

19. This phrase comes from Jason Byassee's work on Augustine's exegesis of the psalms: *Praise Seeking Understanding* (Grand Rapids: Eerdmans, 2007), esp. 205–19.

20. "True" in the simple sense we all suppose when we are not being deliberately sophisticated.

21. Even at the date of this writing, it remains hard for us to remember that the positivistic construal of historical reality is itself only one among many, and far from the most plausible.

22. The Ezekiel homilies of both fathers come and go in Ezekiel's text, those of Origen because of the vicissitudes suffered by his book, those of Gregory because he regularly had to leave off teaching to negotiate with the Lombards who were threatening Rome. Indeed, in his second volume, Gregory begins with Ezek. 40 and gets no further.

23. I do not read Aramaic and am therefore dependent on the English translation in Levey 1990.

24. Rashi is much occupied with what we would now call historical-critical interpretation and little given to allegorical interpretation.

25. For these theories, anything can be a text.

specific set of instructions for achieving such discernment. There is indeed a critical theory at work in this commentary, and it might be called "Nicene theory."

I will not provide surveys of alternative interpretations, nor indeed often specify the reading that may have helped or hindered me to an interpretation, so long as I am not actually borrowing. I am solely responsible for the interpretations presented.

What then did the assignment to write a theological commentary come to mean, as I went to work? It of course meant trying to clarify textual phenomena whose clarification seemed needed, either in the next and for us decisive connection or merely to find our way in the text. It meant a specific attention to the text, looking for what it has to say about God, his people, and their history together, as the church presupposes these realities, rather than for what can be gleaned about other interesting matters. In the theology of Ezekiel, the historical relation of the Lord with his people is decisively determined by the fact of prophecy itself, so that the structure of such phenomena as "the word of the Lord," as these appear in the text, demand our attention. And finally, it therefore often came to mean explicit invocation of points of Christian doctrine that either (in the one direction) are raised by the text or (in the other) demand to shape interpretation of the text. So we will encounter the doctrine of the Trinity, the question of an end of history, election, and other such matters.

The proposition that exegesis of the Old Testament might call up points of Christian doctrine of course offends the modern exegetical academy's chief dogma. That, vice versa, Christian doctrine should shape interpretation of Old Testament passages offends it even more deeply. But the exclusion of the church's doctrine from interpretation of the church's scripture is after all a very odd rule on its face; and it is indeed as Christian scripture that the church reads what she calls the Old Testament.[26] How the academic community came to be committed to an antidoctrinal, and thus in this case ironically ahistorical mode of exegesis, is an often told tale that need not be repeated here.

The present commentary, like the others in the series, thus offers alternatives to the modern academy's prejudices. I will not often argue theoretically the legitimacy of christological or trinitarian or ecclesiological readings I present, but will mostly

---

26. It should not be necessary to recount the following piece of well-known history, but in the present situation it probably is. Rabbinic Judaism and the church have equal and parallel claims to obey the Tanakh/Old Testament as scripture. Neither is a direct continuation of old Israel. In the long run, each could obey old Israel's scripture only by adding a second volume: the rabbis added the Mishnah, and the Christians the New Testament. These second volumes quite properly control each community's way of reading Tanakh/Old Testament. The Mishnah is a legal complex; and rabbinic Judaism reads the Tanakh fundamentally as Torah, given narrative context by the narrative and other nonlegal genres. The New Testament tells and comments on a story that claims to continue one told by the Old Testament; and the church reads the Old Testament fundamentally as narrative with a *telos*, given its moral structure by Torah. The fashion among Christian scholars of calling the Old Testament "the Hebrew scripture" is merely jejune—this being a title meaningless in both communions.

allow them to convince readers by their own sense and appropriateness to the text at hand—or not. I do ask for suspension of a priori incredulity—who knows, the church might be right about how to read her own scripture.

Two Technical Matters

A verse-by-verse commentary on this long book would exceed any normal attention span, including mine. I will instead divide by the text's own units. These can usually be identified with some certainty: a book of prophecy is put together of distinct messages or visions delivered and recorded on different occasions, and the discourse of Ezekiel and his editors and interpolators abounds with formulas that mark beginnings and endings, both of prophecies as delivered or visions as reported and of editorial units of the book.

Some natural units are too long or too theologically or otherwise loaded to make manageable units of commentary, and I will divide them. Thus, for an immediately intruding example, 1:1–28b is clearly a narrative unit and in turn is part of a larger complex that runs through 3:15. But for comment I will separate 1:1–28b from the larger complex; and I will further give 1:1–3 and 1:25–28b separate comment, on account of the number and weight of the theological issues these early verses raise for the whole book.

I will presuppose the text of the New Revised Standard Version unless I see compelling reason to do otherwise.[27] NRSV usually translates the Hebrew text stabilized by late-antique and early-medieval Jewish scholars known as Masoretes. I will from time to time instance the Hebrew; readers who have some Hebrew will very occasionally have a slight advantage in judging the worth of a comment, but no knowledge of Hebrew is needed to understand the comments themselves. I will deviate from NRSV when its translation is seriously bent by the translators' ideology; or when NRSV follows the Masoretes and I am persuaded by the experts that a more plausible Hebrew text can be discerned; or when a more crudely literal representation of the Hebrew is needed to display the thunder of Ezekiel's rhetoric—this last is sometimes important in presenting Ezekiel. I will refer to "ancient versions," translations made before the Masoretes' time, the most important of which is the Septuagint[28]—again, no knowledge of Greek is needed to understand comments that rely on this version.

27. I greatly prefer the original RSV, but must recognize that it is being replaced in use.

28. There is a good argument, urged on me by an editor of the series, that the Septuagint, by way of *A New English Translation of the Septuagint*, ed. Albert Pietersma and Benjamin G. Wright (New York: Oxford University Press, 2007), should be the text for theological interpretation, rather than the Hebrew and the English versions based on it, since the Septuagint was effectively the church's Old Testament in the apostolic period and for some time thereafter. But counterarguments are persuasive: the Latin Vulgate's Old Testament was nevertheless translated—except for the Psalter—from the Hebrew and not from the Greek and was the Western church's Old Testament

To Be Noted in Advance

Since the historical situation and basic message of a prophet do not change every day, longer books of prophecy are very repetitious: however possessed by revelation, no preacher or visionary creates a new set of usages for each discourse, and there are only so many sorts of doom or blessing that can be invoked upon Israel or her enemies. Thus in Ezekiel, usages like "the word of the Lord came to me" or "then they shall know" or "their abominations" recur again and again. I use two devices to cope with this.

One is a liberal use of cross-referencing (using →) to direct readers of one commentary unit to another commentary unit where needed discussion will be found. This has the effect that as we go through the book, the commentary units tend to become shorter or cover more text, since more and more matters are dealt with by referring to previous discussion.

A few phrases and turns of diction are so ubiquitous that cross-referencing them at each occurrence would be extremely tedious. I will therefore discuss them here, once and for all; before turning to the commentary readers should study the following rather carefully.

"The word of the Lord came to me." This clause, which introduces many passages in Ezekiel, is more theologically loaded than one might at first suppose. That the Lord's word comes to a prophet does not simply mean that the Lord comes and speaks to him—remarkable though that also would be. Rather, "the word of the Lord" is a reality in some way *related to* the Lord and so identifiable in and as itself (for the scholarship, see Zimmerli 1979: 144), yet not separable in being from the Lord. The word of the Lord is at once the Lord speaking and identifiable as an other than the Lord.

The phenomenon thus has the same trinitarian structure as some other Old Testament phenomena: most notably "the glory of the Lord" (→1:25–28b), "the name of the Lord" (e.g., 1 Kgs. 3:2–5:5), and "the angel of the Lord" (e.g., Gen. 16:7–12; 22:9–18; or most remarkably of all, Judg. 13:2–23). Each of these realities is *related to* the Lord by the genitive construction, yet as each narrative proceeds turns out also to *be* the Lord.

The rabbis generalized this structure as "the Shekinah." Exodus calls the wilderness temple-tent God's "dwelling place" (משכן, *mishkan*) amidst his people (Exod. 40:34); the rabbis then used a word from the same root for the indwelling itself and extended the word to cover various phenomena of the Lord's dwelling in Israel.

Thus Christian theology could gloss John 1:14 with "the Shekinah became flesh"; the Jewish-Christian disagreement is only(!) about whether this in fact happened. Indeed, by original Christian understanding, the word that came to

---

through most of her history; modern translations in churchly use are of the Hebrew; and theological education has for centuries referred future preachers and teachers to the Hebrew.

the prophets was in fact Christ acting in anticipation of his incarnate coming, and we might even gloss our clause as "Christ came to me" (for this Christology, →1:25–28b).

There is yet another linguistic-theological subtlety in our phrase: the word customarily translated "came" does not mean quite what the English might suggest. The verb *hayah* (היה) does not necessarily specify arrival at one place *from* some place else.[29] By itself, it is closer to "happens to/at. . . ." When in prophetic discourse it is used in the past tense with "the word of God" and takes a preposition with a name or pronoun, we might clumsily translate "the word of the Lord happened, and it happened to. . . ."

"Thus says the Lord." This is the formula with which Ezekiel begins verbal prophecies of the most usual form. In the jargon of form critics,[30] it begins a "messenger-word," and I will use this term throughout the commentary. "Thus says the Lord" makes the claim that the prophet has been sent by the Lord to bring the message that follows, as an official might bring the decree of a monarch to some more distant part of the realm. Thus a messenger-word is not a mere report of the Lord's will; it is the enforcement of it among those to whom the message is brought.

"The hand of the Lord was . . . upon me." This is Ezekiel's invariable way of referring to the onset of a vision, as distinct from a coming of the word. "The hand of the Lord" is a key notion through much of the Old Testament, where it evokes the Lord's *impact* on the course of events (Zimmerli 1979: 117; see also Greenberg 1983: 41–42). Thus Rashi's excellent gloss: "The strength of His might, to lead me against my will" (Rosenberg 2000: 243). In Ezekiel's use, the impact is both on Ezekiel personally and on the swirling history around him; Ezekiel regards the occurrence of vision as itself an act of the Lord in history. More about vision as such will appear in the commentary.

"Son of a man." The Lord always addresses Ezekiel as בֶּן־אָדָם (*ben-adam*). I will throughout translate this phrase as above. The usual translation, "son of man" with no article before "man," carries associations from special uses elsewhere[31] that could be misleading here.[32] NRSV's attempt to avoid this by translating "mortal" is far too polite (and probably too ideologically motivated); moreover, since other

29. Thus the Targum (e.g., Levey 1990: 30) invariably translates "the word . . . was with me."

30. Form criticism sorts out the genres—particularly oral genres—that appear in scripture and attempts to reconstruct the life situation—the famous *Sitz im Leben*—within which an identified genre will have had its preliterary currency. Or vice versa.

31. "One like a son of man" is in some apocalyptic literature a heavenly being; in the canon, see Dan. 7:13. Blessedly, the endless controversy about the identity of beings so named in apocalyptic is irrelevant here. And of course "son of man" is in the Gospels a still not fully clarified designation of the Christ.

32. "Son of man" in fact misled Christianity's first great scholarly exegete, who took Ezekiel himself, because he is called "son of man," to be the presence of Christ in Ezekiel's prophesying (Origen 1989: 59). Christ is indeed present in Ezekiel's prophecy and book, but not as the person of Ezekiel.

creatures are also mortal, it obliterates part of the point, which is identification of the particular sort of creature addressed. Since this is the only way the Lord addresses him, Ezekiel in his own book loses even his name and is identified merely as someone who is not God or one of the heavenly host, but was "born . . . of the will of [a] man" (John 1:13).

"The Lord/the Lord God." Where "the Lord" appears in English translations of the Old Testament, it usually does not straightforwardly translate anything in Hebrew. What is in the Masoretic Text is the personal name—יהוה (*yhwh*)—of Israel's God, with an orthographic device to warn readers against speaking it aloud even when reading scripture.[33] The divine name is marked to alert the reader[34] to pronounce and even to think Hebrew *adonai*—which translates into English as "the Lord"—instead of the name itself.

Despite great scholarly efforts, we do not know where the name יהוה came from or what if anything it might once have meant.[35] In its biblical use it is anyway a true personal name, and that indeed is the whole point (see von Rad 1962–66: 1.179–87). "I am *yhwh*, your God" is God's self-introduction to Israel, accomplished by his name and a following identification, as an incumbent candidate might say to a prospective supporter, "I am John Jones, your representative." By this God's self-introduction with his name, through Moses (Exod. 3) and in the preface of his fundamental Torah at Sinai (20:2), the relation of *this* God to *this* people was established.

Instead of "the Lord" Ezekiel often has—in the usual English—"the Lord God." The Hebrew locution so represented is *adonai yhwh*. When *adonai* is translated in its own character—as it has to be here—it comes into English as "lord." Keeping the divine name in Hebrew, we would have "the Lord יהוה." The double appellation carries some semantic weight: as in the discourse of aristocracy one might refer to "the Lord Buckingham" so here the lordship of יהוה is honored.

If we followed the ordinary rule for avoiding God's name and substituted *adonai* for *yhwh*, or in English "the Lord," and read or translated *adonai* directly, we would have in Hebrew *adonai adonai*, and in English "the Lord the Lord." To avoid this pileup, while not ignoring the fact of a modified phrase (as the Septuagint perhaps wisely did), English translators devised another cover: "the Lord" is now allowed to be the translation of its own Hebrew equivalent and "God" is

33. Christian preachers' and scholars' recent habit of throwing "Jahweh" around out loud is what Ezekiel would call an "abomination."

34. The vowel points in the Masoretic Text are those that represent the vowels in *adonai* ("lord") and are there to remind readers to say *adonai* or, if translating into English, "the Lord." Thus "Jehovah," which is the result of pronouncing the consonants of *yhwh* with the vowels of *adonai*, represents unfamiliarity with this device and is a name that never existed until unwitting translators created it.

35. The authors and tradents of the Pentateuch also did not know where the name יהוה came from or what it meant; the etymology—or what *we* would call etymology—at Exod. 3:14 is plainly ad hoc for the occasion. Ancient exegetes loved this kind of philological play. In modern scholarship, guesses of course abound.

assigned to cover the divine name. This is not a lucky device, since it no longer contains a signal for the underlying presence of the personal name.

"Then you/they shall know that. . . ." This promise or threat provides the conclusion of many of Ezekiel's prophecies.[36] Its paradigmatic version is "then you/they shall know that I am *yhwh* [כִּי אֲנִי יהוה]"; other resolutions of the ellipse shown above depend on the paradigm. In the case of prophecies so concluded, when what is prophesied happens, or sometimes when the event of prophecy itself happens, the intended outcome is experience of the Lord's personal identity, of the personal import of the one thus self-identified. The modality of this knowledge varies with the prophecy: it may be knowledge that the Lord is the one who did or will do what is prophesied; or knowledge that he is the one who has given the prophecy; or knowledge simply that there is this person or that he is God; or some more participatory relation to this God's identity.

A Warning

The purpose of a commentary is to assist readers' involvement with the text. Perhaps readers should therefore take warning before going further. Attention to a text can turn into experience of its matter, and the judgments and promises of God as given through Ezekiel are so extreme that they can easily undo ordinary religiosity—to say nothing of the disastrous spiritual adventures that might be ignited by his visions.

---

36. Walther Zimmerli's *I Am Jahweh*, trans. Douglas W. Stott (Atlanta: John Knox, 1982) is devoted to this formula.

EZEKIEL 1:1–3

A DOUBLE CALL

There was always the problem: someone could simply announce that he was a prophet or be appointed to a staff of temple or palace prophets and then "prophesy" by his own judgment of the situation or from self-induced trance states, usually saying what would please his sponsors. "The prophets prophesy falsely, and . . . my people love to have it so" (Jer. 5:31). Of such sycophants the Lord said by this same Jeremiah, "I did not send them, nor did I command them or speak to them" (14:14). Ultimately, to be sure, sorting out true from false prophets could be done only by God himself, in the course of history (see the whole of Jer. 27)—and Jeremiah's opponents doubtless returned the accusation. But prophets and their literary executors were nevertheless often concerned to claim and where possible recount a divine call and sending. Ezekiel's book provides amply for this, with a narrative complex stretching from Ezek. 1:4 through 3:15.

Ezekiel 1:1–3 introduces this complex, and so the whole book. Indeed, this is done twice. The first introduction, 1:1, is in the first person: "I saw visions of God." The second, 1:2–3a, is the only place in the book where a report of revelation is in the third person, or Ezekiel is referred to by name as the prophet of the book: "The word of the LORD came to the priest Ezekiel."[1] This obviously suggests that the second introduction was provided by an editor. Moreover, the two introductions are of different genres, one tells of an inaugural vision, the other of an inaugural advent of God's word. If either 1:1 or 1:2–3a stood alone, each could be the introduction to a prophetic work of corresponding and different type.

---

1. Ezek. 1:3 is one of only two places where the name Ezekiel appears at all; the other is in a wholly different context (24:24).

In 1:1, Ezekiel writes in the first person of the heavens "opening" to reveal "visions of God" (מראות אלהים). This is in the style of the "apocalyptic" writings that would shortly become the dominant form of prophecy. For exemplification of their general character, we need look no further than to the apocalypse that concludes the Christian Bible: "After this I looked, and there in heaven a door stood open! And the first voice . . . said, 'Come up here, and I will show you what must take place after this.' At once I was in the spirit, and there in heaven stood a throne, with one seated on the throne" (Rev. 4:1–2). The English for Greek *apokalypsis* is "revelation"; what is revealed is God's rule and history as it will unfold under his rule. This mode of prophecy will be essentially literary—throughout the revelation given him, John stands ready with pen in hand.

Corresponding to this sort of revelation is "vision" as a mode of apprehension. The possessive in our text, "visions of God," must be both objective and subjective: God is both the one who is—somehow—seen and the one who gives us such seeing, of himself and other mysteries. In Ezekiel, visionary experience as revelation of God and his future both tends forward to the apocalyptic writings (in the canon see Zech. 1:7 and Dan. 10:7) and harks back to the old seers (e.g., 2 Chr. 9:29), who flourished in Israel before the time of the preachers whom we tend to call "*the* prophets."

Ezekiel 1:3b presents a textual problem, of a sort we cannot pass over. NRSV, following the Masoretic Text, has the pronoun in the third person: "The hand of the Lord was on him." But ancient versions[2] translate a first person, and in the narrative context this seems a far more likely text. In the rest of the book "the hand of the Lord" is invoked only in connection with the impact of visions, never with the coming of the word. If that holds also here, then 1:3b belongs with the narrative of 1:1, 4, rather than with that of 1:2–3a. Ezekiel 1:1 and 1:4 are in the first person. It therefore seems likely that we should read, with the Septuagint, "The hand of the Lord was upon me."

Ezekiel 1:3b thus continues the editorially interrupted first introduction and is Ezekiel's own description of his initial experience of vision. Ezekiel experiences the onset of vision as something like the blow of a hand and feels the impact of the vision also in the history of Israel. In the language of a dominant biblical theology of the previous century, the call of Ezekiel is itself one of the "acts of God in history"— and indeed many of the church fathers understood "the hand of the Lord" as a reference to Christ, who is the agent and content of God's works. Gregory the Great comments on our passage: "The Son is called the hand or arm of the Lord, because all [the Lord's works] are done through him" (1986–90: 1.92).

In 1:2–3a, an editor introduces Ezekiel a second time, as one to whom the *word* of the Lord came. Thus the editor corrects an existing account of the same event, without, however, replacing it.[3] The outcome is that in the canonical text,

2. Including, decisively, the Septuagint: καὶ ἐγένετο ἐπ᾽ ἐμὲ χεὶρ κυρίου.
3. The same combination appears at Zech. 1:7–8, where it seems more forced.

seeing and recording visions of God and hearing and speaking God's word are somehow identified.[4]

Either of the introductions would by itself give us much to think about. What is heaven? What does one see when one sees a vision? What is the word of God, and how does it come to someone? But interwoven as they are in our text, the two introductions pose an additional and theologically intriguing question: How are vision of God and word of God one?

In the theological tradition, heaven is the part of creation that the Creator has made as his own place within his creation. Apart from creation, God is not *in* any place but simply *is* his own place;[5] therefore for him the creation is merely a single other place.[6] But if he is not only to create others than himself, but to live with these creatures, he must have a place within the place made for them, from which to come and go with them.[7] "Heaven" is that part of creation. And what is *in* heaven besides God is the present reality with God of the future that his history with creatures intends, the divine present tense of "the kingdom of God" and of what "must come before" it. Ezekiel's report fits very well with this tradition.

What sort of event is a prophetic vision? For the one who experiences it, such a vision is evidently much like a dream; the wisdom tradition can speak of prophetic "visions of the night" (Job 4:13), and in a passage from the prophet Joel that became central for Christianity, dreaming dreams and seeing visions are paralleled for the prophetic gift of the last time (Joel 2:28). We must not, however, be misled by modern usage: we think of dreams as natural phenomena, but the dreams/visions of seers or apocalyptic visionaries require—in Ezekiel's language—the hand of the Lord. Moreover, they inform about reality and not just about the dreamer's inner reality; they are a kind of looking *at* something (Ezek. 1:4; Rev. 4:1). Perhaps the link between dreams and such waking visions as Ezekiel's is that bystanders behold neither dreams nor visions.[8] Just so the cognitive status of visions is, to be sure, debatable, and has been debated also within theology.

At this point I should note the theological importance of the way in which prophetic books often date and geographically place the advent of word or vision; in the case of Ezekiel, both he and the editor tell us the year, month, day, and place of his call, and someone continues to provide dates through the book. Gregory the Great takes note of this and gives the reason: "In order for the truth to be more firmly displayed, [the prophet] first sinks root in history" (1986–90: 1.83). The opening of heaven in vision does not, like the visions of some mystical

---

4. The phenomenon is not unique to Ezekiel; see Zimmerli 1979: 98.

5. Established for all subsequent theology by John of Damascus, *The Orthodox Faith* 13.11.

6. God's omnipresence does not mean that he is spread out through creation; rather all creation is present to him at its one place with him.

7. For my exposition of this, including the vexed question of where—having regard to Copernicus—heaven might be, see Jenson 1997–99: 1.119–24.

8. Dan. 10:7: "I, Daniel, alone saw the vision; the people who were with me did not see the vision."

practice, take Ezekiel out of history. The prophet does not see what is always and everywhere true; instead, the vision—like the word—seems rather to press him more firmly into a time and a place.

Vision becomes especially problematic when the object is supposed to be God.[9] Can one see God? The doctrine of the Trinity says that we can, in that the second person of God is a particular man, Jesus the Christ, who can of course be seen: "Whoever has seen me has seen the Father" (John 14:9). But without the identification of God as triune, the matter becomes highly problematic. Thus the Targum glosses "visions of God" with "a vision of the glory of the Shekinah of the Lord" (Levey 1990: 20), putting not one but two intermediaries between God himself and what is seen. We will, to be sure, shortly (1:25–28b) need to consider just what sort of intermediary each is.

Thus prophets of a certain kind "see things" and take what they see as real, despite its not being seen by others; moreover what they see is supposed to be a reality inhabited also by those who do not see. The claim to see reality in this fashion may of course be a delusion, and modernity has generally presupposed that it must be—though in fact late modernity is all too ready to embrace plainly superstitious forms of visionary practice. But what warrant, after all, did we have for prejudice against vision as such? If there is the God of scripture, he sees himself and his creation, including heaven, as they truly are; and if we are the fallen creatures that Christian theology describes, we on both counts do not. If then we are to see things rightly, this can happen only if God shows it to us and in such fashion as to penetrate our dim sight.

We must suppose that there are many ways in which God can do this: the "we" who according to Paul now do "see," even if "darkly" (1 Cor. 13:12), certainly included many faithful who lacked overt visionary experience and saw divine truth in other ways. But if for certain purposes or times God employs visions, we must allow him that choice—which still of course leaves the question of how to tell when he has done this.

Finally, we must consider that remarkable identification-in-difference of word and vision that an editor created. The duality of word and vision, hearing and seeing, runs all through scripture, and there are great differences in the way the poles are balanced. Israel at Sinai must not climb the mountain, since "no one shall see [God] and live" (Exod. 33:20), while they are commanded to approach and hear him speak (19:9). But when that same word of God comes in his own person, it is in order that we may *see* his glory (John 1:1–14).

It is something deep in the reality of God that appears in these phenomena. Both in scripture and doctrine, the second person of the triune God is sometimes "Son" and sometimes Word. As Son he is the "image" of the Father (Col. 1:15; Heb. 1:3), so that one who has seen him has seen the Father (John 14:9). As

9. For the deep patristic discussion of this, with specific reference to Ezekiel, see Christman 2005.

Word, he is the message from the Father, the "gospel" of which he is at once the messenger and the content.

This duality carries into the tradition of developed trinitarian doctrine. In one strand—of which Origen of Alexandria[10] is perhaps the great teacher—the Father *sees* himself in the Son, whose being is to reflect the Father's glory. In another—which we may find in Martin Luther[11]—the Logos is so perfect an *expression* of the Father that he in turn is a speaker who answers the Father, to establish the Trinity as a conversation, even a community.

Seeing and hearing are with creatures and in this age two very different modes of perception: we objectify what we look at, but when we hear are ourselves the objects of the one who addresses us. Thus we do not know how to describe the reconciliation of seeing and hearing, nor then how to speak of the second triune person as at once Son/image and Logos. But it is an ancient maxim of theology: God is identical with his attributes, so that these also are identical with each other. Thus we must suppose that "God speaks" and "God shows" name the same reality, as do "God hears" and "God sees," even though we can form no notion of this unity. We may even suppose that when we have been taken into God we too will see by hearing and hear by seeing. Perhaps we may say that prophets are those given to anticipate such wholeness of perception; consider the usage: "The words of Amos . . . which he saw" (Amos 1:1).

---

10. Origen flourished around AD 225 and was the founder both of my home discipline—systematic theology—and of disciplined biblical exegesis.

11. And of course others, e.g., Hans Urs von Balthasar, *Heart of the World*, trans. Erasmo S. Leiva (San Francisco: Ignatius, 1979).

EZEKIEL 1:4–24

THE THEOPHANY

What then did Ezekiel actually see, as an opening of the heavens? He saw God coming to judge and to save, in a place where Ezekiel might well have thought neither judgment nor salvation could reach him. At Jerusalem, the Lord was present among his people on the cherubim throne in the temple's most holy place; and this was doubtless definitive for the piety of the temple priest Ezekiel. In 593 the desecrated temple was still a few years from total destruction. But for the exiles this can have been little comfort: those left behind in Judah might still know some remnant of the Lord's saving presence, but those carried to Babylon were far from it.

Thus a great psalm tells nothing of prayer or praise by Babylon's rivers, only of weeping: "By the rivers of Babylon, there we . . . wept, when we remembered Zion. We hanged our harps upon the willows. . . . How shall we sing the LORD's song in a strange land?" (Ps. 137:1–4 KJV). In a land made impure by idolatry—indeed in the very headquarters of idolatry,[1] the land of Babel, of the united human effort to usurp God—did the exiles even dare to pray?

At first, Ezekiel sees the Lord's advent as a lightning storm heading toward him.[2] This was not a new phenomenon; rather it was a throwback. Before there was the established presence of Israel in her land and of the Lord in the land's temple, Israel

1. In the Revelation, God's final victory over "abominations," that is, idolatries, is announced: "Fallen, fallen is Babylon the great" (Rev. 14:8). There have, to be sure, been recent attempts to interpret the story of the tower and God's action as benign, which convince me not at all.

2. As to why it came from the north, no one really knows. For the guesses, see Zimmerli 1979: 119–20.

had known just such comings of the Lord to rescue his people, riding upon the storm clouds of heaven and deploying his glory in the lightnings (Deut. 33:26). And this was remembered, perhaps in traditions not closely tied to Jerusalem: "He bowed the heavens, and came down; thick darkness was under his feet. He rode on a cherub, and flew; he came swiftly upon the wings of the wind. . . . Out of the brightness before him there broke through his clouds hailstones and coals of fire" (Ps. 18:8–14). Indeed, the Lord's foundational advent to make Israel his people, his redeeming and sanctifying presence to them on Sinai's mountain, had been in just such a storm enveloping the mountain.

Thus the storm advent is merely in itself salvation for Ezekiel and the exiles. And the knowledge of this coming should have been a sort of gospel for them: however it now stood with the Lord's presence in the temple, he could still be present with his people in his more ancient way, and so as well now for exiles in Babylonia as once for wandering tribes in the wilderness or embattled settlers in Palestine's hill country. By the mere fact of his storm oncoming at the Chebar, the Lord shows that he has not abandoned his exiled folk: even by Babylon's rivers they can at least weep to the Lord. To be sure, the Lord's presence in Babylonia may turn out to be as much judgment as what the exiles might regard as salvation.

Then the storm resolves into a theophany of the Lord enthroned. That "the LORD's throne is in heaven" (Ps. 11:4) is Israel's permanent conviction (on the notion of heaven, →1:1–3). It follows that his rule transcends earthly restraints: distance from the temple should not be thought a barrier to his sovereign presence. Nevertheless, an enthronement of God only in heaven could be a soteriologically ambiguous relationship. Now the heavenly throne itself comes to Babylon's river.

In the temple, the Lord's throne was formed and carried by the wings of sculpted heavenly beings, the "cherubim." In his call-vision (Isa. 6), Isaiah saw the Lord seated upon this throne, filling the temple with his "glory," and with the cherubim[3] not sculpted but alive. That the storm from wilderness days should morph into a cherubim throne is therefore consequent, for the ark at the base of the temple's throne was the great locus of God's presence in the days of Israel's journeying, and the statues of winged beings were icons of those "wings of the wind" upon which God rode the heavens.

As literary historians, we might say that the throne of Ezekiel's vision is modeled on the cherubim throne in the temple and on Isaiah's vision. But within the intention of our text, we must say that since what Ezekiel sees is the heavenly throne itself, the throne in Jerusalem was modeled on it. The transcendence of the throne that Ezekiel sees over its earthly icon is marked by its hieratic otherness, its sheer difference from any throne conceivable in wood, stone, or metal. Indeed, the throne is alive, as no crafted throne can be; one "spirit" animates the whole.

3. Now, for some reason, "seraphim."

No doubt all the strange details once had meaning, but their mythic or cultic contexts are mostly lost to us. Why are there four cherubim instead of the two in the temple? We do not know. Why are the four faces all imposed on each "living being" rather than distributed? We do not know (for some implausible suggestions, see Zimmerli 1979: 120). Why do the wheels have eyes? Presumably because also this part of the throne is sentient, but beyond that we do not know. Why are there wheels within wheels? We do not know.

That there *are* wheels is, however, a vital detail indeed. However remarkable their appearance and capabilities, they remain wheels, and Ezekiel insists that they are rolling on earth (1:15). As Ezekiel endures the onset of heaven's throne, he sees the same Babylonian earth under the throne's wheels as he feels under his feet, earth that requires that if there are to be traveling thrones, they must have porters and wheels, however preternatural. The division between heaven and earth thus becomes radically problematic: heaven travels on Babylonian earth. The throne has even carried down to earth a piece of the sky, of the dome that in Israel's theological cosmology separates God's heaven from our earth (1:22).

We need to consider a bit more fully the salvific character of God's coming in vision to Babylonia. Two matters present themselves, so far as I can see.

A first question concerns the actuality of God's saving advent in Babylonia. What good did the throne's advent do anyone in the thirteenth year, in the fourth month, on the fifth day, among the exiles? The event was, after all, in a vision; and Ezekiel did not awake to find the exiles rejoicing, liberated by the Lord's coming. There are at least two things to be said.

First, something immediate was in fact granted to Ezekiel and to the exiles by way of Ezekiel. Earlier in this commentary unit I called it a "gospel." Ezekiel now knew that Babylon was not beyond the Lord's presence with his people, and among the exiles Ezekiel could act and speak on that knowledge. The community now possessed permission at least to lament to the Lord or to petition prophets—such as Ezekiel was to be—for a word from the Lord.

I just interpreted "gospel" with "permission." In this I followed the theological tradition that speaks of "the gospel" as God's permission to approach him and to venture on holy lives. Another and closely related unpacking of "gospel" has been "promise"—thus "*the* gospel" promises the salvation wrought by Christ. We should also remember that what is revealed in apocalyptic vision is "what must take place after this" (→1:1–3). Thus both in the vision and in the promise thereby granted, what is given is the future.

And that poses the perhaps deepest of metaphysical questions. Which is more real—that is, more resistant to our whim and more to be relied upon—the future present in vision or promise, or what we experience if we reject vision and distrust promise? Modernity has tended to suppose the latter. But scripture throughout presumes the former: that what is coming is the very being of what is. Are the exiles "really" saved by Ezekiel's vision? Yes, in the same sense in which Christians can say they are in present fact saved by hearing the gospel promise of coming salvation.

The second matter: readers may have gathered that I regard this vision of the heavenly throne's earthly career as a vision of incarnation. The division of God's place from ours is overcome: the heavenly throne, *God's* place, becomes an item *within our* place. In the next verses to be considered, incarnation will be more than suggested.

Both rabbinic Judaism and modern exegesis have, however, resisted the suggestion. The rabbis made the vision into a purely transcendent opening into heaven. Modern exegesis has done much the same thing from the other side, by discovering that various bits of 1:1–24 are interpolations made by epigones of Ezekiel and judging that as such they should be disregarded. These latecomers were not— according to this exegesis—quite up to the grandeur of the original vision. Fitting out the throne with a mechanism of earthly travel, they made it into a mere portable throne, such as earthly imperial rulers sometimes needed.[4]

In the canonical text to be interpreted, however, the vision presented is precisely of heaven's throne trundling along beside Chebar—however unworthy some may think this to be. We are faced with the same offense as is more precisely posed by the eternal Logos entering earth in a human belly and finding his first accommodation in a feed trough.

The rabbinic speculation is, to be sure, worth reporting for its own sake. Rabbis of the first and second centuries after Christ named the throne "the *Merkabah*," a label provided by the instructions in 1 Chronicles for building the temple[5] and seized upon it as within Israel's scripture the unique revelation of heaven itself. To preserve this revelation from earthly contamination they played down the throne's wheel-enabled travel on earth; and the Targum simply eliminated it, by rewriting 1:15 to read: "And behold, one wheel was placed just below the heavenly heights, beside [each of] the creatures" (Levey 1990: 22), that is, below the sky dome but still in the air. The throne as the revealed secret of heaven thus became the object and inspiration of a daring and esoteric mystical practice, "*Merkabah* mysticism," that was regarded at once with awe and distrust (→introduction).

It is not as though adumbrations of incarnation are rare in the Old Testament. Narrative structures that regularly appear display the same duality as that of the throne, especially in connection with the temple. To instance one immediately relevant to Ezekiel: is the "glory of the Lord" (→1:25–28b) that inhabits the sanctuary an entity related to the Lord, or is it the Lord himself? Is the Lord merely manifested in the temple, or is he himself there? To make sense of the texts, we have to say both. Thus in Solomon's dedicatory prayer, the temple he has built is "a place for *you* to dwell in" (1 Kgs. 8:13, emphasis added), but the dedication is

---

4. Zimmerli is not usually so wooden, but here he is; Zimmerli 1979: 127–28.

5. In 1 Chr. 28:18 the throne is called "the golden *merkabah* [wagon]." English translations of this passage take refuge in a euphemism: "chariot."

affirmatively answered by the coming of "the glory *of*" the one invited. In that same passage, heaven is the Lord's "dwelling place" but prayers to him are to be directed not to heaven but to the temple (8:30). Or in Deuteronomy, Moses commands the people to bring sacrifice to the Lord, but what awaits them when they get to the appointed place is the "name *of* the LORD" (Deut. 12:5–11). Very directly: "The LORD is in his holy temple; the LORD's throne is in heaven" (Ps. 11:4).

We may hear a great Jewish theologian of the just-ending generation, in an essay remarkably titled "Incarnation": "There is no place in which God is not present. But this truth must be combined with the insistence that God also has an address. . . . He dwells in Number One Har Habayit Street [Jerusalem]."[6]

---

6. Michael Wyschograd, "Incarnation," *Pro ecclesia* 3 (1993): 210.

EZEKIEL 1:25–28b

THE MAN ON THE THRONE

These theologically loaded verses belong with 1:4–24, as the last part of Ezekiel's description of the theophany. I take them separately to avoid making the previous commentary unit even longer and more cumbersome than it is.

From above the throne issues a voice, though we are not told what is said. The speaker is nevertheless seen, and what is seen is described. Above the throne there is an "appearance" that is "the figure of a man" (1:26).[1] This human form shines with all the brightness and fire of the whole throne theophany; indeed it now is apparent that the light comes from him. It is thus the enthroned God who here is—somehow—seen and who when seen looks like a man.

Ezekiel 1:28b then concludes Ezekiel's description of the theophany, with a capsule characterization of the whole: what he had seen was "the appearance of the likeness of the glory of the Lord." Within the vision, the segment is concluded by Ezekiel's prostration. It at first seems that this summation, with no less than three qualifications of what Ezekiel sees, must put great ontological distance between the vision and the envisioned reality.[2] But this impression lasts only until we consider that one of the mediating terms, which controls the whole sequence, is "glory" (*kabod*).

---

1. I venture my own translation of דמות כמראה אדם. NRSV's insertion of "something" could be disastrously misleading.

2. Thereby bringing Ezekiel's discourse into unfortunate proximity with theologies that construe our knowledge of God as obtained by peering through the metaphysical distances: recently, feminist theologies that speak of "projecting" or "imaging" God, theologies of "metaphor," and various other conceptually incompetent appropriations of ancient apophaticism.

Ezekiel's concept of "the glory of the Lord" (כבוד־יהוה, *kabod yhwh*) is specific to him and central to his discourse (Jenni and Westermann 1997: 590–602). In biblical Hebrew, *kabod* is initially "weight," in both literal and metaphorical uses. Taken metaphorically of persons, it has much the same meaning as "weight" does in some English uses, as in "he carries a lot of weight in the group," or indeed as English "glory" itself does in "he deserved all the glory." A person's *kabod* is the intrinsic demand for honor that his or her personal presence makes. The presence of the Lord is then infinite *kabod*. Indeed, we may say that the inner meaning of all Ezekiel's variations on "then they/ you shall know that I . . ." (→introduction) is that the identified persons shall feel the impact of the Lord's *kabod*.

In Ezekiel's particular usage, the notion of divine weight melds with another. In Ezekiel and the tradition[3] in which he stands, advents of the Lord occur as light theophanies, displays of godhead in brilliant color, in fire and lightning. Again some English uses parallel Ezekiel's: we can speak of an intensely bright day as "glorious" or of a painter's "glorious" use of shining color. Thus in Ezekiel's conception, the demand for honor that the Lord's presence makes is imposed by his sheer brilliance—we may think of the impact felt from a suddenly appearing and unbearably bright light.

For the glory of the Lord to be present in the temple or at Chebar is, therefore, for the Lord to be there himself. But it simultaneously holds that his presence must be somehow mediated; it remains that no one can directly encounter naked deity and live (Exod. 33:20). It follows from these two propositions together that God can be present only by a mediator of his presence and that this mediator must nevertheless be the same God that he is. We have already seen (→1:4–24) that God both is *himself* present in the temple and is there as the glory *of* God.

The doctrine of the Trinity brings these phenomena to conceptual statement: for God to be present, in the temple or elsewhere, is for him to be present as an other than he—remember always the genitive in "glory of the Lord"—yet as an other that is the same God that he is. In the terminology of developed trinitarian theology, for God to be present anywhere—even to himself—is for him to be a second "person" of himself. In the temple or by Chebar or in St. Thomas Church on a Sunday, or even at the place he is for himself, God is *there* for us—and for himself—as a second identity of the same one God. So far the general teaching of the church fathers.[4] Thus the appearance over the throne can be none other than this "God the Son," the second person of God.

Why does the second person of the Trinity, appearing above the throne in Ezekiel's vision, look like a man? Christian theology must answer: because the

---

3. Ezekiel was part of the priestly tradition (P), which comes and goes through the Pentateuch and may represent the final editing.

4. Foundationally and perhaps most splendidly represented by Irenaeus of Lyons in *Against Heresies* 4.20.10–11.

second person of the Trinity *is* a man—Jesus of Nazareth.[5] After examining this immense claim, that precisely in its offense to all normal religiosity is Christianity's defining theological affirmation, we will have also to ask why then Ezekiel inserts so many qualifiers between the figure on the throne and what it figures.

Gregory the Great simply assumes that the one on the throne is the man Jesus and concerns himself rather to argue the man's ontological status: "We should observe how the order is maintained: above the living beings is the firmament, above the firmament is the throne, and above the throne a man is delineated. For above holy men still living in . . . the body are the angels, and above the angels are superior angelic powers closer to God, and above the powers is . . . the man Christ Jesus" (1986–90: 1.305). Two essential steps of trinitarian orthodoxy lie behind Gregory's assumption; both were accepted doctrine by his time.

The first step is the doctrine that the second person of the Trinity is the perfect and complete word and image of God and is just so identical in deity with the Father. Dogma formulates this by saying that the Son is "of one being with the Father"[6]—that is to say, precisely in and by the relation the Son has *to* God his Father, he is the *same* God *as* the Father. If the Son is the Father's word, he is so accurately and completely his word that any difference in being between speaker and speech—ineluctable with creatures—disappears. If the Son is the Father's image, he is so exhaustively a mirror—as creatures never are to one another—that there is nothing to his being but the Father he reflects.

One consequence of this is that there is no ontological place for other words or images of God than the Son; the Son wholly preempts the relation. Therefore the person who speaks or shows himself in any theophany of the Old Testament must be this God the Son, God the word, God the second person of God.

The second step is the doctrine that God the Son and Jesus of Nazareth are but one "hypostasis."[7] Whatever this proposition may mean, it at least means, in more modern language, that "God the Son is Jesus" is an identity statement. That is, there is no way to refer to God the Son that does not refer to the man Jesus, and no way to refer to Jesus that does not refer to God the Son. The biblical insight behind this insistence is that there is but one protagonist in the story told by the Gospels, whether he does human things like being born in a womb or divine things like forgiving sins. Therefore, the man on the throne who shines as God must be either a mere simulacrum of a man or Jesus the Christ, for no other actual man can have God's *kabod*.[8]

---

5. Most modern biblical scholarship of course regarded applying this doctrine or any of the following to Ezekiel as nonsense or worse. So Eichrodt 1970: 69–70.

6. This is the decisive theological phrase of the Nicene Creed: ὁμοούσιον τῷ πατρί.

7. This doctrine was laid down at the Council of Chalcedon in 451; for the decree, see Norman P. Tanner, ed., *Decrees of the Ecumenical Councils* (Washington, DC: Georgetown University Press, 1990), 1.86.14–87.2.

8. At this point, mainline theology has in my view been sometimes less than resolute; see Robert W. Jenson, "Jesus in the Trinity," *Pro ecclesia* 8 (1999): 308–18. This led already in the

The assertions just made raise metaphysical questions that have divided theologians throughout the church's history. What of the time before Mary conceived? Was there then no Son at all, or was the Son already enfleshed? Was there not rather a Logos who was not yet Jesus, in the language of some theology an "unfleshed Logos"? Taking up such questions and seeking biblically faithful answers would mean undertaking an entire revision of our inherited metaphysics, which we can hardly do in a commentary. But I note the extreme oddity of asking what things were like "before" the birth of one who is eternal God, which may at least suggest that we need to be careful in plotting divine events on a univocal time line.

There is another biblical scene of a human figure shining with divine glory; and on this occasion the figure is straightforwardly identified as a man, and indeed as Jesus (Mark 9:2–8 and parallels). On the mountain of transfiguration the disciples are in decisive ways in the position of Ezekiel: under extreme circumstances they see the figure of a man shining with God's glory. The difference is that the disciples know this man from before, so that identification as *this* man and so as truly *a* man is not problematic.

To be sure, Western theology has tended to domesticate the scene by denying that the glory with which the transfigured Jesus shone was God's own glory, the divine *kabod*. It was, Western theologians have argued, a "created" light, that is, a radiance of the human body in its proper human perfection, a beauty that is enabled only by God's grace but that nevertheless fulfills a possibility of our created nature. Eastern theology,[9] however, has steadfastly maintained that the "Tabor light" was "uncreated," that this human's brilliance on the mountain was the very glory of Christ's divinity, permanently beyond created possibilities, yet really "communicated" to the creature Jesus. In my judgment, the Easterners are in the biblical right of it.

But why then—finally to come to that question—does Ezekiel so qualify what he sees on the throne as an "appearance, the likeness of a man"? Reflection on the transfiguration can suggest an answer.

Both ancient and historical-critical exegetes are agreed: the transfiguration is a resurrection appearance told ahead of time—the church fathers because they thought that God had in fact let the disciples see their master as he would be in the resurrection, the moderns because they thought Mark had for theological reasons transferred a resurrection story ahead of its proper place. Either way, the figure of Jesus on the mountain *anticipates* his own future as the risen and glorified one. It is, one may suggest, this character of the appearance that accounts for the disciples' bewilderment: they see what is yet to come, and so "in a glass, darkly."

---

ancient church to decreasing emphasis on a christological solution to the question "how can we see God?" and increasing emphasis on apophatic qualifications of our seeing, perhaps an unfortunate development. For this history, precisely with respect to Ezekiel, see Christman 2005.

9. The great systematizer and defender here is the fourteenth-century Gregory Palamas, "the Thomas Aquinas of the East." To the present point see, e.g., his *Triads* 3.1.12–17.

If the figure of Jesus transformed on the mountain anticipates his future glory as the risen one, the figure on Ezekiel's throne is doubly an anticipation. To be sure, the meaning of "not yet" in such contexts is—as just asserted—treacherous; but one may perhaps say that the figure on the throne is not yet identified to beholders as the particular man he is and therefore is not fully identifiable as "*a* man."

The event on Tabor was a resurrection appearance, even if ahead of time, and so not a vision.[10] But Ezekiel's experience was a vision and may indeed be called a visionary anticipation of the waking anticipation on Tabor. It is this that makes the man shimmer in Ezekiel's eyes and compels him to be so cautious, for sight is always uncertain when it cannot fix objects in the present.

10. Visions are not seen in groups, whereas most of the resurrection appearances were to gatherings. The appearance to Paul was indeed more like a vision. But according to Paul himself, it was irregular; we should not make it the interpreting paradigm of the others.

EZEKIEL 1:28c–3:15

ORDINATION AND COMMISSION

Seeing visions of God or even hearing him speak does not yet make a prophet. A prophet must not only possess knowledge of God's intentions but be sent by God to tell Israel of them; it was possible to prophesy accurately and still be a false prophet. If the prophet's calling takes place as a vision, the sending may occur within the vision, as it does with Isaiah (Isa. 6:1–10) and here (readers should read the two previous commentary units before continuing here). But since a commission involves the giving of instructions, it cannot be done only by sight; language must intrude. Accordingly, the voice from the throne now speaks intelligibly to Ezekiel, addressing him as the word invariably will, as "you—son of a man," and saying, "Stand up . . . and I will speak with you" (2:1).

The sending is narrated at length and has a liturgical structure. In the middle (2:8–3:3) there is what can be called only a sacramental ordination. This is bracketed by two passages of verbal commissioning. Ezekiel 3:12–15 then narrates the end of the call-vision: the throne departs, and the Spirit transports a shattered Ezekiel to his exilic community, where he waits.

I will begin with the sacramental act. "A hand" appears. Ezekiel refrains from saying that this belongs to the figure above the throne, though within the vision it plainly does. The hand presents a scroll, written on both sides. Scrolls were not normally written on the back; perhaps the overfilling indicates the plenitude of what Ezekiel will be given to say. What is on the scroll is not necessarily a series of lamentations; "mourning" and "woe" are what the contents will produce in Ezekiel's hearers.

The Targum interpolates a characterization of the scroll's contents: "That which was from the beginning and that which is destined to be in the end" (Levey

1990: 24). That is, the Targum characterizes the book as what we have called an "apocalypse" (→1:1–3). And indeed, within the New Testament this very same scroll—identified by being written "on the inside and on the back" just as here—reappears at the beginning of the apocalypse of John (Rev. 5–22). In the Revelation, the scroll contains the plot of history—just as the Targum says—which unrolls in the following visionary scenes as the scroll's seals are removed.

The owner of the hand says to Ezekiel, "Eat this scroll, and go, speak to the house of Israel." With Ezekiel's obedience to the first part of the command, the ordination is accomplished. Obedience to the accompanying commission will then occupy Ezekiel's life.

The idea was perhaps already in place, that God's word can come in a book—written versions of the proclamation of previous prophets seem to have been circulating by Ezekiel's time (Zimmerli 1979: 137). It was not therefore wholly out of the way of the text, when the church fathers made the book a figure of the Bible: "Just as by the prophet the order of preachers is designated, so by the book he receives . . . sacred Scripture is designated" (Gregory 1986–90: 1.369).

"Eat what is offered to you" has obvious and powerful resonance in the church. Eating a book is, to be sure, a drastic sacramental reception, but the word must have *some* path to the inner man—just as in the Eucharist Christ comes to dwell indeed in the heart, but gets there by way of eating. And if this particular book is eaten it will taste sweet, however alarming its content, for God's word is intrinsically sweet (e.g., Ps. 119:103).

In the first commissioning passage, Ezekiel is told to speak to "a people." This turns out not to be the exilic community, as one might have expected, but "Israel." In the Lord's address to Ezekiel, here and often elsewhere, "Israel" denotes a single diachronic entity, existing as one from her beginning in Egypt and encompassing even the partly dispersed northern nation. Indeed, we may say that Israel appears as a single diachronic subject of action, as if it were one person. And this entity is rebellious against the Lord almost by definition, transgressive of his commands and bound to persecute any true prophet.

Correspondingly, what Ezekiel's commission sends him to say is itself abstract. It consists of the standard prophetic opening address, "thus says the Lord," without anything the Lord says. Ezekiel will later be given more than enough to proclaim, but in his defining commission all that could be elided. This fits the intended outcome of Ezekiel's prophesying as here specified: the people shall learn simply that there is "a prophet among them," that the Lord's word is still active in their midst. They will be made to know this just because Ezekiel is there speaking for the Lord, whether or not they hearken to the content of Ezekiel's speech. That they may or may not believe God's word, that this unthinkable choice is open results from their being "a rebellious house." Either way, Israel will have to reckon with Ezekiel, and so with the Lord's word in their midst.

In the passage following the book sacrament, the gist of this is repeated, with additional forebodings. The Lord is sending Ezekiel to a people who speak his language. If he were sent to aliens and somehow made himself understood, perhaps *they* would believe—the story of Jonah and Nineveh is the story of this possibility. But the Lord's own people will not believe. Israel will butt heads with Ezekiel, and all that the Lord can do for him is make his skull as flinty as theirs. It is small wonder that Ezekiel goes home "in bitterness."

Ezekiel is returned to his exilic community. Later instances of Ezekiel's being taken somewhere "in the Spirit," most notably his transports to Jerusalem (8:3; 40:1–3) probably take place in vision, without bodily transportation. In the present case, however, it certainly seems that we are intended to suppose that Ezekiel was physically first by the river Chebar and that when the Spirit was done he was at Tel-abib. What are we to think? It is always good to remember the great motto about "more things in heaven and earth" than "are dreamt of" in anyone's philosophy.

In any case, whether we are credulous or skeptical about physical transportation, the chief thing we need to understand here is the role of "the Spirit." The Hebrew word is *ruach* (רוח), which initially means both "wind" and "breath" (as does its New Testament translation, πνεῦμα). Drastically summarizing the word's primal Old Testament uses, God's *ruach* is the Lord's breath, the storm of his sheer life, that blows about whatever he turns to—thus it was the Lord's *ruach* that blew back the waters of the sea before fleeing Israel (Exod. 15:8–12). If God is bodily to snatch Ezekiel from one place to another, it is his *ruach* that will do it. This will be experienced by the victim as a visionary seizure. And there we will leave the matter.

The Lord's sending of Ezekiel sets us deep within the mystery of history. A "people," Israel, appears here as a single diachronic entity, with so tightly coherent a story that it can be summed in one word, which—sadly—is "rebellion." In the wake of biblical history telling, the great Western historians aimed at discerning similar narratives and slogans also for other "peoples"[1] and indeed, in the wake of apocalyptic prophecy's (→1:1–3) posit of history as a single drama, for history as a whole. In late modernity historians have largely abandoned such ambitions, but thereby they may have abandoned also any secure claim to a discipline of their own. Sociology or literary criticism or political science of a past period could as well be assigned to the several material disciplines. At most, self-labeled historians might be left with the construction of chronologies.

Israel could appear as a temporal entity with a consistent character—even if only rebellion—because it existed by the will of someone other than her, one enthroned to determine the future. And Western historians' erstwhile telling of history as coherent narrative occurred within an intellectual world shaped by the Bible, also when the historian was not Jewish or Christian. Conversely, it would seem that if there is no God, there can be nothing like what the Western tradition has called

---

1. It is hard now even to remember how someone like Arnold Toynbee elegantly construed the character of various civilizations.

history—and in the West's repaganizing culture this is now being demonstrated. Who is to guarantee that there *is* an entity to be called Israel—or Germany or America[2]—and to delineate such an entity? If not God or, in horrid possibility, some human substitute?

To be sure, if there is God to create history, the reality of history *as* history seems threatened from another side. Already in the present passage, the Lord seems close to saying that he has himself determined that Israel's story will be a story of rebellion, and later passages will come even closer to that alarming proposition. But if the Lord determines history, are we not—as it is always said—puppets? And if those who are the *dramatis personae* of history are puppets, why give the process a special name, "history"? Why not acknowledge that the procession of human events is a mere mechanism, as many moderns have thought?

The key—not necessarily a solution—to these problems is in our passage. The Lord's determining of Israel's temporal being is not done by arbitrary decision in heaven. It is done precisely by the presence of his word in Israel's life, by prophets being among them—which is to say that it is done in something like a conversation between the Lord and "this people." The Lord determines, but Israel speaks up in his deliberations—if so far only to say no. Is such intrusion on omnipotence thinkable? It is if Jesus's invitation is valid, that we should approach God, call him "Father," and tell him how we view our situation (Matt. 6:9–13 and parallel). And if it should be objected that there have been no proper prophets since John the Baptist, so that if this teaching were correct history should have ceased, we should remember that according to Christian teaching the church is a single prophetic community in the world (Acts 2:16–18).

Moreover, as the Lord's word in Ezekiel's commissioning is sacramentally embodied, so it is throughout the prophets' speaking of that word—we need look no further than the very next chapters of Ezekiel. And that is to say: the word of God that determines history is itself fully involved amid the clashing and joining bodies that make history. It is in line with the adumbrations of incarnation we have found and will find throughout Ezekiel: God does not rule only from without the rough and tumble of history but also from within it.

2. Is not "America" an invention of nineteenth-century nationalists, etc.?

EZEKIEL 3:16–21

THE SENTINEL

These verses make a clear unit: "the word of the Lord came to me" is Ezekiel's way to begin the account of any revelation that is not a vision. And 3:22 must begin a different prophecy, since "the hand of the Lord was upon me" is the way that Ezekiel reports the onset of vision.

There is, to be sure, a literary problem, again of a kind we cannot altogether ignore: most of the passage appears word for word also at 33:7–9. Moreover, "at the end of seven days" in 3:16a would fit nicely with 3:22 to make a typical vision introduction: "At the end of those seven days, the hand of the Lord was upon me." It therefore seems likely, that 3:16b–21 is the literary unit, created when someone borrowed 33:7–9, added some thoughts, and inserted the result here, breaking up 3:16a and 3:22. As to why this was done, the reader's guess is as good as mine.

Ezekiel 3:16 is Ezekiel's first use in his book of the formula "the word of the Lord came to me" and is therefore an opportunity further to plumb the deep theological waters into which the formula and Ezekiel's use of it plunge us. Modern biblical scholarship has noted that the word that comes to prophets cannot be just a series of messages. What comes to the prophets in their succession is a single living reality (von Rad 1962–66: 1.89 made this fully clear). If we put this contemporary insight together with what I noted in the introduction about the word's coming, we arrive at a conclusion to which I came earlier (→1:4–3:15) from a different departure: the common opinion that the Trinity is not in the Old Testament is false. The word of the Lord that "comes" to prophets is the same word that always "was with God and . . . was God" and is incarnate as Jesus (John 1:1–14). What came to Ezekiel each time he was to speak for God was the one identified in trinitarian doctrine as "the Logos," the "second person" of the Trinity.

When on the present occasion the word happened to Ezekiel, he received no word for Israel, but rather a word for himself. He, this "son of a man," is to be a "sentinel"[1] in Israel. This turns out to mean that he is to watch out for wickedness, warn the wicked to repent, and warn the righteous to stay that way. The stakes for those warned are high: the wicked who continue in wickedness and the righteous who turn from righteousness will die. The stakes are just as high for Ezekiel: if he fails to warn either group, he will die. Behind such stark alternatives and punitive rigor lies the great alternative posed to Israel by the theology of Josiah's reform movement: "I have set before you life and death. . . . Choose life" (Deut. 30:19).

We must, to be sure, take into account the depth of the Old Testament's construal of death. Genesis will suffice at this point. The Lord tells "the man" that on the very day they eat of the forbidden tree, they will die (2:17). They eat and do not biologically die. But they are alienated from God and cast out of his garden. Death in the Old Testament's theological sense includes biological death, but is not identical with it: the former may occur without the immediate supervention of the latter, and the latter does not necessarily involve the former.

Nevertheless, after the stark alternative that the Lord lays before Ezekiel, we hardly expect subtleties. The relation between God's sentence of the wicked and the prophet's warning turns out, however, to be strangely dialectical. The Lord himself sentences the wicked person, "You shall surely die." This is evidently not said through a prophet, since the prophet's work is next mentioned separately. Perhaps we are to think of the law given to Israel as conceived by Deuteronomy, or perhaps of a decree issued in the Lord's hidden enthronement, addressed to the wicked but not intended to be heard.

The Lord's judgment does not, however, deterministically settle the fate of the sinner, since repentance is possible. But this possibility of repentance lies in a remarkable disjunct—which so far as I can see remains unresolved in Ezekiel. After the divine sentence of death is passed, the prophet is to intervene with his warning, which by calling for repentance makes it possible that the condemned will not in fact die. According to this passage, the Lord's legal—and perhaps secret—sentence and the Lord's warning by the prophet can have opposite outcomes.

If this seems to mitigate divine control, another line in our passage makes the antinomy shockingly drastic. In 3:20 we read, "If the righteous turn from their righteousness and commit iniquity, and I lay a stumbling block before them, they shall die." The Lord's act to trip up the previously righteous is not punishment for sin, for "I lay a stumbling block" is in the if-clause of a conditional sentence while the punishment, "they shall die," is the then-clause. But what then? Does the Lord himself trip the once righteous into their sin? And then send the prophet to threaten punishment? Does "I lay a stumbling block" perhaps even refer to the

---

1. The Targum translates "teacher," thereby much dampening the passage's impact (Levey 1990: 26).

same event as "the righteous . . . commit iniquity"? The Lord can be that devious; we will discover that in the wilderness he "gave them statutes that were not good and ordinances by which they could not live" (20:25). If the rest of scripture does not do it, Ezekiel will surely undo simplistic ideas of God's moral relation to history, whether traditional or modern-liberal.

In his call, Ezekiel was not sent to individuals; he was sent to "the house of Israel" as a single reality (→1:28c–3:15). Yet those over whom he is to keep watch, the righteous and the unrighteous, seem to be classes *within* Israel. Later this incipient individualism will become less incipient: "[Only] the soul[2] that sins shall die. . . . The righteousness of the righteous shall be his own, and the wickedness of the wicked shall be his own" (18:20).

The agony of Israel and Judah in the eighth and seventh centuries threatened Israelites' sense of the nation as the reality within which they knew their identity and in whose future they found their reward. Questions pressed that had not before: Why should *I* suffer because the nation of Israel has sinned? Or vice versa: Why should all the *nation* of Israel be punished because many of the elite have sinned, as if Israel were one person?

The question not only distressed later Israel, it perplexes all cultures and centuries: Am I first an individual, who associates with others to make a community, or am I first a member of the community, who just and only so can become an individual? To whom am I first accountable, to the community or to myself? Or to whom are my fellows first accountable, to me or to the community that includes me? Ezekiel—or the Lord as revealed to Ezekiel—seems to have wanted it both ways. One might think that Christian theology should have a way to transcend the alternative, but what that might be is again debated.

Moreover, is the Deuteronomistic doctrine, that death follows sin and life follows virtue, in fact true? Much experience suggests that it is not. The matter came to be fiercely debated in Israel; the entire book of Job dramatizes the question. But if Deuteronomic simplicity is wrong, what then? Is the Lord powerless to maintain justice? If not, how is he God? But if he has the power, how is he just when he does not use it? The problem of theodicy, of justifying God's justice, has occupied minds great and small—and in the judgment of some, including me, it is insoluble within the terms of this age.

May it be that justice, in this age often in abeyance, is nevertheless fulfilled eschatologically? The notion has been mocked as "pie in the sky by and by," and there is no doubt that the Jewish and Christian hope for a final sorting out of moral accounts has sometimes been so cast as to give that appearance. But the promise of the kingdom of heaven, in which God's will must finally be done, is the Lord Jesus's own message, and trust in this promise is the very thing that the church has meant by faith.

---

2. The NRSV, perhaps moved by dislike of "soul-body dualism," has "person." This will not do. The Hebrew is נֶפֶשׁ (*nephesh*, "living being"), for which "person" is anachronistic.

   Or indeed is God's justice too strange to be discussed at all in such categories? It is clear throughout scripture and dogmatic tradition that God does not will sin and therefore is free to punish it. Yet would God's grace—of which also Ezekiel will finally have much to say—really be what Christianity knows as "grace" if we needed no rescue from stumbling? Must not also "the mystery of iniquity" be *somehow* encompassed in the mystery of God's will to save? Could there have been some other incarnate Logos than the one crucified for sin? A passage in the ancient liturgy for the Easter Vigil praises the *felix culpa*, the "happy sin" of Adam, that "occasioned such glorious redemption" as occurred on Good Friday and Easter. Church doctrine has never officially endorsed the sentiment, yet there the passage is, in the most profound of Christian liturgies. Must not God's will to bless creation somehow and unthinkably include that first great stumbling block in humanity's way? The greatest theologians have at least faced the question.

EZEKIEL 3:22–5:4

SIGNS OF THE SIEGE
AND FALL OF JERUSALEM

These verses belong to a complex that continues through 5:17. Though the whole passage reports a single vision, it is too long and unwieldy to manage in one commentary unit, and I divide it for convenience. Making the break at 5:5 is not altogether arbitrary, since there is a strangely unmediated transition there. Even so, the present commentary unit considers a great deal of text.

Ezekiel 3:22–5:17 is not only unwieldy, on inspection it does not hang together very well. This has naturally provoked critical proposals about successive editings, overlapping interpolations by schools of Ezekiel's followers, and the like. The proposals are in my judgment too fragile to be exploited for the kind of exegesis this commentary intends. I will therefore simply take things one at a time and not try to reconstruct coherence where the existing text does not offer it.

The vision is introduced with the formula "the hand of the Lord was upon me." If indeed 3:16b–21 was interpolated into an earlier arrangement of the text (→3:16–21), this introduction once read, "After those seven days, the hand of the Lord was upon me."

Ezekiel is told to go out to "the valley," which is perhaps simply the flood plain of the Euphrates.[1] The visionary character of his experience there is established by a quick—almost perfunctory—reference (3:23) to the inaugural vision reported at 1:4–24: we are to understand that what happens in the valley is like what happened by Chebar. There is another quick reference (3:27b) to the abstract mode

1. KJV's "the plain" may have been the better translation.

of prophecy specified in 2:1–10. What this reference is doing here is unclear, since the messages the vision will now entrust to Ezekiel are if anything prolix. Here as throughout, Ezekiel is addressed as "you—son of a man."

The prophecy granted in the vision is directed to the nation. But when Ezekiel has come out to the valley, the Lord's first word is that Ezekiel should go home again, to the exiles' settlement, and shut himself in his house. Did the Lord bring Ezekiel to the valley merely to impose a moratorium of prophesying, perhaps the same silence as the fit of speechlessness next announced? Or does the Lord, on the contrary, here mandate the location of Ezekiel's prophesying: he is not to go "out among the people" but remain in his own house, so that the exiles will have to seek him out, since they are such a rebellious house?

I hesitantly incline to the second reading, since in the few passages that say where Ezekiel is located when prophesying, he is indeed in his house.[2] If this reading is right, again I must note the remarkable abstraction of "Israel" as the object of Ezekiel's mission: Ezekiel addresses the nation merely by being available, and that to a little group of exiles.

After ordering his return home, the Lord informs Ezekiel of a coming period of physical bondage. It is not clear when this will happen: the apparent narrative succession suggests it will be immediately on his return, but the intrusion of a new introduction, "as for you, son of a man," between "shut yourself in your house" and "cords shall be placed on you" suggests that this appearance may be the result of some now-unrecoverable history of editing.

Nor is it clear who will tie Ezekiel up or why they will do it, but perhaps the best guess is that some of the exiles will not only be pleased that Ezekiel is shut into his house, but will take action to keep it that way. In this politically desperate time, physical restraint of a prophet, in the hope of preventing unwelcome prophecies, was not unknown (Jer. 20; 29:26).

If the binding was to prevent public prophesying, the exiles need have had no immediate worries. The Lord himself will make Ezekiel speechless, until he chooses to speak by him. One day he will so choose, and when he does neither Ezekiel nor the people will be able to hinder it. Whatever other meaning the Lord's imposition of speechlessness may have had in some other context, in the present context it drives one thing home: prophecy is the Lord's gift and the Lord's voice, and he withholds it or gives it as he alone decides.

The main burden of this complex passage follows. When Ezekiel is called from his silence, he is to perform a set of signs, all of which will depict the siege and fall of Jerusalem. Perhaps this context interprets Ezekiel's shut-in time as itself another such sign, of the isolation of the besieged. Perhaps the moratorium of prophecy becomes yet another, of the withholding of the Lord's saving word. Four signs are explicitly mandated, all are provided with stage directions, and some with brief interpretations intended for Ezekiel himself. The import of these signs is all too

2. Zimmerli 1979: 160 interprets in this way. Eichrodt 1970: 77 takes the opposite position.

clear; and comment on this long and chief part of the passage will need less space than has been spent on the preceding formal obscurities.

First sign. Ezekiel is to make a model of Jerusalem and of siegeworks around it. Then he is to take an iron plate and with it squeeze the model. This sign needed little interpretation then, beyond explicit identification of the city, which it will receive at 5:5, and it needs little now.

Second sign. Ezekiel is to lie bound on one side and then on the other, one day for each year of the two kingdoms' exiles. The numbers are plainly round numbers. Instead of the Masoretic Text's 390 days for the years of the northern kingdom's exile, the Septuagint has 190 days, which makes it—barely—conceivable that this sign could actually be carried out. Perhaps this sign has some connection to the bondage predicted at 3:25, but the existing text does not betray what this might be. Perhaps also Ezekiel's "bearing" of Israel's punishment is to be in some way atoning; some of the rabbis interpreted it in this way (Levey 1990: 29).

Third sign. Ezekiel is to live on bread made from miscellaneous grains. The miscellany and the rationing point to the conditions of siege, when people will put together a limited meal of whatever is obtainable. Worse, he is to bake his meager mélange loaf on human dung.[3] For a priest bound to ritual purity (Jenni and Westermann 1997: 482–86, 495–97), carrying out this sign would be a horrifying pollution, and he begs and receives some mitigation. In the coming siege of Jerusalem, people will eat however they can, never mind the laws of purity. The siege will not only impose physical starvation, but also a starvation of holiness.

Fourth sign. The previous signs have been transparent. This of the sword-razor and the batches of hairs is indeed dramatic enough, but in itself carries no obvious meaning. Ezekiel is given the interpretation: the fates of the bundles of hair anticipate the various fates of Jerusalem's population when the city falls. No further interpretation seems required from a commentator.

It is possible that a ray of hope hides in 5:2–4. A third of the hair represents those who do not die in the fall of the city, but are nevertheless later to be killed. But Ezekiel is to protect "a small number" of these in his robe. These may represent those who end up where Ezekiel is, in exile, and just so survive. Also some of this remnant will fall to judgment. Nevertheless there will be a remnant of the remnant of the remnant (von Rad 1962–66: 2.165).

Following the mandate to Ezekiel to perform the signs, and quick personal indications to Ezekiel of what they will mean, the complex concludes with a long continuous interpretation more in the style of a standard prophetic sermon (→5:5–17).

We have before us the first actual body of prophecy given to Ezekiel, which is to be accomplished by acted-out signs. It is time to consider the power of

---

3. For modern Western readers, it may be necessary to note that the use of dried dung for fuel is a usual practice of cattle-raising societies. It is not the use of dung that is ritually polluting but the use of human dung.

prophetic speech and of such signs, as conceived in Israel (von Rad 1962–66: 2.81–98).

Words make things happen. We feel this less urgently than do cultures more dependent on verbal communication and on memory, but the fact is inescapable. If, in the proper circumstances, the jury says "not guilty," the accused goes free and within the law of the community is in fact not guilty. What then if the word spoken is *God's* word? If we creatures can create weal and woe by good words and hard words, what does the Creator do when he speaks? According to the account of creation (Gen. 1:1–2:3), God does nothing less with his word than speak the universe into existence (Jenson 1997–99: 2.3–29): "God said . . . and it was so."

Therefore when a true prophet proclaims "thus says the Lord" and speaks of what is to happen, he does not merely predict what will happen anyway. The speaking of God's word within history is integral to God's action to bring his will to pass—which is why some in Jerusalem foolishly thought that by preventing prophets from prophesying they might prevent the disasters they feared would be proclaimed. As regularly appears in Ezekiel's prophecy and book, the Lord's rule of Israel is not accomplished simply from outside Israel's history, but also from within it: the Lord's throne is at once in heaven and in the temple and in Babylon. The Lord's word spoken by a true prophet is the Lord's sovereign heavenly decree happening on earth.

Throughout the prophetic tradition, the word carried by language was often accompanied by "signs" (Jenni and Westermann 1997: 67–70). Isaiah went naked to signify the suffering of refugees (Isa. 20), and Jeremiah wore a yoke to point to Judah's coming bondage (Jer. 27–28). So much does such action belong to prophecy that the word translated "sign" (אוֹת, *oth*) became a technical term in prophetic speech, as in our passage: "This is an *oth* for the house of Israel" (Ezek. 4:3).

The prophetic *oth* is a specific intensification of the prophetic word's power to do what it predicts (von Rad 1962–66: 2.94–98). Thus Ezekiel's lying bound on his two sides will not only predict the punishments of the two kingdoms but will "bear" them; and when he will throw one bunch of hair into the fire, "from there a fire will come out against all the house of Israel." The visibility and tangibility of the sign embody the word within the bodily human interactions that constitute history. Moreover, prophetic signs were often performed upon the body of the prophet himself and sometimes were painful or shaming: the prophet as himself an embodied actor in history carries in his body the judgments God makes in history. In summary, an *oth* is "a creative prefiguration of the future" (von Rad 1962–66: 2.96), just as a Christian sacrament brings into the present some aspect of the future promised by the gospel.

Indeed, it is impossible to ignore this parallel of the prophetic *oth*, in its unity of bodily action with the word, with the Christian concept of sacrament. Augustine's definition of sacrament became the foundation of Western sacramentology: "The word comes to the element; and so there is a sacrament, that is, a sort of visible word" (*In Johannem* 80.3), where "element" denotes the visible thing with which a sign is enacted. "Our Lord Jesus Christ, in the night in which he was betrayed, *took bread*, gave thanks, and gave it to them *saying....*"

Thus there has been a strand of Christian theology that regards some of Israel's cultic acts—such as circumcision or animal sacrifice—as indeed sacraments "of the old covenant."[4] Perhaps we should not extend this category to cover the prophetic *oth*, for sacraments creatively anticipate salvation while the prophets' signs mostly anticipate judgment. The formal parallel, however, is important for our understanding of prophecy and especially of Ezek. 5:5–17.

---

4. See, for example, Thomas Aquinas's nuanced discussion in *Summa theologiae* 3.62.6 of whether "the sacraments of the old covenant" confer grace.

EZEKIEL 5:5–17

JERUSALEM'S DISASTER

This passage is a classic piece of prophetic preaching. It begins with the formula "thus says the Lord" and continues with usual prophetic forms of denunciation and judgment. The content makes it plain that this is verbal prophecy to go with performance of the signs just previously mandated (→3:22–5:4).

But though this passage is obviously intended to go with the one immediately preceding it, the existing text provides neither logical nor narrative continuity with it. We expect something like, "Then the word of the Lord came to me: 'Speak to Israel and say. . . .'" But instead the one passage is merely set down after the other.

The relation of 5:5–17 to its preceding context is problematic also in other ways. As it stands, the text is a single discourse apparently to be delivered at one time. The signs, on the other hand, must at least in some cases have been performed at different times. Finally, of the four mandated signs, one, Ezekiel's lying bound on his sides, is not mentioned at all.

All this has of course provoked various scholarly reconstructions of the passage's history, especially with respect to its relation to the signs. For our purposes, we may suppose merely that the text before us more or less represents what Ezekiel was initially given to say about three of his signs and recognize one obvious interloper.

The speech begins with explicit interpretation of the *oth* with the model city: "This is Jerusalem." This sets up the whole speech: it will be about Jerusalem. And the identification is already a message of judgment: it is Jerusalem that is to be besieged and taken.

The Lord begins with Jerusalem's previously exalted status: it has been "in the center of the nations [הגוים, the *goyim*—a fated expression]," and other nations have had their place and individuality by their relation to it. In part this claim appropriates the universally encountered mythic nation of a navel of the cosmos (Zimmerli 1979: 174–75):[1] every people thinks that its city—whether Nineveh, Jerusalem, Washington DC, or four mud huts in a clearing—is at the primordial geometric and life-giving center of the cosmos, as the navel is in the human microcosm.[2] But whereas the pattern of myth is that the city's place as a universal center is a fact of the "beginning" and so eternal, the Lord says that Jerusalem's status was given to it by his choice at a time in history and so can be ended in the same way.

Since Jerusalem's place as the center of the nations thus depends on the Lord's personal will for her, Jerusalem's perdurance in that place depends on her correspondence to the moral content of that will, on obedience to his "statutes and ordinances." These were the two forms of law in Israel: *apodictic* divine commands like the Ten Commandments, with their direct and unconditional "you shall not" (e.g., Exod. 20:11–17); and the rulings of daily jurisprudence with their *casuistic* "if . . . is done, the rule to follow is . . ." (e.g., 21:2–22:16). The stereotypical pairing "statutes and ordinances" thus denotes the total moral basis the Lord gave Israel, which rabbinic Judaism calls Torah. Jerusalem, the Lord says, has rebelled against this.

Jerusalem can hardly have managed to rebel against the entire body of her law. Wherein her rebellion specifically consisted, we will learn as we progress through the book. In the present passage we have first indications: it consisted in obeying ordinances of the surrounding nations, and it dishonored the Lord's sanctuary.

This narrows the possibilities: the Lord does not here complain of all bad or even criminal behavior. Certainly there were murders and adulteries and the usual crimes in Jerusalem, together with economic greed and civil decay, and the prophets often made these the burden of their judgments. But the criminal and civil laws of neighboring nations of course no more urged crime or economic or civil degeneracy than did the laws of Israel, and therefore it cannot have been obedience to such laws that was Israel's sin. What other nations did ordain that was forbidden in Israel was worship of Baal and Astarte and all the host of deity. Thus Jerusalem's rebellion was against "you shall have no other gods besides me." As we will find explicitly laid out in Ezek. 8, Jerusalem dishonored the Lord's sanctuary by mixing worship of the Lord with worship of other gods.

Against this direct rebellion against his personal claim to Israel, the Lord will no longer merely send Nebuchadnezzar. The one who chose the city will personally take the field against the city of his choice (5:8), thereby bringing an intrinsically

1. Greenberg 1983: 110–11 thinks this notion pushes the language too far.
2. The navel is the geometrical center of the human body, and even the most observationally hindered society cannot but notice that it also is where the new body is attached to the source of its life.

unrepeatable catastrophe (5:9). This will be constituted by the judgments portrayed in the third and fourth signs.

As Ezekiel hungered under acted-out siege and was threatened with ritual pollution, so the besieged inhabitants of Jerusalem will in the extremity of their hunger turn to the ultimate pollution, cannibalism. For humans to be eaten they must be dead or be killed; and human death is the enemy of life, and so of the God who gives life.[3] In Israel, all dealings with human death had therefore to be purged before approaching God, or approaching other people in their cultic reality as God's people. The miasma extended far: all that emerges from the human body and represents expended life—like the human excrement with which Ezekiel was threatened—pollutes.[4] As for an actual corpse, even necessary and indeed divinely commended contact with one requires ritual cleansing—and eating it is beyond all thought.

The fourth *oth* was the most in need of interpretation but when interpreted is the most fearfully clear, as is here proclaimed at length. As Ezekiel's sword-razor cut through the clumps of hair, the Lord will himself "cut down" the people.

Ezekiel 5:13–17 mostly reiterates the preceding verses, with more strident rhetoric. The passage does, however, develop the speech in two important points, by stipulating the source and purpose of the judgment.

According to 5:13–17 the destruction to be wrought by the Lord will not be a cool judicial punishment, however deserved and duly decreed; it will "satisfy" the *wrath* of God and express his *jealousy*. That God can have any emotion, let alone these, is difficult for modern sensibilities. But it cannot be denied: the God of scripture has these affects. Indeed, at Exod. 34:14, "Jealousy" is a name of God.

The punishment has an intended outcome: "They shall know that I, the Lord, have spoken." This prediction—or threat—supposes that there will after all be survivors to learn the lesson. The event of Jerusalem's disaster will verify for this remnant that Ezekiel's words were indeed prophecy and so verify that the Lord is still active—whether they receive this as good news or bad.

Christianity has often had a problem with "statutes and ordinances." Protestantism has perhaps had particular difficulty; and late modern Protestantism and "progressive" Catholicism have no idea what to do with them. Does not God choose us—as we like to say—unconditionally? Is not his love the very model of inclusiveness? How then can he condemn us for following our own statutes and ordinances, or none? Does not St. Paul teach that we are made right with God apart from law? Why then should we bow to—often apparently arbitrary—divine commands? How, for that matter, do we know that a command proposed to us is divine? Is even its presence in scripture an absolute guarantee? Must we not

---

3. Even accidentally shed "blood pollutes the land," and the Lord commands, "You shall not defile the land in which you live, in which I also dwell" (Num. 35:33–34).

4. That menstrual blood pollutes has nothing to do with low regard for female function, as some feminists assert. The blood is lifeblood that is dying and that is coming from the channel of new life. If the ancients had known what it is intended to carry, they would have redoubled purifications.

rather ourselves determine what is right and good in our time, which is not the time from which scripture or the church's traditions come to us? And may it not further be that we must each do this for him/herself alone?

Such questions press hard on moderns and also on believers. Nevertheless, we should recognize that if we accede to their pressure, we must abandon any thought of divine choice—whether of Israel or the church or of the believer, and whether inclusive or exclusive—and so of divine love.

Antinomianism, the old and recently again flourishing heresy that sees no role for statues and ordinances in the life of faith, may be a temptation built into Christianity: perhaps only on the edge of antinomianism does the true bite of the gospel appear. But falling over that edge is nevertheless the disaster of faith, for the notion of a loving choice that does not impose statutes and ordinances is a mere oxymoron. One person's choice of another—whether it be God choosing Jerusalem or lovers choosing each other—contains an *intention* for the other— if it does not, the choice is not personal but rather arbitrary or mechanistically determined. And the intention of one person for another intrinsically displays some construal of their mutual good, unless again the chooser is a demon or automaton. If God chose Israel in love, then this included his intention that they together live one kind of life and not another, and the difference is delineated in Torah. If according to Paul God in love chooses believers, it is to be persons bringing the fruits of the Spirit and not of "the flesh"; and for all Paul's polemics against "the law," he does not hesitate to tell us at length what the fruits of each are (e.g., Gal. 5:22).

Thus there is a sense in which Jerusalem destroyed herself by rebelling against the statutes and ordinances that made her Jerusalem and not Babylon or Sidon. Nor is the feeling of such self-enforcing morality peculiar to Israel; all integral cultures suppose that communal punishment must eventually follow on communal sin, in a fashion analogous to the connections stated by laws of nature. Evidence to the contrary convinces a culture only as it collapses.

But does that not put Ezek. 5:5–17 in contradiction with itself? Is an immanent connection between Jerusalem's sin and her coming disaster compatible with the proclamation that the Lord himself takes the field to punish her?

Jerusalem is punished by inevitable consequences of sin and is punished by God in person. These are compatible on one condition: if the statues and ordinances that make the moral order do not obtain independently of God (as often in other religions) or do not function merely as a mediation of divine order from afar (as in yet other systems) but simply *are* the Lord's own willing and acting among his creatures.

The supposition that God can be wrathful when rebelled against, and even jealous of his people's love, further offends our prejudices. We may try to escape by the popular supposition that God in the Old Testament could be wrathful and that the New Testament changes all that. But this notion cannot survive the slightest acquaintance with the texts. Paul is not outdone by Ezekiel: "For the wrath of God is revealed from heaven against all ungodliness and wickedness" (Rom. 1:18), which he latter catalogues in truly wrathful detail. And for depictions of divinely ordained destruction of the wicked, the New Testament book of Revelation tops all competition.

Modernity expected God to be disinterested; and if a judge, then a disinterested judge, on the model of one behind the bench of a British or American courtroom. But the biblical God is precisely not disinterested; his boundless personal investment in his creatures is his most determining characteristic. His law is not something he devises and administers, it is his active personal will, which thus defines also who and what he himself is. And therefore when it is flouted he must be personally offended. He is a lover and therefore jealous, for there cannot be an actual lover who is not jealous—the great climax of the Song of Songs, "love is strong as death, jealousy fierce as the grave,"[5] strictly and knowingly parallels love and jealousy. Christian theology dare not retreat a step from these claims,[6] for as the gospel construes our situation, our only hope is God's personal stake in the good he wills for us.

How we are to work out the metaphysics is another matter. In the dominant inherited tradition, deity is defined by a set of characteristics—many beginning with "omni"—that add up to an immunity to temporal created events. But if God can in history be moved to wrath by our deeds, and if his wrath can then be "satisfied" by his acts in time, he cannot be timeless or changeless in any naïve sense of these notions. Which is to say, his deity cannot be construed as it was by those who provided the conceptual armament of our tradition, the pre-Christian religious thinkers of Greece. We must indeed think that God remains himself, come what may in his history with us, but this cannot be because he is unaffected by us or because time is meaningless for him. Proposals of how to think through all this vary greatly, and it is not the function of a commentary to go into them. But the book of Ezekiel surely sets the assignment—as indeed does most of the rest of scripture.

---

5. For the argument that this is the correct translation of Song 8:6, see Robert W. Jenson, *Song of Songs*, Interpretation (Louisville: John Knox, 2005), 90–92. NRSV's translation is tone-deaf, blotting out resonances the poetry expects us to hear.

6. And neither, in my unauthorized judgment, should Jewish theology that takes the Tanakh at all seriously.

EZEKIEL 6:1–14

YOU SHALL KNOW . . .

Ezekiel 6 begins in proper form, with "the word of the Lord came to me," and Ezek. 7 begins the same way. Thus Ezek. 6 makes a clear unit, though there is some division at 6:11, with a new "thus says the Lord." Ezekiel is addressed, as always, with "you—son of a man."

The prophet is again to perform signs (→3:22–5:4) but this time they serve the verbal proclamation rather than the other way around. The first is a bodily orientation of the prophet: Ezekiel is to face "the mountains of Israel" and direct his words "against them." This way of addressing his speech is more complicated than might at first appear.

On the one hand, turning and speaking toward the "mountains of Israel" enacts Ezekiel's peculiar situation. He is to speak to Israel as such, while remaining with a little group in distant Babylon, and perhaps even shut into his house; an *oth* consisting in bodily orientation stands in for personal presence (→3:22–5:4). The mountains in particular can be the focus of Ezekiel's address to Israel because the hill country just west of the Jordan was the heartland of the nation, the part of Canaan they first occupied and where they had lived for generations of struggle.

But for the priest Ezekiel the mountains had another and more ambiguous meaning. Hilltops have throughout religious history been favored cult sites, and when Israel came into the land the existing "high places" of the inhabitants became initial sites also of her worship. Thus the Lord was worshiped on the hilltops well before there was a temple in Jerusalem, and attachment to them was deep in the piety of the people.

But the hill sanctuaries were also the places where the worship of the Lord was most persistently mixed with worship of the local gods, who had after all been there all along. We read that these sanctuaries were furnished with "altars," stone platforms[1] for animal sacrifice, and "incense stands," if that is how an obscure word is to be translated. Both could be used in worship of the Lord—or of whomever. But there were also the "idols." It is uncertain whether the idols here were images or more primal fetishes. In any case, a god who could be presented to his worshipers by the representation of a natural power—by the image of a bull-calf or by a phallic stone or by a figure of Astarte with her multiple breasts—had just so to be some other god than the Lord, for the Lord is no such natural power but is rather Creator of them all.[2] Thus sacrifice in the presence of an idol was merely as such an act of unfaithfulness to the Lord. Ezekiel will later define a righteous man as one "who does not eat [from the sacrifices] upon the mountains or lift up his eyes to the idols of the house of Israel" (18:6).

Ending sacrificial worship at the countryside high places had been a key part of the reform launched by the last fully independent king of Judah, Josiah: the rural priests and sacrifices were to be transferred to the national temple at Jerusalem. This centralizing was of course what in modernity would be called a political move, but in the ancient world politics were always cult politics.[3] We must suppose that Josiah sincerely intended to end the syncretistic religion practiced at local holy places; for what could happen when "all the people did what was right in their own eyes" read, for example, the story in Judg. 17. Evidently, Josiah was only partly successful, for Ezekiel's prophecy is directed against Israelites who continue in their traditional ways.

Therefore the Lord himself must now "bring a sword upon" persistently idolatrous Israel; this continues the theology of the previous passage (→5:5–17). The rhetoric of general destruction is also familiar from that passage: war and its attendant famine and pestilence will devastate the land from city to countryside and from south to north.

Here, however, the destruction has also a more specific target. The furniture and idols of the high places will be broken up and the worshipers slain. Terminology appears that will be crucial in Ezekiel's book: the sacrifices on the high places are "abominations," that is, they are sheerly disgusting to the Lord, they make it impossible for him to dwell in the land. Denunciation of abominations occasions another *oth*: Ezekiel is to show the Lord's disgust by his own (6:11). When the sword of the Lord comes, it will punish one kind of pollution with another: the corpses of the idolaters will be left unburied on the altars and among the shattered idols (→5:5–17).

1. Ancient altars were not raised tables, but more like paved platforms, making provision for slaughter, burnt offering, roasting, and even sometimes for eating.
2. For what remains in my view the clearest exposition of this, see von Rad 1962–66: 2.3–14. In the temple there could be icons of the storm clouds on which the Lord rides, but no image of the Lord himself.
3. And despite all the claims of liberalism, we may wonder whether this has indeed changed.

Pollution by corpses will make the local sanctuaries unfit for worship, of the Lord or of anything else. Nebuchadnezzar will intend this blow to the conquered people's religion, unaware that he is the Lord's agent when he does it. The secularization is both grievous judgment and liberation. Grievous judgment, because it strikes at the heart of old Israel's cultic life, which for most of the people was naturally centered around local worship; a root of Israel's life will have been pulled up. Liberation, because Baal and Astarte and the rest will have lost the sites from which they ruled the people. The drastic treatment in fact worked: straightforward pagan idolatry was not prominent among the problems that troubled Judaism after the exile.

For destruction to cure Israel of idolatry, some sort of Israel must survive it. The previous passage's intimation of a remnant saved in diaspora here becomes explicit (6:8). And new beginnings are now described. The exiles will "remember" the Lord, and that will be the beginning of renewal.

In Israel, the language of "remembering" was not used for mere recollection; remembering was often a cultic act and always established a real presence of what is remembered. Thus, for only one particularly plain instance, Deut. 5 depicts Moses, on the verge of Israel's entering the land, conducting a national remembrance of the Lord's giving of the law. Moses addresses the people: "The LORD our God made a covenant with us at Horeb. Not with our ancestors did the LORD make this covenant, but with us. . . . The LORD spoke with you face to face at the mountain." Moses can be depicted as saying this even though on the occasion Deuteronomy depicts (whether with historical accuracy is a separate question) those who had been personally present at Sinai were all dead but Moses and Joshua, a circumstance that the authors and readers of Deuteronomy—and of course Moses's postulated audience—well knew.

Thus if Israel in exile will be moved to remember the Lord, this in itself will be the reestablishing of broken unity. Israel will remember how her unfaithfulness broke the Lord's heart (Ezek. 6:9). If in the previous passage the Lord's "jealousy" hinted at the true nature of his relation to Israel, this now becomes explicit: the Lord is a lover and Israel the beloved. That of course is why the relation is so exigent. Remembering her sluttish behavior, remnant Israel will repent, and to repent of unfaithfulness in love is to renew love.

Repentance thus has a positive content. The affirmative side of promised repentance is four times predicted in our brief chapter: "You/they shall know that I am יהוה." We cannot proceed without going further into this formula. To grasp the force of the knowledge that the Lord is the Lord, we may look at Exod. 3.

The voice from "the burning bush" first identifies itself by what some philosophers call "identifying descriptions." The voice says, "I am the God . . . of Abraham, the God of Isaac, and the God of Jacob" (Exod. 3:6). But Moses foresees that the people to whom he is sent will not be satisfied with this indirect sort of identification. Before they uproot their lives at this intruding God's behest, they will want to know his personal name. After some of what can only be called sparring, the God gives it up: his "name forever" is יהוה (3:15). Why would the Israelites not be satisfied with the identification of God by adequate identifying descriptions? Why insist on a name?

Within ancient Israel's own grasp of things, the immediate reason is the place that personal names had in their anthropology.[4] A person's name is not for old Israel a mere designator, it bears the personhood of its bearer. It communicates the "soul" itself, with its particular *kabod* (→1:25–28b), and it can do this precisely because it lacks content of its own. To know someone's personal name is therefore to enjoy a mutual commitment with the person—even a kind of hold on him. For Israel to know the name of the God who suddenly intruded in her life was to be provided with access to him, even with a claim: the high priest could go into the most holy place of the temple and implore God by name for the people.

Moderns find this sense for the personal name hard to grasp—though if a friend calls and says, "This is the owner of the hardware shop on First Street," instead of, "This is Jim," we too may wonder what has happened to the friendship. But modern reflection has its own way of seeing why Israel needed the name.

Moderns experience personal identity as fragile: "Is Mary the person she was?"[5] We may run down the list of descriptions by which we would identify Mary to someone who did not know her and find each of them at one or another moment doubtfully applicable. Yet unless we conclude that Mary has over time indeed been simply replaced by one or more alien personalities, the name Mary will persist, if only as the subject term of queries, "Is Mary still the good-hearted. . . ?" Personal identity must be diachronic: we must be able to identify so-and-so *as* so-and-so on temporally separate occasions, by descriptions that nevertheless may not hold at all of them.

Thus we must posit personal identity as the diachronic continuity of an entity whose identifying descriptions can vary through time, perhaps even to the point of contradiction. Such a continuity can only be constituted as *dramatic* coherence. A personal name is given precisely to denote the possibility of such coherence, a coherence that accepts and deploys precisely time and its contradictions. This is why aliases arouse suspicion, and a socially recognized change of name requires legal permission. Unless a personal life is indeed a "tale told by an idiot," the possibility of dramatic coherence is somehow given, and if it is given it is an ultimate fact that cannot be further analyzed. Whether in Israel or modernity, a personal name stands in discourse for this fact.

With gods, the problem is exacerbated. Faced with a claim to be "your god," we desperately need to know that we can rely on the continuing identity of the

4. Johannes Pedersen, *Israel: Its Life and Culture* (London: Oxford University Press, 1926), 1.245–59.

5. Jean-Paul Sartre's novel *Nausée* is the classic representation of this experience.

claimant, that this god will be—in scripture's preferred language—faithful. Otherwise formulated, we must know that he/she is a "soul" and so has a name.

There is a phrase dominant in the Old Testament and in Old Testament scholarship that this commentary has so far not emphasized: "the covenant." The great statement of the Lord's covenant with Israel is "I will be your God and you will be my people." This cannot be a good thing for the people unless they are given a personal name, "Israel," and unless the God in question gives himself one too. How otherwise are they to be in dramatically coherent communion? Indeed, most of what is theologically meant by calling God "eternal" is that he always— "forever"—can be truly called by one name.

EZEKIEL 7:1–9

AN END!

Ezekiel 7 appears in the canonical text as one long prophecy. It is introduced in regular style with "the word of the Lord came to me" and is terminated by the clear beginning of a new unit, a vision introduced by "the hand of the Lord fell upon me" (8:1).

The chapter is rather ungainly in its structure. It is divided into three parts by repetition of Ezekiel's frequent formula for the outcome of a prophecy: "You/they shall know that I . . ." (7:4, 9, 27). Once "thus says the Lord" (7:5) reinforces such a division. Thus Ezek. 7 is probably an after-the-fact collection of three once-separate prophecies, grouped because they deploy similar rhetoric. Indeed, one of these, 7:10–27, seems in turn to be either an editor's repository for fragments or the result of a long history of interpolations.

I will divide the long passage, mostly for convenience sake, though the division is not altogether arbitrary. Ezekiel 7:1–9 encompasses both the introduction to the whole (7:1–2a) and two manageable subunits (7:2b–4 and 7:5–9), both of which are carried by the distinctive and theologically striking rhetoric of "an end!" The run-on 7:10–27, which I reserve for the next commentary unit, is launched by the equally distinctive rhetoric of "the day!"

The whole complex begins with familiar formal elements. The word comes to Ezekiel and addresses him with the invariable put-down: "you—son of a man." Ezekiel is to bring a messenger-word to "the land of Israel," beginning as usual with "thus says the Lord God."

One nuance attracts attention. The prophecy's address of the message of judgment is to "the land of Israel" instead of to "the house of Israel" or even "the mountains of Israel"; and this is a weighty matter. Possession of a land of her own, chosen for her by the Lord, was the singular promise that carried Israel's hope and struggle from Abraham on. "An end" is now proclaimed over all this: Israel's founding hope is over.

Which brings us to that strange word, "end." In a first subunit, 7:2b–4, Ezekiel is instructed to cry "end" three times—the Hebrew קֵץ will have been pronounced something like *qaitz*. The first time it makes a one-word sentence by itself: "An end!" Then it is provided with the definite-article prefix and driven home in a two-word sentence: "Comes—the end!" And then there is a three-word sentence: "Now—the end—upon you!" Hearing this sound hammered in this rhythm must have been a daunting experience.

We may judge the import of this word within Ezekiel's theological tradition (i.e., the "priestly" strand) from its use at Gen. 6:13. In this passage, the word is the key word in God's decree of the great flood, that within the priestly strand of the Pentateuch threatened the reversal of creation itself: "The end of all flesh is come before me."[1]

The subsequent description of the end (Ezek. 7:3–4) employs the rhetoric of previous passages. We hear of judgment and divine wrath, directed against "abominations," practices sheerly disgusting to the Lord. The intended outcome is, again as in previous passages, that Israel "shall know that I am the Lord." Here, however, the coming of this knowledge cannot be a new beginning, for the Lord has foresworn pity. Israel will discover who is God as do the condemned in scenarios of a last judgment.

For all the bombastic description of disaster, nothing in particular is specified to be ended except the land, the embodiment of Israel's hope. There is no talk of ending Israel's idolatry or misjudged politics. Nor is this end to conclude a period in Israel's life, such as the monarchical period in fact then ending. Nor yet does the end of old hope occasion any new hope; if the *land* is to end, what hope can there be? The end proclaimed is absolute. In a brutal saying of our time, Israel will simply "be history."

The second subunit, 7:5–9, repeats the general pattern of 7:2b–4. An opening hammering with "end" is this time done with four two-word sentences in immediate succession: "An end—comes. Comes—the end. It awakes—against you. See—it comes." An artist of Hebrew rhetoric has been at work here. It is a typical touch that the verb translated "awakes" sounds almost exactly like the noun translated "end"—so that also in that line the hearer cannot evade the sound. The auditory incantation is further intensified in that "comes," like "end/awakes," is three times repeated.

The subsequent depiction of doom is more spun out than in 7:2b–4. "You shall know that I am the Lord" is expanded with a participle, "the one doing the striking." The only outcome of all this destruction is that Israel will know who destroyed her.

---

1. So the KJV translation; the rhetorically tone-deaf NRSV paraphrases, to make the Lord sound like a candidate on the stump.

Moreover, there is a pileup of added terminology for "the end": "doom," "the time," and "the day" (→7:10–27). Together these almost seem to describe the "end" as an agent that pursues Israel to undo her. But from 7:7 on the Lord insists that he personally will be Israel's doom. Both identifications surely point to the same doer of judgment—which perhaps is a clue to how we should construe God's identity as wrathful judge. The Targum interpolates an explicitly named mediator of the judgment, the Lord's "word" (*Memra*), and then immediately returns to the first person: "My *Memra* will not spare you, nor will I have pity" (Levey 1990: 32).

The notion of an absolute end—like that of an absolute beginning—is very hard to think. And the difficulties of thinking it have made trouble through the history of Jewish and Christian theology. To have any mental representation to go with the sheer concept of the end, we have to adopt a viewpoint exterior to whatever the end terminates, we have to envisage the end *of* some temporal sequence. But when we do that, the question "and what comes then?" cannot be repressed. The problem appears in its own way in our passage: How is Israel to learn anything, even if only who undid her, if she is simply not there any more?

Christian eschatology is mostly concerned with what comes somehow "after" the end: "the kingdom of God/heaven." When the kingdom has come, there will be no more of the evil and weeping that make the tune of all history in this age, instead there will be total love of God and in God of one another.

But how is that to happen unless there is an entire fresh start, a "new creation"? And how is there to be a new creation unless the old creation comes to an end, much in the sense of our passage? Some recent philosophers have indeed claimed that sheer love is merely impossible within history as it now coheres; and the claim is convincing, both empirically and analytically. If the claim is true, then if the kingdom is in any way a history continuous with the history of this age, there will continue to be sin and evil and weeping, and so not the sheer love that is promised. But if there is no such continuity, how will it be God's people, chosen and guided by him in the history of this age, who are saved?

Perhaps the difficulty is most easily grasped if we consider eschatology with respect to persons. If there is a complete break between this age and the kingdom, how am I in the kingdom to be the same person I am now? If I am to be the same person, it seems that my history will merely start up again, only under more favorable circumstances. On the other hand, if I am not to be the same person in the kingdom, why should I now care about the kingdom?

Probably most believers' mental picture of the kingdom and of our access to it contemplates life in the kingdom as an improved continuation of life now. When our bodies die, the souls we have been all along will transfer to heaven. But that of course means we do not really die, a notion that scripture never countenances. The promise of scripture and the Christian creeds is not the immortality of the soul but the resurrection of the whole embodied person. This elementary point was much stressed in the theology of the mid-twentieth century. But this doctrine seems to make a gap in time between most persons' death and the resurrection, and bridging this seems to require the immortal soul after all. Thus the problem reproduces itself.

The end must be absolute. The end must fulfill that which it ended. Both cannot be together true, unless time works very differently than our traditions have construed it, as a line along which we travel or as Plato's moving image of unmoving eternity. Earlier passages in Ezekiel taught us that the eternal God shares our history in time as his own history. But that means that his eternity must in its own way enact the drama of temporal history, must encompass beginning and goal and reconciliation as we see that he does in time. And then conversely it must mean that our time participates in eternal beginnings and endings and reconciliations. The end of Israel—as that of the church or that of the world—is absolute; and yet, in the twists and reversals and dramatic coherence of the time that God and we live together, it can fulfill what it ends.

EZEKIEL 7:10–27

THE DAY

These verses' presentation as a unit is plainly the result of a long accumulation of glosses and editings (→7:1–9). Even the way it is printed in NRSV displays some of this: we see the difference between the heightened language of prophetic declamation and the plain prose of glosses by less poetic persons. I note that the text has had such a history in order not to be simply bewildered as we read, but the observation has little further exegetical consequence.

Moreover, we do not need to go through the passage commenting on all its accumulated denunciations and judgments, for most of them have the same import: the coming "doom" of Israel will be comprehensive, inescapable, inevitable, and richly deserved. We need to take up only a few pivotal points of the discourse.

Like the two passages (7:2b–4; 7:5–9) to which it is editorially joined, this passage begins with pounding use of a single word, in this case "the day" (הַיּוֹם, *hayom*). We find two pairs of two-word sentences, at the beginning: "See—the day! See—it comes!" and a few lines later: "Has come—the time! Reaches out—the day!"[1] In these phrases "day" is provided with the definite-article prefix and no further description and is paired with an unidentified "it" that is coming and an equally unspecified "the time." Thus the day in question is, with all possible emphasis, sheerly *the* day and nothing else. This has a double import: hearers or readers are expected to know what day this is and to grasp that it is not a day in the ordinary sequence of days.

---

1. Note the chiasmus and the artful shift of tenses.

The day Ezekiel proclaims is certainly the day otherwise referred to in prophetic discourse as "the day of the Lord" (יום יהוה).[2] The phrase had a long history in prophecy, and we must take some space for it.

The earliest appearance of "the day of the Lord" in recorded prophecy is Amos 5:18–20. Isaiah 13:6–9 must be almost as early. In Amos, we see that the phrase "the day of the Lord" had a history before Amos took it up, for he addresses a people who are looking forward to that day, as a great day of deliverance and blessing. Amos turns this around. That day will indeed come, he says, but, "Why do you want the day of the LORD? It is darkness, not light." In Isaiah, Amos's reversal is already assumed, and the day of the Lord is described with what would become standard prophetic depictions of judgment.

What the popular expectation was, and how it could be reversed in this fashion, can be seen in passages from Zephaniah and Jeremiah. "The day of the LORD" is a day of battle, a day when "the warrior cries aloud" (Zeph. 1:14). Among such days, it is the day when the Lord himself will fight against his enemies and be victorious, when his "sword shall devour and be sated" (Jer. 46:10). The prophets can turn Israel's hopes for that day around, because—although Israel apparently had not thought of this logically obvious possibility—everything depends on who the Lord's enemies actually are. They may not turn out to be those whom Israel supposes them to be.

Zephaniah prophesied during the reign of Josiah, probably before the king's great reform effort. In Zephaniah's preaching, the Lord's enemies are a group in Israel herself, the economically exploitative and religiously inclusive elites of Jerusalem (Zeph. 1:4–9). On the day of the Lord, he will fight not against foreigners but against Israelites.

The Jeremiah passage is richly ironic. Jeremiah foretold an actual battle, one that proved decisive for the history of the Middle East. In 605 the Egyptians, aiming to protect recent expansion into Syria-Palestine, met the aspiring Babylonians under their crown prince Nebuchadnezzar at Carchemish, just north from Syria-Palestine. King Jehoiakim of Judah thought Babylon was the enemy and that Egypt would be his protector, which was in any case a pitiful delusion. Jeremiah proclaimed that on the contrary Nebuchadnezzar was the Lord's chosen instrument to judge the nations and that therefore those who opposed Nebuchadnezzar were the Lord's real enemies. Nebuchadnezzar prevailed at Carchemish, drove the Egyptians from Asia, and subdued Judah and the other states of Syria-Palestine.

Thus so much is clear: the context of the phrase "the day of the Lord" was war, with expectation of God's intervention to destroy Israel's enemies—an expectation that prophets could and did turn around. But there may have been also a cultic context of the phrase,[3] for Jeremiah and Zephaniah both describe

---

2. Indeed, the Septuagint has the full phrase: ἡ ἡμέρα τοῦ κυρίου.

3. A chief exponent of this possibility was Sigmund Mowinckel, *The Psalms in Israel's Worship*, trans. D. R. Ap-Thomas (New York: Abingdon, 1962). Mowinckel and others erred in constructing

the slaughter of the day of the Lord as a "sacrifice" prepared by the Lord himself. And indeed the victory of the Lord over the mythic hosts of chaos may have been ritually celebrated in Jerusalem and of course on an announced "day" (see Ps. 96–100).

If there was such a cultic background, that may help explain why in the prophets' rhetoric—as in our present passage in Ezekiel—the Lord's victory on his "day" often seems to transcend any particular battle. In the cult it is universally and timelessly threatening chaos that is defeated.

Thus already Amos used the phrase absolutely, identifying no particular occasion of battle: the day of the Lord is the day of the Lord's unqualified victory. Zephaniah begins his book with the language with which the Lord announced the great flood (Gen. 6:7, 17) and so proclaims a real "end of the world": "I will utterly sweep away everything from the face of the earth, says the LORD. . . . I will cut off humanity from the face of the earth" (Zeph. 1:2–4). Indeed, the destruction of Judah initially appears as just one incident of this general judgment. When Ezekiel turns from absolute invocation of "the day" to description of the disaster, he adds to his customary images an emphasis on the sheer cessation of human activity: there will be no buying or selling, attacking or defending, eating or drinking, prophesying or sacrificing. The assets that sustain life will be worthless. Indeed, in the battle of that day, no humans will actually fight (Ezek. 7:14).

It therefore seems that in Israel's talk of the day of the Lord's victory—popular or prophetic—there was at least an undertone of true eschatology, that is, of expectation not of this or that judgment, but of judgment to end all judgments. The day of the Lord is the day when his will is finally done.[4] This is an undertone also in the rhetoric of our passage, so that its "the day" pairs perfectly with "the end" in the previous passages.

Two further points call for brief comment, before turning to an urgent matter. First, the beginning of our passage depicts the judgment as the inevitable, indeed organic, outcome of sin: "Pride has budded. Violence has grown into a rod of wickedness" (7:10–11). Flourishing evil naturally bears disaster as its fruit. But later the Lord repeatedly insists that he himself will be the agent of disaster; and the conclusion of judgment is, as in the previous passages, knowledge of this personal agency of the Lord (7:27c).

Second, the Lord will accomplish his judgment of Judah by bringing against her "the worst of the nations" (7:24). This is Babylon; we see that proclamation of a nation as the Lord's instrument is not necessarily approval of its character.

Our present passage is eschatological in a stricter sense than any we have so far read. And it is time—perhaps past time—to face Ezekiel's and other prophets' grim affirmations of violence. Who is this God with a sword that must be "sated"?

---

out of hints and pieces a single great annual day of the Lord's ritual "enthronement" at Jerusalem, but the more general point may still be urged.

4. The day of the Lord is the one prayed for in the first petitions of the Our Father.

Eschatology and violence are intrinsically connected,[5] as appears throughout scripture.

A decisive question of all human reflection is the eschatological question, also where that term is not known: Are the events that fill time going anyplace? And if they are, is that place good? Since a sequence of events that is going someplace has what in the West we call a plot, we can put it this way: Does the sequence of temporal events have a plot? And if so, what is its shape and denouement?

Of all the great forms of reflective life, only Judaism and Christianity are unambiguous in affirming that time has indeed a plot, that where it will come out is judgment, and that this judgment will be good, finally resolving the injustices and conflicts that in any drama must come between beginning and end. In introducing the explicit notions of drama and plot, I have, to be sure, drawn not on scripture but on Aristotle's esthetics; Aristotle, however, was adamant that while a great drama has a clear plot, reality as a whole has none, and that this is good, since no great drama has a happy ending. Many great systems of the Indian subcontinent also suppose that reality has no plot, but make an opposite valuation. More perceptive than Aristotle, they grasp that endless undifferentiated time is a horror, and their endeavor is to escape it altogether.

Since Judaism and Christianity do not in either Greek or Indian fashion deny the drama of time, they must then face a hard fact: in what we know as time, there is no drama without violence. There is no plotted sequence of events that arrives at its end without conflict on the way. Nor can there be any penultimate sorting out of history that does not find some guilty of capital evil. If, therefore, God is to be active in the history of this age, he too must be "a man of war" (Exod. 15:3 KJV). Had the Lord not fought for—and against—his people of Israel, he could have had no people within actual history, and so no Christ of that people and so no church of that Christ.

Here is offense. For anyone to claim that God is on one side of a conflict appears to late modernity as a despicable error; God, supposing he exists at all, must stand above the fray. But we must hope that this is not so. For the fray is not going to stop short of an end of what we now know as history, and if God does not fight the forces of evil, they must triumph incrementally.

Surely, after the twentieth century's oceans of shed blood and the beginning of the twenty-first century's even more threatening prospects, we can no longer entertain modernity's great illusion, that our creaturely good intentions are a match for sin's energy and cunning.[6] Moreover, in the conflicts of actual history,

5. The connection is now often used as a reason to purge eschatology from scripture. The problem is that, if we conduct such a purge, nothing is left—as indeed is generally the case when we cling more firmly to ideology than to scripture's narrative.

6. Entire renunciation of violence is the calling of the church herself and doubtless also of certain individual believers. But it can never be the calling of all historical agents, nor can God's actual creation occur without those "who bear the sword." For the opposite position, argued with great force by a friend and theological ally, see any work by Stanley Hauerwas.

there is never a moral equivalency, however flawed and infected both sides may be; and we must pray that God fights for the better side. For if at this time of writing he does not, then the most hopeful scenario for "what must happen after this" (→1:1–3) is a long dark age. As to which side of a particular conflict God is in fact on, we must not presume to know that, since we will inevitably think he is on our side—the very error that according to our passage led to the destruction of Judah.

Such considerations do not, of course, fully "justify the ways of God to man," in this case the violence of the history in which he acts. God need not—we must suppose—have created a historical creature at all; he might instead have created such a timelessly perfect cosmos as Aristotle envisioned. Or with the fall, the collapse of history into self-seeking and so into violence, God might have abstained from further involvement by terminating the creation, as indeed he threatened before commissioning Noah (Gen. 6:7), or by adopting in fact the observer-God position supposed by modernity.

It must be acknowledged: God's continuing involvement in the violence of history is indeed a reason to turn one's back on "the God of history"—as many Jews did after the Shoah.[7] As Martin Luther once said, if we observe how God rules history and judge by any standard known to us, we must conclude "that either God is wicked or God is not" (*aut malum esse deum aut nihil esse deum*). He counseled clinging to the cross and from that vantage defying such reasonings.

---

7. The typical expression of that movement was Richard L. Rubenstein, *After Auschwitz* (Indianapolis: Bobbs-Merrill, 1966), a book still well worth reading.

EZEKIEL 8:1–18

IDOLATRY

In the text as we have it, Ezek. 8–11 seems at first to report one long vision. However, even quick reading discovers that 11:1–21 records a distinct vision, complete in itself (so Zimmerli 1979: 230–31). Often such observations are unimportant for our purpose, but this case is a bit different. A prophetic vision's structure is intrinsically dramatic—indeed the longer of the two visions recounted in these chapters has three formal acts or scenes—and therefore understanding a vision depends in great part on grasping its plot. But if we take the events narrated in 11:1–21 as the continuation of those narrated in Ezek. 8–10, the resultant narrative has no coherent plot. For the central instance, after the extermination of Jerusalem's wrongdoers in Ezek. 9–10, at 11:1 we find the chief villains alive and unaware of a problem. Whereas if we take 11:22–25 as the conclusion of Ezek. 8–10, take 11:1–21 as a separate vision editorially inserted at its present location on account of similarity of theme, and read each vision for itself, both narratives hang together dramatically.

This proposal may perhaps violate the principle that it is the canonical text we are to interpret. It does not seem, however, that the editorial placement of 11:1–21 has created any theologically interesting juxtaposition or indeed anything other than confusion, so perhaps we may allow ourselves so much liberty. There are obvious smaller interpolations and emendations in both visions that need not trouble us. For reasons of convenience, I will divide commentary on the first and longer vision at the chapter divisions—which coincide with its three scenes. Thus our current passage embraces the introduction to the whole and the first scene of the three-scene vision.

Ezekiel 8:1 provides the second date in Ezekiel's book: it is a little more than a year after his call.[1] We find him in his house, where exiled officials are waiting on him. Presumably they have come to seek a divine answer to a query—providing the Lord's answer to urgent questions was what prophets were widely thought to be for. Perhaps their query was about the future of Jerusalem, so that when Ezekiel reports his vision to them (11:25), this is the word for which they came—though surely with a different import than they had hoped. In any case, the chief role of their presence at beginning and end of the account is to provide an earthly context for the visionary events, as the location by the river Chebar did for the call-vision; we have seen before (→1:1–3) that placing revelation within earthly actuality is vital for the truth revealed to Ezekiel. While the elders were there, the "hand of the Lord God fell upon" Ezekiel, that is, he experienced the onset of vision.

The initial visionary presence is modeled on the enthroned being from 1:26–28: the glorious "appearance" that had "the figure of a man."[2] In the present case, however, it is not clear whether this is supposed to be the Lord himself as before or a heavenly being, since when Ezekiel arrives at Jerusalem, the Lord is already there, in the person of his glory (8:4).

It may be that 8:4—and 9:3 in the next scene—are glosses, intended to establish the identity of the God who will now be Ezekiel's guide and interlocutor with the God of the call-vision, for the burden of the vision's third scene (10:1–22) will be the departure of God's glory from the most holy place, riding upon the cherubim. We may accept the theological intent of the gloss and still note that, if 8:5 originally continued from 8:3, the figure who first appeared and stretched out his hand to take Ezekiel to Jerusalem was indeed God himself.

How are we supposed to understand 8:3? The question is not whether shamanistic transportation is possible. The answer to that question is easy and unhelpful: many peculiar things are possible, and as to whether this particular marvel ever happens, who knows? The properly exegetical question concerns the text's intention. Does 8:3 describe such a transportation to Jerusalem as might have enabled people in Jerusalem to encounter Ezekiel? Or does it describe the first event in a vision of Jerusalem, so that during Ezekiel's experience of Jerusalem only the elders in Babylonia would have seen him?

What Ezekiel sees in 8:5–17 is supposed to have been actually going on in Jerusalem, to be seen by anyone taking the same tour as Ezekiel; this suggests Ezekiel's physical presence there. But the journey is said to be "in visions of God" like the call-vision, which certainly transpired while Ezekiel remained by the Chebar. Moreover, the visions of the recording and destroying angels in Ezek. 9 and of the fire from the throne in 10:2–7 are in the exact style of the apocalyptic literature—compare almost any page of the Revelation—and the authors of apocalypses did not make shamanistic flights to attain the scenes they observe. Thus my view is

---

1. This leaves time for the period of binding, if that sign really was carried out.
2. NRSV's translation is no more helpful here than it was there.

that the text intends us to think that Ezekiel saw Jerusalem indeed "in visions" (Rashi supports this view; Rosenberg 2000: 343).

In envisioned Jerusalem, God takes Ezekiel on a tour, from a gate of the city to the inner court of the temple. Much of the description of this route is impossible to unravel, since Ezekiel could expect hearers and readers to know in some detail the plan of the palace and temple compounds at the time, which we do not. A general itinerary of four stops is, however, clear. Each station has its "abomination," that is, a pollution that makes it impossible for the Lord to remain in Jerusalem (8:6). Thus the vision will end with the Lord's departure.

The first abomination is an image and altar at a city gate. What it means that the image is "of jealousy" is obscure.[3] The image itself was probably one of the huge stone statues of lions or mixed animals that guarded the gates of Mesopotamian imperial cities. These were put up not only for pomp, but to guard the city. As for an altar outside the temple, such proliferation of altars presents the very temptation to promiscuous sacrifice that Josiah had tried to overcome.

The next stop may be a room in the palace compound. Why Ezekiel had to break through a wall to get to its gate, we cannot tell. There political officials—two of Ezekiel's contemporaries are actually named—are offering incense to bas-relief images of "creeping things" (always totems of chthonic fertility cults) and "loathsome animals" (probably not simply the animals forbidden Israel for food, but the mixed animals—like the sphinx or gorgon—of mythology). Egypt knew many such gods, which may have been brought to Jerusalem as part of Jehoiakim's dependence on Egypt.

The elders have a rationale. The Lord, they say, has abandoned them, so that they must seek supernatural help where they can. And, anyway, since he has abandoned them he will not notice what they are doing.

The third stop is just outside a gate of the temple. There women are "weeping for Tammuz." Tammuz was a Mesopotamian name for the male of the male-female divine pair of antiquity's universally practiced fertility religion. Tammuz—or Osiris or whoever—dies each year with the harvest, until with the rains he is born anew. The community participates in and indeed maintains the cosmic cycle of fertility through its ritual cycle, which includes mourning[4] during the time when Tammuz is dead, by the fertile members of humanity.

Finally, Ezekiel is brought into the inner court of the temple, the place of sacrifice and ritual prayer, where he sees priests prostrating themselves to the east, with their backs to the most holy place. Their worship toward the east may be sun worship, and their turning their backs on the most holy place is in any case

3. Zimmerli 1979: 239 proposes that it is because the image arouses the Lord's jealousy. Eichrodt 1970: 122 connects jealousy with love and argues that the image was an image of Astarte; this seems to be a stretcher.

4. And temple prostitution—perhaps by these same women—to celebrate and maintain the divine copulation (→16:1–43; →16:44–63).

disrespect. As for the line that NRSV translates "they are putting the branch[5] to their nose," no one knows for sure what that is about;[6] in any case, the Lord regards whatever the priests were doing as the final insult.

This first act of the vision ends with the Lord's declaration of judgment. The most terrible sentence is his determination not to hear Jerusalem's cries, even those properly directed to him.

The four stops of Ezekiel's tour make something like a handbook on idolatry. We will retrace the stations.

How can a statue guard a city? Within paganism's grasp of reality, it can very well do so. Paganism—ancient or modern—envisions the world as bound into one *cosmos*, one beautifully put-together thing, by resemblances and correspondences, visible and invisible. The perception of correspondence can be as crudely powerful as seeing sexual and generative power in an upright stone, or as conceptually and religiously sophisticated as constructing the Middle Platonist ontology of imaginings.[7] Thus a great stone lion at a city gate invokes the whole tribe of lions—empirical and mythic—against hostile intruders.

The gods also are located within this web of correspondences: none of them are what they are except within and by virtue of it. Thus Astarte is fundamentally an image of sexuality and fecundity; her power is finally of the same ontological sort as that of a gate-image of a lion rampant. This brings us to the next stop.

The pagan gods are not, individually or together, creators of this cosmos; they are powers within it. For Israel's faith, which knows a Creator, they are therefore creatures, and to worship them is to worship "the creature rather than the Creator" (Rom. 1:25). This is why the animal images to which the elders of Israel offered incense are "idols" without regard to their further character.

The Lord of Israel is indeed deeply involved with his creatures, but precisely as their Creator and not as creature—indeed, only because of this absolute difference can he be *involved* with them at all. Within a cosmos of correspondences that *includes* the gods, however, deity becomes a predicate admitting of degrees;

5. The Hebrew word denotes more specifically a branch of grapevine.

6. Nobody has been able to discover an ancient ritual or otherwise conventional gesture, pagan or Israelite, that involved putting a sprig of grapevine to the nose; see Zimmerli 1979: 244–45. There is, however, the—admittedly speculative—possibility that the Masoretic Text is hiding the description of a decidedly shaming gesture, as just too much to be read in worship. The Septuagint renders the verse with a vague phrase that avoids "nose" altogether. The Targum does the same (Levey 1990: 37). Perhaps the Masoretic "their nose" is a correction of "my nose," to avoid what scribes thought too objectionable to be possible in scripture—talk of God's "arm" requires explanation enough, but his nose? And then there is the conjecture—it is nothing more—of a possible alliterative use of the Hebrew for "branch" to replace Hebrew for "bad smell." This would yield, "They are putting a stink to my nose." In a large group of persons repeatedly prostrating themselves, unfortunate digestive events may occur, which since these priests were facing away from the most holy place, would indeed have been right in the Lord's nose. Indeed, this interpretation is actually advanced in a rabbinic passage that even interprets the disrespect as deliberate.

7. For a quick summary of the latter, see Robert W. Jenson, *The Knowledge of Things Hoped For* (New York: Oxford University Press, 1969), 34–37.

the gods of Olympus are doubtless more divine than deified Herakles, but only more so—and he can be promoted. And the more extraordinary or uncanny the derived entity, the more it may by correspondence share in deity. So there are monsters on those walls.

What then of Tammuz? It is a chief philosophical question, implicit from humankind's beginning, and in substance asked long before modern philosophers formulated it: Why is there anything at all? Why not just nothing? Judaism and Christianity answer this: because God is his own reason for being and so can will there to be something other than himself.[8] But absent knowledge of this Creator, another answer regularly imposes itself, for all humanity has one overwhelming experience of something new coming to be: the experience of sexual congress and following new being, with all this event's correspondences in the general phenomena of fecundity. To paganism, the cosmos has therefore appeared as a great cycle of sex and procreation; and in one form or another paganism has always worshiped the paired womb-and-breasts goddess and phallic vegetation god. The women at the temple gate have merely joined in with the general religiosity of their world; precisely for that reason, fertility religion was for all the prophets the greatest of abominations.[9]

Finally we come to the priests in the temple. Whether or not their disrespect for the Lord is intentional, they are idolaters simply because they are oriented away from the ark and the cherubim throne. They may well even suppose that they have not abandoned worship of the Lord, but have merely found a more inclusive way to do it: after all, cannot the sun be a powerful symbol of his power? But the Lord is far too jealous to tolerate such reasonings.

Idolatry is a permanent fact of human history, and at a deeper level than the homiletical cliché that we can "make an idol" of money or prestige or whatever, though this is of course true. Our own time of late modernity has relapsed into precisely the vision of reality just delineated. Late modernity's world is again one in which anything at all can be a center of some spirituality, where reality is defined by sexuality, and where priests of the church see no contradiction between panreligiosity and worship of the Lord.

The great expert on late modernity's recrudescent idolatry is G. K. Chesterton's detective priest, Father Brown. In one of the stories, Father Brown speaks to a group of young friends: "It's drowning all your old rationalism and skepticism, it's coming in like a sea . . . , calling all the menagerie of polytheism . . . : dog Anubis and great green-eyed Pasht . . . , reeling back to the bestial gods of the beginning. . . . And all because you are frightened of four words, 'He was made man.'"[10]

---

8. To be sure, Martin Heidegger, from whom I have taken the formulation of the question, regarded this answer as a category mistake, an instance of "ontotheology."

9. They also, of course, found many of its practices simply disgusting.

10. G. K. Chesterton, *The Incredulity of Father Brown* (London: Penguin, 1958), 70–71.

EZEKIEL 9:1–11

THE DESTROYERS

In →8:1–18, I noted that 8:5–10:22 and 11:22–25 narrate a vision in three scenes. In scene one, 8:5–18, the Lord takes Ezekiel on an idolatry tour, from one of Jerusalem's gates to the inner court of the temple. This first scene displays current conditions and is accordingly narrated in something close to realistic style.

The second scene, our present assignment, narrates the future that will be visited upon Jerusalem's idolaters and takes the form of a brief but powerful apocalypse, that is, a visionary unveiling of "what must take place after this" (Rev. 4:1; →1:1–3). The difference in style between this scene and the previous scene has led some critics to separate them, but in my judgment the change of style appropriately mirrors the change of time frames.

Readers of the New Testament apocalypse just cited will recognize both the way in which heavenly beings carry the action and the drastic and abstractly described action that is performed. Unlike the heaping up of literally described miseries in such verbal prophecies of doom as those in Ezek. 7, here everything is abstract drama: the coming judgment will neatly divide the people of Jerusalem into two groups, the one to be slain by angels of destruction and the other to be preserved by a recording angel who has them in his book, with no description of the earthly actuality of the one or other event. In developed apocalyptic writings a new beginning usually ensues on the judgment: here the recording angel returns to report that the righteous will indeed live.

As the scene opens, the Lord and Ezekiel are where the tour of idolatry has brought them, the room just outside the most holy place. The Lord opens the action with "a loud voice."[1] The Hebrew of this cry is confusing; I leave NRSV's translation in place only for lack of reason to do otherwise.[2] The rough import is anyway plain: destroying angels are summoned and appear. That there are six/seven of them doubtless once had significance, but we can at best guess what it was (Zimmerli 1979: 246). The angels arrive on the path earlier taken by the Lord and Ezekiel.

Six are armed; the seventh is garbed as a priest and is equipped to keep records—we should think of the book opened at Dan. 7:10 and Rev. 20:12. Meanwhile, the Lord's presence as his glory, visible above the cherubim throne in the most holy place, has risen from there and is hovering on the threshold (Ezek. 9:3). Like 8:3 this verse may be a gloss, alerting readers to the connection between this scene and the next (10:1–22; 11:22–25), where the Lord's glory leaves the temple and the city.

The Lord instructs the recording angel: he is to go through Jerusalem and mark the foreheads of those in the city who have remained faithful—obviously not an overwhelming number, since there is one angel to do this and six to follow him and destroy the rest. There is wordplay here: the word for "mark" is also the name of the last letter of the Hebrew alphabet, *tau*. We could therefore translate "make a *tau* on the forehead"—which indeed is how rabbinic tradition read the passage (Levey 1990: 37). Thus we know the shape of the mark; in the orthography of ancient Hebrew the *tau* was a cross. It is impossible not to notice: the angel is told to perform the very gesture of baptismal chrism and of Ash Wednesday's marking with ashes.

The executioners are to spare no one who is unmarked, since the Lord has now no more pity and is determined to "bring down their deeds upon their heads" (9:10). To be certain that the angels skip no one, perhaps because of their own pity, the Lord itemizes the census groups.

The temple itself is to be polluted and rendered unfit for worship, for the destroyers are to begin with the unfaithful priests there in the court (→8:1–18) and to leave their bodies where they fall (on pollution by death, →5:5–17). It will therefore no longer be possible for the Lord to dwell in this temple, and the end of the drama will be his departure. If there is again to be worship of the Lord on Zion, it will be either in the open or in a new temple—and in the concluding vision of the book (Ezek. 40–48), the plan and location of that temple are detailed.

After the destroyers have done their work in the court and followed the recording angel into the city, Ezekiel is so appalled by the sight of the dead in the temple and by the instruction to the angels that he forgets that some are indeed to be

---

1. NRSV's "in my hearing" is one of its many flattenings.
2. The Targum has "you who are appointed over the city" (Levey 1990: 36); the KJV agrees and has "them that have charge over the city"; NRSV has "executioners of the city"; and the Septuagint has an abstract singular: "the punishment of the city."

spared.[3] It was part of a prophet's office to not only speak for God to Israel, but to intercede for Israel with God (e.g., von Rad 1962–66: 2.52, 383); the prototype of such pleas is the intercession of the archprophet Moses, to avert the destructions to which Israel in the desert repeatedly made herself liable (e.g., Num. 14:12–15). Here for the first time in his book Ezekiel is jolted into that role; he cries, "Will you destroy all who remain of Israel?" The answer Ezekiel receives is, to be sure, not in itself wholly reassuring.

The Lord indicts "Israel and Judah"; the reference is to the tribes with or without states, and the now stateless northern tribes can therefore be included. The indictment differs somewhat from those encountered earlier. "Perversity" doubtless covers the familiar cultic unfaithfulness to the Lord. But that "the land is full of bloodshed" must indicate violence and crime more generally, such as other prophets denounced—classically, Mic. 3:9–12.

Indeed, the final gravamen is neither religious perversity nor crime for themselves, but their reason. Israel has fallen into particular transgressions because she has come to think two things: "The Lord has forsaken the land"; and, "The Lord does not see." In the end, as we are told throughout scripture, "The righteous shall live by their faith" (Hab. 2:4); Israel, on the contrary, has lost trust in the Lord's promises and fear of his judgments. In such comprehensive absence of faith, a human community must sooner or later fall into idolatry and mutual injustice, which is to be expected among the Gentiles but is terrible apostasy in Israel's case.

The Lord says that he sees very well, and indeed that his eye will be the organ of judgment. The recording angel returns to report, "I have done as you commanded me." And the curtain falls on act two of the vision.

What are we to think of the apocalyptic mode of prophecy that begins to appear in Ezekiel? Modern theology generally regarded the apocalyptic books and passages as a degenerate mode of prophecy: the prophets of the eighth through the sixth centuries, it was thought, had been great moral and religious preachers, but the apocalyptic writers were fantasists and fortune-tellers.[4]

To judge, we need a fuller sketch of the phenomenon. The developed apocalyptic works (e.g., *1–2 Enoch, Testament of the Twelve Patriarchs, 4 Ezra,* and the *Baruch Apocalypse*) of the time between the exiles' return from Babylon and the final end of Israel's political entity laid out schemes of world history in visionary form, hiding the historical phenomena under esoteric appearances—perhaps the parts of a statue or a parade of mythic beasts. Regularly, the scheme displays a final period of this age, in which wickedness has fully ripened. Then there is the

3. There was a talmudic interpretation that also those marked were killed, since no one in Jerusalem could have escaped silent complicity (Greenberg 1983: 177).

4. This evaluation survives in the vocabulary of journalists and some pop theologians. It is the sole basis of the decisions made by the Jesus Seminar: if something Jesus is recorded to have said sounds apocalyptic, it must be inauthentic, since any Jesus the members of the seminar could believe in cannot have been so little like them.

judgment and God's beginning of a new age. Thus the brief but formally perfect apocalypse included in the book of Daniel (7:1–14) begins with four beasts—representing four empires—successively tyrannizing the earth, the last being the worst. Then Daniel sees how "thrones were set in place, and an Ancient One took his throne.... The court sat in judgment," and the beasts were condemned. Finally Daniel sees "one like a son of man coming with the clouds of heaven.... His dominion is an everlasting dominion that shall not pass away."

Three developments in twentieth-century theology have challenged modern theology's negative evaluation of apocalyptic. One was the discovery by New Testament scholars, during that period early in the twentieth century when the historical-critical craft achieved its greatest precision, that Jesus's preaching was apocalyptic in its tone and presuppositions. The famous popularizer here was Albert Schweitzer.[5] Contrary to reigning liberalism's depiction, "the historical Jesus"—they found—did not proclaim a just society to be built in this world by the moral efforts of his followers, but rather a new age to be brought by God's unilateral action, following the judgment and termination of this age. Since the scholars in question were themselves liberal theologians, this was an unwelcome result of their research—Schweitzer himself gave up theology altogether and turned to humanitarian works.

A second development was the painful observation that actual history is more apocalyptic in its course, and in particular more helplessly captive to evil, than liberalism—political or theological—can allow for. Two World Wars provided the demonstration. In this connection there is another iconic name: from his Swiss parish, young Karl Barth watched the First World War and saw the liberal nations of Europe devour one another out of sheer inability to control their own mechanisms. His German teachers, great liberal theologians to a man, had high hopes for him; but he watched them rally to the Fatherland, and he turned against them. Called after the war to teach in a Germany lurching from the horror of a lost war to the horror of the Nazis, he wrote the book that makes the break between standard modern theology and that of the twentieth century: a commentary on Paul's Letter to the Romans that exploits to the maximum Paul's apocalyptic presuppositions.[6] He would later draft the confessing church's manifesto against Nazi theology.

The third development is not so universally affirmed, but is in my judgment important. Does history as a whole have a plot? Indeed, is there such a thing as "history as a whole"? Modernity tended toward a negative answer to both questions. But a broad movement of theology in the second half of the twentieth century contended that at this point modernity had to be resisted, that theology must indeed posit the wholeness of history and its plotted direction. Since there is one

5. Albert Schweitzer, *The Quest of the Historical Jesus*, trans. W. Montgomery (New York: Macmillan, 1910).
6. Karl Barth, *Der Römerbrief* (Munich: Kaiser, 1922).

God and since he creates all things, and since his creating has a goal, there must be one history and it must move meaningfully toward one outcome.[7] Within that broader movement, an intellectually powerful school pointed out that the apocalyptic writings present just such a view[8] and that it is cast from central biblical convictions.

Metaphysically considered, the truth of apocalyptic prophecy must depend upon the presence of the future with God and on its presence with God precisely *as* future. If the future is simply what is not yet, if it is present for no one, it cannot now be shown. But equally, if a future present to God is not present as *future*, perhaps because God's being is an undifferentiated present tense in which temporal distinctions vanish, then the future's presence with him is hidden in his deep timelessness, beyond all revealing to others.

In his mature theology, Karl Barth provided the fundamental insight: what "distinguishes [God's] eternity from time" is that "there is . . . no . . . conflict, but peace between source, movement and goal." They are not distinguished because "in eternity all these distinctions do not exist."[9] The truth of apocalyptic prophecy depends upon the trinitarian insight that in God's own life there is difference between Father and Spirit and so between beginning and goal, source and outcome. Therefore, for God and in God, the future is not the present, yet it has presence. Apocalyptic revelations would indeed be mere dreams, if God were a monad—as of course modern theology for the most part conceived him.

7. There must be precisely a "meganarrative."

8. The leading thinker here was Wolfhart Pannenberg, and the programmatic book is his *Revelation as History*, trans. D. Granskou (New York: Macmillan, 1956).

9. Karl Barth, *Church Dogmatics*, ed. G. W. Bromiley and T. F. Torrance (Edinburgh: Clark, 1957), 2/1.612.

EZEKIEL 10:1–22; 11:22–25

THE GLORY DEPARTS

The two previous passages (8:1–18; 9:1–11) portray two scenes of a three-scene vision (→9:1–11 for the reason for treating these verses separately). The final act or scene of the vision is our current assignment. The break between scenes is not as neat as that between the first and second scenes, since some of the action of scene three is carried by an angel from scene two, and the narrative of his action continues in the apocalyptic style of that scene. But this angel no longer carries a scribe's equipment, and the start of something new is additionally signaled by Ezekiel's "then I looked."

Our passage plainly has several layers of glosses and interpolations; and any attempt to follow the narrative without allowing for some such process will be repeatedly frustrated. We need not try to untangle all this, but attention to one set of interpolations—to which we will shortly come—is essential. What happens in the scene is anyway basically clear: the Lord's exit from the temple and Jerusalem.

The root of Jerusalem's sin was to think the Lord had abandoned the city (9:9). The punishment of that belief is that the Lord makes it true. This pattern is a permanent feature of scripture; so St. Paul writes to the Romans that because humankind has exchanged the roles of creature and Creator, God has given them up to a general and disastrous exchange of roles (Rom. 1:24–27).

God's departure occurs as two coordinated events. The one is the angel's casting holy fire over Jerusalem. The angel is to take coals from the fire "among the cherubim." This is the fire we have seen before: the fire at the heart of the glory in the call-theophany to Ezekiel (1:4, 13), the fire of the Lord's storm-lightnings, the fire on Sinai.

He is to take this fire from "the *galgal* [גַּלְגַּל] underneath the cherubim." What is the *galgal*? The point is minor, but interesting. The usual translation of *galgal* is simply "wheel." But since the word is here in the singular, this would yield the nonsensical "go in between the wheel." Some translators have simply decreed that there must have been an original plural.[1] The only plausible alternative is to take the word as a technical term for some cultic object in the most holy place (Zimmerli 1979: 251), located or used beneath the throne—and that is what I slightly incline to. This construal is supported by the assumption behind 10:13, that it is important for readers to know that the cherubim throne's wheels are the living reality of a known something, "the *galgal*." Unfortunately, no one now can do more than guess what apparatus this would have been. NRSV's "wheelwork" was invented in the literature simply as a placeholder in the absence of an actual identification.

Is scattering holy fire over Jerusalem simply deadly, so that the erstwhile savior angel now turns and completes the catastrophe? The fire of the Lord's glory certainly can destroy, as when it burst from the desert tabernacle to consume Korah and his followers (Num. 16:35). But there is another possibility: that the fire, while indeed it burns away old Jerusalem, is nevertheless cleansing, preparing for a new Jerusalem. This better fits the angel's office in the previous scene and better carries through the conclusion of the apocalyptic scenario in which he functions. This latter reading is therefore my preference.

The fire that the angel receives is the fire "among" the cherubim, that is, the fire that belongs to the glory itself. Even at this extremity, the Lord will not deal with Israel from a distance; it is his own fire that will burn and cleanse his city. The angel leaves with the fire, and our attention is shifted.

The other exit event is the Lord's more personal departure from the temple and from the city. The cherubim throne bears away the glory, the *kabod* (→1:25–28b) that was the Lord's real presence in the temple.

Since we were told that when Ezekiel arrived at Jerusalem the throne was outside the city gate (8:4), we are perhaps to suppose that it has now come into the court to receive the Lord for departure; and this seems to be how 10:1, 3–5 construes the event. But contrary to this construal, the angel has to go "in" to fetch fire from the cherubim, which must mean that he goes into the most holy place. In this case, the cherubim throne of the most holy place has in vision become its heavenly prototype, so that the Lord's fire is to be found amid the living cherubim. On this reading, it is the temple's own cherubim throne that will bear the Lord away from Jerusalem. Such a coming alive of the temple's throne has precedent in Isaiah's vision (Isa. 6:1–5), and indeed, Ezek. 10:4b–5 unmistakably echoes Isaiah's description of that event.

---

1. So the Septuagint and KJV at 10:2 but not 10:13. The KJV translators show they know the word is in the singular by translating 10:13 "as for the wheels, it was cried unto them in my hearing 'O wheel.' "

Thus multiple glossing of this text has resulted in clashing construals of the cherubim throne's identity: Is it the heavenly throne that has now come to the temple, or is it the throne that is already there? In my view, the second construal of events is the original—if we may allow ourselves that slippery word—and I will presume it in the following. Eventually, however, we must consider what the simultaneity of different construals in the canonical text may have to tell us.

It is obviously vital both for Ezekiel and for those who piled glosses on this passage: the vehicle that will bear the Lord's presence away from his temple and city is the very one that bore that presence to Ezekiel in exile—the description of the *Merkabah* at 1:4–26 is pedantically reprised at 10:1, 8–17, 20–22. It also seems to be important that the living *Merkabah* is none other than the cherubim throne in the temple; Ezekiel assures readers that the living creatures really are cherubim (10:21b), that is, that they are the known beings of whom the statues in the temple were icons.

The living cherubim throne rises up from its place—whichever that was—and the glory settles above it. Throne and glory first leave the temple proper and stop at the temple close's east door (10:18–19)—this will be the gate through which the glory will enter a new and eternal temple (43:1–5). Then throne and glory leave the city altogether, stopping on a mountain to the east. And there Ezekiel's three-scene vision ends; he is returned to his house in exile, where he reports what he had seen to the waiting elders (11:22–25). It can be assumed they were not pleased with this answer to their query.

Two theological parties are discernible in the present text's much-glossed narrative of the cherubim throne's movements. Both were of course agreed: the Lord's throne is in heaven. Both also agreed: the boundary between earth and heaven is not absolute, the heavenly throne can—in a certain sense—be on earth. But what sense is that?

In the one construal, the enthroned Lord has chosen a particular place for himself, Jerusalem and the God chamber of her temple. There dwells the Shekinah, the glory, the name. If the Shekinah becomes visible to a prophet's vision, its visible place will be the temple's throne, now visible as what it indeed is, a living throne. And if the Shekinah travels, it will be the temple's throne that bears him—even if someone going into the most holy place would see the statuary there as always. On this construal it was the temple's throne, in its true living reality, that stormed to Ezekiel at the river Chebar.

In the other construal, the Lord's heavenly throne must come *to* the temple—from heaven or for that matter from the river Chebar—if it is to bear away the Lord. The Lord's glory and his cherubim throne may indeed be found in the most holy place, but that is not the primary fact. Primally, the Lord's Shekinah is the glory in the wilderness, and so is at home anywhere, as his people need him. Indeed, the glory of the Lord must come to the temple Shekinah if the Shekinah's departure from the temple is to be the Lord's own departure.

The first construal represents a theology centered on the Lord's covenant with the monarchy and its temple and city. The second represents a theology centered on the Lord's covenant with wanderers in the desert. In a remarkable passage, the prophet Nathan's word to David about his plan to build a temple and about the future of the Davidic dynasty sets the two unmediated side by side. On the one hand, the Lord makes a covenant with David and with the place he has made his capital: "I will make for you a great name, like the name of the great ones of the earth. And I will appoint a place for my people Israel. . . . Your throne shall be established forever." On the other hand, of himself the Lord says: "I have not lived in a house since the day I brought up the people . . . from Egypt . . . but I have been moving about in a tent. . . . [Did I ever say,] 'Why have you not built me a house?'" (2 Sam. 7:1–16; see von Rad 1962–66: 1.308–12).

These two understandings of the relation between the Lord's own reality and his dwelling with us run not only through Israel's theology but also through the theology of the church. Given the incarnation, the question is posed: even though the Logos, God the Son, is indeed the man Jesus, does he not also remain free to act outside this man's presence and power? In the ancient church, the theology centered on Antioch said yes to that question, while that centered on Alexandria said a cautious no. In the long run of history, Western theology tended to say yes and Eastern theology tended to say no. Among the churches of the Reformation, the Reformed quite emphatically said yes and the Lutheran even more emphatically no.

Whether in Israel or the church, this difference in fundamental christological ontology is at once spiritually important—consider, for example, the difference between the interiors of Western and Eastern churches or between those of Reformed and Lutheran churches—and should nevertheless be contained within one church. In my judgment, it is unlikely to be resolved so long as the present churches last.

EZEKIEL 11:1–13

THE POWER OF THE WORD

In the present text, 11:1–22 records one vision. The passage has, however, two parts; the beginning of the second is marked by "the word of the Lord came to me" (11:14), Ezekiel's standard formula for reception of a new verbal prophecy. What relation to each other the two parts once had or did not have need not concern us; the present text coheres well enough. I divide the two parts between two commentary units for convenience, since there is theological matter in each part that requires extended comment.

Like the longer vision into which it has been editorially inserted (Ezek. 8–11; →8:1–18), this vision begins with Ezekiel's transportation to the temple by the Spirit (→1:28c–3:15). We are not told where he was when seized; the account's editorial adjustment to its present context has removed that information. Ezekiel is set down at the ceremonial gate of the temple.

At the gate he sees a caucus of officials. Two are actually named; it is important for understanding Ezekiel's visions that they rarely cut altogether loose from earthly reality. These persons, the Lord says, are much responsible for the city's wrongs and distresses. They appear to be what we would now call "policy advisers," and their plans and scenarios are somehow integral to the deadly political and social processes in which the city is gripped. Indeed, they have by their policies effectively "killed many in this city" (11:6)—and indeed, Jehoiakim and Zedekiah, the kings they have been advising, seem to have been quite brutal despots within their own little spheres.

Two items of the officials' bad counsel are given. The first, that this is not the time to build houses, seems to be city-planning advice given to Zedekiah. Unfortunately, the narrower context is lost and the advice cannot be certainly interpreted. If, as above and with nearly all translators, we take the line as an affirmative proposition, we do not know why refraining from real estate development would have been unjust policy—though from experience, we might suspect that the delay was for the economic benefit of the officials and to the disadvantage of the poor. The Targum, however, reads the line as a question, "Is it not soon enough to build houses?" (Levey 1990: 40). This is not grammatically impossible, and should it be correct, it would be easier to construe the bad advice: the advisers foolishly suppose that doom is not imminent and that Jerusalem should get back to development and other normalities.

The second piece of evil counsel, while more metaphorical, can be more surely interpreted. "This city is the pot, and we are the meat" apparently was a saying going around in elite Jerusalem. The metaphor may seem odd to us who were not there, but its import is clear. A cooking pot and its contents belong together; the pot protects its contents; and if all is in order, the quantity of the contents is right for the size of the pot. In Jerusalem, during the time between the deportations of 597 and the catastrophe that altogether relieved Jerusalem of her illusions, the saying had two sides. The first: we are safe within the city. The second: the city is the right size to accommodate us—and not the exiles. That this last is a point becomes plain at 11:14–16. Thus the evil notions against which Ezekiel is on this occasion to prophesy are the claim to be secure in Jerusalem and the claim to disinherit the exiles.

Ezekiel is to prophesy against the bad officials. The word given to Ezekiel reverses the pot metaphor. The meat in the pot, those who truly belong to the city and even—in a dreadful sense—are protected by it, is those slain by its political and social injustice. And those who trust in the city's protection and claim it for their own will not turn out to be the meat in the pot: they will not be protected in the city or indeed even killed in it. The Lord will expel them from the city and judge them on the border of Israel—which is exactly what happened in 586 to those of Judah's leaders not taken to Babylon.

An aspect of prophecy noted before becomes more explicit in this passage, and we must take some time for it. On this occasion Ezekiel is told to "prophesy *against*" the wicked officials; prophecy is a weapon that can be targeted. Nor is the target the whole house of Israel as in earlier passages, but specific persons active in the history with which the prophecy is concerned. Which is to say, the prophecy functions as an effective curse—indeed one of the targeted officials promptly falls down dead. Targeted prophecy that functions as blessing or cursing was not peculiar to Ezekiel—the paradigm story is the generally instructive tale of the seer Balaam, who was recruited by Balak of Moab to prophesy Israel's defeat and was prevented by God, who said, "You shall not curse the people, for they are blessed" (Num. 22).

The prophesying and its effect both occur within a vision. Are we intended to think that Pelatiah, located also outside the vision, was there slain by it, as all of these officials will indeed be slain when the prophecy is fulfilled and Jerusalem falls? It is likely that we are. This story of a prophesying, so much like that of the older "men of God," is introduced with the formula regularly used of them: "the spirit of the Lord fell upon" them, to make them speak.

In late modernity we have not put much stock in blessings or curses or indeed in the power of words generally. When field anthropologists report that the targets of shamans' curses indeed sicken or die, we explain the connection psychologically. We expect both weal and woe from mechanistically describable factors, not from prophecies—or sermons or stump speeches. "Sticks and stones may break my bones, but words can never hurt me." Whether we are right or wrong about the effects of explicit cursings or blessings is perhaps impossible to know. But modernity has certainly been wrong about the historical agency of utterance in general.

To be sure, it may be that creation is a vast system of purposeless causation, in which case the posit of something specifically to be labeled "history" is itself an illusion. Modernity has often tended to this view, construing utterance also as merely one kind of event within a universal system of effective causation. But in that case Judaism and Christianity, entirely invested in certain narratives, are themselves illusions.

On the other hand, if there is history, then events—at least among persons— carry intentions and indeed intend one another. But the way in which intentions themselves actually occur is by persons addressing one another. If—contrary to possibility—intentions always remained hidden in subjectivity, they would be linked only within whatever mechanistic systems they may also inhabit.

Thus address—by whatever means—is constitutive of human events in their historical connections. Our mutual addresses do not merely describe or invoke or predict what happens among us; without our mutual addresses there would be no happenings among us and indeed no occurrences appropriately to be labeled "events" or "happenings." In the 50s and 60s of the previous century, Rudolf Bultmann's students (most notably Gerhard Ebeling and Ernst Fuchs)[1] developed the notion of the "word event." Every utterance—in whatever medium— somehow "opens the future," opens mutual possibility that would not otherwise have been available, and so is itself a historical event. And every event—or at least every event among persons—says something, is in one way or another a word. Thus, at least if we think of persons, the saying is backward: sticks and stones cannot harm or help, but words can break or mend. And history is just one long conversation.

If then there is the God of the Bible, the conversation that is history is a conversation between that God and his personal creatures. Prophets are those who speak God's word into the created conversation. Prophets' words are therefore not just powerful; they maintain the world of history.

1. See Robert W. Jenson, *The Knowledge of Things Hoped For* (New York: Oxford University Press, 1969), 175–84.

We return to the narrated vision. Ezekiel looks at what his prophesying has done and concludes that if it goes on this way there will be nothing left of Israel. So, as in the previous passage, he is shocked into that other aspect of the prophet's office: to speak not only for God but for the people to God. And this time he receives a wonderful answer, to which the next commentary unit will be devoted.

EZEKIEL 11:14–21

A NEW HEART

I treat this passage separately from →11:1–13 only for convenience of exposition; 11:1–21 reports one vision. The place where I divide is not, to be sure, arbitrarily chosen, since the formula for the advent of a new prophecy, "the word of the Lord came to . . . ," occurs at 11:14. The passage ends abruptly; presumably, it once had some concluding formula, but this has been erased by the passage's editorial insertion in its present place (→8:1–18).

At the end of the previous verses, Ezekiel is appalled by the drastic result of his prophesying against Jerusalem's evil counselors. He cries to the Lord, "Will you make a full end of the remnant of Israel?" It must indeed seem that if things continue in this way, there will be no Israel left. It may also be that Ezekiel still thinks that the real Israel is those left in Jerusalem, so that an end of them is an end of Israel; if so, this is an idea of which he is about to be disabused. It is in response to his intercession that—still within the vision—the word of the Lord comes again to Ezekiel.

The Lord's first word is for Ezekiel himself (addressed as always "you—son of a man") and concerns the exilic community and its relation to Jerusalem and her inhabitants. The Lord's concern is the Jerusalem elites' attitudes; the context is still the vision of evil officials.

It was being said in Jerusalem that by being removed from access to the temple the exiles had been removed from access to the Lord. And indeed the exiles themselves feared the same thing. If earlier prophets were to be believed, the exile was punishment for Israel's sin; therefore those in exile must be the sinners and their exile must be exile also from the Lord. But that fear should have been alleviated among the exiles by the glory's appearance to Ezekiel in the land of exile, on the living cherubim throne (→1:4–24). Indeed, it apparently had actually aroused some hope in the community, since we now find exiled leaders seeking a word of the Lord from Ezekiel and receiving it.

It was being further said that the land of Israel no longer belonged to the exiles, but now belonged only to her current inhabitants.[1] To the contrary, the Lord here refers to the exilic community as "the whole house of Israel." Not those in Jerusalem, but the exiles are the remnant Israel, to whom city and land belong.

Then Ezekiel is given a messenger-word, to be delivered with the standard "thus says the Lord." It is the first unreserved and conceptually expanded promise of restoration in Ezekiel's book—and indeed somewhat out of place in the general structure of the book (→25:1–17).

The good news starts in the present tense. Even in an exile imposed by God himself, the exiles have not been beyond his salvific presence. God himself has been "a little temple" for them (11:16).[2] The glory on the wings of the cherubim can—as shown by Ezekiel's call-vision (→1:4–24)—be present also beyond the realm of the Jerusalem temple. This does not relativize his presence there; so long as the Jerusalem temple stands and is the place of the appointed sacrifices, it is, so to speak, the big temple. Nevertheless the freedom of the Lord's presence enables prayer and prophecy also in Babylon, and the Lord has in fact granted this, partly in the person of Ezekiel himself. The Targum paraphrases: "I have given them synagogues, second only to My Holy Temple" (Levey 1990: 41)—and the institution of the synagogue may indeed have originated in Babylon during the exile.

Then begins a series of promises to the exiles, probably including those of the northern kingdom (11:17–20). Fulfillment within history of the first two is conceivable, if just barely. The first promise is that the exiles will be gathered from all the countries to which they were scattered and given "the land of Israel." And indeed, exiles did return from Babylon, but not all of them, and we hear of no return of the northern kingdom's scattered deportees. The second is that the nation created by the returning exiles will be free of idolatry. So far as our record of events in Jerusalem goes, this promise was eventually fulfilled.

The third and fourth promises are, however, the chief matter and the most astonishing. The new Israel will no longer hanker for idols, because the Lord will have given the returning exiles a new "heart." And then the great covenant promise—which has carried the whole history of Israel, "They shall be my people, and I will be their God"—will at last be fulfilled on both sides.

1. Jeremiah, actually situated in Jerusalem, reports no such antiexile sentiment.
2. NRSV's "I have been a sanctuary to them for a little while" seems to be another case of the translators' inability to believe scripture can mean to say the strange things it says. If for a passage to make sense, a Hebrew adjective—here מעט ("little")—must be translated as what we would call an adverb, this can be done. But what here is the necessity? Older translators were not so skittish. KJV has "a little sanctuary" and the Septuagint has ἁγίασμα μικρόν ("little holy place"). For critical argument for the translation proposed here, see Zimmerli 1979: 262.

Here we hear promises that are in the strict sense eschatological—we have encountered eschatological judgments earlier in the book, but not eschatological promises, though subsequent chapters will display many such. In the usual scholarly usage, a divine promise is eschatological if in principle and not just in fact it cannot be fulfilled within the terms of history as we in this age experience it—if it requires an "end" in the sense of Ezekiel's more absolute judgments (→7:1–9) and a new start of creation.

Through the Old Testament, we see the promises to Israel grow in scope, from ordinary historical hopes, through hopes implausible within what we know as history, to promises that reach decisively beyond all terms of that history. That the descendants of Abraham should be a great nation was certainly feasible; such things have happened. That by that nation "all the families of the earth shall be blessed" (Gen. 12:3) pushes the limits, but there have been nations that were a blessing to others, and perhaps a people could indeed appear in history that was a blessing to all—it could be argued that the Jews have in historical fact been a general blessing, if one widely unappreciated. But that, under the Davidic dynasty or any other regime, that blessing will be "endless peace" (Isa. 9:7) pushes the limits of this age to their breaking point. And that "mountain of the LORD's house" shall become "the highest of the mountains" and be a center of a universal worship of the one God and therefore of universal peace (2:2) must require a complete reworking of the regularities of created history.

So to the spectacularly eschatological promises in our passage. The first: collectively and singly, Israel, which now has a "heart of stone," will return from exile with a "heart of flesh."[3]

"Heart" (לֵב, *lev*) is a key term of Israelite anthropology[4] and is closely related to "soul" (נֶפֶשׁ, *nephesh*), which denotes simply the person, as a living organized whole with an individual stamp. A heart is the pulsating active center of such a soul.[5] "Heart of stone" is therefore a deliberate oxymoron, a metaphor for a heart that is no heart, a personal center that no longer feels or acts, but has only a physical object's inertia. A heart should be of flesh. Since "flesh" (בָּשָׂר, *basar*) denotes the creaturely as over against the Creator, a "heart of flesh" is a personal center that receives and acts in the way proper to a creature, that is open to the Creator's love and the statutes and ordinances of his love and follows them without hesitation. The Targum rightly glosses the new heart as a "faithful" heart (Levey 1990: 41–42). And it is noteworthy that in our passage there is no third possibility besides "stone" and "flesh."

Is such a transformation conceivable? A conversion literally from death to life, from stony immobility to life open to God? A replacement of the personal

3. On the whole complex of Ezekiel's promises of new moral agency, able to obey the Lord's will, see Lapsley 2000.

4. One had perhaps best not speak of Israelite psychology—not, anyway, with the sense that Anglo-Saxon discourse gives the word.

5. Johannes Pedersen, *Israel: Its Life and Culture* (London: Oxford University Press, 1926), 1.99–106. This work remains the classic anthropological study of the Old Testament.

center with a new one? It is the question Nicodemus put to Jesus, "Can one enter a second time into the mother's womb and be born?" (John 3:3–5). But is faith a possibility of this world? The preaching of the gospel in the New Testament certainly calls for nothing less and purports to achieve nothing less: if anyone is in Christ he is a new creature (2 Cor. 5:17).

Christianity believes that the fullness of everything promised to Israel, though not a possibility within what we now experience as history, is nevertheless actual in the case of the one Israelite, Jesus the Christ. It is precisely because of the impossibility of such a life in this age that he had to die. And eschatologically new life, which can only follow the "end" (→7:1–9), is the life into which he was raised.

For their own persons, Christians join Jews in waiting for new birth and new creation to be completed beyond this age in the kingdom. But they also claim to know this radical new start as something that happens now—ahead of time—at baptism and in baptized persons' new freedom with respect to sin. Both in the kingdom and in the pilgrim church, believers' freedom from a heart that is dead to righteousness and their possession of a heart that is alive to God depends on their union with Christ, who has himself already made the step (Rom. 6:1–14).

Our passage has a second great eschatological promise: "They shall be my people, and I will be their God." Particularly in the priestly tradition from which Ezekiel came, this double promise locates the covenant between the particular God, "the Lord," and the particular nation Israel (e.g., Lev. 26:12). There is, however, a twist in Ezekiel: the order of the clauses is reversed. The formula normally begins with "I will be their God" because this condescension of God is the surprising point to be made, and Israel's status as his people simply follows. But by Ezekiel's time there has—at least in Ezekiel's view—been a long history of Israel's unwillingness to be the Lord's people (e.g., the story of Oholah and Oholibah in Ezek. 23). Thus the miracle is now not that God commits himself to Israel but that Israel at last will be faithful to God, because of God's eschatological act to recreate her at her heart.

So when is Israel at last faithful? At "the end of the days" and already—by Christian conviction—in the person of the one Israelite whose own heart was never stony, but who was killed by our stony hearts and who lives as the new heart of all God's people.

EZEKIEL 12:1–16

INTO EXILE

This commentary unit takes up the first of two passages (12:1–16 and 12:17–20) that were probably put side by side in our text because both mandate a prophetic sign, an *oth*, and both prophesy the imminent fate of Jerusalem. Both passages begin in the style standard for Ezekiel: he tells us that "the word of the Lord came" to him and addressed him as "you—son of a man." We are not told about the occasions or circumstances.

The passage continues with a word about Israel addressed to Ezekiel himself. We have heard before that Israel is, almost by definition, "a rebellious house" (→3:22–5:4). Here a more specific characterization of the rebellion is added: they "have eyes to see but do not see" and "ears to hear but do not hear." This trope appears in other prophecy of Ezekiel's general time (e.g., Jer. 5:21; Isa. 43:8). The trope's application here is that those to whom this prophecy is addressed have experienced the first catastrophe in 597, have heard of events in Jerusalem since, have heard the prophets, and have learned nothing.

In Isa. 6:9–10 it is very explicitly the Lord who has himself blinded and deafened Israel. If the trope carries that aura with it here—which in my view it surely must—then there is a powerful dialectic set up with the next verses. The performance Ezekiel is to stage is repeatedly specified as done in Israel's sight, in the hope that "they," being unable to avoid seeing the sign, may "perhaps" be brought to see also their true situation as a "rebellious house" (12:3–5).

Thus God is said both to blind and deafen Israel and to send prophets in the hope that they may see and hear and repent. This is not mere incoherence. It is rather one manifestation of a logic that runs through all scripture.

The questions always come up, wherever the realities of God and faith are taken seriously. Putting them in the popular language about salvation: If salvation depends wholly on God, and if not everyone is saved, then if God does not choose to save me, what is the use of my faith or works? Or if I am responsible to open my own eyes, how can I fully rely on God as my Savior, since I may at any moment undo everything by failing that responsibility?

What we must come to understand is that neither question is appropriate, for the simultaneity of "God decides and works all things" and "see, hear, and be saved" is itself the truth about our situation with God. Believers are bound to "work out [their] own salvation,"[1] precisely *because* "it is God who is at work" in them (Phil. 2:12–13). Both propositions can be true, and true only together, because between God's will and a creature's will there is no "zero-sum game." When you and I must decide some matter, to the extent that you choose I do not, and to the extent that I choose you do not. Thus we are always negotiating, for we are both finite creatures with a limited scope for choice. But it does not work that way when God decides to open my eyes and I must, in response to his simultaneous appeal, myself decide to open my eyes. High medieval Scholasticism's statement of the relation between God's choice and ours is so simple and so patently right that it is very hard to grasp: God's will is impeded by *nothing*; therefore if he chooses that I shall do x, I will do it; *and* if he chooses that I shall do x of my own free will, that is how I will do it.

The appeal for repentance is here made by an *oth* (→5:5–17). Ezekiel is to act out a deportee's or refugee's exit from a ruined city, making way through the rubble of its wall with a few belongings in a pack carried on his shoulder. Ezekiel is to stage this *oth* in the light of day, so that "they" cannot fail to see it.

Who are "they"? If the onlookers are the exiles—who are the only ones in position to see Ezekiel leaving his house—then it is the exiles who will ask, "What are you doing?" And then it is the exiles whom the Lord here describes as "the house of Israel, the rebellious house" (12:8–9) and calls to repent. If this is the right construal, then the *oth* portrays before the exiles the very miseries they themselves once experienced, in the hope that "perhaps" they will be jogged finally to see and understand their own true situation, as a rebellious house that brought exile upon themselves.

But we have seen before that Ezekiel can address the entire house of Israel—including those still in Jerusalem and Judah and even the northern populace and her deportees—most of which is of course physically distant from him. Perhaps he is to stage this *oth* for the same audience. Then it is the nation that somehow queries Ezekiel and that is called to repent before it is too late for Jerusalem and Judah, the nations remaining more or less intact entities.

If it is not clear to whom the *oth* and its accompanying verbal prophecy (12:10–20) are addressed, the elucidation plainly specifies whose fate the *oth*

---

1. Rather than having it worked out for them by someone else, in this passage, by Paul.

anticipates: "the prince" and "the house of Israel" in Jerusalem (12:10). The prince is Zedekiah, and the house of Israel is here all those who in 586 would indeed make their way through Jerusalem's ruins with emergency baggage, whether as refugees or deportees.

There is a problem that we may not notice at first. At what time of day did these folk leave Jerusalem? Ezekiel 12:12 says, with deliberate emphasis, that Zedekiah will leave Jerusalem in the dark. And we know that this is what he and others in fact did, in trying to escape (2 Kgs. 25:4). But Ezek. 12:3, the initial mandate of the *oth*, is equally emphatic that the whole action must be performed in the light of day. Thus the interpretation in 12:12 does not match the sign it is to interpret. It would seem that someone has noticed the difficulty and patched it up by interpolating several lines in 12:4b–6, dividing the *oth* into daytime preparation and nighttime journey—though so far as plausibility goes, this only makes matters worse. Which raises the question: Why did the author of 12:12—whoever he was—create this pother in the first place?

The answer is irresistible: 12:12–13 and some other parts of our text were interpolated by someone who knew what had actually happened to Zedekiah and the elites with him, that they were captured outside the city as they fled, that many of the captured were not thereupon deported but were summarily executed, and (most notably) that Zedekiah was blinded before being taken to Babylon—every item of which appear in 12:12–14. The suggestion is that parts of our passage—we need not sort line by line—are *vaticinia ex eventu*, supposed prophecy composed after the fact and based on knowledge of what had in fact happened.

I said in the introduction that a theological commentary should not worry about most historical-critical problems. But the presence in the canonical text of alleged prophecy plainly composed after the event is surely itself a theological problem. There are of course mitigating considerations. Ancient historians of all nations routinely composed speeches and plans for the characters of their narratives, with no intent to deceive; verisimilitude was the goal. Pseudonymity, often anachronistic, was standard practice throughout antiquity, from motives both good and bad. And, very much to our case, the disciples of an ancient prophet or teacher did not clearly distinguish themselves from their master; the disciple who added to his master's text felt himself to be acting for the master. These considerations, however, do not quite do away with the problem.

The usual move of modern scholarship has been to regard interpolations—and assuredly interpolated *vaticinia ex eventu*—as secondary and therefore, if one worries about theological authority at all, not to be taken with full seriousness.[2] If we are not to make this move, which undoes the authority of the canonical text, we must, in my judgment, excise a metaphysical prejudice that has lurked at the back of Western minds.

---

2. Eichrodt 1970 is particularly given to this practice. He does not even bother to comment on the parts of a passage that do not appear in his reconstructed original.

Even though we may suppose we know better, we tend to construe the relation of God's eternity and our time as if eternity and our created time line were lines running parallel to each other. Thus we suppose it makes sense to ask what the word was like "before" he became incarnate of the Virgin.[3] And it may indeed be that some god or other might be related to time in this fashion, but not the God who appears in scripture, whose life does not run neatly parallel to ours but rather intersects with created history in strange and convoluted ways. We may perhaps better capture something of the biblical God's relation to our time if we think of created time as a sequence that God opens in his eternity to accommodate us, so that our time line is *encompassed*—not paralleled—by his triune life.

If we make this turn in metaphysics, we are then in position to pose an audacious question: Why should a word formulated after an event *not* belong to the word of the Lord that invokes that same event? The Word of the Lord who comes to one prophet after another is not a succession of words but a person (→3:16–21) and is the same person on each occasion; this theological fact precludes thinking of the succession of prophetic words—or even successive interpolations by disciples—as bound to their chronology. If indeed our text includes words interpolated after the fact and by someone other than Ezekiel, the text as it stands can nevertheless very well be a word of the one Word and be powerful to evoke the history of which it speaks, even after the chronologically linear fact.

We return to the text, now taking it as it presents itself. The Lord, through the instrumentality of his hunting net, Nebuchadnezzar, will slay and scatter the elites who attempt to escape the judgment of Jerusalem (12:14–15). Then "they shall know that I am the Lord." In the present instance, this ubiquitous and variously nuanced statement of result must have the following force: those who survive will know that the one who has done this is the Lord, their own God, and that just so the Lord is not helpless and has not departed the stage.

Finally, those who survive will bear a strange witness to the nations among which they are scattered (12:16). They will tell of their own "abominations," of their faithlessness to the Lord their own God, and of their worship of the gods of the very nations amidst which they now find themselves, and they will be in person a demonstration of what came of that. Then the nations too will know that there is the Lord.

3. Not noticing that this is a version of the famously nonsensical question about what God was doing before he created time.

EZEKIEL 12:17–20

DESOLATIONS AGAIN

This short prophecy is something like a standard Ezekiel prophecy. In teaching, one could use the passage as a model, to display the elements of prophecy in Ezekiel's style. Ezekiel introduces the prophecy with his usual formula for prophecies other than visions: "The word of the Lord came to me." The Lord addresses Ezekiel as he invariably does: "you—son of a man." The layout is exemplary: first Ezekiel is given a sign, an *oth* (→3:22–5:4), to perform; then he is given a verbal prophecy to interpret it, a messenger-word beginning with "thus says the Lord." And the passage ends with the outcome formula of much of Ezekiel's prophesying: "You shall know that I am the Lord."

We are not informed of the occasion. Even the editorial placement is common to many passages: Ezekiel or someone else has located it here because in matter and form it is similar to the preceding passage.

Also the content is standard, indeed routine. Imminent judgment is proclaimed on the inhabitants of Jerusalem, who unlike the exiles are still "in the land of Israel." The land will be stripped and its cities laid waste, on account of the general wickedness[1] of the inhabitants. The *oth* depicts the overwhelming anxiety under which people live in such circumstances: Ezekiel's hand is to shake as he brings a morsel or cup to his mouth. These predictions are, to be sure, grim enough, but are a mild depiction of disaster compared with many in Ezekiel's book.

A few particular matters may call for comment. The *oth* and the verbal prophecy are to be addressed to "the people of the land," the *am haaretz* (עם הארץ). Who are they here? The matter is disputed and probably not certainly to be decided. The

---

1. "Violence" is a comprehensive term for all sorts of mutual harm.

usual referent of the phrase is those who rightly possess a territory, but that makes little sense here. Given the rest of the passage, the addressees must be the exiles or perhaps some group of them, who for some reason—that we do not now know and are unlikely to discover—are here peculiarly denoted. If the addressees were the people currently in possession of the land, we would have another instance of Ezekiel's strange address to persons not physically present.

If the prophecy is indeed addressed to the exiles, it is they to whom Judah's desolation will make it known that "I am the Lord." The meaning of this saying is slightly shaded from prophecy to prophecy. Here it must mean that the exiles will learn that all who, like the inhabitants of Jerusalem, continue in disobedience to the Lord's "statutes and ordinances" do so at their peril.

At first thought there is something incongruous about a routine prophecy. Should not an intervention of the Lord's own word always be in some way new and startling? Can we give the present passage any weight in our understanding of Ezekiel? But a second thought will perhaps see the point also of routine.

In the New Testament, the church emerges as an entire prophetic community (Acts 2:14–18). Thus her apostles and local preachers and teachers were like Israel's prophets to speak God's own word into history. Since the church's word is the report of a past event, the crucifixion and resurrection of Jesus, there is indeed a certain routine of her prophesying. Alike in mission and catechesis, the church from the beginning needed standard patterns of proclamation and teaching: the "kerygma" (the short missionary message that "Jesus is risen") and slightly later the "rule of faith" (the second century's generally accepted though never uniquely formulated list of essential doctrine). We should perhaps construe our present passage on those same lines.

EZEKIEL 12:21–28

ON IGNORING PROPHECY

This commentary unit will consider two prophecies together. They deal with tightly related phenomena in Israel, and the Lord's response to these phenomena is single. Moreover, the second passage (12:26–28) is extremely short.

The two also form a thematic unit with the following chapter. All three passages deal with prophecy itself and with its currently precarious position in the life of Israel. To list the topics in a preliminary way: 12:21–25 rebuts general skepticism about prophecy; 12:26–28 rebukes those who think it concerns only a distant future; and 13:1–23 takes up—at length—false prophecy, for its own sake and because it is one cause of skepticism.

Both prophecies dealt with here display formal features standard in Ezekiel's discourse. In both, Ezekiel's report begins "the word of the Lord came to me"; in both the Lord addresses him "you—son of a man"; and both actual prophecies begin "thus says the Lord God."

The Lord's opening words report to Ezekiel what some people in Israel are saying about prophecy. Then follows the Lord's response, which Ezekiel is to convey.

The mere fact of the report and the mere fact of the response are both theologically remarkable. On the one hand, so exclusively is the Lord in charge that he even tells Ezekiel what Ezekiel already knows or could find out for himself. On the other hand, God reacts to human creature's opinions: he not only speaks to his people and so carries on a history with them; what he—precisely as sovereign!—says is in part determined by what they antecedently say. The history of God with his people is thus a jointly reactive history—as indeed all real history is.

That the Lord reacts to his people in his history with them should, to be sure, be no surprise to Christian faith or theology. But it often is, because it is nonsense to those currents of our intellectual tradition that derive too unbrokenly from the theology of the pre-Christian Greek theologians. In the theology of an Aristotle or Plato, the very definition of deity is that it is superbly and blessedly unaffected by human claims or objections. Indeed, the propensity of human religion as a whole is to posit some high deity that does not deign to react to mortals, leaving such things to lower divine beings. Ezekiel's God, however, does react, even argue, which Christian theology sees validated when the incarnate Son of the Gospels is in constant debate with friend and foe.

So to our first passage and to the way in which some shielded themselves from taking prophecy seriously (12:21–22). A saying—a *mashal*, that is, a more or less fixed form of pithy discourse[1]—is circulating in Israel:[2] "The days go on and on,[3] and every vision comes to nothing"—referring to prophecy generally as "vision" is usage from earlier times, perhaps persisting in sayings (Zimmerli 1979: 281).

History, these skeptics say, continues: there have been many prophecies of utter disaster and many of glorious fulfillment, and here we still are, neither wholly undone nor yet fulfilled. Surely, they conclude, there is little reason to attend to prophets. Here we hear the voice of simple skeptics. The Lord's response is in three steps.

First Step. A straightforward contradiction of the *mashal* is done by a rhetorically elegant reversal. To "the days go on" he opposes "the days are coming near." "The days" here, like "the day" in →7:10–27, must denote the event that other prophets called "the day of the Lord." To "every vision comes to nothing" the Lord's *mashal* opposes the vindication of all authentic prophecy on that great day of the Lord's triumph.

Second Step. It seems that the skeptics have been able to justify their attitude by pointing to the many prophecies that have failed. And some prophecies must indeed fail when there are false prophets, so that seeming prophets contradict each other. The Lord acknowledges the excuse and says that on that day he will remove it, by eliminating false prophecy.

Third Step. On that day—with no false prophecy creating discord—the Lord will speak unmistakably, and his word will be promptly and unmistakably fulfilled. This immediate linking of prophecy and fulfillment will occur within the lifetimes of those who now hear Ezekiel; indeed, it seems to be the prophecy the Lord now sends by Ezekiel whose inescapable fulfillment he proclaims by Ezekiel. And when Ezekiel's prophecy is so quickly fulfilled, prophecy as such—"every vision"—will be vindicated.

Something like this immediate fulfillment of Ezekiel's prophecy did happen. Between 596, when Ezekiel probably performed his first sign, and 586, when his visions of doom were unmistakably fulfilled, there are after all only ten years.

---

1. Why NRSV wants to make our saying a "proverb," which it is not, is a mystery.
2. KJV's "in the land" is just as possible as NRSV's "about the land" and surely makes more sense in context.
3. Getting the flavor of this clause in English is hard.

Nevertheless, at the time, the skeptics doubtless received this prophecy of an end to their skepticism as just another prophecy to be skeptical about. And no sooner had Ezekiel's prophecies about Jerusalem been fulfilled, than things became ambiguous again.

Thus the skeptics had and have a point. Theology must in fact deal with the fact of at best partially fulfilled biblical prophecy: Israel has not yet met either her final end or fulfillment, nor have all nations thereupon gathered to make peace around Mount Zion. Nor does it quite eliminate the problem that the final reaches of Israel's prophecy are properly eschatological, in that what they promise cannot be contained within history as we experience it, for the end itself is remarkably delayed.

So how *are* we to deal with the delay of fulfillment? It was all very well for the author of 2 Peter, probably still writing within the lifetimes of initial converts, to insist that "the Lord is not slow . . . as some think of slowness" (2 Pet. 3:9), but what might he say now, after two millennia?

The second of our prophecies displays one way that Israelites dealt with delayed fulfillment—a way that remains common among the pious. Again the Lord quotes a popular saying: what "he"—the antecedent is probably whatever prophet was making waves at some time—prophesies will indeed come to pass, but in so distant a future that we need not worry about it now. Obviously, this works out to the same result in practice as the skepticism previously denounced. Therefore the Lord's response is the same: he will by Ezekiel speak a word that will not delay but will be promptly fulfilled. Which, to be sure, lands us back with the general problem: What when fulfillment *is* delayed?

The history of Christian theology displays a succession of attempts to answer this question. Premodern theology generally said that all the promises and threats of Israel's prophets had in fact been fulfilled in the events of Christ's coming, mission, death, and resurrection and in the existence of the church. Of the delay of Christ's own final advent, premodern theology usually taught some version of 2 Peter's apology.

Modernity was generally blind to the way that actual stretches of history display thematic figurations, anticipations, paradigms, and the like, acknowledging only supposed historical "causes." And most modern critical biblical scholarship insisted—indeed, as a sort of dogma—that the Old Testament cannot really be about Christ or the church, that premodern exegesis had been an alien imposition achieved by fantastic "allegory." Thus the traditional argument has been implausible to most modern Christians. But what then?

The theology of modernity for the most part solved the problem of seeming nonfulfillment by spiritualizing and moralizing the fulfillment—that is, by ruling actual eschatology out of theological discourse. Christianity was construed as a species of religion, which deals with timeless spiritual and moral truths. The prophets were read as religious preachers within their time and place, and what could not be read in that way was set aside.[4] The kingdom proclaimed by Christ was interpreted as a structure of morality to be erected within history by the freedom that the gospel enables for believers.

An earlier commentary unit (→9:1–11) noted the overthrow of this construal by rebels from within neo-Protestantism itself. The kingdom proclaimed by Christ, it was acknowledged—in Karl Barth's case, proclaimed from the housetops—was not the outcome or ideal of our moral labors. A new beginning in theology was then marked by the "dialectical theology,"[5] which set out to reclaim the eschatological character of biblical faith. These theologians, in one way or another, made the notion of an "end"—or of irresolvable "crisis"—central. The preached message of Christ's crucifixion, they said, brings our temporal strivings to a halt; it sets us in a moment "in and out of time" that is both an absolute end and contains a new beginning within itself. The eschaton is real, but the future in which it appears is not itself a future event; it is the "eschatological moment" that occurs whenever finitude is truly confronted with infinity.

Dialectical theology's great achievement is again not to be doubted. But a moment's reflection will see that these rebels against neo-Protestantism did not in fact emancipate themselves from Schleiermacher's dogma that prophecy of the eschaton provides no determinate information. To caricature the position of the school of Bultmann, "authentic" or "eschatological" existence is the moment of openness to the future—the future of being able to be open to the future.

Let us suppose that we find neither neo-Protestantism's nor dialectical theology's resolutions satisfactory. What then?

We should—in my view—begin by retrieving the church's premodern construal. The New Testament does in fact think that all the promises of God are fulfilled in Christ (e.g., Rom. 15:8), and so should Christian theology. It is becoming ever more obvious: modern scholars' insistence that the original sense of Old Testament anticipation cannot be christological or ecclesiological is not itself a scholarly result but an antecedent ideological construal of how history works. There is no need to share this construal.

We must, to be sure, be very careful not to suggest that, because the promises have been fulfilled in Christ, they no longer apply to the Jews as a people. But a nonsupersessionist construal is indeed possible and in some part already achieved.[6]

If we go on from the fulfillment of the Old Testament in Christ, the problems of delay devolve into one: the so-called delay of the parousia. And here the first

4. One of the scholars to whom this commentary often refers regularly makes this very move; Eichrodt 1970: e.g., 162.

5. Dialectical theology flourished very briefly, roughly from 1922 to 1932. The more familiar names will be Karl Barth, Rudolf Bultmann, Friedrich Gogarten, and Emil Brunner. After 1932 they went separate ways.

6. The enterprise is in fact flourishing; see, e.g., Carl E. Braaten and Robert W. Jenson, eds., *Jews and Christians: People of God* (Grand Rapids: Eerdmans, 2003).

thing to say is that the failure of primal Christianity's expectation of Christ's immediate advent is a plausible reason not to believe the gospel that proclaimed it. If after nearly two millennia we find that gospel so compelling that we continue to hope, we should acknowledge that such a hope speaks a great "nevertheless."

Finally, if we ask why the Lord is so slow, we may indeed adapt 2 Peter's answer. Those who write and read this commentary should not complain that God did not end history millennia ago; he lingers to make room for us. Moreover, we cannot control the unpredictable ways in which the sequences of God's eternity intersect with those of our created time. As the same passage from 2 Peter puts it: "With the Lord . . . a thousand years are like one day."

EZEKIEL 13:1–23

BLACK WORDS AND SACRAMENTS

Ezekiel 13:1–23 and the two immediately preceding passages (12:21–25 and 12:26–28) make an editorial grouping on a theme: the situation of prophecy in Ezekiel's time. Ezekiel 12:21–25 takes up general skepticism about prophecy's fulfillment, in part occasioned by the prevalence of conflicting prophecies; 12:26–28 rejects an evasive way of dealing with the problem; and our present chapter takes up false prophecy directly.

The chapter is a clearly marked unit that records the Lord's giving a single continuous prophecy to Ezekiel. It begins with the standard introduction, "the word of the Lord came to me," which is not repeated; 14:1 then begins discourse of a different genre.

There is, to be sure, a new beginning at 13:17. But examination of the rhetoric by which the new start is made shows that the move is not from one prophecy to another; rather, the second set of verses is artfully constructed as a mirror of the first, so that the two make a sort of diptych. Ezekiel 13:17 mimics 13:2: in both verses the Lord gets Ezekiel's attention by addressing him as "you—son of a man" and then instructs him to "prophesy against" those "who prophesy out of their own inwardness,"[1] falsely proclaiming "thus says the Lord God." This analysis is further confirmed if we, as it were, close the diptych to match the patterns of prophecy given to Ezekiel on the two sides: on both, indictments of spiritual malpractice

---

1. The Hebrew that NRSV here and elsewhere translates "imagination" is לב (*leb*), normally translated "heart" (→11:14–21). Thus KJV translates "out of their own hearts," and the Septuagint ἀπὸ καρδίαις αὐτῶν. Why NRSV reduces this comprehensive concept of Israel's anthropology to "imagination" can only be guessed at.

come first; and on both, condemnations follow immediately, introduced with "therefore thus says the Lord God." Finally, 13:17–23 can be shorter than 13:1–16, even cryptic, precisely because the later passage presupposes the former.

We may ask why so much art is devoted to welding 13:1–16 and 13:17–23 formally together. The reason is that otherwise hearers or readers would surely separate them and interpret each without reference to the other: the evils for which the two sets of spiritual charlatans are indicted are at first glance only distantly related. But if we did read them separately, we would miss the dark mystery that in fact binds them, the mystery that it will be the chief task of this commentary unit to uncover. It is thus central to the meaning of both parts of 13:1–23 that they be read together.

On the first side of the diptych, those indicted are some of "the prophets of Israel"; this generic designation serves to apply the indictment equally to prophets in exile and prophets in Judah. The wrongdoers are those who prophesy despite having been provided no prophecy by the Lord (13:3) and not having been sent by him (13:6). They have no source for their message other than their own inwardness, their own "hearts." Thus their word is only their own word, and their claim to bring the word of the Lord (13:2) is a lie. The indictment is then specified, with two images.

The first image (13:4–5) is taken from the situation of a besieged city, that is, from the recent and immediately future situation of Jerusalem. When a breach in a city wall is made, faithful citizens must rush to repair it. In Jerusalem's crisis, some of the prophets have not been among these faithful, but have instead found personal opportunity in the ruins, as jackals do.

Each citizen will of course contribute to repair of the breach in a way that accords with his role in the city. It is the particular task of prophets to speak the truth: in this case, that the attack on Jerusalem is "the day of the Lord" (13:5; →7:10–27) and that therefore nothing but immediate and unconditional repentance will ward off catastrophe. And it would have been the task of prophets to intercede for the city, to be the voice of such repentance—the Targum glosses the text to make this explicit (Levey 1990: 44). The false prophets have done neither, which is why they are false.

The second image is harder to make out. It is perhaps taken from building practice (Zimmerli 1979: 295). If we assume that background, the comparison must run something like this: the structure of Jerusalem's security is like a lightly constructed temporary or interior wall, plastered to make it look like solid masonry. It would have been the task of prophets to reveal the wall's fragility; instead they are the ones who applied the plaster. The judgment of such shifts is always the same: "The rain fell, and the floods came, and the winds blew and beat against that house, and it fell" (Matt. 7:27).

The malfeasance of the prophets can then be summed up: they have proclaimed "peace" where there is no peace (Ezek. 13:10). The famous phrase " 'peace,' when there is no peace" is not Ezekiel's coinage; he shares it with his near contemporary in Jerusalem (Jer. 6:14; 8:11). In both their mouths, it is a daring reversal. Amos and other prophets had reversed expectation for "the day of the Lord" (→7:10–27) but reversing the meaning of "peace" was yet more daring, for it had been a slogan not of a popular piety but of the great Isaiah's message of salvation (e.g., Isa. 9:7) and of the tradition he founded. By Ezekiel and Jeremiah's time, however, "the feet of the messenger who announces peace" were not "beautiful," as at Isa. 52:7, for they brought not "good tidings" but fatal illusions.

The prophets that Ezekiel denounced could of course reply—and probably did—that whether there was in fact to be peace or no peace had yet to be seen. And we must acknowledge that Ezekiel does not provide a criterion of true or false prophecy that is available until it is too late for application: too late for repentance if prophecies of judgment turn out to have been the true ones, or too late for faith if prophecies of peace turn out to have been the true ones.

Telling true prophecy from false at the time of the prophecy could be only Spirit-worked like the prophecy itself. For the Old Testament prophets themselves, more prosaic verification had to come after the fact. This aporia could be resolved only when the word that comes to prophets became in such fashion personally present as to be available as the criterion. Thus the church's criterion of true prophecy was laid down by Origen in comment on our passage: "If . . . I find in Moses and the prophets the sense of Christ, then I do not speak according to my own heart but according to the Holy Spirit" (1989: 50).[2]

The punishment of the false prophets will be loss of their influence, exclusion from "the register" of Israel—which the Targum interprets as the register of those to be given "eternal life" (Levey 1990: 44)—and exclusion from the exiles' return (13:9). A backhanded promise is contained in this judgment: also after the day, there will be an Israel, for false prophets to be excluded from; there will be a book of life, to lack false prophets' names; and there will be a return from exile, for false prophets to miss.

Turning to the second part of the chapter, we see why 13:17 must work so exactly to make clear that what it introduces belongs with what precedes it, for in what follows we seem to enter a very different milieu. The difference is not that we encounter women prophets; they are not uncommon in the biblical record, where we hear of Miriam (Exod. 15:20), Deborah (Judg. 4:4), Isaiah's wife (Isa. 8:3), and others. It is that Ezekiel's "women who prophesy" would not in the previous passage have appeared as prophets of any kind, false or otherwise.[3] They are practitioners of the sort of petty but sinister magic that seems to be a permanent affliction of humanity: charms to obtain the disaster of an enemy or to counter the enemy's charms, love amulets, divinations of

2. Origen 1989: 2 applies Ezekiel's judgments directly to incompetent or heretical teachers in the church, as indeed I do throughout this commentary unit.

3. As to why it is women who are depicted as practicing the minor black arts, the answer is that in all cultures they have in fact predominated among its practitioners. Why that is so is a question beyond the scope of this commentary.

where to build a house or launch a venture—very popular on the American West Coast—and so on and on.

We do not know what sorts of conjure devices the "bands" or "veils" were that figured in the women's magic (Zimmerli 1979: 297; the Targum is at sea [see Levey 1990: 45]), but they were dark enough, since they served to "hunt down lives" and by way of fees (13:19) to preserve the sorcerers' own lives. The text does not say that these practices, whatever they were, did not work. On the contrary, when the Lord will tear away the "bands" he will thereby liberate lives bound to death. There is a dark truth in magic, that we are cautiously approaching.

But why then are these "women who *prophesy*"? And why do their practices profane the *Lord* among his people? Part of the answer is explicitly provided in our text: they seek and obtain advice by some mechanism of divination, and the advice will have been represented as a word from the Lord, although the Lord had not given it (13:22–23). But there is another and more important point. Ezekiel can take something for granted in his readers: knowledge that amulets and all such devices do not work by themselves, that they must be accompanied by the proper words. Power must be granted to the medicine bag or crystal or horoscope, and those who use it must in turn use the right words. And in Israel, even Israel in her superstitious dregs, the name to conjure with was יהוה. The profanation of the Lord's name is that humans attempted to manipulate events to their own desires by conjuring with the name, tried to obtain blessing by unauthorized imitation of prophetic or priestly intercession.

St. Augustine defined sacraments with a formula that became the foundation of Western theology's sacramental teaching: "The word comes to the element"—to an object and gesture with it—"and so there is a sacrament" (*In Johannem* 80.3). A parody of this formula can define magic: "The conjure word comes to the element and so there is a charm." Wherever it appears, traffic with conjure words and their embodiments is black parody of the sacraments, also when the practitioner has never heard of them.

Within Christianity, people have smuggled consecrated hosts to use against the evil eye and mumbled what they heard of the Latin consecration as an all-purpose charm (*hoc est corpus meum* is often thought to be the source of English "hocus-pocus"), while at a yet more debased level of superstition whole churches now construct sacramental rites according to the dictates of their own "hearts," deaf to the Lord's mandating word, "Do *this*." In like manner, there were in Israel, paired with the "sacraments of the Old Covenant,"[4] the antisacraments purveyed by these women—and we know that such witchcraft was indeed practiced in Israel, from the rigor with which the law condemned it (Exod. 22:18).

There is a second slogan of Western theology: all God's provisions for our final good are summed together as "word and sacrament." The *and* here is not exclusive: under this rubric we can equally say that a sacrament is a "visible"—that

4. As Christian theology has often described Israel's central cultic practices.

is, tangible—word and that the word of the gospel is an audible sacrament. It is precisely this mutuality of word and sacrament that is God's saving presence among us. The same was true in Israel: Torah/prophecy and sacrifice belonged together.

Whether it is old Israel's prophecy and her practices of the covenant, or the church's gospel and her sacraments, word and sacrament is always shadowed by dark parody—and this is finally the fearful secret insinuated by the mutuality of 13:1–16 and 13:17–23. God's proclaimed word in Israel and in the church is always shadowed by lies, and his old or new sacraments by magic—together, God's grace is shadowed by Satan's tricks.

The "mystery of iniquity" is that this negation of grace is allowed its own sort of actuality: magic sometimes works, and lies can be Satan's own penultimately effective intervention in history. Augustine said that evil is the darkness where being has ran out; the shadow that lies over our lives is the gloom that deepens as the light dims. Karl Barth said that evil is what God eternally leaves behind him and that the shadow is the trace of his doing this. But perhaps the shadow's sheerly negative reality is best acknowledged and exorcized by doing what Martin Luther famously did, throwing things at it.

EZEKIEL 14:1–11

THE SIGN OF JONAH

Ezekiel 14:1–11 makes a straightforward unit. The passage begins as did the visionary complex of Ezek. 8–11, with leaders of the exilic community waiting on Ezekiel. The beginning of a following unit is marked by the formula for new verbal revelation at 14:12. We will, however, see the genre of the passage take strange turns.

The elders have come to solicit a word from the Lord. They are this time identified as elders "of Israel," rather than of "Judah" as before, perhaps because we are to take them as representative of their type, whether in exile or in Jerusalem. We are not told what their query was about, for the word of the Lord comes incontinently to Ezekiel and disrupts the proceedings, making not the elders' question but they themselves the matter at hand.

Thus the object of the prophecy now provided to Ezekiel is a group of persons characterized by their behavior, as before in Ezek. 11 and Ezek. 13, where we had foolish Jerusalem officials and false prophets. In Ezekiel's attention to individuals and particular groups, here as elsewhere, we see him fulfilling his sending as a "sentinel" in Israel, to discern the righteous and the unrighteous in Israel and warn each person or group appropriately (→3:16–21).

The Lord's initial word (14:3) is directed to Ezekiel himself. The Lord tells him about those elders: they are persons who have "taken their idols into their hearts" or, perhaps, have "exalted idols within their hearts."[1] If read in this latter way, the indictment against them is perhaps that old idolatrous practices had

---

1. The verb is a causative form of עלה (*olah*, "to rise up"). KJV's "set up their idols in their hearts" is surely better than NRSV's "taken into."

remained in memory and now have risen into—doubtless cautious—practice. We are not told precisely what sort of idolatry the elders are given to. It is anyway a stumbling block into "iniquity,"[2] into the sort of guilt that altogether excludes from God's people.

In any case, the transgression that triggers our passage is that these elders at once indulge in idolatry and seek a word from the Lord. By daring to appear before him while not renouncing all idolatrous practice, they indeed stumble into iniquity. And they display two great theological failings.

First, they have not caught on about their God, the Lord, even though they doubtless knew the declaration by heart: "I the LORD your God am a jealous God" (Exod. 20:5). They are about to discover what this jealousy means.

Second, they are following human religiosity's universally followed path of least resistance. Humanity's ability "to believe six incompatible things before breakfast" becomes almost a defining characteristic when it comes to religion. Never mind if, for example, the Lord and Moloch are declared opposites, we will, if given the chance, worship both at once—and whatever else seems powerful in the neighborhood.

As Karl Barth insisted, all religion is in itself our attempt to secure our own wants and preferred construals, by invoking whomever or whatever we think powerful enough to help. Since there is in the world a multitude of apparent powers, religion has therefore an inherent inclination to polytheism. It can be rescued from itself only if the one God himself imposes the sort of radical judgment and promise of new beginning that he does by Ezekiel. Those elders are about to experience the judgment, in service of others' new beginning.

The Lord asks Ezekiel: Why should I answer the queries of such as these, who dare appear before me with idols in their pockets? Then he nevertheless gives Ezekiel something to say to them, but in a way crosswise to their intention, both in content and form. The content is familiar: the Lord will undo these folk. It is the form that is startling.

We have so far made little use of form-critical study. There are two aspects of form criticism: identification of the genre to which a piece of discourse or narrative belongs, and the attempt to reconstruct the "location in life" within which that genre has or had its function. With our present passage, this kind of scholarship provides vital insight (Zimmerli 1979: 306).

The genre of the message given to Ezekiel (14:4) leaps to the eye, so soon as one asks the form-critical question: the dictum is in none of the second-person forms of judgment and promise characteristic of prophecy, but rather is a third-person proposition of the law. Indeed it is holy law, the law laid down by priestly oracles, as we know it from Leviticus and elsewhere, with the fixed form "anyone who . . .

---

2. עָוֹן is a comprehensive word for moral disaster, even for damnation. The two-word phrase—literally "a stumbling block of their evil"—can be construed either as making evil the stumbling block (so NRSV) or as making their evil the horror into which idolatry precipitates. It will be seen that I prefer the second construal.

shall be . . ." (e.g., Lev. 17:3, 10, 16). And among the offenses that can appear in the if-clause of such a law, worshiping other gods or making images of any god at all is the gravest, as the Old Testament makes clear by putting it first in the list of crimes prohibited by the Ten Commandments (Exod. 20:1–17; within Ezekiel's priestly tradition Lev. 19:4).

Thus the Lord does not give Ezekiel any new word for the elders; instead he tells Ezekiel to recite law they have known all along. The indictment is not only in what is said, but in the contemptuous way in which it is said.

Then the genre breaks again. The proper then-clause of a sacral law is judicial statement of what is to be done with the one who has done such-and-such; but in our passage the Lord disrupts both form and syntax, replacing the legal specification with personal presence. He leaves no room for priestly judicial process, instead announcing: I, the Lord, will in this case act as myself both judge and executioner.

The biblical God is not a distant origin and enforcer of the laws that govern his people's lives; he is himself actively present in them. Here his presence bursts out in the passage's disruption of genre and grammar. Law—sacral or otherwise—lays down appropriate consequences of specified misbehavior for judges to determine and pronounce. But here the Lord personally comes to judge and punish. He is indeed always hidden in his law; but our passage's formal break reveals his presence there. We are not at first told what the Lord will do with the present malefactors, but when he himself emerges to punish violation of the first commandment, the least that can be expected is manifest exclusion from Israel (14:8), like that of the false prophets in the previous chapter (13:9).

The formal twists and turns continue. The Lord, without marking the shift, turns again to talk with Ezekiel and tells Ezekiel his motive in personally taking over judgment of idolatrous leaders: he intends by their fate to "take hold of the hearts of the house of Israel" and so to call them finally back from estrangement (14:5). Then he provides Ezekiel with verbal prophecy to accompany this demonstration, shifting genre again: Ezekiel is instructed to address "the house of Israel" with a classic direct second-person prophetic call for repentance (14:6). And then in the next verse, we are back again with law, indeed to repetition of the same law previously cited, with the same appearance of the Lord as a sort of personal apodosis.

This second law citation is very slightly expanded and in such fashion as to justify our speaking of citation. The addition of "aliens who reside in Israel" is irrelevant materially and surely appears here only because it was an existing legal ruling that is here invoked. But why the repetition? Some scholars see it as a sure sign of interpolation, in which case it is 14:4–5 that has been interpolated. But why would someone have done that?

There is another possibility: the discourse had to follow the course it does to mirror its import rhetorically. Having started with legalities, it had to break through them with the personal advent of the Lord and his intent to reclaim Israel, and having done that it had to give Ezekiel an actual call for Israel to repent. But then it had to get back to legalities because that is how the Lord is dealing with those elders, who are after all the occasion of the discourse.

So we finally arrive at what the Lord intends to achieve by his judgment of those elders. Their judgment before all eyes will be an *oth* (→3:22–5:4), a prophetic sign, that he is indeed the Lord the jealous God who brooks no divided worship. And this time, the people will finally learn that (14:8).

One more thing must be attended to before the Lord can utter the great promise that has been the goal of all these zigs and zags. The presenting situation is between the elders and a prophet. What of the prophet? If he goes along with the elders' request and provides a "word from the Lord" at their request, he sins as do they, and his own fall will be included in the *oth* their fall will make (14:10). But how can a prophet be thus deceived—whether he is a real prophet like Ezekiel or a false prophet who does not know he is false? In either case, there is only one possibility: the Lord himself has deceived him (14:9).

We encounter again the mysteriously simple relation between the Lord's will and our wills. The antimony appears everywhere in scripture. Jesus tells his hearers that no one can come to him except those whom the Father gives him, and he does this in a speech aimed at bringing his hearers to him (John 6:65). In the case always adduced when theology takes up this matter, the Lord hardens Pharaoh's heart against letting Israel go and then destroys him for not letting Israel go (Exod. 7:3–5; →12:1–16).

We should ask ourselves: if we find predestination offensive, what would we rather have the Lord do? Let us go the ways of our rebellion, to the destruction that terminates those ways? Or turn history over to our wise rule? Or, as Ezekiel here portrays God's rule, be himself in some utterly mysterious way responsible also in our iniquities? One may of course say that God is surely not bound by such dilemmas. But that would be true only if he withdrew from his history with us; if he soldiers on with creatures who are both finite and fallen, he too faces alternatives. One may say that God should not in the first place create a history that poses such choices. But what other sort of history would we, in our great wisdom, institute?

In any case, the goal is what it has been since the covenant made at Sinai. The house of Israel shall at last be faithful to the Lord. In Ezekiel's present version of the great covenant formula, they shall indeed be his people and he shall himself be fulfilled as their God. And then even those foolish elders will have been prophets, performing their assigned *oth*.

EZEKIEL 14:12–23

THE LORD'S THEODICY

This unit is in many ways a standard instance of Ezekiel's prophecy. It is marked out in his usual fashion: beginning with the word of the Lord coming to Ezekiel and addressing him as "you—son of a man" and ending with a variation on the "you shall know" formula. To be sure, the prophecy that Ezekiel is to bring to the people does not actually begin until almost the end of the passage, with "for thus says the Lord God" at 14:21, but such delay is not uncommon in Ezekiel. The announced agents of judgment when we get to them—famine, encroachment of the wilderness with its wild beasts, war, and pestilence—are standard for Ezekiel and indeed for the prophetic tradition. Nor is the ferocity with which judgment is proclaimed novel.

In other ways, however, our passage is a new thing in Ezekiel's book. In 14:12–20, the word addressed to Ezekiel himself, the Lord does not speak of Israel or Jerusalem or erring groups within them. Instead, he lays down—indeed hammers home with one legal dictum after another—general principles of his rule of history, rules that apply to any nation at all. Reading some other parts of Ezekiel's book, one might think that the Lord's only concern for other nations is their ad hoc availability as instruments to punish or bless Israel. Here we discover something different.

Indeed, the Lord is at pains to make clear that the law now enunciated applies specifically to *Gentile* lands: the three named as examples of the righteous whose presence in a rebellious land will or will not mitigate its fate are none of them Israelites; all are what the rabbis called righteous Gentiles. This is unproblematic in the cases of Noah and Job, biblical figures explicitly located outside the specific story of Israel, yet renowned for their righteousness—though we have to excuse an alcoholic coma in Noah's case (Gen. 9:20–23). But also the Daniel to whom the Lord here refers—and who appears again at Ezek. 28:3—can hardly be the Daniel of the Old Testament book by that name, since that book presents Daniel as Ezekiel's contemporary. As the archeological luck would have it, we know of a "Daniel" of general Middle Eastern legend, a ruler widely famed for righteousness and wisdom (Zimmerli 1979: 314–15), with whose story Ezekiel could well have been familiar. Given the matter of our passage, it may also be useful to note that in their stories all these three somehow let down their children.

What the Lord then says of his relation to the Gentile nations is theologically remarkable. When a nation sins, whether it be Egypt or Babylon—or, presumably, China or the United States or whoever—the sin is always directly against Israel's particular Lord (14:13a). That the Lord's claim to universal lordship is put so backhandedly is of course typical of Ezekiel, at least as his book has recorded his prophecy. Moreover, the sin consists in acting "faithlessly," or perhaps "treacherously," to the Lord; the discord between the Lord and Babylon is just as personal as the Lord's discord with Israel. The Lord—and we must remember that "the Lord" is cover for יהוה, the personal name of the particular God of Israel—here presumes that all nations owe their faith or loyalty immediately to him, and says that he personally will raise them up or bring them down, accordingly as they remain faithful to him or not. Moreover, in our text this does not depend on their relation to Israel; the general principle is laid down first and only then applied to Jerusalem.

Babylon cannot well be faithful or unfaithful to the Lord if she has never met him. Thus the sort of universal direct rule that the Lord here claims must involve some sort of universal personal self-revelation of the Lord—and lines of biblical teaching that imply this are found not only in Ezekiel. Every confession and school of theology therefore has some label under which it tries to understand this implication—"natural law," "general revelation," "the covenant of creation" are among the historically prominent.

Whatever concepts we employ, the problem is to acknowledge the fact of such revelation to the nations, while also obeying the prophetic judgment that the gods of the nations are idols. It is not that, as is often said, there is truth in every religion, not if we have any determinate notion of truth: if the worship of Phoenician Moloch is true in any way at all, the worship of יהוה is not. But we can indeed say that all religion is response to a self-introducing word of the one true God. The response to the Lord's word may well be perverse and even evil— like burning children alive in honor of Moloch—but the word itself is a true offer of communion. And we may locate that word, that must, like the word to Israel, somehow come by human speakers, in the word that in mutual discourse establishes our humanity, but that none of us can finally claim as his or her own, the reciprocal word "thou shalt. . . ." There has been and can be no human community in which that word has not been heard, however faintly and with however perverse a response.

The general principle of 14:12–20 is then applied to Jerusalem. Does that mean that God's rule of Israel is an *instance* of his general rule of nations? Not necessarily, as we see in 14:21–23.

The drumbeat of doctrine in 14:12–20 is clearly directed against some contrary teaching. It is apparently presumed both by those rebuked and by the Lord, that the righteous remnant in a doomed land will be saved by their righteousness. Some—perhaps among the exiles—apparently also expect that these righteous persons will effect the salvation of others than themselves; obviously they are thinking of the righteous and unrighteous in Jerusalem, whose fall was imminently threatening.[1] The question is this: Whom does this false hope number among those others? And wherein is that salvation thought to consist?

One possible reading of the false hope limits it drastically: the righteous who escape the catastrophe of their land will be able to bring members of their families along. Exegetes who read in this way ransack Jewish legal and other precedent for the background of such opinion (Eichrodt 1970: 187–88).

In my view, however, opposing this rather trivial error can hardly demand such big legal and rhetorical guns as the Lord here mounts. Moreover, in reading our text it is impossible not to think of a different background for false hopes: the famous exchange between Abraham and the Lord about the judgment of Sodom and Gomorrah (Gen. 18:22–33). Abraham urges that the presence of even a few righteous persons in the cities of the plain should avert their destruction; and the Lord agrees to save the cities if they contain even a tiny number of such persons. To be sure, they were nevertheless not saved, for none righteous were found in them, except for—presumably—Lot. He escaped, notably bringing along his children.

If we take this story as background, then the hope that the Lord so emphatically contradicts is far more consequential than the first reading supposes: there are those who maintain that the Lord will yet spare Jerusalem, for the sake of the righteous within her, few though they may be. Against this, the Lord says that not even the combined righteousness of Noah, Daniel, and Job could save any but themselves. The force of 14:12–20 is then that the righteous who escape a land's destruction will save *not even* their own unrighteous sons or daughters, much less any others. Indeed, the hopes of exiles for—unrighteous—sons and daughters they had left behind may have been the occasion of the prophecy; this may be suggested by the choice of the particular righteous Gentiles adduced, each of whose stories connect his fate with those of his children (Greenberg 1983: 261).

Finally the Lord turns explicitly to Jerusalem (14:21). Jerusalem is indeed in a special position, and perhaps false hopes for her had been based also on this. The Lord had "set her in the center of the nations" (5:5); should that not confer some

---

1. Zimmerli 1979: 313 thinks our passage dates from immediately *after* the fall of Jerusalem. It makes slightly better sense of the passage to construe it as done here. Readers who side with Zimmerli will have to change a good bit in the following.

immunity? But here the conclusion from this placement is not that Jerusalem will be more leniently treated than other cities. The rule holds with double stringency for Jerusalem: if there are a few righteous persons within the unfaithful city, their righteousness will avail only for themselves.

The passage then ends with a rather shocking reversal (14:22–23). It turns out that some unrighteous sons and daughters of the righteous who escape will after all be rescued, and that these also will join the exilic community in Babylon. The Lord's purpose in this is, however, to show the exiles, by the behavior that these persons will display among them, what people had been doing in Jerusalem. If the catastrophe of Jerusalem had made them worry about the Lord's justice, they will be "consoled": they will learn from the unrighteous lives of their rescued sons and daughters that it was "not without cause" that the Lord destroyed Jerusalem. Like many other texts of Ezekiel, this one ends with "you shall know" the Lord—but here in a very particular connection.

Thus the outcome of the law laid down in 14:12–20 and of the events prophesied in the remainder of our passage is a demonstration of the Lord's justice in his punishment of Jerusalem. That is, the passage as a whole is a theodicy, a justification of "the ways of God to men," conducted, however, not by men but by God. Perhaps the exiles did not find it convincing, and perhaps neither would we in similar circumstances.

Be that last as it may, in my more usual role of systematic theologian I am convinced that any justification of the ways of God to humankind would have indeed to be performed by God himself. By no standard of justice known to us, could we examine the facts of history and conclude that "God is just."

We cannot achieve a theodicy, but Christians believe that God has indeed performed his own theodicy, with the cross and resurrection of Jesus. Just as God in Ezekiel makes himself responsible for the evil his creatures do, and judges them for it, so God the Son dies as "the chief of sinners" and is judged innocent by his Father, together with the other sinners with whom he identified himself.

EZEKIEL 15:1–8

THE VINE-BRANCH

This short chapter is clearly a unit. It begins with the formula for new word-revelation, "the word of the Lord came to me," and the usual address to Ezekiel as "you—son of a man." It ends with "says the Lord God."

Ezekiel 15:2–5 is addressed to Ezekiel. The verses' genre is a puzzle. Form critics are required to provide a label and so call these verses a "picture word,"[1] which is a fairly obvious description and advances understanding very little. NRSV prints the passage as verse, apparently because of the occasional parallelism of its lines.[2] Eichrodt points to the style of some wisdom literature (1970: 192–93).

What strikes me, however, is that the verses beg to be read as specifying an *oth*, a prophetic sign (→3:22–5:4), except that a command to carry out the action is missing. The instructions would have been to take a length of vine and first try to make it support something, as a solid peg or pole would; after failing in this, put it in the fire so that it catches at both ends, and display it as it burns toward the middle. One might even suppose that Ezekiel was in fact instructed to perform this *oth* and did it, and that for some reason the mandate or account of that performance has devolved into what we now have.

If no *oth* was performed, Ezekiel must have displayed the picture in some other fashion before delivering the interpretation in 15:6–8, for this would have been incomprehensible to hearers who had not experienced the imagery. Nor could he have done this by proclaiming 15:2–5 as verbal prophecy, for 15:6–8

---

1. *Bildrede*, in the native language of form criticism, at least sounds more serious.
2. Hebrew poetry consists of couplets or triplets of lines with—in most cases—the same number of emphasized words, paired by common reference.

is very explicitly interpretation of the verses about the vine, and verbal prophecy as interpretation of another immediately antecedent and sufficiently clear verbal prophecy would have been even more baffling.

In any case, so soon as the interpretation identifies the vine-branch as the "inhabitants of Jerusalem" and the vine's fate as their fate (15:6), the picture becomes transparent and hardly needs interpretation. We are to understand that the inhabitants of Jerusalem have never been able to bear much weight. And in consequence of one too many collapses under the Lord's burden, Jerusalem's population has been given over to the fire and in 597 was partially burnt, so that what is left is charred and even less reliable than before. Finally this remainder too will go; none of Jerusalem's inhabitants will finally escape the judgment.

And with that, what more is there to say about the passage? The Lord will undo Jerusalem and her people on account of their faithlessness (15:8); if we have read anything earlier in Ezekiel, we have heard that to surfeit. And then they will know the identity of the God who destroys them, that their own God, יהוה, has done it (15:7); we have encountered this too. Do we really need to be told yet again how faithless Jerusalem was and how their Lord has himself become their destroyer?

The initial readers of Ezekiel's book apparently did. Whoever put the book together and placed this passage where it is—whether Ezekiel or an editor—of course knew very well that readers would have heard or read it all before.

Just this, perhaps, is the chapter's particular theological message for us, in context of the whole book: the word of the Lord that assails his people's faithlessness does indeed need to be said and enacted again and again. The theology of the Reformation spoke much of "law and gospel," of God's two words for us, one that uncovers our need of grace and another that conveys that grace. Neither word can be spoken once for all, though both are final words that between them bespeak absolute end and absolute new beginning.

Indeed, a recently flourishing school of Protestant theology—Rudolf Bultmann and followers—held that the moment when the words of law and gospel impact the individual *is* the eschaton—in Ezekiel's language, "the day," "the end" (→7:1–9; →7:10–27). It is a moment when the time of this world stops for the hearer and when the hearer thus lives authentically before God—or misses the moment and just so is truly judged. Since the eschaton is on this interpretation indeed an end of time but one that happens to a person who continues on in time, the word that brings it must always be spoken anew, since in the next moment time starts up again. Most readers will surely find this existentialist restriction implausible as a complete representation of the Bible's eschatology and assuredly of Ezekiel's. But there is at least partial insight in the Bultmannian construal that should not be lost.

EZEKIEL 16:1–43

THE WAYWARD BRIDE

The whole of Ezek. 16 is an editorial unit, but is too long and too freighted to treat in one commentary unit. Since there is a new beginning of sorts at 16:44, I will divide there. Even so, this commentary unit will be long. The passage begins with the full array of items that in Ezekiel introduce a new revelation, all by now well known to Ezekiel's readers. The word of the Lord comes to Ezekiel, addresses him as "**you**—son of a man," and tells him to prophesy to Jerusalem, beginning with "thus says the Lord."

That he is somehow to address Jerusalem from distant Babylon is an aspect of Ezekiel's calling noted before. That Jerusalem's sins are "abominations" signals that we are again to hear of sheerly disgusting practices, fit to revolt not just the Lord but any righteous human observer.

But when, after this familiar beginning, we come to the prophecy itself, we are confronted with a new and strangely fractured mode of discourse. The Lord narrates the history of Jerusalem under a figure, of a foundling bride and her wayward married life. We might therefore be inclined to call the passage an "allegory," and many have. But the Lord appears also as a speaker *within* the story that he tells, and there directly addresses his bride Jerusalem, so that the line between the figure and what is figured is constantly erased. The erasure shows up in various ways; temple prostitution, for the central example, appears simultaneously as an actual abominable practice within Israel and in the allegory as the figure for Jerusalem's general unfaithfulness.

It is a constant structure of Ezekiel's theology: the Lord does not remain merely the author of the history that the prophet's word is to animate, but lives also within it as his own history. Indeed, that the Lord is in this fashion at once the sovereign author of his people's story and a *persona* within it is decisive for the Bible's whole account of God. Here this trinitarian pattern shapes the literary form itself.

The matter of the allegory—we will for want of a better label call it that—is a summary of Israel's history of judgment and salvation. The biblical tradition of such summary accounts of salvation history runs from the creedal formula of Deut. 26:5–9 through such passages as Ps. 106 to Stephen's long recital in Acts 7.

Ezekiel's account, however, does not begin as usual with God's election of Abraham or his rescue of the tribes from Egypt, but with the origins of the city of Jerusalem. When Abraham or the exodus tribes are the starting point in Israel's memory of her past, they are from the first *personae* in God's history with his people. But Jerusalem had a well-known antecedent existence that was no part of Israel's salvation history: before David captured the city and made her his capital she was a stronghold of the Jebusites (1 Chr. 11:4). Thus in both history and the allegory, it can be said that Jerusalem's "father" was an "Amorite"—which was by Ezekiel's time a general designation for the pagan population of Canaan—and that her "mother" was a "Hittite," like David's mercenary captain Uriah (2 Sam. 11:3–26).

That is, Jerusalem's inheritance was on both sides Canaanite and therefore compromised by all those abominations on account of which the Canaanites forfeited their land in the first place—the very abominations that will now appear as the transgressions of Jerusalem. Ezekiel 16:3 implicitly asks, What could anyone, even the Lord, expect of a city with such a background?[1]

Nevertheless, the Canaanite taint of Jerusalem's birth might not have persisted. For when the Lord comes across newborn Jerusalem (16:4–8), she has been repudiated by her parents; indeed, she has been denied all recognition as a human person of any sort. The practice of "exposing" unwanted children, especially girls, was widespread in the ancient world.[2] Abortion was perilous for the mother; an alternative way of denying the unwanted child's human status was to bring her to term, deny her both the community's welcoming rituals and medical care, and discard her to die of exposure. It is this practice that is detailed in 16:4–5. Thus in the version of salvation history here narrated, Jerusalem is outside humanity when the Lord comes along.

The Lord does come along. And "come along" is the right phrase, since the divine election that is now described is contingent; the Lord is on his way to somewhere else and might have gone a different route. As it is, he finds this reject

---

1. Origen catches the tension between this depiction of Jerusalem and that found elsewhere in scripture, including in Ezekiel, and resolves it, fully—one may think—in accord with Ezekiel: "When [Jerusalem] did not sin, she had Abraham and Isaac and Jacob for her source; when she sinned, Canaan became her source" (1989: 216).

2. When Israel was obedient to her own calling, she did not share in this practice. And the primal church included in the description of her "way," as opposed to the "way" of the world, the command "you shall not murder a child by abortion or kill a newborn" (*Didache* 2.2).

from humanity in his way, "flailing" in placental blood. And he chooses her for himself.

The choosing has two steps. In the first encounter, the Lord gives back the human life that had been denied her, with a creating word modeled on those in Gen. 1: "Live," he says, and she lives. When he comes again—the time we expect between the first and second encounters is collapsed—he finds her sexually mature[3] but still outside humanity. He marries her.

The description of marriage ceremonies in 16:8 is not now as clear as we might wish, but the spreading of the man's cloak over the bride is documented as such ritual (Zimmerli 1979: 340) and by covering her nakedness here serves also as rescue from her social exclusion. The Lord's making a "covenant" with her is the self-commitment that will somehow appear in any marriage ceremony and here is also a figure for the Lord's making covenant with Israel. Thus Jerusalem replaces Abraham or the tribes at Sinai as the original recipient of the covenant—to cast her ominous shadow over Israel's whole history.

Why does the Lord take foundling Jerusalem for his bride? There is not a word of explanation. He just does. The simplicity and utter primacy of the Lord's choosing his people, though attested throughout scripture, has always been hard to accept, and doctrines designed to mitigate election or predestination have proliferated.

However unmotivated God's election of Jerusalem, his *character* in doing so is clear, and the theological consequences of observing this are weighty. Origen of Alexandria—in the midst of a perhaps rather arbitrary but theologically deep exegesis (1989: 229–30)—caught it: what humanity did not show the child, *pity* (16:5), is exactly what the Lord shows in doing for her what humanity did not—washing her, clothing her, and so on. And Origen catches the profound implication for scripture's understanding of God, as against that of his own world and education: for pity is an *affect*, a "passion"; specifically, it is for Origen the affective aspect of love (*caritatis . . . passio*). According to Origen, if God did not experience the affect of love, he would not so involve himself with humanity (*in conversatione humanae vitae*) as this text shows him doing and as he fully does in the incarnation. The great dogma of the Aristotelian and Platonic theology was Origen's intellectual heritage: God is utterly without affect (*impassibilis*), that is, he does not in any way "suffer." Contemplating this passage, Origen is nevertheless led to say: "Not even the Father is without affect" (*ipse Pater non est impassibilis*), for it is his antecedent pity that commits the Son to suffer the human condition.

Not only did the Lord marry foundling Jerusalem, he adorned and supported her extravagantly, and she flourished and became beautiful (16:9–13). The rich

---

3. The Hebrew is not altogether clear. Perhaps a better conjecture than NRSV's "full woman-hood" would be "at the age to have her period"; Zimmerli 1979: 339. And the hair in question is of course pubic; NRSV is sometimes oddly prim.

and beautiful city the figure evokes is of course Solomon's capital. The fame of this city indeed "spread among the nations" (16:14); we may instance the pilgrimage of the queen of Sheba (1 Kgs. 10:1–5)—which if legendary is all the more telling.

The honeymoon, however, did not last long, as indeed Solomon's splendor did not. The Lord tells Jerusalem the reason: "You trusted in your beauty" (Ezek. 16:15).

The ground of a way of life is always trust in someone or something. Jerusalem was to trust in her bridegroom. Instead she trusted in his gift, her beauty, for its ability to bring her what she wants. And this too became the ground of a life, a life of "whoring."

That whoring is in the allegory the figure for Israel's general unfaithfulness derives from two circumstances. One is that in the allegory—as elsewhere in scripture[4]—Israel is very realistically conceived as the Lord's beloved, to whom he has pledged himself and all that he has. Therefore Israel's turning from him to other lovers could be thought of as adultery, from which it is an easy figurative step to soliciting the lovers.

It is, however, the other circumstance that more controls our passage. Jerusalem/Israel is in this prophecy denounced for three specific and actually practiced Canaanite abominations. One of these, the worship of the fertility goddess Astarte, funds the allegory.

The cult of Astarte—who still appears in the New Testament as "Artemis of the Ephesians" (Acts 19:28)[5]—quite literally made whores of its female devotees, who took their turn in sacrificing their bodies, offering themselves to regenerating unification with the male power in "every passerby." The lack of choice, like a commercial prostitute's lack of choice, was the very point.

The Astarte devotees built "shrines" and "platforms" (Ezek. 16:25, 31) for their activities. Some parts of Ezekiel's description are now obscure,[6] but the reference to "platforms" is plain. We should remember that ancient sacrificial altars were not little tables, but rather were broad platforms for the whole business of animal sacrifice. Depictions of Astarte altars have been preserved: they were smaller such platforms, on which the women were spread out and on which the sacrificial copulation occurred (Zimmerli 1979: 342–43). In the allegory, that is Jerusalem's posture for all comers but the Lord—and the figure is developed with brutal explicitness.[7]

---

4. Most powerfully in the Song of Songs, if read according to its place in the canon; see Robert W. Jenson, *Song of Songs*, Interpretation (Louisville: John Knox, 2005).

5. The KJV translators made this phrase be "Diana of the Ephesians," in the then reasonable supposition that readers would know the Greco-Roman equivalent.

6. What exactly Jerusalem or the Astarte worshipers made with their colorful garments (16:16) is unknown.

7. NRSV's rendering of 16:36, "because your lust was poured out," is a mere guess at the meaning of a corrupt text. The word translated "lust" is manifestly an irretrievable corruption; the lexicons give "copper"—and the Septuagint translates that way—which of course makes no sense.

The trope of whoring and its connection to the Astarte cult are not original in Ezekiel. Hosea had fully developed it (Hos. 1–6). Indeed, Hosea seems actually to have carried out an enacted sign, an *oth*, of the Lord's betrayal by Israel's cultic promiscuity: he was ordered to "take for yourself a wife of whoredom" and did it (1:2).

A second abomination is the use of images. Here we should probably think of fertility religion. The phrase that NRSV translates "male images" (16:17) could less smoothly be translated "images of the male" and were very likely phalluses. Cosseting a golden phallus could very well be thought of as whoring.

The third abomination is child sacrifice. This was widely practiced in Israel's milieu, in worship of Molech. Moreover, there is evidence that this practice was also linked to temple prostitution, that children conceived in it were returned to the god by fire (Zimmerli 1979: 344).

Here we must pause to make two more general points. First, the Canaanite religious practices on account of which the Lord judged the Canaanites and now judges Jerusalem/Israel were—and are—real and are indeed abominations. The notion that religion as such is a good thing could occur only to such religiously sheltered persons as Western inclusivist theorists or to those who are themselves captives of some religious nightmare. The decisive question is not "is there God?"[8] The decisive question is "who is God?" We must hope that most answers historically on offer to the second question—that evoke the affectless God of the old Greeks or Molech or Astarte under whatever names or the distant high gods of animism and so on—are simply false.

Second, Ezekiel's version of Israel's salvation history, starting with tainted and helpless Jerusalem rather than with Abraham or the exodus, and continuing with intractably whoring Jerusalem rather than with the glories of the possession of the land and the building of the temple, was a brutal assault on his hearers' religious self-understanding. Centuries later, this self-conception was still invoked by Jesus's interlocutors: "We are descendants of Abraham" (John 8:33). Moreover, we will see the stringency of Ezekiel's attack only when we recognize that this self-understanding is religiously honorable, by no means to be dismissed with Christianity's usual pseudo-Pauline antinomianism.

Indeed, the Targum found the passage as written simply intolerable and re-wrote it. Using bits of 16:1–14, shading some of them, and interpolating at great length, it replaces Ezekiel's story with a standard salvation history, from Abraham through exodus and so on. All references to the Astarte cult are eliminated. Jerusalem is not denounced, but rather some persons in Jerusalem; apparently on the principle that Jerusalem may have sinful inhabitants but is herself pure (Levey 1990: 47–54).

Greenberg 1983: 285–86 argues convincingly that the reference is to vaginal secretion under intense arousal, so that a better guess would be something like "because your liquid was poured out."

8. By sufficiently attenuating what you mean by "god," you can always make the answer be yes. And so what?

We return to the allegory. In it the passersby who copulate with Jerusalem are identified (16:26–29). They are the powers who see Jerusalem on their imperial excursions and desire her: Egypt,[9] Assyria, and Babylon.[10]

But did Jerusalem actually solicit their embraces, as the allegory says she did? At least in the cases of Egypt and Babylon, she did indeed: Israel's relation with each involved an alliance on which Israel counted for defense against a third party (Greenberg 1983: 282–83). More to the allegory's point, however, is that each successive overlord brought its gods with it, whom Jerusalem then took to her bosom. And unlike a sensible whore, Jerusalem paid for the privilege (16:31b–34), with tribute and political subservience.

We may well ask whether Jerusalem could have done otherwise. Could her leaders really have said, "We won't have your image of . . . in our city"? Or, "We won't pay tribute"? In fact they sometimes attempted at least the latter, and it led to disaster every time; indeed, another prophet, Jeremiah, denounced resistance to Babylon's impositions as resistance to the Lord's own chastisement. Moreover, in the verses immediately following Ezekiel's peculiar salvation history, he also will proclaim the catastrophe of Jerusalem's revolt against Babylon as the Lord's own act, done precisely as punishment for Jerusalem's faithlessness (16:35–43).

Thus what was demanded of Jerusalem/Israel, and what during her entire existence as a national state or states she never quite managed, was total trust in the Lord and in him alone. She was not, like other nations, to depend on armaments or financial power or judicious tribute or alliances—and assuredly not on the gods of the nations—but solely on the Lord. Only insofar as the allegory measures by *that* standard is its depiction and judgment of Jerusalem's history just and coherent.

But again: Is trust only in God a possibility in this age? Is it possible even for persons, never mind for nations? Is not the sort of faithfulness the Lord demands by Ezekiel and other prophets possible only in a new kind of history, with utterly different dynamics than those now in force? Would not in fact the present age inevitably kill any person or community that lived as Israel is told to live, as though a better world had begun?

Christian faith says that Jesus the Christ—and in this age only he—managed pure trust in God and that the power structures of this age did indeed kill him for it and have with little interruption continued to kill those of his disciples who have followed most closely in his footsteps. Thus the coherence and truth of Ezekiel's allegory is finally established only by this Jesus's resurrection into a new creation and his commitment to bring God's people after him.

---

9. NRSV translates with its usual primness; a faithful translation would be "Egyptians with their swelling flesh."

10. Philistia is out of order in this list—and indeed does not really belong in it. What motivated its inclusion and whether the inclusion is a later interpolation are both disputed.

EZEKIEL 16:44–63

SISTERS

I divide 16:44–63 from the preceding verses mostly to avoid creating a too long commentary unit. In the chapter's canonical state it is a unit: 16:44–63 continues the strangely broken allegory of →16:1–43. Nevertheless, the division is not wholly arbitrary: 16:44–63 starts over from the beginning of Jerusalem's allegorical story, introduces new characters, and tells the story of Jerusalem's unfaithfulness and its results in rather different fashion.

We may perhaps think of this second run of allegory as a sort of riff on the first: inspired by it, varying it, exploring new allegorical possibilities. The riff may have been added by Ezekiel himself[1] or by a follower or followers; we need not decide. In any case, it was composed some time later than its model, since it presupposes Jerusalem's final catastrophe, which for the model is still impending.

The passage opens by citing a saying: "Like mother, like daughter" (16:44).[2] This seems to have a double purpose. It sets up an abstract—indeed, rather artificial—framework, encompassing the original allegorical figures and those now to be introduced. And it specifies one aspect of the disgrace (16:52) that ruined Jerusalem must now face: the wise[3]—"those who use proverbs"—will judge her

---

1. Eichrodt 1970: 214–16, to be sure, provides powerful reasons why Ezekiel himself cannot have been the author, and it is certainly true that the variation's use of the original allegory's figures confuses their references.

2. NRSV's translation gives the familiar English saying. The Hebrew does not have the double comparative; a more literal translation would be simply "the daughter is like the mother"—which is how the Septuagint and KJV translate.

3. There is another interpretation, which I seriously considered: "wise guys."

---

as in fact no better than her inauspicious Canaanite background should have made one expect.

Then we are presented with an entire sisterhood of cities born to the Canaanite parents of the original allegory, all three disastrously faithful to the lineage. The allegory is rather stretched: Sodom was straightforwardly Canaanite, so that no figure is involved, and there is no recorded Canaanite prehistory of Samaria. Moreover, since Sodom and Samaria were not related to their nations as was Jerusalem to Judah, we should probably from this point on read also Jerusalem simply as the city of that name.

For Ezekiel and his hearers or readers, Sodom and Samaria were both, though in different ways, memories from the past. Sodom appeared in Israel's stories of ancient days as the example of an entire society's ruination by notorious perverse sexuality (Gen. 19), and it is rather surprising that she is here indicted instead for injustice and pride (Ezek. 16:49–50)—unless Ezekiel exploits the causal relation of sexual chaos to general civil disintegration.[4] Following the Lord's famous negotiation with Abraham, the Lord found not even ten righteous in Sodom, and she perished in "fire and brimstone." Samaria, the capital of the northern kingdom, had been a center of fertility religion within Israel (Hos. 8:5–6), and the Lord had judged her by the Assyrians over a century before.

It had apparently been common in Jerusalem to adduce Sodom as a wicked contrast to Jerusalem's righteousness (Ezek. 16:49) and the catastrophe of Samaria as a contrast to the security guaranteed Jerusalem by the presence of the true temple (e.g., Jer. 7:4). But now the Lord says that Jerusalem's abominations imitate and indeed outdo those of them both (Ezek. 16:47).

There are some obscurities in the verses that set up the allegory (16:45–46). What is the allegorical point of mother and daughters all despising their husbands? Probably the reference is to the same unhappy marriage: Jerusalem despised the Lord her husband, as he is identified in the original allegory, and literary formalism has extended the accusation to the mother and her other daughters. Or perhaps the Lord is supposed to be the despised husband also of Samaria and Sodom. This reading is easy in the case of Samaria; but in the case of Sodom it would imply some sort of marriage covenant of the Lord with a nation outside Israel.

Again, who are the daughters of the daughters, who are in turn despised? We know from the original allegory what Jerusalem's being despised by her parents meant: she was left out to die (→16:1–43). My best guess is that the daughters' daughters are simply the dependent towns that all three had and that each metropolis indeed abandoned to die in the catastrophe she brought upon herself.

The body of the allegory then presents a series of shocking and calculated reversals. A marked-off unit is devoted to each.

4. Or was there perhaps an alternative tradition of Sodom's wickedness? See Eichrodt 1970: 216.

Ezekiel 16:48–52 is introduced by a renewed "thus says the Lord." The passage depicts a sort of judgment scene. "Bear your disgrace" comes from the language of cultic law, and the judge opens proceedings with his own oath: Jerusalem must confess and be disgraced before an assembled court. She has committed abominations far worse than those of Sodom or Samaria—what these were is presupposed from 16:1–43. And then the surprise: the guilt of Jerusalem is so dominating that by contrast it "justifies" Sodom and Samaria; that is, it secures their acquittal (16:51–52).[5]

This scene of judgment comes close to being a depiction of *final* judgment, since of course neither Sodom nor Samaria was available for trial in Ezekiel's time, nor has been since. And in the last judgment, we are told, just such surprising reversals will regularly occur; as the Lord said to Capernaum: "On the day of judgment it will be more tolerable for the land of Sodom than for you" (Matt. 11:24).

Ezekiel 16:53–58 promises restoration and salvation, following on the judgment. But the promise starts with the salvation of Sodom and Samaria—to which any righteous Israelite would have had to say, "Samaria, maybe—but Sodom?" Justified by contrast with Jerusalem, the two sisters will be restored to "their former state," which of course does not mean their former state of wickedness but an hypothesized state of righteousness before a fall. Then Jerusalem too will be restored, but only "with" Sodom and Samaria, as a sort of appendage (16:53). And she will be restored only in order that she bear her disgrace and pay her penalty (16:54, 58). Indeed, she will be restored in order for the sight of her disgrace to provide part of Sodom's and Samaria's renewed happiness (16:54). The first shall indeed be last and the last shall be first.

The final verses, 16:59–63, are a more explicitly eschatological prophecy of salvation, though still remarkably backhanded. The unit is again marked by a renewed "thus says the Lord."

The Lord has dealt and will deal with Jerusalem according to her faithlessness. Nevertheless, although she has rebelled against the marriage covenant he made with her—as the original allegory described it—he will "remember" her. That is, he will be bound by it, so that he cannot permanently cast her off. Indeed, a phrase suddenly appears that we would surely not have expected in this context: the Lord's restoration of Jerusalem will establish an "everlasting covenant," a *berith olam* (ברית עולם), with her.

The notion of covenant (Jenni and Westermann 1997: 256–66) is not otherwise central in Ezekiel.[6] Here, however, it is decisive, as it is in other parts of the Old Testament.

5. RSV/NRSV's "you have made your sisters appear righteous" is a substitution of what the translators could accept as plausible for what is said by the text, which contains nothing at all about appearances and should simply be translated on the lines of "you have justified your sisters," as the Septuagint and KJV do.

6. This has led scholars to doubt that this passage comes from Ezekiel or indeed from close disciples. In my judgment, however, Ezekiel's use of the notion is not intrinsically unlikely, since the

A *berith* was not a mutual agreement—as it is still sometimes characterized in textbooks. A *berith* is one person's unilateral self-commitment to another; and so determining is the notion of *self*-commitment that in a few secular uses of the term there is no partner at all, the person makes a promise simply to himself or herself. It is anyway plain from the texts: where the Old Testament speaks of a covenant of the Lord with Israel, this is made by the Lord's sole agency (Gen. 15:18; 17:2; etc.). Of course a covenant can, depending on maker and content, enable particular corresponding actions by the recipient or even obligate to them; thus it is that Israel can break—or try to break—the Lord's covenant with her.

The Lord's new-old covenant with Jerusalem will be "everlasting" (*olam*). We must be careful not to import into the word *olam* doctrines of abstract eternity that are alien to the Old Testament. The model "everlasting covenant" is the one that God makes with Abraham (Gen. 17:5–7); it is everlasting simply in that God's self-commitment to Abraham's offspring covers all future generations and contingencies. That is to say, the eternity of the covenant resides solely in the Lord's unshakable faithfulness through his history with his people. Since in our allegory the covenant appears as the Lord's marriage covenant with Jerusalem, the covenant's being made eternal means simply that divorce is henceforth impossible: no matter how Jerusalem strays, the Lord will—and indeed must!—regard her as his wife.

To be sure, if we consider the *content* of the Lord's promise to Abraham we discover that while it is not a timeless arrangement, it is eschatological and thus eternal in that sense. That all nations shall find their blessing in the nation to spring from Abraham, and that in this shared blessing universal peace will occur (e.g., Mic. 4:1–4), was in successive waves of prophesy revealed ever more clearly as a promise unfulfillable in this age. So in the present case, the Lord's self-commitment to Israel is unshakable through history. But when will the marriage be happy?

A final turn of the screw concludes this remarkable chapter. Jerusalem—that is to say, her remnant population and restored future existence—will abide by the covenant precisely because she will be so ashamed she will never open her mouth again, even to rebel (Ezek. 16:62–63). She will "remember" the Lord, as he has promised in his new covenant to remember her. And to remember God is itself salvation, in that remembering is in Israel's conception always the reestablishing of a positive relation to what is remembered.

We may think it a strange way to be saved: to acknowledge and remember guilt and to be saved by being taken along in a package with others saved in their own right. But we should consider this: If, for a key example, the rich can be saved only because all things are possible for God (Mark 10:25–27 and parallels), wherein

---

covenant appears particularly in the Deuteronomistic literature surrounding Josiah's reform—not long past in Ezekiel's time—and in Ezekiel's own priestly tradition.

will their final salvation consist? Perhaps in blessed exchange with the condition of the poor?

Finally, as so often, the general formula for the outcome of the Lord's saving or judging acts—or as here of both in one—is that Israel and Sodom and Samaria shall "know that I am the Lord." To know who is God, or that the God who addresses us is indeed יהוה and not another, is in itself salvation.

EZEKIEL 17:1–21

EAGLES AND THEIR PLANTINGS

Ezekiel 17 is an editorial unit, whether put together by Ezekiel or by someone else. It has three parts, not necessarily simultaneously composed, of which the first two will be treated in this commentary unit. The third is so theologically loaded that it will be given its own commentary unit.

The first part (17:1–10) is introduced in proper Ezekiel style, with the coming of the word and an address to Ezekiel as "you—son of a man." There is a textual problem with the passage that we may as well deal with here: the Masoretic Text of 17:7d–8 is plainly corrupt (Eichrodt 1970: 221). NRSV has rearranged the text, without making greater sense of it. Perhaps more plausible would be a version on these clumsy lines: "[The vine] stretched out its roots to [Egypt], for [Egypt] to provide better water than did the garden plot in which it was planted. [It did this despite] being planted in good soil with plentiful water."

The second part (17:11–21) is again introduced by the coming of the word, but without specific address to Ezekiel, who is simply instructed what to say next. This suits the verses' relation to part one. The third part (→17:22–24) is set off from the first two mostly by the ending of the second (17:21), a version of the "you shall know" formula. It is itself introduced somewhat uncertainly, with an unmediated "thus says the Lord."

The first part of Ezek. 17 is another of the symbolic tales that cluster in Ezek. 15–17. The second is a more ordinary prophecy that explains the tale, much as 5:5–17 explains the prophetic signs mandated by 4:1–5:4. The third is rather awkwardly attached to the first two. And it utterly changes the tone, from judgment to promise of salvation. I suggest that, as with 16:44–63, this third part is best taken as a riff on what precedes it, here the antecedent tale of eagles and their horticulture. It is likely that this riff was composed later than its model, whose fulfillment it seems to presuppose.

The text itself specifies the initial story's genre (17:1), the story of the eagles and their horticultural endeavors (17:2–8) is a "riddle" that Israel is challenged to solve (17:9–10). This is further specified, by parallel construction, as a "saying" (משל, *mashal*),[1] that is, a formulated and memorable locution; the hearer or reader is to pay attention to the precise words and constructions.

The sense of the word translated "riddle" is perhaps best suggested by its use in two typical stories: the puzzle that Samson set before his banqueting companions was a riddle (Judg. 14:12–19); and the tests that the queen of Sheba put to Solomon (1 Kgs. 10:1) were riddles. Like these, our story of avian horticulture and a self-willed plant is a riddle in that it hides a secret that the hearer or reader is to divine or not—in this like the parables of Jesus. Indeed, the devising and solution of riddling tales was a craft cultivated among the wise men of Israel; thus the queen of Sheba appears in 1 Kgs. 10:1–10 as a competing savant.

This riddle is transparent once unriddled, whether by the hearer on his own or by a reader instructed by the solution provided. Eagles are universally totems for mighty kings like Nebuchadnezzar or Pharaoh Neco, with whom Zedekiah hoped to conspire. One of the proverbially upright and imposing cedars of Lebanon can well stand for the house of David—or at least for its pretensions. The leader/shoot of the cedar, snipped off and taken to Babylon, is plainly Jehoiachin and the other elites exiled in 597. The cutting planted in Judah by Nebuchadnezzar is the vassal king Zedekiah and is not from a cedar but from a grape vine, intended to become a plant humble in stature but fruitful. And the vine's yearning toward yet better sustenance than provided by Nebuchadnezzar's garden plot is Zedekiah's appeal to Egypt to support his rebellion.

Readers of the Gospels will think of tales to which our riddle is very similar: the story of the eagles, of their improbable setting out of a cutting, and of the wholly impossible subsequent behavior of the plant (17:7b–d) make a story very like some of Jesus's longer parables. The parable of the sower (Mark 4:3–10 and parallels) comes immediately to mind, with its impossibly careless farmer, and the following rabbinic explanation (4:11–20 and parallels) functions much as does that provided here.

Why did Jesus speak in parables? It is popularly supposed that they were everyday stories told to make a clear moral or religious point in images familiar to hearers. But most of the parables were not at all clear in everyday terms, since they distort the agricultural and commercial images past all recognition—hearers' reaction to the parable of the sower could only have been, "But no sower behaves that way!" And the explanation given to the puzzled disciples is that Jesus speaks

1. The term covers everything from a fixed popular proverb or comparison to an elaborate construction of the wisdom tradition; see Zimmerli 1979: 280–81. There seems to be little reason for NRSV's more specific translation of *mashal* by "allegory" except the translators' personal judgment that what follows is in fact an allegory.

to the multitude in parables in order to *prevent* their understanding.[2] Jesus even cites the Lord's commission to Isaiah: "Go and say to this people: 'Keep listening, but do not comprehend; keep looking, but do not understand' . . . so that they may not . . . turn and be healed" (Isa. 6:9–10)—a style of commission with which Ezekiel also was only too personally acquainted. Only those to whom it is given can divine the secret.

Why did the Lord speak by Ezekiel with similarly riddling stories? At least this one seems to have had a purpose very like that just cited for Jesus's parables. That the story functions as a riddle rather than as an illustration is itself a rebuke to its hearers, for the Lord's people should need no explanations to grasp "these things"—that is, the evil of unfaithfulness—and would not in fact need one were they not a "rebellious house" (Ezek. 17:12). An explanatory prophecy must follow precisely because it is expected that Israel will not get the point. Thus it is in not supposed that the tale makes anything easier to understand.

There is another and decisive commonality between many of Jesus's parables and this one of Ezekiel's: the stories themselves are strictly secular, God does not appear in them. Indeed, to explicate the tale itself (17:2–10) and the first part of its interpretation (17:11–15), I could have simply directed the reader to the introduction's sketch of relevant history. Zedekiah's revolt against Babylon and appeal to Egypt for support is presented by the riddle and by the first part of its resolution simply as a piece of foreign policy whose foolishness should be obvious to anyone, worshiper of the Lord or not; the questions of 17:9–10 anticipate the answer "no—this policy obviously will not thrive."

One part of Zedekiah's foolishness may need some comment: its character as the breaking of a covenant, a *berith* (→16:44–63; 17:13–18). When Nebuchadnezzar installed Zedekiah as vassal king, he will have imposed a *berith* on Zedekiah, stipulating the terms of Zedekiah's tenure and Nebuchadnezzar's support (Zimmerli 1979: 365–66). Zedekiah was required on his part to render an oath of allegiance and as was customary will have sworn on his own God, יהוה. When he conspired with Egypt, he broke both Nebuchadnezzar's *berith* and the oath by which he was bound to her. Can such behavior succeed in the long run? It still remains just within the reach of secular judgment to say that it cannot; even international relations can absorb only so much perjury and treachery.

God does not appear in the overt tale; he is hidden behind it, and his presence is to be divined by the hearer—or not. When we divine rightly, or when the written account lets the secret out, we find that God is the one behind the eagles—just as he is the reckless sower of his blessings in Jesus's parable. And it

2. It is of course generally supposed that the explanation is a product of the primal church, to bend the parable to their own distress, which was not at the behavior of the sower but at the behavior of the recipients. One need not deny that the primal church allegorized the explanation to fit her problems, but this does not mean that the main point did not stem from Jesus.

is God who will enforce the oath taken in his name, even though it was made to a Gentile oppressor.[3]

The exegetical problem finally posed by the canonical written text is that in this book version—as in the Gospels' written accounts of the sower parable—the tale loses its force as a riddle, for no secret remains to be divined. Having read the riddle we need only read on to be presented with the cat ready out of the bag: it is the Lord who will undo Zedekiah (17:19)—just as in the Gospels we are told in a sort of rabbinic lecture that the sower is the Lord spreading his word. What then, in the written versions as we have them, can be the point of the stories themselves? Why not just replace them with their interpretations, once the secret has been published? When the tale appears in this now-literary context what can it bring to the reader? A cute illustration of a point that the sermon makes plain without it? Evidence of the preacher's ingenuity?

What 17:1–21, recorded in literary form together with its resolution, enforces on the reader is that the story of God's judgment of Zedekiah can indeed be told as a story of ordinary political foolishness, so ordinary indeed that it can become a *mashal*. When the Lord destroys Zedekiah's armies you will not see the glory (→1:25–28b) or the *Merkabah* (→1:4–24) rampaging on the battlefield. You will see only the very image of military defeat caused by foolish statecraft. Whether Ezekiel or an editor had such a subtlety in mind cannot of course be known. My suggestion is that in any case the text presents it.

Nor was the Father's glorification of his Son on the cross visible to the multitude. The story of the crucifixion can be told as a secular tale of the triumph of political calculation over justice—perhaps even one so archetypical as to make a *mashal*. Those who tell of the Son's crucifixion as a mere moral or religious paradigm do not necessarily speak falsely; they have just not caught on to the secret. Only great and faithful artists have seen the angels depicted in icons of the scene, holding eucharistic chalices to catch life-giving drops of blood. Nor did anyone see the Father raise the Son from death; indeed, no one saw the resurrection at all.

3. It is likely that prophets in Jerusalem assured Zedekiah that an oath made—as they judged the situation—against the interests of Jerusalem was not binding.

EZEKIEL 17:22–24

THE LORD AS EAGLE

The previous commentary unit called 17:22–24 a riff on the riddle of eagles and plants (→17:1–21). The riff is not fully intelligible apart from its model. Also our passage's unmediated literary attachment to the earlier parts of the chapter—with an unprepared "thus says the Lord"—enforces its dependence on them.

To be sure, this is a drastic riff—like one of those flights whose celebration of the original theme is audible only to the player and any equally gifted hearers. The initial riddle and its interpretation proclaimed the Lord's judgment; without transition, the present passage proclaims salvation. The imagery of the initial riddle was realistic, within the limits of a riddle's characteristic improbabilities; now suddenly the imagery derives from myth. And this new tale of an eagle is not a riddle at all; it is more like the broken allegories of →16:1–43 and →16:44–63.

With the very first word the Lord breaks into the story, to appear there in the first person, as he did intermittently in Ezek. 16. The literary solution (17:11–21) of the riddle had revealed that the tale of eagles and transplantings was in fact about God and his actions; now God sheds even this reserve and appears openly as himself the eagle protagonist of the new parable of salvation. The Lord's seizure of the action in his own person is made unavoidable for the reader: twice in 17:22 a verb already firmly in the first person is augmented with the independent pronoun "I," to make a construction that NRSV rightly translates "I myself will. . . ."

Every theology must devise some construal of the relation between God himself and created carriers and representatives of God's action, like the eagle/Nebuchadnezzar in the initial riddle. Thus Martin Luther called such historical agents of God's work "masks" behind which God hides (*larva dei*). In our passage the Lord takes off the mask of earthly powers. But what will happen when he does that? And when may we expect it? What is the scope of the passage's future tense?

The first thing to note is that the Lord does not say he will simply unmask himself. He will no longer hide behind Nebuchadnezzar and his like; nevertheless he will not appear as naked deity—which by biblical lights would no longer be deity—but as the eagle of the riddle. If in this new masking he is nevertheless to act as *himself*, it must be that he and his mask will now be one, that he will himself be the eagle as which he masks himself.[1] Within Christian theology, it is the doctrine of the Trinity that asserts and accounts for this.

The second person of God is another than the Father, indeed he is the man Jesus, who looks not at all like God; thus according to Luther, the incarnation does not unmask God, rather it reveals him precisely by masking him absolutely. Yet this suffering servant—Isa. 52!—is the same God as the Father, is "of one being with" him (ὁμοούσιον τῷ πατρί), as the Nicene Creed has it. If the Lord can indeed appear as in this way himself-as-other-than-himself, the eternal difference and identity between Father and Son in God is the possibility.

As to when this "will" happen, the answer depends on the context of the question. We may say that the relation of the Son to the Father—that the Son is different from God the Father, in such fashion as just so to be the same one God—is an eternal relation. There is no time when the relation does not obtain. But we may also say that, looking forward from Ezekiel's time, it is Mary's conception of the man who is the Lord that is the future moment denoted by the repeated "will" in our passage. In this direction, it is when Jesus is "conceived by the Holy Spirit" that the Lord puts on his eagle self.

But yet again, in our time after the Lord's ascension, he is indeed incarnate but nevertheless the end is not yet; we must still await the eagle's coming at the end. Then Jesus the Christ will not be another than Mary's child, but we will see him differently. As the English collect for the first Sunday of Advent has it, the Son came once "in great humility," but on "the last day . . . he shall come again in his glorious majesty."

There is no escaping the strictly eschatological reference of our passage: an Israel on a high mountain, whose fruit nourishes all nations and shelters all creation, is not a possible phenomenon of this age, also not in the time of the church. Which brings us back to the story now told of the eagle and his planting.

One way in which the Old Testament evokes the eschatological reach of its hope is by recruiting images from antiquity's myths, for their transcendence of given reality. Earthly cedars do not grow from cuttings, but the Lord will break a twig from the cedar of Israel, plant it, and see it grow. He will plant it on "a high

---

1. In the West, Tertullian gave us the language of triune "persons," *personae*. In ordinary Latin usage, a *persona* was first a mask through which an actor spoke, then the role the actor played—as in *dramatis personae*. Then it became a role also off the stage, a role in society. Tertullian adapted the notion for the triune identities by abolishing the difference between the social agent and the role: a triune *persona* simply *is* the role he plays with the other two; see Jenson 1997–99: 1.118–19.

and lofty mountain"; that is, on the world-mountain from which all creation is seen. There this new Israel will grow into the great tree that in the myths of many peoples supports the world (Zimmerli 1979: 367). And though earthly cedars do not bear edible fruit or provide thick cover, the Israel-cedar will feed and shelter all creation. The outcome of this eschatological act is that not only Israel but all nations, "all the trees of the field shall know that I am יהוה" (17:24). "They will not hurt or destroy on all my holy mountain; for the earth will be full of the knowledge of the LORD as the waters cover the sea" (Isa. 11:9).

The promise that Israel or Jerusalem or, as here, the world will know that "I am יהוה" is the conclusion of many of Ezekiel's prophecies; but in 17:24 it is given a twist. The prophecy goes on to say *what* we will know when we know that יהוה is יהוה. We are given something like a description of what it is for יהוה to be יהוה and not another, something like a definition of his particular deity.[2]

To be יהוה, we are told, is to "bring low the high tree" and "make high the low tree," to "dry up the green tree and make the dry tree flourish." In his relation to creatures—in his works *ad extra*, as the theological tradition has it—this God simply *is* the one who reverses the judgments and outcomes of this age. When he comes masked in himself as Mary's child, his message is that "the last shall be first and the first shall be last." When he comes "in glory" this will be the glory of the humility in which he was among us: the lamb is "slain from the foundation of the world" (Rev. 13:8 KJV).[3] Which, of course, is the possibility of our salvation, who before God are all last.

Reversal of the given order of things can be God's work outside himself because reversal of what otherwise might be the order of things belongs to his reality in himself.[4] The Son's humble obedience to the Father makes obeying belong to deity equally with the Father's sending and commanding of the Son, for the Son is equal in deity with the Father. It is a chief role of the doctrine of the Trinity to insist that the God who in his history with us casts down the high and raises up the lowly can do this because he is in himself just such a God—indeed, because this history with us is his own personal history.

---

2. It must be "something like" because Jewish theology and all branches of Christian theology are agreed that we cannot in this life know God's "essence," that is, what it means for God to be the God that he is.

3. RSV and NRSV are linguistically just possible, but will be adopted only by those who suppose the text cannot say what it surely seems to.

4. The distinction appears in the tradition as the difference and relation of "the immanent Trinity" and "the economic (historical) Trinity."

EZEKIEL 18:1–32

IT'S NOT FAIR!

Ezekiel 18:1–32 is a coherent ordered unit, not, however, marked out by formulas, as is usual in Ezekiel, but rather by strong internal structure. There are three parts, plainly intended to make a sequence: the second and third parts begin at 18:19 and 18:25 with "yet you say," which is a short following version of the challenge that begins the first part: "What do you mean by repeating this saying?" At the end, the passage simply comes to a splendid climax and stops.

There is, to be sure, the usual opening, "the word of the Lord came to me." But then the Lord launches directly into speech to Israel, without any address or instructions to Ezekiel. It is hard to know what to make of this—unless we take the usual critical refuge in textual history. Perhaps in the text we actually have, the haste is a literary expression of the intensity of the Lord's concern: he cannot pause for the formalities.

The Lord, as he speaks to and by Ezekiel, is a master of many forms of discourse; in this chapter we encounter yet another: formal debate. Popular sayings (reported at 18:2, 19, 25) are circulating, to which the Lord takes strong exception, in much the same fashion as earlier at 11:3 or 12:22. This time, the Lord rebuts each of the three in turn. I will order this commentary unit by taking up the offending sayings in sequence, discussing the Lord's rebuttal with each.

The first is explicitly identified as a *mashal*, a formulated and memorable saying:[1] "The parents have eaten sour grapes, and the children's teeth are set on age."[2] This appears here as a cynical version of what had been a fundamental tenet of Israel's faith: when the Lord gave nothing less than the Ten Commandments, he described himself as one "visiting the iniquity of the fathers upon the children unto the third and fourth generation" (Exod. 20:5 KJV). In the bitter mouths of some in Israel this has now become: Persons dead and gone sinned, and we are the ones God punishes for it. What moral sense does that make?

It is an observable phenomenon, and one present to the moral self-consciousness of every intact community, that the culpable folly of one generation brings catastrophe on a subsequent generation—thus the slaveholding of the United States' founding fathers was visited not on them but on their great-grandchildren. Intact communities are extended in time—they are in fact the very bearers of temporal continuity—and the relation between communal deeds and consequences is therefore seldom instantaneous, but spans stretches of time that are often much longer than an individual lifetime.

In some communities, as in that of ancient Greece, the distribution across time of blessing or disaster, with its often attendant lack of apparent individual justice, is attributed to the rule of impersonal cosmic law, for which no one, not even the gods, is responsible. But Israel, with her understanding of God's personal presence in history, understood the moral plot of the community's history as the free doing of the Lord himself—as indeed was straightforwardly asserted by the traditional doctrine just cited.

So long as individuals in Israel saw themselves as chiefly identified by membership in the temporally extended community, so that past or present deeds of the community were their own deeds and the community's fate their fate, this occasioned no theological or moral problem. That the Lord visited the sin of the community upon individuals—also when these were committed before (or for that matter after) an individual's life—did not seem unjust, since individuals did not decisively distinguish their moral status or happiness from that of the continuing community. But in the later monarchical period, the individual's identity with the community loosened (there are sociological explanations for this development, but these are not relevant here).

However it was that a limited individualism developed in Israel, the question of the justice of the Lord's rule in history was then bound to arise. Lonely people in exile had to think: it appears that the Lord has punished us for sins we did not ourselves commit, by destroying our community and condemning us to individual suffering in Babylon.

---

1. That NRSV translates more specifically "proverb" is puzzling. A proverb is supposed to be a piece of wisdom, which this saying emphatically is not.

2. The saying is cited also by Ezekiel's Jerusalemite near-contemporary, Jeremiah, with the same sense (Jer. 30:29–30). Perhaps it had a different use in other contexts; there is no way to be sure.

The reflection itself was unavoidable. One possible outcome was rejection—not necessarily denial—of the Lord's rule of history. Observation of what had in fact happened around and to the exiles, and of their own consequent situation, could be encapsulated in that bitter *mashal*.

The Lord first responds to this attack by proclaiming his absolute lordship not only over nations but also over individual lives: over parent and child and righteous and unrighteous (18:4a). Modernity has convinced itself that being in the hand of God is a threat to "human autonomy"; what we have forgotten and are painfully relearning is that the disastrous alternatives to being in God's hand are to be in some fellow human's hand or to have no recourse from the workings of impersonal fate.

Then the Lord announces an unexpected rule of this lordship: "It is only the person who sins that shall die. If a man is righteous . . . he shall surely live" (18:4b–9). If a righteous father has an unrighteous son, the son will not be saved by the father's righteousness (18:10–13); and if an unrighteous father has a righteous son, the son will not die for the father's sins (18:14–18).

Is this a reversal of the Lord's earlier asserted visitation of folly across the generations? It certainly seems to be. If it is, Ezekiel undoes also the basis of his own usual prophecy, which like that of other prophets announced communal catastrophes as punishment for communal past history and proclaimed salvations that those who heard of them might not live to experience. Rabbinic tradition saw the reversal and affirmed it: Moses had indeed brought the "severe decree" that sons would be punished for the sins of their fathers, but Ezekiel was sent to repeal it (Levey 1990: 59n1).

Eichrodt proposes a different reading, which readers may wish to consider (1970: 237–38). Perhaps the new maxim was not intended as a new general principle of the Lord's rule. Perhaps it was instead a specific promise to certain Israelites in the situation of their particular time. The Lord announces: you, upon whom Jerusalem's catastrophe and your isolated existence as exiles weighs so heavily, are released from history's ordinary patterns. I am the Lord, and as I shape and enforce those patterns, so I can release from them. Thus I will now not judge you by the deserts of the nation, but will judge each of you by his own deeds.

Or perhaps the announcement is an eschatological promise. Much modern reflection has dealt with the general problem in that way. Immanuel Kant regarded it as an argument for life beyond death, that in this life righteous individuals are nevertheless often smitten by the evil of their communities, so that if universal order is just they must receive their reward elsewhere; and liberal theology generally followed him in this.

To derive comfort or warning from this message, in whatever construal, the hearer or reader of course needs to know who is righteous. The Lord provides an explicit answer, with a list of "statutes and ordinances," such as are found throughout Exodus and Leviticus (Zimmerli 1979: 379–81). Indeed, he provides no less than three lists (18:6–8, 10–11, 15–17) containing roughly the same items—the repetition is a powerful rhetorical enforcement. The one who obeys these commands is righteous and will live.

The Ten Commandments is the paradigm of such lists. Thus Ezekiel's first and model list starts as the commandments do, by commanding exclusive worship of the Lord (18:6a). Then, in parallel to the "second table" of the Ten Commandments, crimes against and obligations within the community are listed.

Most of these latter need little explanation (on the prohibition of intercourse during the woman's period [18:6b], →5:5–17). The ban on charging interest does not prohibit making profit on an investment whose risks are shared among all involved, but only transactions where the profit for a lender is stipulated in advance and where the borrower must provide it however his affairs may have gone. This is of a piece with the Old Testament's general sympathy for unfortunate debtors.

Before proceeding to the second popular saying that is unacceptable to the Lord, I will take this as a convenient place to insert a general point. Throughout Ezek. 18, the Lord's judgments are "he shall live" and "he shall die." We should not, however, think simply of longevity or of sudden death legally or naturally inflicted. In Israel's grasp of things, life was more than biological existence; it was fellowship with God among his people. Biological death was horrid precisely because it excluded from such life, but one could be excluded in other ways. The judgments have primary religious and moral force.

The second saying (18:19a) is uncertainly related to the first. If we translate with the NRSV (and RSV, but not KJV or Septuagint), then this saying must come from a group in Israel who did not share the view of those rebuked in 18:2–18. This other group asks, "Why *shouldn't* children pay for the iniquity of their fathers?" Then the Lord intervenes in a dispute within the community, rebuking both sides. He rejects this saying with the same decree with which he rejected the first. Children, says the Lord, *should* not have to pay for parents' sin for the very same reason that they now *will* not in fact pay: I do not choose to rule history in that way (18:19b–20).

There is, however, another possible translation of the saying. The modal force that NRSV's "should" gives to the saying may be misplaced, since it represents nothing explicit in the Hebrew. The text could just as well be translated, "How is it that the son does not suffer for the iniquity of the father?"[3] Read so, this second saying is a counter to the Lord's rebuttal of the first: It has been Israel's ancient experience and certainly ours that one generation in fact bears the iniquity of a previous generation. If this was never really or is no longer the case, how comes the generational link to be broken? On this reading of this saying, the Lord's rebuttal is a slight variant of his rebuttal of the first saying: righteousness now trumps inheritance (18:19a). As to how that can be so, it is because the Lord decrees it (18:19b–20).

3. This is in fact how the Targum reads the passage (Levey 1990: 58).

Without further debate, the Lord then proceeds to what the whole passage has been aiming at, a call to individual repentance (18:21–24). If an unrighteous person turns and does "what is lawful and right" he shall live. And this is indeed a definite step beyond what has previously been asserted.

There is a logic behind the move. The moral bond between generations remains, after all, a reality. If then the son is not bound by the iniquity of the father and can break with his familial past to be a righteous person, this is a real break in a continuing lived story. Which is to say, it is a kind of repentance. All the prophets called the community to such repentance; Ezekiel has now extended the possibility to individuals. But such an extension once made, it cannot stop with the possibility of breaking the bonds only of others' past iniquity: the living individual cannot be bound even by his own past iniquity. If a wicked person turns and does "what is . . . right" he becomes a righteous person.

We remember from early in the chapter that all lives are in the hands of the Lord. Therefore the possibility of all these liberations must lie in the Lord's character. We come to the final secret, here twice revealed, once in our present verses and once at the end of the chapter: "Have I any pleasure in the death of the wicked, says the Lord God, and not rather that they should turn from their ways and live?" (18:23, varied at 18:32).

Some theological traditions speak of "gospel," a word of God that, unlike the word of judgment (i.e., in the language of this tradition, "the law"), frees from the past and its evil and opens a future of righteousness (i.e., "justification"). Here is the gospel by way of Ezekiel, and a central message of all Ezekiel's prophesying. It is repeated in slightly altered form at 33:11, in a passage that goes over much the same ground as this chapter, though in more usual and less rigorous form.

By way of general remark, it cannot be said that Ezekiel fully resolves the problematic relation between community and individual. Nor can it be said that subsequent history or reflection has done so. Late modernity has experienced the disaster of individualism, and much current theology—including my own—seeks to understood personhood as constituted in communal relations. But "seeks" perhaps remains the right word.

The third complaint (18:29a) hardly achieves the dignity of a "saying." The speakers are reduced to humankind's immemorial childish wail, "It's not fair!"[4] What is not fair? That the Lord visits iniquity upon those who come after—or that he does not? That the Lord permits wicked individuals to repent—or that he does not? It hardly matters. So long as I am not in control of history, I will find its course unfair, whatever it may be. And since Israel's God was supposed to be in control, an Israelite will wail to the Lord about it.

4. The Targum is unable to voice even the possibility that the ways of the Lord are unfair and suppress the text. In its place we find "the good ways of the Lord have not been declared to us"—that is, an excuse for bad behavior (Levey 1990: 59). The Targum cannot here have read an earlier Hebrew text, since that would mean that the Masoretes or their tradition had replaced a rabbinically acceptable text with an offensive one.

Appropriately, the Lord hardly bothers to respond: You think me unfair? How would you manage matters better? Indeed, how in fact do you now manage your own little affairs? (18:29b). The Lord is in haste, again, to make his concluding appeal.

This (18:30–32) is an urgent—indeed passionate—plea for the remaining members of the "house of Israel" to respond to the possibility of repentance—they are not now addressed as an inevitably "rebellious house" (Eichrodt 1970: 241). Why do you want to perish? *I* do not want you to. Live!

EZEKIEL 19:1–14

THE DEATH OF
THE HOUSE OF DAVID

This chapter seems to have been dropped into its location at random. It has no introduction or opening formula, yet neither does it continue the preceding passage. Nor does it have a thematic or formal relation to the following chapter. The Lord addresses—presumably—Ezekiel without identifying him and launches directly into instruction for what he is to do.

The chapter is allegory of a sort and so fits with the editorial group of picture discourses in Ezek. 15–17; it seems likely that Ezek. 18 has—for reasons not now apparent—been interpolated without regard for the integrity of this grouping, thus producing this chapter's naked presentation. No doubt this observation alleviates some puzzlements, but reading Ezek. 19 immediately after Ezek. 17 does not contribute materially to our grasp of either.

Was the chapter written before or after Jerusalem's final catastrophe? Or, since there is an obvious break at 19:10, was 19:1–9 written before it and 19:10–14 written after it? Or vice versa? There are persuasive arguments for three of the four possibilities. As will become apparent, in this case one must make a choice. I propose: 19:1–9 seems not to presuppose the final catastrophe, whereas 19:10–14 is easier to construe on the supposition that it does; therefore the first part was probably composed shortly before 587/586 and the second shortly thereafter. There is no reason to doubt that Ezekiel himself wrote both parts, with perhaps the exception of a few glossing lines that need not occupy us.

The genre is specific and certain, and this will be theologically important. Ezekiel is told to intone a *kinah* (קינה, "a lament"), and when the chant is done we are assured (19:14d) that it is indeed a *kinah*. Indeed, since a *kinah* has an immediately recognizable meter,[1] we would not have needed to be told. The bracketing with this label also establishes the chapter's unity, at least as the canonical text.

A *kinah* is a lament for the dead (Zimmerli 1979: 391–92). Initially, singing a *kinah* appropriate to the deceased belonged to actual ceremonies of mourning and burial. Later such chants came to be composed also for communal or figural deaths, and the genre in that extended use was adopted by some prophets. Ezekiel shares the practice especially with his Jerusalemite near-contemporary Jeremiah, from whom we have an entire collection of such compositions, the book of Lamentations.

Additionally, this particular *kinah* takes the form of broken allegory somewhat like those in →16:1–43 and →16:44–63. Figures carry the story, and the figuration is for the most part maintained, but Egypt and Babylon are identified by name.

The lament is for the "princes of Israel" and their "mother": 19:2–9 mourns them under the figure of a lioness and her cubs, 19:10–14 under the figure of a vine and its shoots. Since the two passages were composed separately, I will first read each allegory independently, then put them together; there seems to be no other way to sort out the figurative references.

In 19:2–9 we have three figures to identify: the lioness and her two cubs. One identification is certain: only one Judean king was ever taken captive to Egypt— Jehoahaz, who immediately succeeded his father Josiah in 609 and was dethroned and carried off by Pharaoh Neco that same year. But two kings, Jehoiachin and Zedekiah, were taken captive to Babylon. Which of the two is the second cub? And who is the lioness? When we read 19:2–9 by itself, the fairly obvious proposal must be that the lioness is the actual mother of Jehoahaz and Zedekiah, Hamutal.[2] That a royal wife becomes kingmaker on behalf of her sons has happened in many societies and is plausible here. So we have Hamutal as lioness and Jehoahaz and Zedekiah as the cubs.

We need not take the rhetoric about the prowess of the cubs too seriously, whether to their credit or discredit. The rhetoric simply belongs to the trope of the monarch-as-lion. The outcome of the verses is that Zedekiah's voice will be "heard no more on the mountains of Israel" (19:9d). Thus the prophecy made by this allegory—read by itself—is that the exiles should invest no hopes of restoration in him, as some may have done.

When we turn to the second allegory (19:10–14) we have to look for different identifications, for the story of the vine does not easily fit Hamutal—which of course may be an argument against the identifications proposed for the previous story. That the lament is more for the vine than for the shoot, and the prevalence of stem and shoot imagery for families, makes it likely that the vine is the family

---

1. That is, couplets, with three accented words in the first line and two in the second.
2. This is Eichrodt's proposal (1970: 252–58) for the whole chapter.

line itself, the Davidic dynasty.[3] Reading this way, the "strong stem" of the vine (19:12), in whom revanchist Israelites briefly placed their hopes, is Zedekiah, and the other "branches," who burned with the vine (19:14), are other princes of the line, whom Nebuchadnezzar summarily executed (2 Kgs. 25:7). If these identifications are correct, then what this second allegory says is that the Davidic line itself has been uprooted and has desiccated and burned, root and branch.

In the canonical text, the two allegories are to be read as one: there is no new start for the second except "your mother," which only emphasizes the relation of the two by repeating the beginning of the first. Since we can subsume the import of the first allegory under that of the second, and not vice versa, I propose that this is how we should read the composite whole. Not only will Zedekiah not again roar on the mountains of Israel, no Davidic king will. The composite passage is a funeral chant mandated by the Lord for the whole house of David; as prophecy, it says, "It is over." Indeed, whoever affixed 19:14d certifies that the death for which the *kinah* was written had in fact taken place.[4]

In the first allegory, we are told who captured the young lions: Egypt and Babylon. We are not told who uprooted the vine,[5] a reticence that often in scripture indicates that God has been the agent. And then—was the Lord also one of the mourners at the funeral? Can we attribute also this affect to God (on the passibility of God, →16:1–43)? It is, after all, the Lord's own *kinah* that is to be sung for David's line.

The dethroning of the house of David was a theological event of immense weight. However the establishment of a monarchy may have clashed with the tradition of the desert covenant (Jenson 1997–99: 1.66–71); once the step was taken and David ruled Israel, the Lord's covenant with him and his line was unequivocal: "Your house and your kingdom shall be made sure forever before me" (2 Sam. 7:16). There are not many ways to construe the termination of something that has been promised to continue forever. Perhaps the Lord lied. Or perhaps he has simply failed and institutes the *kinah* for himself and his project with Israel. Or if neither of these is true, Israel must now look for the promise to David to be fulfilled in another history than that of this age.

Exilic and postexilic Judaism's hope for the Messiah, the finally anointed one, was pluriform and contested.[6] But one constant factor was hope for a literal or figurative descendent of David who would at last do what the kings of Judah

3. This is Zimmerli's proposal (1979: 393–94) for the whole chapter. The Targum also makes the mother a community, but in its cavalier fashion makes this be "the Congregation of Israel" (Levey 1990: 60).

4. The construction ותהי לקינה has been translated with various tenses. Eichrodt 1970: 250 has "and has become a lament," which I think makes the most sense in context. The Targum's paraphrase of the line is arbitrary but interesting: "It is a prophecy, but it shall become a lament" (Levey 1990: 60).

5. The Targum identifies kings from the east (Levey 1990: 60).

6. Sigmund Mowinckel, *He That Cometh*, trans. G. W. Anderson (Oxford: Blackwell, 1956), 280–345.

were supposed to do and never quite achieved, or in many cases never wanted to achieve: he would "reign in righteousness" (Isa. 32:1) and just so "command peace to the nations . . . from sea to sea" (Zech. 9:10).

There is a way in which the Old Testament can be said to conclude with two questions posed by the book of Ezekiel. One is explicit: the Lord shows Ezekiel the dry bones of all Israel and asks, "Son of a man, can these bones live?" (Ezek. 37:3). We will of course spend time with that. The other is implicit in our chapter: Will a true shoot yet somehow spring from the vine stock of Jesse and establish eternal righteousness and peace? Christianity is faith that Mary's child is God's personal answer to both questions.

EZEKIEL 20:1–31

A STRANGE HISTORY OF SALVATION

In all the book of Ezekiel, two passages—the opening vision of the *Merkabah* in 1:4–28b and the present retelling of the Lord's history with his people—propel us most abruptly into theological depths we should perhaps fear to enter. In the passage before us the Lord narrates his history with Israel not as a "history of salvation" but rather as a story of uninterrupted spiritual disaster—the only similar account in scripture is Stephen's recital at Acts 7. Israel, as readers of Ezekiel will have read many times, is "a rebellious house"; in this account of her history she is nothing but that. And in the midst of the dismal tale, the Lord says that he himself was at one point the agent of Israel's rebellion: "Moreover, I gave them statutes that were not good and ordinances by which they could not live. I defiled them through their very gifts" (20:25), that is, through the sacrifices they were commanded to bring.

The chapter begins with the third of the datings scattered through the book. In our calendar, the year is 591, a year later than the previous dated prophecy at 8:1–18. Just as on that occasion, a scene is set: Ezekiel is in his house and leaders of the exilic community have come to "consult" the Lord. That is, Ezekiel is asked to lay a question before the Lord and bring back the Lord's answer. Again as before, we are not told what their query was, although it is tempting to find it alluded to in 20:32.

As the elders hoped, the word of the Lord does come to Ezekiel. He is addressed as "you—son of a man" and told to speak to the elders with "thus says the Lord," all of which is with Ezekiel the standard beginning for a prophecy, also for a prophetic *responsum*. But when the Lord responds, what Ezekiel is told to do, instead of bringing an answer to the elders' query, is to bring the Lord's refusal to be queried by them. He is to pronounce a judgment that these persons have no standing to consult the Lord because of the "abominations," the sheerly disgusting religious practices, of their ancestors, in which they have continued (20:3–4).

Ezekiel is to establish this judgment by reciting a version of Israel's creed that the Lord dictates to him (20:5–29). Israel's creed was never laid down as a stable text—though Deut. 26:5–9 reports a version much like one of the concise Christian creeds. But Israel in cultic situations certainly confessed narratives of the Lord's saving deeds that cited items from a more or less standard repertoire—we may take the entire Pentateuch as a very long such confession, much as we may regard one of the Gospels as a long version of a trinitarian creed's second article.

In the version the Lord now dictates to Ezekiel, three events are adduced: the Lord's self-revelation to Israel in Egypt (20:5–8a), the exodus with giving of the law (20:8b–13a), and the entry into the land (20:13b–31a). On this occasion it is the Lord himself who recites the history. Uniquely among such recitals, each event is made to be nothing but an instance of Israel's unfaithfulness. One may contrast this with a passage from Ezekiel's contemporary, himself sufficiently attuned to disasters: "I remember the devotion of your youth, your love as a bride, how you followed me in the wilderness" (Jer. 2:2).

The creedal history terminates in a repetition of the rebuff to the elders (Ezek. 20:31b). As happens several times in the book of Ezekiel, this passage is then followed by another of similar theme but somewhat different character: 20:32–44 was probably composed at a later date but in the canonical text is nevertheless intended to be read with what precedes it.

The creedal recital begins, "On the day when I chose Israel" (20:5). This is Ezekiel's only explicit use of the concept of God's "election" or "choice,"[1] which makes its appearance all the more striking. Indeed, the clause is a sort of title for the whole passage, which as a whole is about God's election and his people's rejection of it.

God's election of this people occurred on a particular "day," the day when the Lord introduced himself by name to them in Egypt. Election is not here conceived as happening in the timeless eternity in which some Christian theology has located it. In Ezekiel, and indeed generally in the Old Testament, even God's primal election of his people occurs *in* his history with them.

One story nicely shows both what may be the original context in which Israel spoke of divine election and a decisive aspect of the act. First Sam. 16:6–13 recounts the Lord's choice of David to be king, emphasizing that he is chosen *instead* of Jesse's other sons. Election in the Old Testament is regularly such choice of one possibility from several; and the earliest theological use of the explicit concept

---

1. Other passages, notably Ezek. 16, of course display the election itself, but they do not use the concept. For the lexicography of the root בחר (*bḥr*) and for what amounts to a history of the concept in Israel's theology, see Jenni and Westermann 1997: 209–26.

may as here have been for God's choice of a king (Jenni and Westermann 1997: 213–15).

If this suggestion is correct, then at some point the notion of divine choice was extended from election of the king to election of the people. And around Ezekiel's time, the doctrine of the Lord's election of Israel was highly developed, to became central in the Deuteronomistic theology. One passage of Deuteronomy itself displays the resultant theologoumenon: the Lord has "chosen" Israel "out of all the peoples on earth," to be "his treasured possession" and, as in this way affiliated to God, to be "holy." He made this choice sheerly because he "loved" Israel, with that lack of further motivation that attends falling in love—Israel was in herself an insignificant nation (Deut. 7:6–8). In this theology, which Ezekiel plainly shares, the Lord's election of Israel is an act of sheer grace, and what Israel is elected to is holiness in the strictly theological sense of closeness to God.

Since election is the choice of one possibility among others, there must evidently be those who are not chosen; Jesse's other sons are explicitly *not* to be king. Are then nations other than the chosen one not called to holiness, not to be united to God? Or those who do not belong to the church? In respect of individuals, the notion of double predestination has haunted Christian theology at least since Augustine—and when it has not, this has always been a sign of theological cowardice.

There perhaps will be no accepted resolution short of the final vision of God. But it may be that Ezekiel provides a clue. Israel is chosen on a day in the Lord's history with her. Thus at least one picture is rejected: we are not to think of a God sitting before and above all time, sorting fates. And the church's Christology, in which the temporal person of Christ is eternal God, suggests a way to a different construal: the day of encountering Jesus *is* the moment of divine decision.

Israel's election took place when the Lord revealed himself to the people as "יהוה your God" (Ezek. 20:5) and bound himself with an oath to bring them to a fertile land he had picked out for them (20:6). Israel thus begins with the Lord's unilateral self-revelation and unilateral promise of blessing. The obligation placed on Israel by this gift of covenant was to put away their Egyptian gods, since now the Lord is their God (20:7); the Israelites, however, continued in their old ways without a moment's pause (20:8a). In the exodus accounts themselves, we do not read of Israelite idolatry in Egypt; but Ezekiel is here determined to leave no moment of Israel's history untainted by it—and indeed if the Lord needed to introduce himself to the people, presumably they had been worshiping some other god or gods.

The Lord, he says, might at this point have terminated Israel (20:8b). He decides not to, "for the sake of [his] name." Having entrusted his personal name to this people, the Lord is so identified with them that their disaster would profane his own personhood "in the sight of the nations" (20:9). This motivation will appear less egocentric if we remember that the Lord is in fact God also of those "nations," who also would be dishonored by his disgrace, and that all this is said in a context established by a divine choice made out of sheer love. The Lord cannot dispatch Israel without harming himself because no lover can wholly distinguish himself from the beloved. Moreover, in Christian theology there is a maxim: nothing but God can be the final goal of righteous intention, even for God himself.

Thus the Lord does lead Israel out of Egypt and in the desert blesses them with his "statutes and ordinances" (→5:5–17) and with the institution of the Sabbath (20:10–12). The exodus itself, with its Passover and the miracle of the parted waters, is not mentioned. The Lord does not here tell a tale of wonders and sacraments, but of gifts and rejections.

Late-modern antinomianism is likely to regard "statutes and ordinances" as restrictions of personal autonomy and so as dubious blessings; and Israel in the desert evidently had the same view. The Lord, however, gave his commandments not as restrictions but rather—in Karl Barth's illuminating language—as *permissions*, words that open the possibilities of human life. Ezekiel 20:11, perhaps better translated "by the observing of which man shall live,"[2] is language from Ezekiel's priestly tradition (see Lev. 18:5) and reflects the Deuteronomistic challenge to obey God's commandments and so choose life (Deut. 30:15–20). Israel, in the better moments she of course did in fact have, knew all this: "Lead me in the path of your commandments, for I delight in it" (Ps. 119:35).

Again the Lord might reasonably have made "an end of them" and refrains only for his name's sake (Ezek. 20:13b). As in the account in the Pentateuch (Num. 14:22–23), he condemns the rebellious generation to remain outside the promised land (Ezek. 20:15–16) and turns his hopes to the next generation. These promptly adopt all the ways of their parents (20:18–21). Thus another generation was set to languish in the wilderness, except that again the Lord acts for the sake of his name (20:21c–22) and so—as will shortly be narrated—does bring them into the land (20:28a).

This time, however, the Lord takes additional measures. First, before Israel ever enters the land, the Lord determines that he will drive her out of it again—into the very exile Ezekiel and the elders are enduring—and swears to this on the spot (20:23–24), in a black parody of the election and oath that began this recital (20:5) and made Israel the Lord's people. This is an event unrecorded elsewhere in scripture. In unparalleled fashion, it binds the evils of Israel's total history into one guilt: the sins of Israel in the land are one with her sins in the desert, and in such a way that the punishment of both is one, that is decreed before the sins in the land are ever committed.

Second, the Lord there "gave them statutes that were not good and ordinances by which they could not live" (20:25). What the bad laws were is stated in the next verse: they commanded the ritual sacrifice of firstborn sons (20:26).

Such a command is in fact found in Israel's divine law, at Exod. 22:29: "The firstborn of your sons you shall give to me"—the horrid sense of which is made

---

2. Is NRSV's bizarre "everyone shall live" an attempt to avoid saying "man"?

plain by its position as the first item in a list that goes on: "You shall do the same with your oxen and with your sheep." The surrounding peoples indeed sacrificed children by fire,[3] and no doubt Israelites who had most thoroughly adopted their cultic practices adopted this one also; even during the time of exile there are apparently those who "slaughter [their] children in the valleys" (Isa. 57:5). Here, however, it is supposed that the very Israel that knew and handed on the Lord's own statutes and ordinances at least sometimes regarded sacrifice of the firstborn son as mandated by them.

The Targum, always concerned to preserve God's reputation, simply edits out the Lord's attribution of this law to himself (Levey 1990: 63). Less venturesome exegetes commonly try to mitigate Exod. 22:29 by pointing to the command, in other collections of law, to redeem the firstborn son by substitution of an animal; so at Exod. 34:19–20: "All that first opens the womb is mine. . . . All the firstborn of your sons you shall redeem." But the passages that provide for redemption only reinforce the principle that the life of the firstborn son is indeed forfeit to the Lord; and they do not change the fact that in the particular coherent code of divine law preserved in Exod. 19:1–23:19 there is no provision for substitution. Jewish theologian Jon Levenson argues from a wide base of evidence that while the sacrifice of the firstborn was never generally enforced in Israel, it was long regarded as a work of devotion and was ended only by the prophets' and the Deuteronomist's polemic against it, as we see in Jer. 7:31 or here in Ezekiel.[4]

The Lord speaking by Ezekiel now calls child sacrifice a sort of ultimate proof of Israel's wickedness, a defilement incurred by their worship itself (Ezek. 20:26a), and the command to perform it an ordinance that does not promote life. But he also says that he himself gave the command. He provides a reason: he did it to punish Israel for inveterate rebellion by driving them into rebellion's final depth, into sheer horror, where they might finally acknowledge their desperate situation (20:26b).

Thus the Lord, by his own account through Ezekiel, once commanded great evil, to bring evil to its self-annulling perfection. Whatever the status of our passage, it poses with unmatched severity the problem of evil's place in the Lord's salvation history. It is not, moreover, the only passage of the Old Testament that attributes sin to the Lord's instigation: for example, the "evil spirit" that drives Saul to murderous rage is "from the LORD" (1 Sam. 16:14–23), as is the "lying spirit" in the mouths of certain false prophets (1 Kgs. 22:22–23).

3. Just one excavated area at the Phoenician colony at Carthage contains the ashes of 40,000 sacrificed infants. I have been there and never forgotten it.

4. Jon D. Levenson, *The Death and Resurrection of the Beloved Son: The Transformation of Child Sacrifice in Judaism and Christianity* (New Haven: Yale University Press, 1993), 3–44. Levenson goes on to argue that while the practice of firstborn sacrifice ceased, the conception that the beloved firstborn is intrinsically devoted to the Lord continued and underlies theology and practice in both Judaism and Christianity. The whole book is important, but I cannot follow it further here.

That our sin has—somehow—a place in the Lord's agency in his history with us is a persistent theme within Christian thinking. The central liturgy of the Western church, the liturgy of the Easter vigil, in the great song of the *Exultet*, notoriously celebrates Adam and Eve's disobedience as "the happy fault [*felix culpa*] that occasioned such great redemption." Martin Luther—and that in a catechism!—taught that God created us "just in order to redeem" us. And the question—if not the answer—has always been there: Is not God's act to rescue us from the fall a greater love than would have been possible simply as love for unfallen creatures? If the incarnation is the eternal secret of God (Eph. 3:3–9), what would an incarnation have been that was not the man hanging on the cross for our sin? The undoubted greatest theologian of the past century, Karl Barth, pressed the question with unique energy.

Surely we must at least acknowledge that modern theology's frequent picture of God as transparently good and kind cannot be squared with scripture—again, however we treat the present passage. His ways to his purposes for us are devious, at least by any standard of straightforwardness available to the fallen and redeemed creatures who actually exist and can worry about such things. If the Lord is—as Ezekiel precisely in our passage asserts—his people's utterly committed lover, we must admit that this love often indeed passes our understanding. Christians see both the guarantee of this love and the revelation of its off-putting mystery in the sacrifice of the only beloved Son.[5] If we try to penetrate beyond that, perhaps the Lord will "horrify" us also.

Eventually—and in this recital it is almost an anticlimax—the Lord does bring Israel into the land, whereupon they eagerly adopt every religious practice of the antecedent inhabitants (20:28–29). Therewith we are in the present tense, with a denunciation of Israel's persistence in idolatry "to this day" (20:30–31). "Oh house of Israel. . . . I will not be consulted by you."

---

5. That some reduce this to child abuse betrays a truly remarkable philistinism.

EZEKIEL 20:32–44

A FINAL EXODUS

This passage is clearly intended to be read with the foregoing passage, whether or not it was written at the same time. They are here separately discussed only for convenience (→20:1–31).

Ezekiel 20:32 is a hinge between the two passages—and indeed it could be discussed in either commentary unit. Formally, it belongs with what precedes it: it has no introduction of its own and a following "says the Lord" introduces a new subunit, 20:33–38. Materially, however, it belongs with the latter passage, as the provocation for its amazing judgment and promise.

The "thought" attributed to exiled Israel—or perhaps to a faction within it—can be read in two ways. In my judgment, it is now impossible to decide between them with certainty; we lack some key presumed by the text.

Perhaps the "thought" is an intention; NRSV translates in that sense. In that case, those among whom the idea circulates consider that in view of all that has happened and of their present circumstances, they might as well forget the promises made by this יהוה, who clearly cannot or will not keep them, and join the other nations in more usual patterns of religion. There are grounds for this reading: 20:32 seems deliberately to echo premonarchical Israel's demand to have a king "like other nations," a request that the Lord saw as rebellion against him (1 Sam. 8:5–7); moreover, if this echo is in Ezekiel's mind, that explains the sudden appearance in the next verse of the Lord's intention to be himself "king" in Israel, a divine title that in Ezekiel appears only here.

But if the exiles were proposing to go all the way in worship of the gods of the nations, it seems unlikely that to state this they would adopt Isaiah's language, who called those gods "wood and stone" precisely to say they were

---

powerless (Isa. 37:19). And the Hebrew text could just as well with KJV be translated as a straightforward prediction, "We will be as the heathen [nations]." I incline slightly to this other possibility: the "thought" is not an intention but instead a lament. If present trends continue, suppose at least some exiles, Israel will inevitably be altogether assimilated to the nations amid which she is scattered and be no better than they with their dead idols. This thought too is an unbelieving thought.

Either way, the Lord will have none of it. Israel is his, and he is going to keep her: "I will be king over you." And in the future proposed, this will be the case regardless of Israel's faithfulness or rebellion (20:33, 44); somehow the divine act now prophesied will transcend even the limited reciprocity of the covenant (→16:1–43) and guarantee Israel's place unilaterally.

The proclamation of the Lord as Israel's "king" (מלך, *melek*) belonged to a strand of theology and piety associated with the Jerusalem temple.[1] There it seems that on certain occasions the ritual included the acclamation, "O come, let us sing to the LORD. . . . For the LORD is a great God, and a great King above all gods" (Ps. 95:1–3); or again, "Say among the nation, 'The LORD is king!' . . . for he is coming to judge the earth" (96:10–13). Such cultic acclamation had a deep mythic background in ancient Mideastern cultures, where the kingship and deity of the earthly and heavenly sovereigns were mutually dependent in the cult, where the king's "coming" to his throne was the image of the god's advent. And Israel knew such myth, since it was from Canaanites that Israel learned about kings in the first place. Just how alive these notions and practices ever were in the relation between palace and temple at Jerusalem is, to be sure, unclear. And in any case, in the coming rule of the Lord now proclaimed, all reciprocity is over: he is going to reign in Jerusalem come what otherwise may, and so with or without a king in the palace.

Ezekiel 20:39d–44 describes the reality of that God-ruled kingdom. Israel will be gathered from her diaspora among the nations. The sacrifices will be reestablished in purity, with no admixture of polluting foreign rites—whether once commanded by the Lord or not (→20:1–31). And by performing these marvels—for given the record, marvels they will be—the Lord will show his "holiness among" his people (20:41), that is, he will demonstrate that he and with him the nation are separate, incomparable,[2] always unexpected, and impenetrably mysterious.

It must be understood that the original context of holiness is not ethics but what moderns somewhat feebly call "religious experience." A landmark work in the modern study of religion described "the holy" as encountered reality that is at once "fascinating" and "terrible."[3] When the holy intrudes on us we cannot

---

1. A *Thronbesteigungsfest* ("ritual of the Lord's enthronement") was earlier postulated by Sigmund Mowinckel (*The Psalms in Israel's Worship*, trans. D. R. Ap-Thomas [New York: Abingdon, 1962]) and others.

2. In a German phrase that has become standard in all languages, they are *das ganz andere*.

3. Rudolf Otto, *The Idea of the Holy* (London: Oxford University Press, 1936).

turn our gaze from it, even as it overwhelms us, even as it resists all analysis and utterly repels every effort to deal with it.

The Lord's presence in Jerusalem amid his people will be like that, the Lord says, for all the world to experience (20:41). And in reflex from the nations' fascination, Israel also will finally understand that יהוה is incomparable, unavoidable, and ungraspable, that he is in fact the Lord and not another (20:42). And indeed they will at last grasp what it means that they are one with this God, that they are themselves—as originally promised—a holy nation (Exod. 19:6).

It is apparent that this promise has not yet been fulfilled, and by hindsight it is apparent that it could not be fulfilled under the conditions of this age—unless that is what happened on Golgotha, at almost predictably great cost to the holy God himself. Prophecy has here again reached beyond what we know as history, to become eschatology.

In the middle of our passage, the Lord describes how he will establish this final and holy kingdom: he will redo the exodus entry into the land (Ezek. 20:34–38). These verses follow the order and stations of the previous passage's recital of the exodus as a string of disasters. But now the language with which Israel herself confessed the original exodus appears, as it did not there: the Lord will act with "a mighty hand and an outstretched arm" (Deut. 26:8). And the signs are now reversed: where in the previous recital there was the rebellion of Israel, now there is the unilateral action of the Lord.

As he brought them out of exile in Egypt so he will bring them out of the many lands of their present exile. As he brought them into the wilderness adjacent to Egypt, now he will bring them into the "wilderness of [these] peoples." Obviously this wilderness cannot be any one geographical area; wilderness has become an eschatological figure for the place of that judgment after which there will be no occasion of judgment. The giving of Torah is not here adduced; that does not need to be repeated or undone.

As the Lord judged the people in the Egyptian wilderness, he will judge them in that final wilderness. This judgment will be "face to face," as was the original meeting between the Lord and Israel at Sinai (Deut. 5:4). But whereas in the first wilderness he condemned a generation to remain there but passed the promises—and so the possibilities of renewed rebellion—on to their children, in this eschatological wilderness he will separate sheep from goats for good, judging according to each one's faithfulness to the covenant (Ezek. 20:37–38).

This judgment will be final. In the eschatological wilderness, the Lord will dismiss all those of the "house of Israel" who want to serve their idols, to go and do so. They will then remain in the eschatological wilderness and be no part of the future Israel and thus will no longer be in position to profane the Lord's name (20:39). The others will march into the unshakable kingdom.

But what, we cannot help asking, guarantees that those who make this new entrance into the land will not simply rebel again, as did those brought in the first time? In our text, this question is not directly addressed until the last verse, to which we will come. We may say that this judgment and this entry into the land are plainly, in our language, eschatological, so that the question of further history does not arise. But what establishes it in that finality?

If we—as we must—read this passage together with what precedes it, we may perhaps suppose that the depths to which the Lord has reduced Israel are the unsurpassable end of rebellion and so themselves the possibility of radical new beginning—from the bottom of the pit there is no way but up. Israel's rebellious past will not disappear; the new Israel will remember the old and "loathe" herself (20:43). Just this remembrance (→6:1–14) will be their knowledge of the Lord's identity (20:44a); and it will be their side of a union with him constituted on his side by sheer grace, as he deals with them not according to their sins but according to his own identity (20:44b–c).

It is at the cross—or never—that this threat and this promise have been carried out. There at last is fulfillment of our rebellions and their consequence, when precisely the perfect one among us must cry, "My God, my God, why have you forsaken me?" And in the resurrection of the crucified we see the last end turned into the last beginning. As for where that leaves the rest of us, according to Paul God's final judgment will be precisely the final justification of the ungodly, and this will include a refining by fire that burns away all the hay and straw built into the persons we have become in our lives and leaves only the pure gold and silver of faith (1 Cor. 3:12–15).

Or perhaps for our understanding of Ezekiel we may even more appositely turn to a theologoumenon of—again—Martin Luther. God, Luther said, is profoundly hidden by his "alien work," his work of judgment or earthly rewards. As he does this work he is a *deus absconditus*, a "hidden God." When he turns to his proper work, the "work of his right hand," he does not, however, cease to be hidden. On the contrary, he reveals himself and acts in sheer grace precisely by redoubling his hiding, in the suffering and injustice of the cross.

EZEKIEL 20:45–21:7

THE SWORD, PART 1

This passage is the first of three, four, or five prophecies that have been grouped together at 20:45–21:32, whether by Ezekiel himself or by an editor, because all invoke the image of "the sword." Without much commitment I will suppose that we are dealing with four prophecies and will devote a relatively short commentary unit to each. The present passage is in turn divided into three parts: 20:45–49; 21:1–5; and 21:6–7.[1]

The relation between the first two parts is much the same as we find between the two parts of →15:1–8 or of →17:1–21. Here 20:45–48 develops a figure, 21:1–5 provides an interpretation, and 20:49 connects the two. This latter linking verse also confirms the figural nature of the first part: the story of woods and a fire is specified as a *mashal*, a formulated saying, and moreover one in such need of interpretation that it exasperates the hearers. Thus the announced disaster should not be taken as a literal forest fire, however destructive, Following the figure and its interpretation, 21:6–7 prescribes an *oth*, a prophetic enacted sign, that, however, differs from other actions mandated for Ezekiel in that the prescribed action would hardly have needed mandating, since it is Ezekiel's natural reaction to the judgment just announced—which is why I read these verses as the third part of a continuing passage.

The figural and interpretive prophecies are both introduced in standard fashion: the word of the Lord comes to Ezekiel, addresses him as "you—son of a man," and instructs him to prophesy, beginning with "thus says the Lord." For

---

1. Ezek. 20:45–21:7 in English Bibles is numbered 21:1–12 in the Hebrew and Septuagint texts.

both prophecies, Ezekiel is to "set his face against" a geographical location. This substitution of orienting bodily gesture for presence on the spot is a regular aspect of Ezekiel's peculiar God-imposed situation.

In the figural prophecy, the target is "the south" or "the Negeb." The interpreting prophecy tells us that this is Jerusalem. It is not clear why "the south" is a figure for Jerusalem: perhaps it is simply because Judah is in the southerly part of Syria-Palestine, or perhaps because Babylon's armies will attack Jerusalem from the north and Ezekiel in Babylon adopts that point of view, or perhaps because in myth the north is often the origin of evil. In the Old Testament Negeb can be the name of a region, the arid southernmost part of Syria-Palestine, or it can be simply another word for "the south" (Zimmerli 1979: 423). Since the target of the prophecy is in any case Jerusalem, we may suppose that the Negeb is here merely a rhetorical variation for "the south."

Having announced that the Lord will set a southerly forest fire, making a conflagration so fierce that living and dead trees alike will be burnt, Ezekiel is understandably met with incomprehension. Indeed—and again understandably—he is accused of regularly purveying such obscurities. This time he complains to the Lord about this aspect of his mission (20:49). So he is given an interpreting prophecy (21:1–5).

The fire—we are now told—is the war that the Lord will bring against Jerusalem and "the sanctuaries," these last probably the syncretistic holy places that persisted after Josiah's reforms. Indeed the Lord will personally come to wield the sword, no longer leaving it to Israel's creaturely oppressors. "The sword" of course is itself another figure, but one so obvious as not here to be felt as such.

That the Lord punishes Israel by bringing war against her is a staple of prophecy, which we often see in Ezekiel. In this case, however, two features stand out. The Lord, having once drawn his sword, will not sheath it: God's war with Jerusalem will not allow for repentance—this despite the demand for repentance that pervades Ezekiel's prophesying. And Jerusalem's faithful and unfaithful will alike perish—this despite the separation of the righteous from the wicked formally proclaimed in Ezek. 18 and elsewhere. How are we to understand these contradictions?

We might think of this war of God against Jerusalem as an eschatological event, like some others prophesied by Ezekiel, and so as occurring on the other side of possible repentance. But the "news" referred to in 21:7 must surely be either the message that Jerusalem has fallen or Ezekiel's just uttered prophecy taken as news of the disaster's imminence; we are therefore firmly within history. But neither do I see much prospect of harmonizing the present declaration of divine total war with more usual parts of Ezekiel's prophesying that demand repentance and insist the righteous shall live.

Probably we must simply let the contradictions stand. A prophet's utterances, moving with the very history they are to move, cannot form a logical system. Their coherence is instead dramatic and rhetorical. With respect to this passage, perhaps we must simply suppose that in a particular context not now fully known to us, and amid discussion or argument among the exiles just before or immediately after Jerusalem's fall, this terrible word was the demanded utterance.

Ezekiel laments Jerusalem's fall (21:6). It is entirely typical of Ezekiel's situation over against the Lord, that Ezekiel's natural reaction to Jerusalem's fall is not reported as such, but only by way of the Lord's instruction to behave in this fashion; Ezekiel is not permitted to own even his emotions. When the people ask why Ezekiel is carrying on, he is to tell them that he is anticipating what they too are about to experience: the word of Jerusalem's fall will undo them as it has him (21:7).[2]

And then the last word of the passage does after all give the whole an eschatological edge: "See, it comes and it will be fulfilled!" We encounter this "it"[3] earlier in Ezekiel, in →7:10–27, where it belonged to the rhetoric of "the day of the Lord," the great and terrible day when God will triumph once for all—and not necessarily as we might hope.

The occasional logical incoherence and overall rhetorical coherence of Ezekiel's prophesying give occasion to consider the way in which the scriptures in general cohere—and cohere they must if they are God's word. Christianity reads the scriptures fundamentally as narrative, of the coming of Israel's Christ and his kingdom. For Christianity, therefore, scripture coheres in the way that a long and agitated narrative coheres, a mode of continuity that I call "dramatic coherence." In a drama, the author can very well at different times promote principles and decisions that are formal contraries, particularly an author who—as often in Ezekiel and in some high-modernist plays—appears in his own drama. And this mode of coherence rules not only in scripture as a whole, but in at least some of its parts, notably within that scene of the Lord's story that is the book of Ezekiel.

2. NRSV's translation "all knees will turn to water" evades a crudity—as NRSV often does. Almost certainly the phenomenon of urination caused by intense fear is intended. We should translate "water will run down to their knees"; see Greenberg 1983: 152.

3. The Hebrew has third-person singular verbs with no subject.

EZEKIEL 21:8–17

THE SWORD, PART 2

Ezekiel 21:8–17 is the second in a group of prophecies editorially brought together around the image of "the sword."[1] It is possible that 21:8–13 and 21:14–17 were intended to be two poems; but since we do not know the function of "says the Lord God" at 21:13b—for reasons we will come to shortly—we cannot be sure there is an ending there, whereas there is a clear ending with "I the Lord have spoken" at 21:17. And even if Ezekiel or an editor once regarded 21:8–17 as two poems, nothing will be lost by taking them as one. Ezekiel 21:8–9 provides Ezekiel's standard introduction to a messenger-word beginning with "thus says the Lord": the word comes to him, addresses him as "you—son of a man," and tells him what to say.

NRSV prints the passage as poetry broken by a prose gloss; and this seems right. To be sure, something has gone seriously wrong with the text. Thus, for example, KJV, translating what is actually there in Hebrew at 21:10b, comes up with "it contemneth the rod of my son, as every tree."

Since translators are not supposed to leave blanks, we may forgive both KJV's gibberish and NRSV's desperate attempt to make sense. But I will pass over 21:10b and 21:13 in silence and read 21:8–17 as a poem with a few lost lines.

It is, moreover, a remarkable poem, a chief justification of the introduction's description of Ezekiel as a true poet. In speech occurring under such spiritual and conceptual tension as that under which prophets spoke, we may expect the appearance of something like poetry, and passages of verse and exalted prose are

1. Ezek. 21:8–17 in English Bibles is numbered 21:13–22 in the Hebrew and Septuagint texts.

scattered through the prophetic books. But Ezekiel—divine inspiration aside—has claim to be a powerful poet also in the usual sense (forcefully argued by Eichrodt 1970: 292–96). Indeed, the phenomenon poses the major theological matter to be considered in this commentary unit.

The first thing to do with any true poem is to pronounce it, at least in one's head; and the main commentary to our present passage must be an exhortation to do just that. That done, we may as literary critics note Ezekiel's subtle yet powerful variation in handling his unifying image, "the sword": sometimes this sword is wielded by a swordsman, sometimes it has its own life and indeed can be addressed, and sometimes even its edge and polished surface have their specific force. We may discover the suggestion, made not by statement but by the parallelism of lines, that the Lord himself mourns for his people and his princes (21:12). We should follow the way in which the identity of the swordsman is intimated, but then held back until the end, when the Lord unmasks himself (21:17).

Descending to more prosaic analysis, 21:8–11 evokes the making of the sword and its terrible beauty, and 21:14–17 evokes its action in judgment. Ezekiel 21:12 and 21:14a unite the two parts by their affect on the Lord and his prophet; here we again—as decisively at 16:1–43—encounter Ezekiel's depiction of the Lord as affected by emotion. The sword's victims do not simply fall in battle; rather, the language suggests that they are more executed than defeated, though doubtless Nebuchadnezzar's siege is the means thereof. According to 21:15 the preternatural panic that struck Israel's enemies when the Lord led them in holy war (Exod. 23:27) will now afflict Israel herself instead. One wishes we could be more certain about the meaning of the gestures instanced. Context suggests that striking the thigh (Ezek. 12:12) must be a gesture of sorrow, but is striking hand against hand (21:14, 17) a gesture of triumph or of threat? And what does letting the sword fall three times (21:14) do? The imperative sentences at these places should not here be taken as mandating prophetic signs; they belong to the poetry.

Thus reduced to prose, the message of these verses is all too familiar to readers who have come this far in Ezekiel: Israel's rulers and people will be punished by deadly force, and the attacking warrior will finally be the Lord himself. Israel's particular guilt is this time not specified, nor can we be certain precisely when the prophecy was uttered. Translated into prose, our passage is less interesting in its depiction of judgment than many others.

We do not, however, have a prose speech before us. We may be moved to ask: Why does the word of the Lord sometimes take the form of poetry? That is, of language specifically elevated into beauty? Of course, Ezekiel is not the only biblical poet—consider the Psalms or Mary's song (Luke 1:46–55)—nor have poets been lacking in the history of the church. If we cut straight to the deepest reason, the Lord's word must be beautiful—and icons of that word, and music for that word, must be beautiful—because beauty is a primary attribute of the Lord himself, and the Lord's Word is a second identity of himself. In the theological tradition, beauty has been classically defined as the *splendor veritatis*, the "shining of truth." God *is* the truth, and therefore he is also the original shining of truth, the original of all beauty. Indeed, beauty as classically defined is very close to what Ezekiel's tradition called "glory" (*kabod*) (→1:25–28b). A theologian of the just-previous generation, perhaps the greatest Roman Catholic theologian of the twentieth century, Hans Urs von Balthasar, produced what amounts to an entire systematic theology built around this theme, blended with a history of the Western notion and experience of beauty.[2]

---

2. Hans Urs von Balthasar, *Herrlichkeit: Eine theologicsche Ästhetik*, 5 vols. (Einsiedeln: Johannes, 1961–69).

EZEKIEL 21:18–27

THE SWORD, PART 3

Ezekiel 21:18–27 is the third in an editorial grouping, joined by the image of "the sword."[1] It begins in standard fashion: the word of the Lord comes to Ezekiel, addresses him as "you—son of a man," and gives him instructions. On this occasion Ezekiel is to begin by performing a prophetic sign, an *oth* (→3:22–5:4). The Lord specifies the sign (21:18–19) and provides him with an interpretation (21:20–23). Then, linked to the sign and its interpretation with "therefore," the Lord dictates a messenger-word (21:24–27) that begins with the standard "thus says the Lord." This is directed to an unspecified "you" that in view of the foregoing must be the people of Jerusalem; as so often, Ezekiel is to prophesy at a distance.

As the *oth*, Ezekiel is to "mark out" a location[2] with two diverging roads leading from it and put up a signpost indicating the two destinations. We are not told how he was to do this; perhaps the best guess is that he was to make a model. Nothing is recorded about Ezekiel's performing the sign, about how he communicated its interpretation, or about how either was received.

At 21:20 prescription of the sign spills over into its interpretation. The alternative destinations to appear on the signpost are Rabbah, the capital of the Ammonite kingdom,[3] and Jerusalem. Ezekiel and his hearers of course knew what we know from

---

1. Ezek. 21:18–27 in English Bibles is numbered 21:23–32 in the Hebrew and Septuagint texts.

2. Given the following interpretation, this may have been Babylon itself or Nebuchadnezzar's field headquarters at Ribla, or perhaps the fork in the road is entirely notional. Greenberg 1997: 427–28 argues for the last option.

3. At present this same city is the capital of much the same territory, under the name Amman, which does indeed derive from Ammon.

history, that Zedekiah made his rebellion against Babylon in alliance with the Ammonites.[4] Now "the sword" will follow the road to one or the other of these cities.

Ezekiel 21:21–23 then unveils the historical reality figured by the *oth*. Nebuchadnezzar is just beginning his final campaign against the rebel states of southern Syria-Palestine. He must choose which rebel city first to attack. As was universal practice in the ancient world, he consults the auguries, and they indicate Jerusalem.[5] It is against that city that he will march to erect his siegeworks.

At Jerusalem they think—or pretend to think—that this heathen divination will betray Nebuchadnezzar into folly (21:23a). But in fact the auguries spoke truly, for it was the will of the Lord himself, and not that of whatever gods Nebuchadnezzar invoked, that determined Nebuchadnezzar's decision—and Israel did not regard augury as itself improper.[6] Zedekiah and—presumably—other notables had sworn allegiance to Babylon (21:23b), and the oath they broke will have been sworn by the Lord. Nebuchadnezzar will make them remember that (21:23c) and justly take the oath breakers of Jerusalem into exile (12:24d).

The auguries that Nebuchadnezzar consults are of mixed provenance. "Shaking the arrows" is clearly a warrior's form of drawing labeled slips; it is not otherwise documented for Babylonian practice. We do not know what "teraphim" were, except that they must have been some form of small amulet or image;[7] whatever they were, their use is documented for Syria (Gen. 31:19) but again not for Babylon. On the other hand, inspecting the liver of a sacrificed animal, or of one whose behavior was itself regarded as an omen, was a Babylonian obsession;[8] every detail of the shape and condition of a liver from each kind of animal has stated meaning in books of augury that have been preserved. Why Ezekiel depicts Nebuchadnezzar as practicing a sort of international medley of augury is not clear.

We come to the tremendous messenger-word from the Lord that follows on all this (21:24–27). A proem (21:24) recapitulates the preceding verse, with a switch: it is Jerusalem's own persistent behavior—and not finally Nebuchadnezzar—that has brought her guilt into remembrance and will be punished with exile. Then the poet of the previous passage (→21:8–17) is given full voice (21:25–27). Again we must violate the poem by prose exposition.

The Lord by Ezekiel directly addresses a "vile, wicked prince of Israel." This must be Zedekiah, the chief oath breaker, whose removal from office and capture makes the surface of the prophesied judgment—the Targum makes this identification

---

4. The Targum, evidently unwilling to countenance an alliance of Jerusalem with Ammon, changes Rabbah from a target of Nebuchadnezzar to a cobelligerent (Levey 1990: 66).

5. The meaning of 21:22a is perhaps undecidable. NRSV supposes that Nebuchadnezzar draws an arrow with his right hand. But there are other possibilities; see Greenberg 1983: 429–30.

6. The high priest carried the "Urim and Thummim," which were lots of some sort, with which to obtain the Lord's answer to queries brought to him (Exod. 28:30).

7. In Israel, teraphim appear as part of the apparatus where worship of the Lord was conducted with idolatrous practices (Judg. 17:5). At Gen. 31:19, NRSV translates תרפים with "household gods," which it does not do elsewhere.

8. The practice was not limited to Mesopotamia; we find it also in Rome and elsewhere.

explicit and for good measure includes a wicked high priest for removal (Levey 1990: 68). From the first, however, the temporal event is clothed in eschatological rhetoric. Zedekiah's impending disaster is his "day"; we are to remember the unique and final day of 7:10–27. To feel the force of the next phrase we must preserve the Hebrew's thudding procession of three nouns and translate with something like "in the time, of punishment, the end";[9] here we are to remember the absolute "end" that "comes" in 7:2b–7.

Description of the "day" then begins with Zedekiah's historical removal from power (21:25). But the prophecy quickly goes beyond that: *no* established order is to remain as it is. The casting down of Zedekiah suddenly becomes the universally stated casting down of "that which is high"; and to this, with equal lack of preparation, is correlated the exaltation of whatever is "low" (21:26).

Jesus will tell a parable on this theme[10] that concludes, "For all who exalt themselves will be humbled, and those who humble themselves will be exalted" (Luke 14:8–11). His mother celebrated his birth with "[God] hath put down the mighty from their seats, and exalted them of low degree" (1:52 KJV). And it was a chief theme of his promise of the kingdom: "So the last will be first, and the first will be last" (Matt. 20:16).

Is then the general upset of order proclaimed here fulfilled by Zedekiah's fall or first in Jesus's fellowship with "publicans and sinners" (e.g., Mark 2:15–17) and the resurrection of this offensive person to be Lord? Or does it further await the kingdom whose coming he proclaimed? So soon as prophetic promise acquires an eschatological edge, time begins to behave peculiarly, by our lights: God's upset of reality, to bring down and raise up, occurs when the last king of Judah falls, perhaps to open a new historical order, *and* when the friend of publicans and sinners dies and is raised, *and* when he will come in glory to judge all history; and these events are somehow both the same event and historically different.

Ezekiel 21:27 is our poem's concluding burst and indeed begins with an actual magical incantation, "A ruin, a ruin, a ruin!" That is what the Lord will "make it." But what is "it"? Jerusalem? The people of Israel? The creation? Exegetes cannot settle their quarrel because, I suggest, the answer is "all of the above." Indeed, the poet knows that the day and the end of his prophecy are absolute: "Such has never occurred." And then there is that last line.[11]

The clause that NRSV translates "until he comes whose right it is" (21:27) picks up Jacob's blessing for Judah (Gen. 49:10): "The scepter shall not depart from Judah . . . until he comes to whom it belongs."[12] Anciently, and by both

---

9. The word translated "end" is קץ (*qaitz*) as before. To feel the rhetoric, we must not, with NRSV, translate with an adjective, required as that may be for smooth English.

10. A fact that most modern commentators contrive not to notice.

11. Typically, the Targum simply ignores this whole verse and provides a different discourse in its place (Levey 1990: 68).

12. The word presented by the Masoretic Text of Genesis, שילה, seems to be a proper noun and is so translated by KJV: "until Shiloh come." Ancient and modern conjectures take it as a variant

Jews and Christians, "Jacob's blessing" has been taken messianically, and in my judgment properly so. That suggests a messianic reading also of the piggybacking line in Ezekiel.

There is, to be sure, another possibility. A key word in the Ezekiel passage (*hamishpat*, המשפט) can be translated either "whose right it is" (so NRSV) or "who administers the right."

Those most impressed by Ezekiel's appropriation of the Judah blessing will tend to read this word in the first way and so to take Ezekiel's prophecy as messianic: the ruins will remain until the one comes to whom the ruined kingdom belongs by right; then the Lord will give it to him. Others read it the second way and take Nebuchadnezzar as the subject who, as in the foregoing 21:23b, administers judgment and will be given that office by the God he unwittingly serves.

There does not seem to be a knockdown linguistic argument for either reading (see Greenberg 1983: 434–35). I lean to the messianic reading, because of the eschatological rhetoric of the whole poem and because ending merely with Nebuchadnezzar would be a poetically disastrous anticlimax, unlikely in so powerful a poet.

---

of שילה, which can be translated either "until what belongs to him comes," which is what NRSV presupposes by translating with "tribute," or "until he comes to whom it [the scepter] belongs," as I prefer. And who knows? KJV may be right, in which case "Shiloh" is a name for the Messiah.

EZEKIEL 21:28–32

THE SWORD, PART 4

Ezekiel 21:28–32 is the fourth and last of a group of prophecies brought editorially together by the image of "the sword."[1] The passage is chiefly interesting for two matters, both extraneous to the content of its message. As to that content, those reading through Ezekiel will by now be all too familiar with the disasters proclaimed (→7:1–9; →7:10–27).

The first point of interest is that in the recorded book of Ezekiel's prophecies, this is the first where the traditional dooms are to befall a Gentile nation. There will be an entire block of such prophecies, occupying Ezek. 25–32.

The second point of interest is that the passage is extraordinarily difficult to read; indeed, it is quite impossible to discover an overall sense without extensive rewriting (Greenberg 1997: 435–38). It relies on the preceding sword prophecies for its logic and rhetoric, yet its relation to them resists clarification. The reference of some lines is so obscure as to suggest that the history of the text has simply obliterated it.

Finally, even the target of the prophecy is confused: the passage starts straightforwardly enough, announcing "the Ammonites" as the target, but this nation promptly vanishes from the scene. I will take up the difficulties in the order just displayed.

Ezekiel 21:28–32 must have been composed later than the first three sword prophecies, since while these threaten the final catastrophe of Jerusalem, the present verses seem to presuppose it. Moreover, our passage is in considerable part put

1. Ezek. 21:28–32 in English Bibles is numbered 21:33–37 in the Hebrew and Septuagint texts.

together of citations from the earlier prophecies and so again presupposes their existence. But just here the difficulty appears, for the appropriated bits are used very differently than in their source (Zimmerli 1979: 447–49; Eichrodt 1970: 305–7). So differently indeed, that one may wonder if the author of 21:28–32 at all understood the texts he was exploiting. Thus, for example, the "vile, wicked" one of 21:25 was there Zedekiah; but this identification in the singular can hardly be carried over to the plural but still seemingly specific persons of 21:29. Who then are these? The text offers no clue. What did someone think he was doing by appropriating "vile, wicked" here? One guess is as good as another.

The matter of the "vile, wicked ones" (plural) brings us next to the obscurity of the verses' reference. A central problem is posed by 21:29: Who are "they" who inflict "false visions" and "lies" on someone or something? The lines pick up the account of Nebuchadnezzar's resort to augury from 21:21–23: there the Jerusalemites' opinion that its results were false was erroneous. But the diviners now adduced cannot be Nebuchadnezzar's augurs, and the divinations are here presented as indeed false. Then, the singular "you" of these verses has to be "the sword," which throughout 21:8–27 is Nebuchadnezzar and his army. But when were actually false auguries inflicted on the Babylonian force? All in all, we cannot tell to what persons and events the prophecy refers.

Finally, against whom is the prophecy directed? The initial instructions to Ezekiel specify the Ammonites. And we can indeed read 21:28b–29 as prophesying their doom: the sword from the great poem (21:9–11) will again glitter and rage: as once against Jerusalem now against Rabbah. But this identification promptly fails us, for 21:30 cannot be directed against the Ammonites, but must surely be directed against Babylon. However obscure 21:29b may be, the line does play on the destruction of Zedekiah, and if this borrowing is to have any force at all, the sword of 21:28–29 must be the sword that undid Zedekiah, that is, it must be Babylon's army. Moreover, in 21:30, it is this army's destruction in its homeland that is announced.

For our purposes, we should probably resign ourselves to things as they stand: a prophecy against Babylon has intruded into a prophecy against the Ammonites, or a prophecy against Babylon has been relabeled as a prophecy against the Ammonites. Whether this phenomenon reflects some event of which we know nothing, represents an editorial intention we cannot now recover, or is the result of editorial incompetence or textual misfortune is again undecidable. We must make do with what we can separately discern of a judgment against the Ammonites and of a judgment against Babylon.

The Ammonites are denounced for taunting[2] Jerusalem, for malicious glee over their recent ally's misfortune. We may perhaps be permitted to guess the taunt: "We both rebelled against Babylon, and only you have been ruined for it!

2. In context, NRSV's "reproach," while linguistically possible, obscures the only possible point.

Ha ha!" (21:28). The Ammonites' punishment is proclaimed with citations from the opening lines of the great sword poem (21:8–17): the sword that once turned aside from Rabbah to ravage Jerusalem will be turned against Rabbah after all. Unidentifiable persons devise false divinations and will thereby aim this sword against unidentified persons for whom Zedekiah is somehow a model. And that is about all that can be gleaned.[3]

Babylon's army is ordered back into its sheath (21:30a): its slaughtering—of whom?—is over. And now this force by which the Lord judged Jerusalem will itself be judged (21:30b–c). As the Lord used Babylon against Judah, so now he will use a "brutish" warrior nation against Babylon; this must be the Medes and the Persians, who would shortly perform just this function and who on their first emergence into history were indeed impressively ferocious warriors. And that is about as far as we can come.

What are we to make of biblical passages that so resist being read? Patristic exegetes sometimes regarded a text's lack of historical or semantic sense as a good thing, an opportunity for figural or otherwise more profound explorations. Indeed the greatest of them, Origen of Alexandria, taught that God had deliberately provided meaningless or offensive bits of scripture to frustrate our preoccupation with scripture's surface sense and open us to its spiritual depths. It will probably be apparent that this is one principle of premodern interpretation with which I am uneasy, despite my admiration for the theologians who employed it—indeed, this is perhaps a point where I and other commentators in this series will go different ways.

It should not be denied that the Spirit can make use of invincibly obscure passages and the free figural or speculative appropriation for the edification of the church and that this too belongs to scripture's "inspiration." But the historical sensibility that emerges with modernity, however problematic we may find it, inhibits modern—even postmodern—Christian scholarship from divining spiritual meaning without some basis in historical or otherwise plain meaning, however hard it often is to discover what exactly a plain meaning is. Sticking to a perhaps plain reading of "plain," I have to regard the inhibition as a blessing: it is not true that the figural exegesis of the church fathers and medievals was in general arbitrary or uncontrolled, but when the text before them was obscure they were sorely tempted. If refraining from opportunity posed by texts like the present one means that sometimes the fruit of exegetical labor is slight, so be it. Anything more we must leave to the Spirit's guidance of a reader seeking edification, or of a preacher or teacher assigned a text he or she does not know how to deal with, or simply of our turning to scripture in the many other places where scripture lives in the life of faith.

---

3. I am indebted to Zimmerli 1979: 449 for even this much construal of the judgment against Rabbah; the indebtedness is so complete that it must this time be explicitly acknowledged.

EZEKIEL 22:1–16

THE CITY OF BLOOD

The prophecy begins normally with "the word of the Lord came to me" and with the word's address to Ezekiel as "you—son of a man." But provision of the messenger-word we expect to come next is delayed, to be fitted into a more specific assignment: Ezekiel is to be the accuser of Jerusalem in what we might now call a "virtual" judicial proceeding. The emphasized "will you judge?" does not ask about a possible antecedent desire on the part of Ezekiel, but recruits him to the role, rather as the Lord in the story of Isaiah's call asks, "Whom shall I send?" with no one there but Isaiah (Isa. 6:8). Ezekiel's call to "judge" is not to sit as a neutral magistrate behind the bench, but to act as the accuser; thus the juridical term is paralleled, in the language of Ezekiel's priestly tradition, with "declare to [Jerusalem her] abominations."

Ezekiel's prosecutorial brief from the Lord is compressed in a new name the Lord inflicts on Jerusalem: she is now "Bloody City." The name is transferred to Jerusalem from no less bloodthirsty a city than Nineveh herself (Nah. 3:1), of universally evil memory.

Ezekiel 22:3 then begins the word given for Ezekiel to proclaim, to be introduced as usual with "thus says the Lord." It has three parts, which—continuing the virtual trial—are steps in the prosecutor's side of a legal proceeding: 22:3–5 is an exordium; 22:6–12 recites a bill of particulars; and 22:13–16 stipulates the punishment to follow conviction.

The exordium develops Jerusalem's naming as "Bloody City" with rhetoric that carries a hidden argument. Jerusalem is filled with civil and ritual crimes (22:3–4); both together are bloody. We can perhaps supply the conceptual link that Ezekiel presumes: life—which in Israel's anthropology is represented by lifeblood—belongs to God, and when life is taken, whether legitimately or il-legitimately, he must be given a "reckoning" (Gen. 9:14–15). Crimes within the community are crimes against the Lord because they shed or can lead to shedding blood that belongs to the Lord; idolatrous sacrifices are crimes against the Lord because they devote the lifeblood of the animal to a god other than him. It is Jerusalem's failure to honor the Lord's claim on all life that here condemns her.

"Thou shalt not kill." We repeat it, and even in secularized societies do not invoke it only in synagogue or church. But *why* shall we not kill? A defining fea-ture of modernity, and even more of postmodernity—whatever we take that term to mean—is forgetfulness of the reason: that all lives belong exclusively to God, so that human creatures are not in their own interest to take life.[1] The sense of the commandment is not that putting to death is in all circumstances forbidden, but that humans are not to make decisions over life and death by their—even justified—desires, but only by command of the one to whom all lives belong. As our forgetfulness of this deepens, the boundary of the forbidden recedes: the blood of the unborn child is shed to preserve the autonomy—from whom?—of the mother; the life of the hopelessly diminished gives way to their or their care-takers' desire to escape; the criteria of a just war are conformed to the desires of *Realpolitik*. The bill of particulars in the next part of our text (22:6–12) will at its end explicitly state the origin of all crimes, civil or cultic: "You have forgotten me" (22:12).

By Jerusalem's sins against lifeblood, she has brought herself to her "time," she has brought her "day" near (22:3–4a). If we have been reading through Ezekiel, we know about this unqualified "time" and "day" (→7:1–9; →7:10–27). "The day" is the day when the Lord triumphs; "the time" is that appointed for the event. It is a feature of prophecy from Amos through Ezekiel that the Lord's triumph can—contrary to Israel's ideology—be his triumph over Israel rather than her enemies; and such is the case here. Moreover, the Lord's triumph of "the" day is for good and all; "the" time is not a time in the sequence of times. Is then the day that Jerusalem has brought on herself the day of her destruction in 586? Or is it the day of a last judgment and the beginning of a new age? Or indeed is it the day of Christ's crucifixion and resurrection? We should not distinguish.

Through most of this exordium, Jerusalem is the agent of her own downfall: she has brought it on herself (22:4a–c). Then suddenly the Lord identifies himself as the immediate personal agent of Jerusalem's punishment, of her "disgrace before the nations" (22:4d). This rhetorical switch is a manifestation of the way in which the particular God of Israel relates to his creation: the moral continuities that govern history and that eventually bring the cumulatively wicked to their downfall are not independent laws, but his personal willing and speaking presence.

1. Indeed, the initial sense of the commandment was probably simply the prohibition of vendetta: vengeance belongs to the Lord and to those he appoints to carry it out, not to the ag-grieved themselves.

Turning to the bill of particulars in 22:6–12, it seems unlikely that it is assembled from observation of daily events in Jerusalem, whether ordinary or in vision. Rather it directly invokes a code or codes of divine law, particularly of the sort we find in Lev. 17–26, the so-called Holiness Code. Israel has been told by the Lord what to do and not to do, inasmuch as the Lord is holy and she as his nation is to be holy (→20:32–44). She had done the opposite.

The list of crimes divides into three lists, of different sorts of crime (22:6–8, 9–11, 12). Each list begins by naming a crime that is done "to shed blood." This maintains a link to the indictment; and each of these crimes is of a sort that can in fact lead to literal bloodshed. The crimes that follow in 22:6–8 come straight from the kind of law that appears in the Ten Commandments. Those in 22:9–11 are idolatry and sexual pollutions.[2] These are always closely related in Ezekiel's judgments; indeed, rampant sexuality is his most powerful metaphor for Israel's general idolatry (→16:1–43; →16:44–63), linked by the actual practices of Canaanite fertility religion. And the crimes listed in 22:12 are financial crimes, a frequent subject of Israel's law. The bill of particulars is concluded and driven home with a second "says the Lord."

Now the Lord—speaking by Ezekiel—wraps up the prosecution by stipulating punishment (22:13–16). The Lord's handclapping gesture is perhaps to launch the agents of execution. Jerusalem expects to survive the onslaught of Nebuchadnezzar; she does not realize that the Lord himself is her enemy, against whom her bluster will not avail (22:14). The announced exile will be more severe than that of 597, which left the exiled community more or less intact; now the inhabitants of Jerusalem will simply be scattered (22:15). This scattering did not happen, and Ezekiel or editors will have known that when shaping our book; again, "the day" and its judgments cannot simply be identified with any temporal disaster.

The goal of judgment is to purify Jerusalem from her ritual and moral pollution. We are expected to understand that a bloody city is just so unclean, that is, excluded from contact with the Lord or his people: death is the Lord's great contrary, and shed blood is therefore the great pollutant (→5:5–17). This doctrine does not contradict that noted earlier, that all lifeblood belongs to the Lord. Insofar as shed blood is dying blood, even the burial of the dead requires ritual purification. The frightful purification imposed in our passage is for all the blood wrongly and willfully shed in Jerusalem's whole history, taken as one horrid event.

If the final disaster is to be Jerusalem's final purification, it would appear that at least some of Jerusalem's people must survive to be pure. And we are told wherein their purity will consist: this remnant will at last acknowledge the person of "the Lord," that is, in this context, they will acknowledge that they belong to the one whose name is יהוה and that he himself has been the agent of their disasters as he will be of their purified life. Given the tone of finality that runs through 22:13–16,

2. One perhaps requires explanation: to uncover a "father's nakedness" is to have sex with one of his wives.

we may ask whether this remnant is the exiles of 586 or the 144,000 of Rev. 7:4–8 or Jesus on his cross. In my judgment, we are yet again not to choose.

Finally, just before this conclusion, Ezekiel makes one of his leaps into theological depths. By scattering his people, the Lord will himself be profaned[3] in the eyes of the nations (22:16a). The Lord has publicly identified his name with this people; when they are scattered he is humiliated in his own person. In Ezek. 22 we saw him again and again spare Israel precisely to prevent this; now he accepts it. And then the further astonishment: this too will enable the remnant's knowledge that there is יהוה.

How can that be? Perhaps construals of this passage might be devised to mitigate the offense. But finally, יהוה can be revealed by his own humiliation only if humiliation somehow belongs to his divine identity. Christians believe that the one humiliated on Maundy Thursday and Good Friday is the second identity of God, and intrinsic to his being.

---

3. Faithful to its theology, the Targum converts this into its opposite: "I shall be sanctified through you" (Levey 1990: 69).

EZEKIEL 22:17–22

THE WRATHFUL REFINER

Ezekiel 22:17–22 is a "picture word" like the one in Ezek. 15. Here, however, the picture is neither introduced nor interpreted; a figure is simply presupposed and used in the course of direct address. The passage is thus very like a parable, and I will sometimes refer to it as one.

The text's formal organization is plain. The verses begin with the usual coming of the word to Ezekiel and the word's address to him as "you—son of a man." Ezekiel 22:18 is then addressed to the prophet himself. The Lord tells him what Israel has become in his eyes: she is "dross," the useless stuff that is produced and thrown away in the course of refining precious metal—within this figure, the precious metal is silver. Ezekiel is then provided with a messenger-word for this population of dross (22:19–22). The prophecy concludes with a variant of Ezekiel's regular "then you shall know" formula.

Commentators are agreed that Ezek. 22:17–22 is dependent on Isa. 1:24–25: "I will pour out my wrath . . . , I will smelt away your dross." And Ezekiel not only picked up the image; it was a standard prophetic trope, as we see from its appearance at Zech. 13:9 and Mal. 3:3. The currency of the figure is perhaps a reason why Ezekiel can be so sparing with context and explanation.

Very soon in the text we encounter a textual-exegetical problem that cannot be ignored: the way the word "silver" is placed in NRSV's version of 22:18 conflicts with what otherwise is surely the import of the verse and of the following messenger-word. NRSV lists silver as a component of what Israel has become in the smelting pot. Silver is of course not dross, but is rather the desired end product of the smelting. But 22:18 is supposed to set up the messenger-word of judgment that follows, in which Israel is pure dross, an amalgam of useless metallic by-products. The way NRSV rearranges 22:18 thus undercuts the verse's function.

In the Masoretic Text of 22:18, "silver" does not in fact appear in the list of the smelting pot's components. The word appears rather at the end of the sentence, as a dangling anomaly. If one translated the Masoretic Text with crude literal-ness, 22:18b–c would read: "The house of Israel have become dross to me, all of them—brass, tin, iron lead. In the smelter they have become dross. Silver." NRSV has emended the Hebrew text, and one can see why even while not approving the result: the dangling "silver" is indeed unsatisfactory.

A chief step in the ancient technique of refining silver-bearing ore was to mix it with base metals and melt them together: the base metals bonded with the ore's unwanted components and were then discarded, leaving purified silver. The NRSV translators have supposed that "silver" is displaced in the Masoretic Text by scribal error or other accident and must originally have belonged with the other metals in the smelting pot. While the resulting text accurately describes a smelting pot's contents at the beginning of the smelting process, the emendation wrecks the point of the instruction to Ezekiel, since the burden of his message is what Israel has turned out to be in the smelting—pure dross. But is not a silver smelting that produces no silver either a failure or strikingly peculiar? Indeed it is, and that, in my view, is the very point.

How then shall we read 22:18? I will keep as the text: "The house of Israel have all become dross to me—brass, tin, iron, lead. In the smelter they have become dross." I will leave the dangling "silver" to some future solver of textual mysteries.[1] And in consequence of this somewhat arbitrary proceeding, I shall indeed lack complete confidence in my exegesis of the prophecy.

Following the word to Ezekiel, he is given a messenger-word for the "house of Israel"—that is, whoever is left in the land. It begins, "Because you have all become dross, I will gather you into the midst of Jerusalem" (22:19). Therewith the figure is further resolved: the dysfunctional smelting pot is Jerusalem. The gathering of the people into this pot undoubtedly refers to a historical event actually in progress at the time of the prophecy: the flight of Judah's population from Nebuchadnezzar's troops to supposed safety in fortified Jerusalem. In fact, says the Lord, it is he who is driving them, into a Jerusalem that is a refiner's melting pot.

From here on, the figure is used against its own intrinsic suggestion, and in my judgment that is intended. As Isaiah and others in his train used the figure of a refiner and his pot, the point of the smelting was to rid Israel of her dross, leaving her silver. Here the melting down has no other outcome than itself (22:19–20). If there is indeed silver in the pot, its fate too is simply to be melted (22:21).

A refiner is expected to aim at a gratifying result of his smelting, the purified precious metal. Even when Isaiah and others use the refiner's fire as an image of

1. Or perhaps we should follow the Vulgate, which translates "they are become the dross of silver."

the Lord's wrath, that fire of wrath is also expected to produce a purified people. But as the Lord here tells of his smelting, there is no such goal; the messenger-word—in my judgment, deliberately—derails the expectations evoked by the image. Parables (→17:1–21) sometimes work that way. Hearers of Jesus's parable of the sower will have first reacted with, "But no proper sower would act like that!" The question then posed was, "That's right. But who might?" A similar but purely negative shock is intended here—or so I propose.

It was the exiles' and Jerusalem's last hope if everything was after all to come right: despite our idolatries, the Lord will not finally let us down, his wrath will end when Israel has been purified. But this parable advances in the expected story of the refiner and his pot to "you shall be melted" (22:21–22) and then simply breaks off. To "no refiner would stop there!" the parable leaves us with "but the Lord will now." Thus hearers and readers are left with "the fire of my wrath." Finally, this passage's version of Ezekiel's favorite concluding formula, "you shall know," brings the same message: the only knowledge of יהוה that Israel will gain from her disaster is that he is the one who has done it.

A general principle for interpreting prophets is that their messages of doom are intended to provoke and enable repentance. This is generally the case with Ezekiel, but—at least to all appearances—not always and not here. How are we to understand unqualified prophecies of destruction of the Lord's people? That is, how are we to understand prophecies that seem to say salvation history will just break off?

If for the moment we may look at the history of Israel's prophecy as if it were the history of a complex of ideas, we might say that as the prophets penetrated ever more deeply into the reality of the Lord and of human rebellion against him, that is, as their message became ever more clearly eschatological, more open to the final outcomes of the Lord's promises, they came to see that there could be no simple continuation from the actual history of Israel into a history in which God's loving will is unequivocally done. Pushed to clarity, even the notion of a righteous remnant will not work—for if the remnant is simply a selection from the existing people, what is to prevent them from beginning the process of rebellions and remnants anew? In Ezekiel's messages, the Lord sometimes simply asserts that it will not do this—"I *will* be king over you" (20:33)—but why not? Moreover and more important, the picture of a God who "pours out" his wrath until he gets over it, and then is nice to the survivors, does not finally fit Ezekiel's and the Old Testament's general story of God's judgment and love.

Much Christian theology will at this point suggest that the people of God in what we now know as history and the people of God in the kingdom of God are one people only as they are taken into the life of God, and so are one in the unbreakable unity that the triune persons have with one another. The Son is other than the Father; and in the cross and resurrection that otherness is stretched across the abyss between the rebellion of the people of God and

God's love of that very people. The unity of judgment that is love and love that is judgment is given only in God—that is to say, only in the unity of the cross and the resurrection—and is in God as pain inconceivably suffered there and nowhere else. As the dogma has it: "One of the Trinity suffered for us" (*unus ex trinitate passus est pro nobis*).

EZEKIEL 22:23–31

AFTER THE DAY

Ezekiel 22 gathers three proclamations of Jerusalem's destruction. The last, 22:23–31, presupposes the fall of Jerusalem and should be dated immediately after it. The account begins with a slightly compressed version of the familiar formulas: the word comes to Ezekiel, addresses him as "you—son of a man," and gives him the word to be spoken.

Ezekiel is to address the "land" in the second person, speaking to her[1] as a land made waste by "the day" of the Lord's indignation. The text and proper translation of the first phrase of 22:24 are uncertain (Zimmerli 1979: 465–67): is the land polluted or is it metaphorically draught stricken?[2] But the import of the verse as a whole is clear enough: the day of Jerusalem's fall has come and gone, and in its wake Judea is a desert.

Ezekiel is then given a list of the transgressions on account of which the Lord has inflicted this doom, and immediately the discourse shifts to the third person: "Her princes are . . ." and so through the catalogue. We will shortly attend to this bill of particulars itself, but already a formal aspect of the opening verses is theologically suggestive: the second and third persons seem to have been manipulated. Ezekiel is to begin in the second person, and when he speaks in this mode the addressee is evidently the land as such and not its population, since the land is explicitly said

---

1. It is no great matter, but the Hebrew pronoun is feminine both here and throughout the passage, and KJV, RSV, and the Septuagint all translate that way. One fears that someone among the NRSV translators was ideologically offended by the Hebrew and English custom of making cities and nations feminine.
2. NRSV punts with "cleansed."

185

to be deserted. But so soon as Ezekiel must mention people and their doings, in order to explain this desolation, he is directed to exclusive use of the third person. Thus it seems that address to hearers is carefully avoided—though we may assume there were in fact exiled hearers. Can this be because there is a sense in which, in the eschatological time frame that much of the passage's rhetoric evokes, there is indeed no longer anyone to hear? Is the prophecy to be spoken into something like a human void? As in the day announced at 7:10–17, there is a cessation of all human activity.

A similar vacancy is evoked by the second clause of the address to the land: the "day of indignation" has come and *gone*. This day is certainly the great day of the Lord's final victory, proclaimed by prophets beginning with Amos as the Lord's triumph over all rebellion—including that of the "rebellious house" of Israel—and invoked several times by Ezekiel. Prophetic discourse about the day (→7:10–27)[3] always tended to be absolute, to transcend any particular day with its particular divine triumph. Now this day has come, and the Lord, Ezekiel, and Ezekiel's hearers or readers look back at it. But can that day really become past, to be looked back at? If it does, what reality do we inhabit on its other side?

The absence of hearers and the oxymoronic past tense of the term "the day" together suggest that the Lord by this prophecy situates Ezekiel and his hearers and readers in something like an eschatological no-man's land. Yet this is not sheerly a state of nonbeing, for the prophet is there and we are there to read what he writes. The logic and rhetoric of the prophecy thus locate us somewhere between the "end" of this age, the day of this world's final judgment, and a here unidentified future, for the prophet's speech to invoke. But what future would that be?

Other prophets during the exile—including the great Second Isaiah (Isa. 40–66)—proclaimed a great new salvation, of supernaturally triumphant return to Jerusalem and of the city's universal glory as the center of a new regime of universal peace. But the historically[4] actual return from exile was far from matching such predictions, peace did not come and has not come, and the Second Temple lasted but a while.

Thus when we come to the great question of Ezek. 37, "Son of a man—these bones are the whole house of Israel. Can these bones live?," I will suggest that the history of old Israel effectively ends with this question. Israel is dead, and the question is whether she can rise again. From this point of view, even the return from exile happens in a sort of eschatological pause, in a long moment before— what? Christian faith will say that the rhetoric of 22:23–31 locates us just before the crucifixion and resurrection.

The bulk of 22:23–31 is then a record of the transgressions on account of which Judea has been desolated (22:25–29). The list is ordered by classes of society:

3. That it is here the day of "indignation" results from our passage's dependence on Zephaniah, which I will discuss shortly.

4. Again, of course, the question arises of what "historical" might mean.

kings, priests, state officials, country gentry. There was a prophetic tradition of such class-differentiated accusations in which Ezekiel shares; indeed there may be direct literary dependence on Zeph. 3:3–4.

The urban and rural proletariats appear only as anonymous victims of the listed classes, for the class located at the bottom, "the people of the land," are not those later despised under that label. These country people are in a position to oppress the needy; thus they are landowners who hire labor. If Ezekiel had been asked, "But do not the poor also sin?" he would doubtless have agreed that they do; but he does not advance their sins as a cause of the Lord's judgment on the nation. This is no doubt partly because ancient societies generally did not think of laborers or the poor as historical agents or as being responsible for weal or woe. But it is also because the Old Testament makes the welfare of those who cannot act on their own behalf a chief duty of those who can, a duty that Judea's elites have sloughed off.

Much recent Christian discussion of politics and social ethics has spoken of scripture's "preferential option for the poor." The first thing to be said is that there is indeed such a scriptural option and that the church and her theology must attend to it. The Lord "executes justice for the orphan and the widow, and . . . loves the strangers" (Deut. 10:18).

Nevertheless, the notion of a sort of fundamental option among economic classes—like many other such generalizing maxims—must be carefully wielded. It must not be made an overriding slogan by which all Christian social or other teaching is constrained. Nor are all movements aimed to combat some real or alleged oppression merely thereby made allies of the church. Thus recent liberation theology fruitfully appropriated some Marxist concepts; but those liberation theologians who made Marxism a general framework of their thought and saw Marxist parties as natural allies often came to theological disaster. Also the recent American cultural phenomenon that abstracts from the actual conditions of the poor and oppressed to construct a vague general class of "victims" and then proliferates groups who claim that status and its privileges is far removed from scripture's version of a preferential option.

The Lord concludes (22:30–31) with the judgment "poured out" because of the enumerated transgressions. The first of the two verses is another of Ezekiel's shocking surprises. Regularly in prophecies given to Ezekiel—including the two others gathered in Ezek. 22—the Lord insists that he himself is in person the one coming against Jerusalem, that Nebuchadnezzar and that his host are but masks (→17:22–24). Thus he appears in this verse as the very one who assaulted the breach by which the city was taken. But here he also tells how he looked for someone in the city to repair the walls and defend the breach against his own onslaught, thereby preventing him from destroying the city. He finds no such person and so enters the city.

By entering the city he destroys the whole land; the break in the trope from walled city to land is needed to bring the end of the prophecy around to the beginning. The verse does not say what would have qualified someone as defender of the breach, but the context suggests it would have been a king or prophet or other magnate who did not participate in the evils of his class and who led the people in returning to righteousness. The figure of Josiah may well be suggested.

The involvement—and indeed emotional involvement—of the Lord in his people's history could hardly be more drastically pictured than here. We find the Lord on both sides of Jerusalem's walls: assaulting the city for its evils and seeking someone to fend off his own attack. We have earlier found the Lord both pouring out his wrath on Israel and taking no "pleasure in the death of the wicked" (18:23). But we have not before found him doing both at once; we have not before heard of the Lord's internal conflict, of his hope for a savior from his own wrath.

Is such a conflict in God conceivable? Not according to the usual construals of deity. But much scripture suggests that we should reexamine some of those construals. Might we use the doctrine of the Trinity to construe the Lord's fighting on both sides of Jerusalem's walls? Does Christ's "My God, my God, why have you forsaken me?" express just such a conflict between God the Father and God the Son? It would go too far to say[5] that it expresses an actual break of divine oneness. But we should indeed think of the crucifixion as a moment in the life of the triune God that calls for reconciliation. The Lord's emotional position on both sides of the breach in Jerusalem's walls is an anticipation of the crucifixion and resurrection.

---

5. With Jürgen Moltmann, *The Crucified God*, trans. R. A. Wilson and John Bowden (Minneapolis: Fortress, 1993).

EZEKIEL 23:1–27

OHOLAH AND OHOLIBAH

Ezekiel 23 presents a combination of literary-theological features that those who have been reading through Ezekiel will have encountered before (→23:28–49).

First, the chapter is an editorial construction, consisting of a main passage (23:1–27) followed by attachments that are on the same theme but do not necessarily make quite the same point. Here the additions are plainly marked, by the formula that usually introduces a new messenger-word: "Thus says the Lord" or once "the Lord said to me." Since the additions are intelligible only if one knows the main passage, it is unlikely that they were ever independent prophecies; but we probably cannot reconstruct their historical relation to the main prophecy, and for our purposes need not try.

Next, the main passage is a broken allegory, formally much like the story in Ezek. 16 of Jerusalem as a wayward bride. Here as then, the Lord tells a story that we would readily classify as allegory—in that its referent is a set of events other than the one it overtly narrates—except that the Lord breaks into the story and addresses figures within it, thus appearing not only as the teller of the story but as an agent—and victim!—within it. In the discussion of Ezek. 16, I suggested that this is a literary form appropriate to the Lord's specific way of being with his people: he at once directs a history with them and is an actor in that history. It is the doctrine of the Trinity that displays the coherence of this dual role.

Finally, the story is told as an unrelatingly negative parody of Israel's salvation history with the Lord, a genre peculiar to Ezekiel in the Old Testament. Perhaps the most powerful such narrative is the one at 20:5–31, which tells a complete version of Israel's creed and allows Israel no single moment of faithfulness. But the present piece is a close second.

Our passage begins with the usual "the word of the Lord came to me." What first follows is not an instruction that and how Ezekiel is to prophesy, but a private recital to him. Only much later, with "therefore" (23:22), does the discourse turn into a messenger-word to Jerusalem, beginning as usual with "thus says the Lord." But even then there is no instruction to Ezekiel to relay the message; the Lord simply carries on with his discourse, so that he seems to speak as his own prophet; the general impression given by the text is of a God breathless to utter his indignation. Thus we encounter in the very rhetoric—as often in Ezekiel—the Lord's emotional involvement in his history with his people, however unwelcome such a phenomenon may be to those who with the pre-Christian Greek theologians[1] and many moderns construe deity as sublime immunity to temporal events.

The version of Israel's history that the Lord here recites to Ezekiel does not mention the patriarchs or the descent into Egypt or even the exodus. It begins with Samaria and Jerusalem, as juvenile wildlings in Egypt—one may here as elsewhere contrast Ezekiel's account with that of his near contemporary Jeremiah, "I remember the devotion of your youth, your love as a bride" (Jer. 2:2). Presumably the sisters' names in the allegory, Oholah and Oholibah, had some significance, but we lack the key (Zimmerli 1979: 483–84; Eichrodt 1970: 321–23).

Just as in 20:5–6, the covenant is made in Egypt, but that passage's theology of loving choice is wholly absent: we are told that the Lord marries two promiscuous young women, and nothing more. We are also told that the Lord and the two have children, presumably the people of Israel. That יהוה should actually have children born of sexual congress is of course an utterly impossible notion within Ezekiel's theology,[2] and that it here appears without further comment shows how little attention the reader is to pay to the allegory in its own terms. We then read nothing of wanderings in the wilderness or of the conquest of the land; the narrative skips straight to the monarchical states in Syria-Palestine.

There Oholah prostitutes herself to the Assyrians, to whom she submits for their glamour as warriors. At the same time she continues to yearn for the Egyptians who awakened her sexually. Therefore the Lord gives her up to the Assyrian lovers with whom she has thus played a double game, and they rape her and kill her children (23:5–10). The allegory could hardly be more transparent. Samaria submitted to the Assyrian warriors in 732, but simultaneously turned to Egypt for help against them. Samaria's destruction in 721 was then the Lord's judgment on these proceedings. We must shortly ask what exactly her transgression is supposed to have been.

Next it is Oholibah's turn (23:11–21)—and perhaps we can abandon separate consideration of the allegory and its referent. Jerusalem sees what happened to

1. In their own account, Plato and Aristotle and Plotinus were theologians of Parmenidean-Homeric religion and not the religiously neutered "philosophers" that the Western tradition has made of them.

2. It has been suggested that the widespread myth and cult of *hieros gamos* is the background. But Oholah and Oholibah are decidedly not goddesses.

Samaria but does not learn from it. She too submits to the Assyrians, then calls on the Babylonians to deliverer her from them,[3] having seen depictions of them as even greater warriors.[4] So she submits to Babylon. But then she dumps[5] Babylon also—here we are to think of Jehoiakim's rebellion. Thereupon the Lord abandons her, to the sack of 597. Even this does not wean her from entangling alliances, and she turns to her original seducers in Egypt.

At this point in the narrative we are in the present tense of the story, the time of Zedekiah's rebellion and appeal to Egypt for aid (23:19–21). The following verses, 23:22–27, are thus the Lord's message to Jerusalem, of the final disaster he will bring on her.

Three things are especially striking about the allegory in 23:5–21 and its use in 23:22–27. One is the constant presence of Egypt as temptation. Another is how strictly political the referent of the allegory turns out to be, despite the sexual imagery. And of course there is the remarkable imagery itself.

First, in Israel's normal confession of her history with God, Egypt always played a central role. It was of course the place of her bondage, but reference to Egypt also evoked Israel's founding deliverance at Passover and at the Reed Sea.

Reliance on Egypt against Mesopotamian powers was always the great temptation during the time of the Jerusalem monarchy's decline. In the allegory, Ezekiel makes this be an inability of the sisters to get over their first paramours. It is as if Israel had never really come out of Egypt. In the narrative of Exodus and Numbers, Israel in the wilderness repeatedly "murmurs" about how much better she had it in Egypt; Ezekiel here sees that longing as the real truth of her existence. Israel, says the Lord by Ezekiel, was from the start and always remained a liberated and chosen people who did not want to be free or different. A question is hidden in most of Ezekiel's prophesying: How is such a contradiction to be remedied?

Second, in the earlier allegory in →16:1–43 and →16:44–63, of Jerusalem as a whoring bride, the Astarte cult makes a material link between prostitution as an allegorical figure for unfaithfulness and the false worship by which Israel was in fact unfaithful, since the defining practice of Astarte's worship was temple prostitution. In our present passage, there is no such link. Thus in the present case the relation between the figure and the referent is unmediated: we have to leap directly from the allegory to the political history that it images. Perhaps this was a history of foolish policy, but how does political foolishness deserve the Lord's obliterating judgment?

The allegory's figure must supply the answer: the politics of appeal to Egypt or Babylon against Assyria or to Egypt against Babylon is worthy of judgment because it is unfaithful to the marriage bond with the Lord: if his bride is to be saved, he will do it, and he tolerates no rivals in this role. The story of Gideon's war

3. There was in fact such an embassy; see Zimmerli 1979: 486.
4. Examples of which have been preserved; see Greenberg 1997: 478–79.
5. The American slang is perfect for the point.

against Midian perfectly displays the Lord's position: he does not permit Gideon to attack until Gideon's force is too small to have any hope of victory, lest Israel "take the credit away from me" (Judg. 7:2–7). Even our passage's sole reference to idols (Ezek. 23:7) is here a political reference: an alliance, particularly between a great power and a dependency, always involved the weaker partner making room in the temple for the stronger partner's gods.

Plainly there is a practical problem with the Lord's claim: How are Samaria and Jerusalem supposed, in quotidian national existence, to live as the Lord demands? In recent theology, Stanley Hauerwas has urged, with unique and disquieting persistence, the defenselessness that must characterize God's people.[6] And indeed God's people as church or synagogue must and can eschew violence, even in self-defense; but God's people as Samaria and Jerusalem were a nation among the nations. Is the appearance in history of a peaceful *nation*—or tribe or empire or other political entity—possible? Is it conceivable? Could it perdure even long enough to be a community? Could the United States withdraw from all armed engagement simply because peace is always intrinsically preferable to violence?

In any event of these questions, those in the palaces of Samaria and Jerusalem were unable to see how they were to preserve the state without resort to military force and, if their own resources were inadequate, without resort to alliances— how, in effect, they could follow Gideon's example. But in taking the prudent course, they found themselves fighting not against Assyria or Babylon only but against the jealous Lord, a battle they could not win. In their dilemma lies the deep point of our text.

From its place after the fact, Christian theology can perceive that a king of Israel—whatever may be true of the rulers of other nations—would always find himself either defenseless against the world or fighting against the Lord. And Christian theology therefore supposes that in the last extremity no king of Israel could fulfill his role except by dying in the world, rising before God, and taking his people with him. It thus lay in the nature of Israel's national existence that her hope finally devolved to hope not in the next anointed one, but in a last Anointed One. And that when he appeared he would be crucified and rise.

Third, what are we to make of the extraordinary sexual imagery?[7] Ezekiel's understanding of the Lord's covenant with Israel as a marriage naturally suggests appropriation of love imagery for their relation, as in the Song of Songs.[8] This in turn suggests parody of such language for the adulterous relation between Israel and other lords. And the parody will want to make the adulteries of Oholah and Oholibah as gross as possible. Even so, there is a strange energy behind all this talk of fondled breasts and male emissions.

6. One should first turn to the book that made Stanley Hauerwas known: *The Peaceable Kingdom* (Notre Dame: University of Notre Dame Press, 1983).

7. The Targum is so shocked by it that it suppresses it altogether (Levey 1990: 70–72).

8. Robert W. Jenson, *Song of Songs*, Interpretation (Louisville: John Knox, 2005).

The ancient world was almost as soaked in gross sexual language and imagery as is late Western modernity—consider only the depictions on the choicest Attic vases. Moreover, the source of this pansexuality was religion: in one way or another, humanity has generally supposed that the congress of Father Sky with Mother Earth is the primal fact from which all derives and by which all is to be explained, and the ancient Middle East was zealous in this conviction. Ezekiel had only to look about to find his parody.

It lies in the nature of religion to have this sexual afflatus. The great religious-metaphysical problem has always been—in one formulation—that of "the one and the many." The world in which we find ourselves seems to be a bewildering and manifold chaos; if we are to master it we must suppose that it nevertheless hangs together somehow, that somehow it is one. And the great presenting instance of unity-in-multiplicity is the physical fact and ecstatic experience of sexual union. Moreover, from that oneness new multiplicity derives: all the ancient accounts of derivation of the many from the one—even the sublime emanationism of the Platonists—are modeled on the emergence of children from the womb, children who are at once like the mother and distinct from her.

There is of course truth in humanity's primordial association of deity and sexuality, and Judaism and Christianity also reckon with it. The question is: Do we interpret God and his relation to the world by antecedently experienced sexuality, or do we interpret our sexuality by antecedent knowledge of God and creation? Does God show the image of our passion, or is our passion a mystery that shows God's antecedent love for his people? " 'For this reason a man will leave his father and mother and be joined to his wife, and the two will become one flesh.' This is a great mystery, and I am applying it to Christ and the church" (Eph. 5:31–32).

Finally we come to the actual messenger-word to Jerusalem, that unveils the—not very well hidden—secret of the allegory (Ezek. 23:22–37). By now it is almost an anticlimax. Summarizing: the Lord will do to Jerusalem what he did to Samaria; he will bring all the nations with whom she was unfaithful against her and "commit the judgment to them" (23:24). That the Lord can thus marshal whatever nations he needs, and moreover that their laws will suffice for Jerusalem's condemnation, is simply presumed.

The place of the closing formula "they/you shall know that I am . . . ," which is regular for this sort of judgment, is here taken by "I will put an end to your lewdness. . . . You shall not long for . . . Egypt any more." Whether this final cure of Israel's unfaithfulness is to be a new beginning—and then necessarily eschatological—or is to be accomplished simply by the abolition of Israel is not resolved in this passage.

EZEKIEL 23:28-49

THE SISTERS AGAIN

Ezekiel 23:28–49 is a series of attachments to →23:1–27. The collection is unmistakably an editor's grab bag, bringing five pieces of varying form, message, and quality, united only by being somehow related to 23:1–27. The divisions between them are easily discernible, marked by the formula that introduces a new messenger-word: "Thus says the Lord" or (once) "the Lord said to me."

Ezekiel 23:28–31 is a messenger-word in proper form. It presents a short version of the indictment and announced judgment of the main text and may well be a word spoken to Jerusalem just before her fall—at, of course, Ezekiel's frequent long distance. The Lord will give Jerusalem into the hands of the lovers she has turned from, the Babylonians, and they will treat her in accord with her treachery. The allegory has all but disappeared, as has the name Oholibah.

Two material deviations from 23:1–27 should be noted. The religious aspect of Jerusalem's faithlessness is in the foreground as there it was not: Jerusalem will be destroyed because she has "polluted" herself with Babylon's idols. This returns to Ezekiel's more usual emphasis. And the outcome of Babylon's revenge will be that Jerusalem's failed policies will be "exposed" as the religious promiscuity they are at heart. This threat to unveil the truth is more in the line of Ezekiel's usual thinking: formally it more resembles his favorite "then you/they shall know" than does "you shall not . . . remember Egypt," which ended the original version.

Ezekiel 23:32–34, though presented as a messenger-word, is a powerful poem built around an image widespread among the prophets.[1] Jerusalem will be given

1. For the Old Testament variations and allusions, see Greenberg 1997: 492–93 and Zimmerli 1979: 490–91.

her sister's "cup," from which she will drink the same "horror and desolation" as did Samaria. The poem ends spectacularly when in a frenzy of self-loathing the woman tears out the breasts that so many have fondled. A relation to the main text appears only in the reference to sisters in 23:31, and that may be an editor's construction to attach the poem to the collection.

The "cup" of "the wine of wrath" is a figure that runs through later scripture. The image obviously offers itself: draining too "deep and wide" (23:32) a cup of wine leads to disaster in especially plain fashion. At the image's earliest appearance in scripture, Jeremiah is given the cup and sent to make the nations drink from it (Jer. 25:15–17, 27–28). The present prophecy then says that Jerusalem herself must drink the cup. And when this prophecy had been fulfilled, the Second Isaiah called Israel back from disaster with "rouse yourself, . . . you who have drunk at the hand of the LORD the cup of his wrath" (Isa. 51:17).

The cup reappears as the suffering that Jesus must undergo, that his disciples will endure in his train (Matt. 20–23), and at the end will be the cup from which worshipers of the beast will drink "the wine of God's wrath" (Rev. 14:10)—and in the American Civil War the armies fighting slavery saw the Lord "trampling out the vintage where the grapes of wrath are stored." If we were to trace the whole tradition of the cup of the Lord's wrath, we would find something like an entire doctrine of incarnation and atonement.

Ezekiel 23:35 is a prophecy in one sentence. But it is not so routine as may appear on quick reading, for in Israel's ontology forgetting is a freighted matter. That past events are remembered means that they are cultically or morally reenacted and that when this is done they are effectively present—as at every Passover the participants pass over from Egyptian bondage into life. Thus the remembering here in question is like that of the Eucharist: "Do this, for my remembrance." Conversely, to forget something is to sever the living relation to it; thus if Israel has forgotten the Lord, this means that they have cut themselves off from his saving acts—from exodus and Sinai and the promise of the land—so that Israel is now a crowd of individuals with no sacramentally bonding history.

Ezekiel 23:36–45 is a literary and logical chaos—unless there is some coded order invisible to the naked modern eye. Oholah and Oholibah are back, though we cannot tell whether the prophecy is supposed to target both or one of them. The opening line is simply borrowed from 20:4: "You—son of a man, will you judge?" The declaration that follows is sometimes directed to Ezekiel and speaks of "them" in the third person, and sometimes is directed in the second person to those being judged; within the present text there is no apparent reason for the shifts. And indeed, who is being judged? Where there is direct address the verbs have a singular object suffix, so that the addressee is singular and is presumably Jerusalem. But when the discourse abruptly changes to the third person in 23:44b–45, the target is explicitly identified as both sisters. The punishment of Samaria and Judah seems to happen at the same time, though of course Samaria fell a century and a half before Judah. Plainly there is a complicated and rather chaotic textual history behind the text as we have it, a history that is now not likely to be untangled.

The content of the indictment will for the most part be familiar to readers of 23:1–27. Two features are new, not appearing in the model prophecy.

First, the sister/sisters is/are shown dressing and making up for lovers and setting the scene for assignation. This reminds us of the Astarte-worshiping Jerusalem of →16:1–43 and →16:44–63. But it can hardly be by accident that they are also so remarkably like the seductress of Prov. 7. Whether or not there is a an actual literary relation to the wisdom tradition, the imagery now has a different context than it had in the main text.

Second, the "abomination" of child sacrifice, central to the problematic of 22:1–31, recurs here as Ezekiel's chief indictment of Jerusalem. Not only do Jerusalem's mothers sacrifice the Lord's children—the people of Israel—giving them to the idols "for food"; when they are done they appear in the Lord's temple, bearing their pollution with them. Ezekiel →7–8 told how pollution by death renders sanctuaries permanently unfit for the Lord—or indeed for any sort of worship. What then must be the pollution brought from such death as this, of children offered to Molech?

We come to the last attachment. Ezekiel 23:46–49 seems to misunderstand the primary text (Zimmerli 1979: 492). An assembly is summoned to judge "them"; presumably these are—at least in the present text—supposed to be the sisters of the original allegory. But—insofar as I can at all make out the purpose of this assembly—this glossator has taken the allegory literally,[2] for the assembly is to try and punish certain degenerate women;[3] thus the stipulated punishment is stoning, which the law prescribes for fornication (Deut. 22:24). This is to be done as a warning to women generally not to "commit lewdness" (Ezek. 23:48). It may be that the sexual rite of the Astarte cult (→16:1–43; →16:44–63) is specifically intended, since "lewdness" and "sinful idolatry" are paralleled in 23:49. Thus what was an allegory of the two Israelite states here becomes a moral and religious exhortation to women at large.

It is tempting to note that this last attachment to 23:1–27 has misunderstood that text (Zimmerli 1979: 491–92). But this observation would be hasty, for there is in fact a causal connection between sexual disorder and general civil and political disorder (Jenson 1997–99: 2.73–94). Probably the deviser of 23:46–49 did not have this connection explicitly in mind; the connection in the canonical text may authorize us to consider it.

There is one and only one place where the synchronic and diachronic dimensions of community intersect: the heterosexually based family, in which persons are joined with unique intensity, by union of the bodies as which persons are present

2. Eichrodt 1970: 333 unconvincingly presses the other possibility: that the loose women are still Samaria and Jerusalem and that the "other women" are the Gentile nations.
3. The Targum supports this reading (Levey 1990: 73).

to one another, and from which union the next generation derives. It is a platitude to say that the family is the base unit of any society; but it is a platitude because the saying so ineluctably describes a simple fact. Only a society that dualistically thinks of the body as one thing and the person who "has" that body as another thing can overlook that fact.

A society that displaces sexuality from its place in this structure, that does not by law and custom hold its core community together, will lack intrinsic coherence and over time will be able to hold itself together only by force; sexual liberation and political tyranny are ontologically coupled. It is a grimly laughable delusion to suppose that society and polity have no stake in what people do "in the privacy of their bedrooms"; there is nothing else in which the public has so primary an interest. Thus an editor's attachment of 23:46–49 to 23:1–27 in fact traces a profound connection—that may even have been felt by the editor.

We are done with Oholah and Oholibah. One may think it is none too soon.

EZEKIEL 24:1–14

THE COOKING POT

We come to another of the dated prophecies that appear at intervals through Ezekiel's book—in our calendar, the date works out to mid-January 588 (Greenberg 1997: 496). As before, the date begins the passage; after it we read that the word of the Lord comes to Ezekiel and as usual addresses him as "you—son of a man." The following instruction, however, is unique in the book: Ezekiel is to write down the date. The command to write is typical of the apocalyptic mode of prophecy that we find elsewhere in Ezekiel (→1:1–3), and indeed if the following verses were cast as a vision we would unhesitatingly assign the passage to that genre.

In this case, to be sure, insistence on noting the date in writing is not in itself surprising, since it is the date of a long-feared event, and one decisive in many connections: Nebuchadnezzar has begun his final siege of Jerusalem. Ezekiel proclaimed the end of Jerusalem throughout the years since it was first sacked; now the judgment has begun. Will it be as total as he has said? Ezekiel is given prophecies suited to the occasion.

That the tenth day of the tenth month of the ninth year from the beginning of Jehoiachin's reign was indeed the day on which Nebuchadnezzar invested Jerusalem is apparently confirmed by the historical notice at 2 Kgs. 25:1. Precisely this confirmation, however, has "repeatedly given trouble to commentators" (Zimmerli 1979: 498). How did Ezekiel in Babylon acquire this information on the very day of the event?

Could Ezekiel see at a distance? Or is Ezekiel's agreement with 2 Kings a coincidence? Or was Ezekiel after all in Judah at the time? Or did Ezekiel just guess, and 2 Kings then take the date from his book, so that neither can be trusted? Eichrodt (1970: 336–37) and Zimmerli (1979: 498)—our two historical-critical stalwarts—conclude that the date must have been inserted or altered later, perhaps when information arrived in Babylon or perhaps from 2 Kings or its documentary source. The one possibility not canvassed by either or by the many whose views they report is that what the text says happened really did happen: on a day whose date Ezekiel knew or later checked, the word of the Lord came to him in such fashion that he knew the siege was just then beginning.

The exegetes' struggle here gives occasion to pose a hermeneutical decision that is fundamental for interpreting Israel's prophets: Do we believe that what the prophets understood as prophecy can occur, or do we not? Modern exegetes—even such pious persons as Eichrodt or Zimmerli in fact were—have not believed it. I agree that Ezek. 24:1 may in fact be a later editorial dating; independent linguistic and historical arguments can be marshaled for this (Zimmerli 1979: 498–99), which may or may not be decisive. But we should surely question the dogmatic assumption that it *cannot* have happened as the text says it did, that it is merely unthinkable that God can have enabled a prophet to know a fact he would not otherwise have known.

The question marks a sharp line between premodern and modern exegesis of biblical prophecy: Can actual prophecy have happened? Not moral or religious interpretation of events—which, after all, the false prophets could do—but knowledge of God's own intention by human persons?

Christian theology should remember: according to the doctrine of the Trinity, God's sharing of knowledge and intention belongs to his very being; the Son simply *is* God's knowledge and intention; and he is this *as* an other than the Father. Moreover, as it in incarnational fact happens, the Son is a human person; thus human sharing of God's knowledge and intention certainly is real in his case. Moreover, Christian faith supposes that to be a human is precisely to be over a lifetime conformed to this human. It must follow that actual prophecy is possible also with other humans.

Ezekiel is next commanded to "utter a *mashal* [משׁל]"—a formulated saying— "to the rebellious house," which must in this instance be the exilic community. The simplest possibility—though perhaps not the only one—is that the *mashal* is the poem that follows at 24:3b–5, here cited as a messenger-word to Israel with "thus says the Lord."

Taken for itself, the poem is nothing more remarkable than a—nicely—versified instruction to make a good meal for a substantial company.[1] It is possible that we are intended to think of the earlier use of a pot-and-contents image at 11:3; there it appears as a saying circulating in Jerusalem after the first capture, expressing the cozy fit between the city, as the pot, and the remaining local elites, as the choice bits. The interpretations that here follow the *mashal* should then be understood as judgments upon this presumption. I am, however, inclined to think that the

---

1. Eichrodt 1970: 338 accepts a form-critical suggestion that the poem was originally a "working song" for cooks.

poem is too long and irrelevantly detailed to carry such a point; moreover, nothing but the existence of 11:3 suggests that it might.

If the instruction were addressed to the prophet, it would be a typical mandate for a prophetic sign, an *oth*: cook a big meal in public view and wait until someone asks what this is for.[2] And on reflection we may think that 24:3a indeed mandates an *oth*, which varies from the norm only in that the prophet is to recruit others to participate in enacting it, by telling them to "make a good meal in a big pot" and enforcing the command as a word from the Lord. I will adopt this reading. We should envision Ezekiel and others standing around a full pot set over a good fire, with Ezekiel waiting for them to ask, "Why are we doing this?"

Ezekiel 24:6–14 is then a series of verbal prophecies, each interpreting the *oth*. There seem to be too many of these for one *oth*: a first starts at 24:6, a quite different one at 24:9, and perhaps another at 24:12. Moreover, their mutual references are very hard—in my view impossible—to straighten out. These phenomena have of course occasioned proposals about interpolations and relative datings. I will not depend on any such reconstruction, but will take up 24:9–10 first and so out of textual order, since the connection of these verses to the *oth*—or anyway to the poem, if no *oth* is intended—is direct and clear and that of the intervening verses is not.

The Lord sends his word by Ezekiel: "Woe to the bloody city!" Thus the pot and its contents are identified as Jerusalem and her inhabitants. The first word after the lamentation is "I": the Lord himself will take up cooking—just as in earlier prophecies of judgment the Lord says that he himself will wield the sword. He will build an immense fire and cook the contents of the pot until the meat is boiled to nothing[3] and the marrow and bones are burned up. As an evocation of the Lord's wrath and the doom it will inflict, this could hardly be surpassed.

Why, however, is the city "bloody"? To answer that, we have to go back to the previous prophecy (24:6–8). It may therefore be thought that we should have begun with that passage. We did not because it condemns the pot for something that has no correlate in the *oth*: the pot is eaten with rust, from the blood in it—and the food seems to have disappeared.

As repeatedly noted, in Israel's law shed blood pollutes both those who shed it and the place where they do this. And blood unjustly spilled calls from the ground for vengeance, which notoriously belongs to God—thus the Lord says to Cain: "The voice of your brother's blood is crying to me from the ground" (Gen. 4:10 RSV). But those who spilled blood in Jerusalem have not so much as bothered to kick earth over the blood to hide it, or even to choose a place where this could be done; they think themselves immune, and their violence is heedless (Ezek.

---

2. The Targum is apparently so puzzled by the instructions that it eliminates them altogether and replaces them with a composition of its own (Levey 1990: 74–75).

3. The motivation for the NRSV's idea that the Lord is only going to cook the meat "well" escapes me: the lexicons give "finish," "do . . . totally," etc., and that is surely the obvious point here.

24:7). Indeed, the Lord himself has so ordained it, in order that the call to him for vengeance may be apparent (24:8).

Since it is the city herself that has shed this blood (24:7a), we should probably not think of the general rate of assaults and homicides in Jerusalem. The reference must be to blood shed by agents of the state; and in Jehoiakim's and Zedekiah's repressions of opposition to their rebellions against Babylon, there will have been enough such blood (Eichrodt 1970: 338–39). If the famous and feared Jeremiah could be thrown into a cistern filled with filth and saved only by influence at court (Jer. 38:6–11), what could not be done with less prominent citizens? "Jerusalem, Jerusalem, the city that kills the prophets and stones those who are sent to it!" (Matt. 23:37).

Turning to the verses before and after Ezek. 24:9–10, we find that the figure they develop is not cooking in a pot but some pot's own rusty condition, of which there is no suggestion in the *oth*. Thus these verses do not seem to interpret the *oth*, yet neither can they be disentangled from 24:9–10, which do. I will not try to explain this, but simply carry on with the text.

Jerusalem is like a pot deeply eaten by rust; since the woes are pronounced upon a bloody city, the rust is probably the social and legal disintegration that follows violent political repression. The Lord has worn himself out trying to remove the rust, to no avail; repair is hopeless (24:6b, 10a, 13). And now we are partially returned to the image of cooking (24:11): when the Lord has cooked the pot's contents to nothing, he will set the empty pot on the fire and keep that burning until the pot melts. Finally he will be rid of the rust.

At every step in Ezekiel we encounter some offense to Western theology's generally presumed construal of deity, of what it means to be God, according to which deity means immunity to the affects that temporal events inflict on mortals. But in Ezekiel we regularly encounter the Lord's emotional involvement in the historical vicissitudes of his people. Now we even find him *laboring* in that history and, moreover, failing to achieve his goal by the methods initially employed. It does not ameliorate the clash to speak of "metaphor" or of allowable "anthropomorphism." Of what is this consistent portrayal supposed to be a metaphor—unless that somehow the Lord is not immune to affect? Or what is the ground of the anthropomorphism's possibility—if not a humanity of the Lord?

Ezekiel 24:13b brings divine frustration and emotional affect together: "You shall not again be cleansed, until I have satisfied my fury upon you." No further attempts at reform will be made. Jerusalem will be melted down—then we will see. This concludes the interpretation of the *oth*—if that indeed is what the verses about rust and melting are. Ezekiel 24:14 then concludes this whole proclamation of Jerusalem's imminent doom: be under no delusion, I will act, it is too late for petition, "says the Lord יהוה."

EZEKIEL 24:15–27

NO MOURNING

The word of the Lord comes to Ezekiel, addresses him as "you—son of a man," and speaks to him, at first directly. If we have been reading in Ezekiel generally, all this is routine.

But what the Lord then says to Ezekiel (24:16–17) may be the most shocking passage in his book: the Lord first says he will take away Ezekiel's wife and then commands him to take the event as occasion to put on a performance—to enact a prophetic sign, an *oth* (→3:22–5:4). It is, however, vital to restrain our protest long enough to discern precisely what offenses the text actually presents. To do that, we must notice and remember how rhetorically ascetic, how stripped of narrative or logical connectives, this word of the Lord to Ezekiel is. We may be tempted to supply the missing connections; if we are to understand the passage, we must not yield to temptation.

The Lord informs Ezekiel that his wife will die suddenly. But the Lord does *not* say why, he does not give an ulterior reason for her death. He indeed says that her death will be his act, that he will "take" her. But he does not state his motive for taking her. In particular, he does not say that he is doing this in order to set up the *oth* that he will next ordain—tempted though we may be to suppose this connection. The death is announced as a fact; the sign is mandated; the relation remains contingent.

The beloved woman's death is indeed announced as the Lord's own act: he will "take" her. This may alarm modern sensibilities. But we must ask: How else would we have the matter stated? Among some raised in the faith, the locution still appears: as comfort ("the Lord took her in her sleep") or as complaint ("why did the Lord take him now?"). And there was reason for the locution—that such language is disappearing in much of the church is not a good sign. If a human person's death is no one's act, if it is simply an impersonal something that occurs, then it is meaningless and with it the life that it ends—for then it is not the conclusion of a human story with some shape to it, but simply a cutoff. But if then someone acts here, who would we want that to be, if not the Lord? Simply the doctor who slipped, or the enemy combatant? Or if there is no other person to be blamed, perhaps Satan?

"The Lord gives and the Lord takes away" can be followed in two ways: "Therefore all human life is vanity" or "Blessed be the name of the Lord." It depends on what we think the Lord is like. And the final answer to that is the Father's resurrection response to the Son's "why have you forsaken me?"

In my opinion, the first shock we *should* feel is the ordinary one inflicted by Ezekiel's sudden loss. It is, to be sure, some relief to discover that he loved his wife—with prophets you never know (Hos. 3:1–3). But that of course only sets up the wound. In my opinion, readers are intended to be jolted simply by the event itself—the ending of a mutual love can eclipse the fall of cities, even of Jerusalem. And to the ineluctable question "why her, and why now?" there is no answer; or anyway none avowed by Ezekiel. When the beloved dies, we *should* protest and set the burial rites in motion and not be quickly comforted. Which leads us to the second shock that the passage delivers.

This is not that the Lord takes the death as occasion to lay an *oth* on Ezekiel, but rather the content of the *oth*. Ezekiel is forbidden all expressions of his loss; only interior anguish is permitted. He is forbidden both the wailing and visible depression that are—at least in the Middle East—the natural expression of loss and the rituals of mourning established within his culture: hair loosed from the turban,[1] bare feet, a wake with its special food, and whatever the business with the upper lip was. Both natural and conventional signs of grief have the function of regulating it, lest in one chaotic explosion it destroy the bereft person. Ezekiel is forbidding this negotiation.

Ezekiel is then told to appear in public, displaying his apparent lack of affect and ritual conformity. Thereby his behavior becomes a sign: members of the exilic community predictably ask him why he is acting this way (24:19), and this gives him opportunity to deliver his interpreting messenger-word from the Lord (24:21–24).

The function of the sign depends upon the analogy between Ezekiel's wife as his love and the temple as the exiles' love, with the added poignancy in the case of the exiles that they are separated from it, so that it has been their "desire" (24:21). The message Ezekiel now brings from the Lord is that the Lord will take away the temple as he has taken away Ezekiel's wife—and for good measure the loved ones still in Jerusalem, who are a sort of secondary analogue to Ezekiel's love. He will take away the temple by profaning it, which here must be by allowing Gentile

---

1. The Targum has "wear your phylacteries" (Levey 1990: 74–75).

troopers to trample its courts and mock its God. Again, we are not told why the Lord will do this; here also the style matches that of the announcement of Ezekiel's bereavement—and in any case any who have read through Ezekiel to this place will know more than they want to know about Jerusalem's transgressions.

It is not, however, the destruction of the temple that is the chief matter of this prophecy, but rather that when the exilic community hears of the event they will replicate Ezekiel's strange behavior (24:24). Despite the opinion of some exegetes (e.g., Eichrodt 1970: 343; Greenberg 1997: 514–15), we should probably follow most English translations and read the verbs in 24:22–23 as imperatives: "You shall." The Lord does not foretell that the news of Jerusalem's fall will so undo the exiles as to deprive them even of mourning, he commands them to abstain from it.

But how are we then to understand this "you shall"? As fully parallel to that laid upon Ezekiel, and so as a mandate to be obeyed? What, however, would be the point of such a mandate? The parallel can hardly extend to the purpose of Ezekiel's behavior, for to whom would Israel's abstention be a gain? It is when the news of Jerusalem's fall arrives that the exiles will or will not begin to mourn; and if they indeed do not mourn, the sign-relation between Ezekiel's earlier behavior and theirs will become apparent (24:25–26). But what sign-relation would at that time emerge between the exiles and some other people or nation? We might perhaps imagine one, but our construction could claim no attachment in the text.

I propose that in the "you shall" addressed to the exiles we see a grammatical form of the prophetic word's effective power. The Lord commands Israel to be like Ezekiel, and precisely so they become those who must experience this. They are commanded to refrain from natural and ritual mitigation of their loss, and just so they are in fact deprived of it. And when the command becomes their lot, they will indeed know that the one who spoke it is *yhwh* and that he is the only Lord (24:24). If support for this reading is needed, it can be found in the effective force generally attributed to the prophetic word, and with special insistence in the case of Ezekiel.

The final verses of this prophecy (24:25–27) are a nest of problems. The first verse recapitulates the deprivations just proclaimed for the exiles. The subsequent verses mostly double 33:21–22, which seems to say that someone will arrive from Jerusalem on the day of its fall, with the news of that event. Considering the distances, this is a manifest impossibility—barring a shamanistic wonder that the text does not adduce—and the final editor of Ezekiel's book will have known that. But what then?

Finally among difficulties: although the scope of these verses is Ezekiel's release from a God-imposed period of speechlessness, they do not say when or why this period began. It may be that it was very short: 33:22 is probably the original within the doublet, and there we read that "the hand of the Lord" had been "upon" Ezekiel the previous evening, perhaps inflicting silence by the onset of a vision (→1:1–3).

For the purposes of commentary, we need not speculate about the textual history behind these phenomena. What is clear is enough to be going on with: after Jerusalem has fallen, one of the new group of deportees arrives to inform the earlier exiles of the event. This restores Ezekiel from an unspecified time of dumbness.

That God sometimes made Ezekiel dumb and later released him to prophesy seems indeed to be somehow decisive for his sending, for it appears early in the book's account of Ezekiel's ministry and in connection with defining events of that ministry (3:15, 26–27). Ezekiel 3:26–27 may even suggest a sort of regular divine procedure in Ezekiel's case: imposed speechlessness as preparation for prophecy.

It is certainly true that when God's word comes to be spoken by creatures, it silences our chatter. As a great hymn has it, "Let all mortal flesh keep silence, and with fear and trembling stand . . . ; for . . . Christ our God to earth descendeth." We must not reverse this: whatever may be true of other alleged gods, the triune God is never silent, for he is eternally in himself the Word that enables all words. But *we* must sometimes be silent, if there are to be prophets. And if the church is to be what she claims to be (Acts 2:16–18), a sort of communal prophet, she too must sometimes be silent.

EZEKIEL 25:1–17

BAD NEIGHBORS

I must begin with a few paragraphs about Ezek. 25–32 as a group. In the middle of Ezekiel's book, these chapters are a collection of prophecies against Gentile nations, which may indeed have once circulated on its own. The group's location in Ezekiel's book is important for the book's structure in that it makes the transition from prophecies of judgment to prophecies of restoration. It does this in two related ways.

The prophecies collected in Ezek. 1–24 are with few exceptions directed against Israel, imposing judgment for her unfaithfulness. The prophecies collected in Ezek. 33–48 are, again with few exceptions, prophecies of Israel's restoration, indeed of eschatologically new existence, of a fellowship of God with his people that is intimate and fixed beyond the bounds of what is possible in this age. The interposition of prophecies directed against enemy nations makes a hinge for the shift: first prophecies against Israel, then prophecies against those who have acted against Israel, and then prophecies for Israel.

More materially, these prophecies in the center show the Lord as Lord not just of Israel; also enemy or treacherous nations will be made to "know that I am יהוה." Moreover, he will enforce this claim on them by whatever created instrumentality he chooses, whether Nebuchadnezzar or raiders from the Arabian steppes (25:4–5). These chapters display the universality of the Lord's rule as the possibility of his action to restore Israel: if the Lord is Lord outside of Israel, then he is not bereft of power even when his particular people have none. He can even if he chooses use one of the other nations to restore Israel. And indeed, the other great prophet of the exile, Second Isaiah, will acclaim Cyrus, the Persian conqueror, as the "shepherd" who will carry out the Lord's decision to restore Jerusalem and the temple (Isa. 44:28).

The prophecies are transitional also biographically and historically. The prophecies of Israel's punishment were obviously delivered before Jerusalem's final disaster. The prophecies of restoration mostly follow that event. The prophecies in Ezek. 25–32 are structured by a series of dates; and the dates fall in the tenth through the twelfth years of Jehoiachin's exile; thus these prophecies cluster around the disaster itself. Ezekiel's prophesying had itself a history: God's word in Ezekiel's mouth not only moved history but moved with the events it impelled. We should not think of the word of God as a static content that simply is what it is, not even when we say that the Word is eternal with God, as at John 1:1 or in the developed doctrine of the Trinity. The Word of God is precisely the agent and content of God's history with us and with himself.

As for the actual prophecies we find in this chapter and the rest of the group, they belong to a long tradition of oracles against enemy nations. Amos 1 is the form's earliest appearance in the writing prophets, but already in Amos the condemnations have a stereotyped form: "Because . . . has done . . . , I will. . . ." Prophesy against enemy nations must therefore have had some shaping context earlier than the preaching of the writing prophets—I allow myself a bit of proper form criticism. This was probably the presence of "men of God" in the camp when Israel went into battle, who were there to proclaim—indeed to invoke—the disaster of the enemy; we have accounts of this practice at 1 Kgs. 20:13 and 20:28 and an extended display of the notion of such prophecy in the wonderful story of the pagan prophet Balaam (Num. 22–24).

Ezekiel's oracles against enemy nations denounce seven of them, with messenger-words beginning "thus says the Lord" and with evocations of their guilt and punishment done in various genres. That they are seven surely once had some significance; perhaps it makes the nations mentioned represent the general hostility of the Gentile world, seven being commonly regarded as signifying totality.

The division of space is very unequal. Our present chapter takes care of four of the seven: Ammon, Moab, Edom, and Philistia, denouncing them much in the form we see in Amos 1. Tyre gets almost three more interesting and original chapters (26:1–28:19). A bare two verses (28:20–23) pick up Sidon, almost as an afterthought and perhaps merely to make up the seven. Finally and massively, Egypt has Ezek. 29–32 all to herself.

So to our present chapter. It is directed against Judah's nearest Gentile neighbors, who were indeed not notably good neighbors. The chapter has a customary introduction: the word of the Lord comes to Ezekiel, addresses him as "you—son of a man," and tells him to address messenger-words of doom to the Ammonites. As the chapter continues, this introduction is made to serve also for other near neighbors. In keeping with the stereotyped form of the four messenger-words, we can take them together.

All four nations will be destroyed as national or political entities. The announcements of judgment are very much in the style traditional from Amos on. Only one passage is lively enough to deserve special note. Ezekiel 25:4–5 describes what happens when nomadic tribes intrude into an agricultural society: they pitch their tents where they choose; though they grow nothing themselves, they eat up what peasants and merchants grow or have stored; and they degrade the cropland.[1]

The transgressions for which Israel's near neighbors are judged are more interesting than the announced punishments: their sins are not crimes or religious "abominations" such as Ezekiel denounces in Israel, but rather their hostile attitudes toward that same Israel. The chief of the Ammonites' several transgressions is that they laughed when the temple was profaned (25:3). Moab was delighted to see Israel's claim to be a special nation apparently refuted (25:8)—the Targum translates Moab's saying as a rhetorical question: "Why should those of the House of Judah fare differently from all the nations?," thereby capturing the point precisely (Levey 1990: 77). Edom found in Nebuchadnezzar's campaign an opportunity to avenge ancient humiliations by Israel (25:12; →35:1–36:15) and will be punished by similar humiliations (25:14). And from Israel's first entry into Canaan, the Philistines contested her independence there (25:15).

All these charges can be brought under one rubric: hostility to Israel's claim to be the special people of an exclusive God (as suggested by Eichrodt 1970: 356–64). The outcome of God's acts against the four nations will be, in each case but one, that they learn "that I am יהוה," that is, in this context, how very specific the God of Israel indeed is and how universally sovereign he just so is. The different formula in Edom's case should be no comfort to her: Edom will know the very particular vengeance of "the Lord יהוה," offended on behalf of his people (25:14).

The Gentiles—who include me and doubtless most readers of this commentary—have never fully shed the resentment shown by Ammon, Moab, Edom, and Philistia, our predecessors as Gentile neighbors of the Jews. The root of the world's inveterate and pervasive anti-Semitism has always been and still is offense at the claim that the one who is supposed to be God of us all has a special love and purpose for some of us, for this particular people. And even when Jews have themselves shied away from the claim to be a chosen people, the Christian scriptures keep on making it for them.

Judah's neighbors rejoiced to see the Lord seemingly abandon or be unable to sustain his people. And the Lord has continued again and again to appear in the same light, in the case of the Shoah so utterly as to call his very reality into question. And yet—where are the Nazis now? Vengeance was indeed visited upon them, by nations with no more love of the Jews than Nebuchadnezzar had when he worked judgment on Israel's neighbors.

1. Once upon a time, the Canaanites would doubtless have described the encroaching Israelite tribes in the same way.

God's continuing investment in the descendants of Abraham has regularly been questioned in the thinking of the church. Theology that went so far on this line as simply to deny any continuing special status of the Jews is now called "supersessionism." This theological opinion held that the church has in such fashion superseded old Israel, that there is no room for another true superseder: the church is a "new Israel" and continuing rabbinic Judaism is not.

No church has ever officially taught supersessionism, but the opinion was widespread. Following the Second World War and the Shoah, Christian theologians have regularly condemned supersessionism, and several churches have explicitly disavowed it. Exactly *how* Christian theology is to affirm the continuing status of the Jews in God's history with his people continues however to be a matter of debate.[2]

So-called inclusive Christian attitudes toward "the other religions" originate in offense at the biblical God's particularism in exactly the same way as does supersessionism. Inclusivism is only a typically modern form of the offense: Israel and her now paired successors—rabbinic Judaism and the church—are not to be allowed any special role between God and humanity.

---

2. For a symposium that proved significant for thinking on the problem, see Carl E. Braaten and Robert W. Jenson, eds., *Jews and Christians: People of God* (Grand Rapids: Eerdmans, 2003). For a particular and well-argued statement, see R. Kendall Soulen, *The God of Israel and Christian Theology* (Minneapolis: Fortress, 1996).

EZEKIEL 26:1–21

THE FALL OF TYRE

This is the first of two and one half chapters directed against Tyre, a group that is in turn part of a larger grouping (Ezek. 25–32) of oracles against Gentile nations (→25:1–17).

Anciently, the city of Tyre occupied an island just off the coast of what is now southern Lebanon. Her island location made Tyre secure from all but the most determined attackers and shaped her prosperity as a mercantile port and colonizing sea power, with wide connections over the Mediterranean. At the beginning of Israelite statehood, King Hiram of Tyre is said to have been David's ally (1 Kgs. 5:1). And at the end of the Davidic monarchy, Jerusalem and Tyre were briefly allied as leaders of the Syrian-Palestinian rebellion against Babylon.[1]

Our present chapter is a clearly marked unit, and its structure is one common in Ezekiel: there is a primary prophecy (26:1–6) to which three other germane passages have been attached (26:7–14; 26:15–18; 26:19–21). The dating is uncertain,[2] but the prophecies must have been given either immediately after the fall of Jerusalem or during the siege.

The primary prophecy is in the classic style of oracles against Gentile nations (→25:1–17). First the crime is adduced: "Because Tyre . . ."; then the punishment is announced in a messenger-word: "Therefore, thus says the Lord." That Ezekiel

1. Jer. 27:3 tells of a meeting of this coalition; it may be significant that the meeting was held at Jerusalem.
2. The Masoretic Text, the Septuagint, and even different manuscripts of the Septuagint vary; see Greenberg 1997: 529–30.

in Babylonia could be the Lord's messenger to far-off Tyre is an instance of the strange prophecy at a distance that was regularly mandated to him.

Tyre's sin, like that of those denounced in the previous chapter, was taking pleasure in her former ally's disaster. Jerusalem had been "the gateway of the peoples"; now Tyre expects that role to fall to her—foolishly, since she is next on Nebuchadnezzar's list. It is not clear what it meant to be "the gateway of the peoples" (Zimmerli 1983: 34).[3] Does the phrase refer to a position in international trade, or to a specific or dominating role in the politics of Syria-Palestine, or to something of a different sort altogether? Whatever position of honor or power it was that the saying attributed to Jerusalem, Tyre is delighted to see it vacant and available. And that is her crime, because Judah had been her friend and because disdain for Jerusalem is disdain for the Lord, whose city it remains—even when it is in ruins.

"Therefore, thus says the Lord יהוה: 'See, I am against you, O Tyre.'" The imagery of the following passage of not-quite-verse (26:3–5) is obviously taken from Tyre's location: as the waves of storms have beaten upon the city walls, now nations will. We learn later (26:7) that these "nations" are the various troops of an imperial force, the army of Nebuchadnezzar. The imperial waves will knock down Tyre's walls and even scour away her soil. Tyre's site will become just another barren island, a conveniently empty place for fishermen to land and spread their nets. A tacked-on passage (26:5c–6b) adds that Tyre's "daughter-towns"—that is, her mainland possessions— will also be sacked. The result is one with which we are familiar if we have been reading Ezekiel: those who see these things will learn who יהוה is.

The next of our chapter's words against Tyre (26:7–14) should probably be read as an explaining and supplementing exegesis of the first. The attacking horde is now identified as Nebuchadnezzar's army, complete with infantry, cavalry, armor, and siege engines (26:7). And the brief announcement of 26:4, "they shall destroy the walls of Tyre and break down its towers," is expanded into a long description of siege warfare and of what ensues when the walls are eventually breached (26:8–15). The end is as before: the island will be barren,[4] but with the terrible additional judgment, "You shall never again be rebuilt" (26:14).

A hard question is jointly posed by these prophecies—one that readers of the prophets must face sooner or later. Nebuchadnezzar did not in the event sack Tyre, but after a long siege—perhaps mostly a blockade from the mainland—went away, in return for tribute and recognition of his overlordship. Nor did he take the city on any later occasion. We, who after the fact know this bit of history, cannot but ask: What are we to make of prophecy that seems so straightforwardly unfulfilled and thereafter unfulfillable?

In the texts immediately before us, we perhaps have three clues to an answer. There is the circumstance that the editors of Ezekiel's book knew that

---

3. Indeed, it is not altogether clear that this is the right translation.
4. Rashi glosses, "First it was given into the hands of Nebuchadnezzar, and ultimately the sea came up and inundated it" (Rosenberg 2000: 225).

Nebuchadnezzar did not do what Ezekiel said he would do—indeed, they will later include a prophecy that explicitly describes Nebuchadnezzar's frustration (29:17–21)—yet saw no need to remove or adjust this text. There is the phenomenon of Ezekiel's prophecy at a distance, which in this case may disclose its deepest import. And there is the heavily emphatic "I have spoken" at the end of both prophecies, which the editors also allow to stand.

Whatever may have been the personal intentions of Ezekiel's final editor or editors, the text they left us is simply unbothered by Nebuchadnezzar's departing from the historical scene without carrying out his prophesied part in the doom of Tyre. To go with this diachronic unconcern, the texts of Ezekiel's book often, as here, display a synchronic one, blandly locating Ezekiel far from those he addresses. I suggest that these marvels can occur because all prophecies implicitly end as two here end explicitly, with "I, יהוה, have spoken" (26:5, 14). Whatever may be adduced to the contrary, if יהוה has indeed spoken that settles the matter: Tyre will hear the word of her fall and will fall to Nebuchadnezzar, for "the word of our God will stand forever" (Isa. 40:8).

The Word of God is not impeded by time or space, for he is the second identity of the God who creates both time and space (John 1:1). Therefore faith in the word of God can be "the assurance of things hoped for, the conviction of things not seen," a faith that transcends present appearances (Heb. 11:1). If a word from God has not yet been fulfilled, indeed if it cannot be fulfilled within the time and space of this age, we may nevertheless depend on it. For when the word of God is spoken, time and with it space do not display the linearity we in our finitude and fallenness assume. Christian thinking has for two laborious millennia been learning—and forgetting and relearning—to interpret time by biblical phenomena such as this: the man Jesus, born many centuries after Abraham's death, can say, "Before Abraham was, I am" (John 8:58).

Moreover, the Word that thus shapes time and space to his own contours does not exercise this agency because he simply "transcends" time and space. The Word that shapes time and space is himself firmly located in time and space. It is the word in the mouth of prophets like Ezekiel, pinned to history by careful dating (→1:1–3). It is the word on which our text relies when it continues to proclaim Nebuchadnezzar's coming judgment of Tyre. And in the denouement of God's conversation with us, the Word that is "in the beginning" and "through whom all things were made" is Jesus of Nazareth, the Christ of the nation Israel.

When will such faith in such a word be vindicated? At any unpredictable time, and at the end. Christian hope expects a "last judgment," a judgment to end all judgments, that will be not so much an evaluation of individual merits as a sorting out of all the mutual injustices that constitute our history. Perhaps the most audacious statement of this is by Jonathan Edwards:[5] "The causes and controversies

---

5. Jonathan Edwards is America's greatest theologian to date and perhaps her greatest intellectual of any sort. On his theology, see two standard studies: Sang Hyun Lee, *The Philosophical Theology of*

that must be decided by the supreme Judge" are violations "of our union . . . in society"; these will at the end be put right. Moreover, many of these are between nations or other collectives—as between "the Spanish and Portuguese . . . and [the] nations of South America"—or even between generations.[6] So why should not the supreme Judge at the end summon Nebuchadnezzar and Israel and Tyre to their mutual resolution? Why indeed should not Nebuchadnezzar at last be the Lord's servant to judge Tyre and be judged in his turn?

If 26:7–14 is an exegesis editorially cast as a messenger-word of judgment, the next bit of our chapter, 26:15–18, is a literary composition appropriated in a similar way. The rulers of Tyre's sister sea powers are depicted as descending from their thrones, putting on mourning, and singing a funeral lament, a *kinah*, over Tyre's grave. The depiction is striking, and the lament is elegant—these lines are a confirmation of Ezekiel's gift. Within the composition itself, neither God nor his acts are mentioned.

We may ask: Why would a book of prophecy include such a composition? Or why, for that matter, would such a book include the previous passage's recitation of siege tactics, so much like the catalogues of armaments and tactics in Greek epic? The answer, in my view, is that they are included sheerly because they contribute to the grandeur of the discourse and because grandeur belongs to the Lord's word. We have encountered the question before in connection with →21:8–17.

Finally in our chapter, 26:19–21 is a formally proper messenger-word from "the Lord יהוה." It has, however, its own peculiarities: only its location identifies it as a word against Tyre in particular, and it takes us deep into myth.

The ordinary storm waters that in 26:3 provided an image for enemy attack on an island city have here become the watery chaos of general Middle Eastern myth (26:19c). The priestly theology of Gen. 1—Ezekiel's own theological tradition— tells us that the Lord simultaneously created and overcame these waters as the beginning of creation (Gen. 1:2–3).[7] Once thereafter—continuing in Genesis—he unleashed the chaos-waters to bring creation to the verge of undoing (Gen. 6–8). That he then promised never again to threaten all creation with chaos does not mean he cannot sink Tyre into it.

A bit of "demythologizing"[8] is surely here called for: What is the theological import of the mythic picture of a primeval and always threatening "watery" state

Jonathan Edwards (Princeton: Princeton University Press, 1988), and Robert W. Jenson, *America's Theologian: A Recommendation of Jonathan Edwards* (New York: Oxford University Press, 1988).

6. Jonathan Edwards, *Miscellanies 853–1152*, Works of Jonathan Edwards 20 (New Haven: Yale University Press, 2002), no. 1007.

7. To see this structure, we must translate with RSV and KJV and reject NRSV's insertion of "when" in Gen. 1:1—an insertion that remains alien to the text despite its recent popularity. It is quite inconceivable that the priestly theologian who wrote these lines can have thought of a reality antecedent to God's creation other than God himself, whatever may have once been the case in mythic traditions he mined.

8. This is Rudolf Bultmann's famous slogan. Bultmann's particular criteria for what constitutes myth are theologically unacceptable, but that scripture and tradition often appropriate myth's

of reality, in which all is "formless" and "void" (Gen. 1:2)? Karl Barth's teaching is most convincing: chaos (*das Nichtige*, in Barth's language) is what the Lord in creating rejects and so leaves behind; it is the intrinsically past—which just so casts its "shadow" into the present, since every present indeed has a past, if in this case a past that never was.[9]

These verses present also a second picture: the Lord will make Tyre descend into the realm of the dead (26:20). Here the past tense is explicit: the pit is the realm of peoples long absent from history, who dwell in "primeval ruins"—such as already in Ezekiel's time a traveler in Mesopotamia would have seen. The passage needs very little demythologizing: the Lord will shut Tyre into that permanent past tense into which many nations have already entered: "Though sought for, you will never be found again" (26:21).

Finally for our understanding of these mythic pictures, the Old Testament regularly identifies or almost identifies the watery chaos with Sheol (→32:17–32) despite the impossibility of a combined picture. So, for example, Ps. 69:15 in parallel construction: "Do not let the flood sweep over me, or the deep swallow me up, or the Pit close its mouth over me."

When Israel's scripture in this fashion recruits into its discourse bits and pieces of Middle Eastern myth, it is for the sake of the absoluteness that this language can be used to evoke. Tyre will be brought to no mere ending in time, but to an eschatological end, an end with no future. She will be swallowed by the past tense. It is not, to be sure, obvious why the Lord should single out precisely Tyre—and not, say, Edom—for this distinction. For whatever reason, he does. Tyre will be with Sodom and Gomorrah, locked into the past.

And so our chapter presents another theological hard question: How are we to think of such damnation? What are we to think of the eschatologically excluded? In my view, Ezekiel and Karl Barth suggest the beginning of an answer: the damned are those who have no future, and these need not merely be individuals. Whether those with no future[10] can be said to exist at all is a question that has divided all theological history, and will no doubt continue to do so. The correlated question of whether the pit will finally have permanent occupants is equally unsettled, and again may remain so.

---

language—and that to read that language we sometimes need to reverse the appropriation—is surely correct.

9. Karl Barth, *Church Dogmatics*, ed. G. W. Bromiley and T. F. Torrance (Edinburgh: Clark, 1960), 3/3.349–68.

10. Or as it has more often been put in the tradition, those separated from God.

EZEKIEL 27:1–36

IT WAS SAD WHEN
THE GREAT SHIP WENT DOWN

This long chapter is the second of three that prophesy the downfall of Tyre; the group is in turn part of a collection (Ezek. 25–32) of oracles directed against Gentile nations (→25:1–17).

The prophecy begins in the fashion to which readers of Ezekiel are accustomed: the word of the Lord comes to Ezekiel, addresses him as "you—son of a man," and gives him a messenger-word addressed to Tyre. On this occasion, however, the word given Ezekiel is not an accusation or judgment, but is a funeral chant, a *kinah* (27:2b), sung for the death of Tyre. Nevertheless, it is introduced by "thus says the Lord." Thus what is before us is the Lord's own lament over Tyre. The passage must be dated after Tyre was invested but before it developed that Nebuchadnezzar would not in fact sack her, so that no funeral lament was needed (→26:1–21).

The *kinah* runs from 27:3d to 27:11, is interrupted, and resumes at 27:25b to run to the end of the chapter. Tyre was in fact located "at the entrance to the sea" and traded with "the peoples on many coastlands" (27:3a); thus the lament is appropriately composed around the images of the excellence and foundering of a great trading ship, with all the riches she carried. Ezekiel 27:32b–36 is a lament within the lament, the voice of those most shocked by the ship's destruction. Ezekiel 27:9c–11 is probably from a narratively challenged interpolator who ignored the image of a ship and reverted to literal description of Tyre as a fortified port-city.[1] Ezekiel 27:12–25a interrupts the poetry with a prosaic list of trading partners and the sorts of merchandise they had brought to Tyre, a sort of obituary in the business pages. It was doubtless inserted to emphasize what a general economic disaster Tyre's undoing was and probably also in service of ancient literature's general love of lists, this one being at hand and more or less relevant.

The first half of the poem (27:3d–9b) praises the great ship for herself. Her builders made her "perfect in beauty,"[2] drawing on the finest and most elegant materials from all parts of their trading world. She sailed with a crew of the best specialists, again recruited from wherever they were to be found. She was altogether a supreme achievement of international human endeavor. And it is the Lord himself who lavishes this praise and who by doing so with a *kinah* laments the loss of this human achievement.

The second half of the poem (27:25b–36) describes the richly laden ship's foundering and laments this both for itself and as an economic disaster. It is important that most of this part of the poem (27:29–36) records the human horror of those who see and are affected by the disaster, their rites of mourning, and the lament (27:32b–36)—within the lament—that they raise. Thereby human evaluation of the ship and human mourning for its loss are incorporated into the Lord's own valuing and mourning.

There is little need for point-by-point comment on either the poem or the interrupting list of trading partners; both are clear as they stand. Extensive prose explanation inflicted on a poem that does not need it usually hinders understanding; and the list is what it is. Despite the length of the chapter, the commentary unit on it can therefore be brief, since within the scope of this commentary we are not interested in such things as the poem's manipulation of *kinah* meter, the detailed architecture of the ship, ancient trade patterns in the eastern Mediterranean, or other such matters—which does not mean that in another context of concern they are not interesting indeed.

It is an old problem: What relation do the specific goods granted to the Lord's people by his historical acts and promises, and the fidelity demanded by his historically communicated commands, have to goods granted to humanity in general and—at least apparently—given independently of his particular history with his people? Our poem depicts the Lord as celebrating the humanly created power

1. By determined rewriting, the Targum manages to abolish the image of a ship altogether and conform the whole poem to these verses (Levey 1990: 79–82). The purpose of this poetic desecration is not obvious.

2. The NRSV reading of 27:3c—correctly translating the Masoretic Text—could suggest that the praise of Tyre's beauty is her own hubristic self-congratulation. But this reading would surely fight with the body of the poem, which is the Lord's own praise of the ship's beauty, as something that in fact obtains (27:4b). A very plausible conjecture attributes the Masoretic Text of 27:3c to an easy scribal error, the correction of which would yield "Tyre, you are a ship of perfect beauty"; see Zimmerli 1983: 42.

and beauty of the great pagan city Tyre and the prosperity that her position enables, and moreover depicts the Lord as mourning their passing—even though readers of the book are of course expected to know that the disaster is the Lord's own doing.

In theological tradition, the problem has been most frequently posed as a question about the relation of "nature and grace," or "nature and supernature." In this scheme, "nature" is the complex of capacities and opportunities that are ours whether or not we belong to God's people; "supernature" is whatever God's particular people are given over and beyond these. Supposing the distinction, the question is: How does God value our natural gifts? And how therefore should we? Are those outside God's people rightly satisfied with their natural gifts; or is the absence of supernatural grace a deprivation of human nature itself? If I am doing what is possible for me as a natural human, how, if at all, does that relate me to a supernatural end?[3] And how, correlatively, should God's people regard their own natural gifts? As preparation for grace? As neutral to grace? As something grace must overcome?

In our text, God regards humanity's natural achievements with admiration, but he does so within a context of sorrow for their failure, a failure that is measured by the supernatural demands and promises made to his own people. This suggests, for one thing, that the gift of natural goods to all humanity is not finally independent of the gifts made in history to God's people: the story of the Lord's conflicts with and benefits to his people *encompasses* the stories of the Lord with the Gentile nations—how that is to be worked metaphysically currently divides the theologians. And it further suggests that the Lord's supernatural regard to natural gifts is always at once affirming and mournful.

3. For the most penetrating recent discussion, that of some French theology in the period leading to the Second Vatican Council—the *nouvelle théologie*—and for my own view, see Jenson 1997–99: 2.65–68. Perhaps the most mature work of the "new theology" is Henri de Lubac, *Surnaturel* (Paris: Desclé de Brouwer, 1991).

EZEKIEL 28:1–19

THE DOWNFALL OF DIVINE KINGSHIP

Ezekiel 28:1–19 brings the last two of a group of oracles (26:1–28:19) directed against Tyre, a group that is in turn part of a larger grouping (Ezek. 25–32) of oracles directed against seven Gentile nations. The remainder of Ezek. 28 is devoted to Sidon (→28:20–26). Readers should read the opening paragraphs of the two previous commentary units before continuing here.

In our present passage, we find first a messenger-word (28:1–10) directed against Tyre, cast in the traditional form of oracles against Gentile nations: "Because … has … , therefore …" (→25:1–17). To this is attached, in a way that readers of Ezekiel will have seen before, a passage (28:11–19) on the same theme but of different character, here yet another funeral lament for Tyre.

Ezekiel 28:1–10 begins with the standard introduction to a messenger-word: the word of the Lord comes to Ezekiel, addresses him as "you—son of a man," and provides the word. This is not directed against Tyre herself, as in the previous two chapters, but against her prince.[1] The indictment following "because" is that Tyre's prince has thought and said "I am a god,"[2] when in fact he is but

---

1. This is presumably the reigning prince. Rabbinic tradition, however, thought of David's ally Hiram, who had been—à la the next verses—living in paradise all along and had grown proud; Levey 1990: 83.

2. אֵל (*el*) may mean "the God," or be used as an appelativum (so NRSV), or be the name of a particular God. I am convinced by Zimmerli 1983: 77–78 that NRSV's reading is correct.

a man—the Targum provides a gloss, "and not indispensable," which indeed is much to the point (Levey 1990: 82).[3]

Thus the Lord speaking by Ezekiel judges the ruler of Tyre by a distinction foreign to that prince's own grasp of reality. For Ezekiel—as for the rest of scripture and for Judaism and the church—any reality must be either the only true God or one of his creatures; there are no midway entities. But for ancient paganism there were—and in late-modern paganism are again—indefinitely many levels of slightly less than fully divine entities on the one hand and of more or less divinized creatures on the other. Even where sophisticated religious reflection has produced a "monotheism" within paganism, the principle remains: thus even after Greek religious thought attained the notion of one abstract deity "whom men [only] call Zeus," Zeus himself and some of his clan retained their cultic and interpretive functions, to say nothing of the deities and half-deities involved in the "mystery" initiations and festivals. The princes of Tyre indeed thought that their throne raised them above mere humanity and into the sphere of the divine and within their grasp of reality supposed that this was obvious, that it simply went with being the prince. It belonged to the royal theology of all Judah's monarchical neighbors: elevation on the throne is elevation into divinity.[4]

The crime for which Tyre's prince is here condemned is therefore not—as we might at first reading suppose—simple overweening pride, but rather a culpably false understanding of reality. Since there is the Lord and since he is who he is, the supposition that anything other than the one God can be in any degree divine must be false—whether the creature involved is the host of heaven or the life-giving power of the rains or the Caesar or the prince of Tyre or whatever. And the error is culpable also in those who do not know the Creator, because the advent of death by mortal hands refutes divinity (28:9) and because it should have been obvious to anyone in the Fertile Crescent that kings can be killed, since they regularly were.

Indeed, death is God's standing refutation of humanity's inveterate self-deification. Through the millennia, from Adam and Eve's eager assent to the serpent's suggestion to recent Wall Street "Masters of the Universe," powerful humans have said, "I sit in the seat of the gods" (28:2c), lesser creatures have striven to share the delusion, and all have died.

The great decision falls in Christ's crucifixion and his disciples' martyrdoms. These deaths make the conclusive end of humankind's attempt to be God, since as the death of the human who indeed is God, and of those who belong to him, these deaths simply leave no more ontological space for human self-exaltation. If you have contemplated these deaths, you know there are no more-than-human humans or partial deities. The reality of the one who is indeed "true God" and

3. Rashi quotes a midrash: "He made for himself in the air over the sea, a mechanism that was a replica of the seven heavens, and he sat down on the highest one" (Rosenberg 2000: 239).

4. For Phoenician cities, the documents from Ugarit make this explicit; see Eichrodt 1970: 391.

"true man" without shading either, and of the death that this meant for him, sort out Creator and creature forever.

Ezekiel 28:11–19 then attaches a distinct but thematically closely related word about Tyre, which Ezekiel is again to introduce with the messenger formula "thus says the Lord." As in the previous chapter, however, what follows is not in fact a message; it is a funeral lament, a *kinah*,[5] now for the "king" (מלך) of Tyre—but it does not appear that much should be made of the different title. The passage is again the Lord's own lament, as in the previous chapter for the great ship Tyre. In →27:1–36 I discussed the problem posed by the circumstance that Ezekiel's evocations of Tyre's fall were, on the time scale of this age, premature.

In what may seem at first glance to be in tension with the main prophecy's denunciation of divine kingship, the king whom the Lord here laments is himself not a being in the usual order of humanity. It is no historical prince of Tyre whose beauty and fall are lamented—none of these inhabited paradise or were once upon a time pure and innocent. This "king" is rather the mythic prototype of Tyrian kingship.

In depicting this figure, Ezekiel appropriates various mythic traditions. The most prominent is a version of one behind Gen. 2–3: as "the Adam," the prototype human, dwelt in "Eden, the garden of God," so does this prototype king of Tyre (Ezek. 28:13a); as the Adam was "blameless" until he unaccountably sinned, so was this figure (28:15); as the Adam was barred from paradise by cherubim, so a cherub casts out this king (28:16c). It is the glory and fall of Tyrian kingship as such that is sung, in the language of a myth of the primal "Adam"—and indeed the Targum read the whole passage as referring to the biblical Adam as the primal and prototypical human (Levey 1990: 83).

Ezekiel 28:12b–15 praises this Tyrian kingship in its intended blamelessness. Some of this praise is in more or less plain language: Tyrian rule—not necessarily any historical Tyrian ruler—is said to be distinguished for "wisdom" and "beauty" (28:12c). Some of the mythic language is fairly transparent. "The [holy] mountain of God" (28:16b) appears in many religions—including that of Israel, with Horeb and Zion—and here parallels the image of God's garden: if the primal king of Tyre is not quite a god, he does inhabit God's vicinity. The significances of his being "the signet of perfection" (28:12c), of the precise royal regalia (28:13),[6] or of his living among "the stones of fire" (28:14c) are lost to us (for some unconvincing guesses, see Zimmerli 1983: 91), pending new discoveries or unpredictable strokes of scholarly ingenuity.

5. For the intricate and sophisticated structure of this composition, see Greenberg 1997: 587–88.

6. Greenberg's observation (1997: 582) that the list of precious stones in 28:13 covers nine of the twelve stones in the Jerusalem high priest's vestment (Exod. 28:17–20) is typical of the minutiae, most of them leading nowhere, that he loves to report and for which his commentary is a treasure house.

Nevertheless, contrary to a central supposition of all intact myth, the poem insists that Tyrian kingship, even in its transcendent prototypical being, is a creature—with all that scripture means by that (28:13, 15). The language is emphatic: Ezekiel uses the technical term of Gen. 1, *bara* (ברא), that in his theological tradition was strictly reserved for God's unique act as Creator. Moreover, the Lord in his lament explicitly claims credit for the prototype kingship and its glory (Ezek. 28:14). It is thus the great point of the passage: Tyrian kingship, also in its mythic being, is the Lord's creature. This has of course two sides. One was hammered home in the main prophecy: the king—mythic or historical—is no god. But the other side is here to the fore and is astonishing: the preternatural reality of a pagan dynasty is instituted by Israel's God. Indeed, he mourns its passing.

Our poem thus does not deny the reality of the mythic figure; rather it cuts it down to creaturely size and then endows it with a creature's very different glory. The great parallel is again from Ezekiel's theological tradition, at Gen. 1:14–15: "the host of heaven" were universally worshiped in paganism; in Genesis they are revealed as lamps and clocks and glorious decorations that God has put up there for the general convenience and for beauty, and that just so are "good."

It is this Tyrian kingship-as-such whose fall and punishment are then narrated in 28:15c–19—just as it is "*the* Adam" whose fall and punishment are told in Genesis. The fall appears in the actual historical working out of Tyrian king-ship's particular mythic virtue, practical wisdom: that is, in the city's economic dominance. Tyre's economic power falls into injustice and oppression (28:18) just as "the Adam" falls into disordered desire, in a history transcendent to history. And in that same history the Lord casts her "to the ground" (28:17) below the mountain of gods and outside Eden.

The Lord takes "no pleasure in the death of the wicked" (33:11) and so, as in the previous chapter's lament, mourns both Tyrian power's corruption and his own consequent imposition of her "dreadful" eschatological end (28:19b). Yet again, we encounter the Lord's emotional investment in his creatures, and here we find it extended to the pagan world. "How good God is, who mourns even those who deny him! And this derives from the affect of love. For no one mourns someone he hates" (Origen 1989: 410).

It is time to consider: What sort of reality does myth evoke, that the scriptures can appropriate its language, if only in bits and pieces? Myth tells the story of how things are in a beginning that abides, to be the hidden reality of its historical outworkings:[7] for example, the patron god of Babylon, Marduk, once overcame the chaos monster and divided her body into dry land and channeled water to produce the habitable world, and this event repeats itself in the Mesopotamian irrigation system's annual flooding and draining.

---

7. Rudolf Bultmann's famous "demythologizing" works with a very different—and idiosyn-cratic—notion of myth.

Israel and the church also know of a beginning behind which we cannot penetrate and which abidingly determines creation's shape and value. This beginning, to be sure, differs greatly from that told by myth, in that the Lord does not need to overcome anything to be the Lord and to create and in that the Lord's act of creation does not thereafter repeat itself. Scripture thus tells no intact myths. But throughout Israel's and the church's history, broken pieces of mythic narrative have provided dramatic language with which to evoke an absolute and continuing formative beginning. Our passage presumes that such a phenomenon as Tyrian kingship, precisely as created, has such a beginning in the intention of the Lord.

It is because the act of what scripture calls creation is directed to a future that it does not merely repeat itself. This indeed is the great difference between myth and scripture's narrative. The Lord's creation does indeed have an abiding beginning that shapes all that is and happens—which is why bits of myth can evoke that shaping. But it has also an outcome, the kingdom of God, that shapes God's history with us yet more deeply, since it is the very purpose of the beginning. It is the maxim of all properly Christian metaphysics: we most deeply are what we will be in God's kingdom. If we are now "justified by faith," this is because faith is "the assurance of things hoped for" (Heb. 11:1) and because in the hoped-for kingdom we will in fact be just. It is this futurity of all being that breaks myth and endows us with its fragments.

EZEKIEL 28:20–26

FAREWELL TO THE SIX

Within the collection of prophecies (Ezek. 25–32) directed against seven Gentile nations, six are directed against Judah's hostile close neighbors. Ezekiel 28:20–23, the oracle against Sidon, is the last of these. Ezekiel 28:24–26 then provides a theological conclusion for the set (→25:1–17).

We might have expected to find 28:20–23 with the similarly short oracles gathered in Ezek. 25. Doubtless it is located here, after the chapters against Tyre, because "Tyre and Sidon" were always thought of as a pair, and at Ezekiel's time in that order. The two were recurrently powerful cities of the Phoenicians, an ethnic grouping whose territory was more or less that of modern Lebanon.

The prophecy against Sidon is introduced in Ezekiel's standard fashion. The word of the Lord comes to Ezekiel, addresses him as "you—son of a man," and provides a messenger-word, to be delivered to Sidon with "thus says the Lord." Ezekiel, of course, is far distant from Sidon; as on other such occasions, a prophetic *oth* (→3:22–5:4) spans the separation. Ezekiel is to "set [his] face toward Sidon"; the embodying gesture replaces physical location. Throughout Ezekiel, we encounter such ways in which the word bends time and space to his own contours (→26:1–21).

Unlike the other prophecies against Gentile nations, the message to Sidon includes no indictment; there is no "because Sidon has." This is a notable departure from the standard form of prophecies against Gentiles, in Ezekiel or elsewhere. Perhaps we are expected to assume the indictment specified for the other bad neighbors—glee over Jerusalem's disaster—but there is another possibility.

Only one aspect of this oracle arrests special attention: the Lord's announced aim in destroying Sidon. The messenger-word begins with something like a challenge to single combat: "I am against you, O Sidon" (28:21b). In this combat, the Lord will "gain glory" for himself, so that observers will "know that I am יהוה"—this is twice repeated (28:22c, 23c). To this proposition, there is a momentous parallel. Before Israel's crossing of the sea, the Lord says to Moses, "I will harden Pharaoh's heart, and he will pursue them, so that I will gain glory for myself over Pharaoh and all his army; and the Egyptians shall know that I am the LORD" (Exod. 14:4, repeated with slight additions at 14:17–18). In this passage there is no indictment to explain the Lord's action. And we are given an explicit other explanation: the Lord hardens Pharaoh's heart to provoke the battle in which he will gain glory.

We must remember what "glory" (*kabod*) is in the Old Testament: the sheer impact of a personal presence (→1:25–28b). Both here in Ezekiel and in the passage from Exodus, that the Lord gains glory and that people come to know "that I am יהוה" are parallel. Thus both passages give Ezekiel's favorite outcome formula a particular specification: in this case, to know the Lord is to feel the sheer power of his presence. And in both the Lord demonstrates—indeed gains—that presence by combat with his enemies, entered into at least partly for the sheer victory.

The Old Testament's frequent picture of the Lord as a warrior seeking glory has been a great offense to modernity's sensibility. Liberal theology elided this aspect of the Old Testament's vision of God by calling it "anthropomorphic" and so "pre-Christian." The problem is: if we remove everything that might be called anthropomorphic from the Old Testament's talk about God, little or nothing is left. And indeed liberal theology could finally maintain its concord with modernity only by in general denying the Old Testament's theological authority. What was not always noticed at the time was that the New Testament's authority depends internally on that of the Old Testament. If we are unwilling to abide by the offense of the Lord's quest for glory by combat, we will finally have no scripture at all.

In my judgment, the offense cannot be fully rationalized and indeed constitutes a plausible reason not to believe in the biblical God. What we can do is try to grasp how the picture of the Lord fighting for his glory fits the whole biblical story of God, and then ask if we really wish to remove ourselves from that story. We will do this in two steps.

Does God really need to "gain glory" before the nations? The answer, in the case of the Bible's God, is not so automatically no as we might first think. From the call of Abraham on, the Bible tells the story of the Lord's entry into his creatures' history—to be the particular God of a particular nation, to be incarnate as the particular man Jesus, to send the particular communities of Judaism and the church—in order by acting within history to reclaim his creatures' worship. The heavens may declare the glory of God to all humanity, but humanity's response to that display has been that "they did not honor him as God or give thanks to him" (Rom. 1:21). Nor is God's action to regain humanity's worship selfish, for creatures that do not honor the Creator are lost. Thus God does need to act within history to regain the glory that belongs to him—unless he is to let us go our way into nothingness.

But does the Lord need to *fight* to gain glory? Again, the answer is not so clearly no as modernity has demanded. Our failure to give him glory is not passive; it is active rebellion: the Lord has enemies, of which some fight directly against Israel, Christ, synagogue, and church. Thus insofar as the Lord acts within history there are specific historical figures who oppose him, in our passage—for whatever reason—Sidon. If God does not take sides within the violence of history—if, for an instance more immediately palatable to modern sensibility, he does not have "a preferential option for the poor"—the forces of violence must triumph altogether. To be sure, from faith that God works also in the violence of history, it does not follow that we are to guess what side he is on and jump in to help.

Perhaps we may—at considerable theological risk—draw from the long theological tradition about "just war." According to the mainline of this reflection, Christians may not use violence in their own cause, but are not excused from defending their neighbors amid the violence of a fallen world. What then of God himself, insofar as he too acts within our history? With him, love is so absolute that the distinction between his own cause and that of his creatures does not apply. It no doubt stretches language to speak of a divine dilemma, but if we make that stretch we may say that God finally resolves his use of violence against violence on the cross, where his victory over his and our enemies is accomplished by utterly abandoning self-defense. On the cross, absolute pacifism worked.

We may still ask: Why did the Lord wait so long for the cross, and why does he now wait so long to bring the end, leaving all that room for continuing violence? That of course is the kind of question that can hardly be asked, never mind answered. But perhaps we may venture: because he has wanted to include the readers and author of this volume among his rescued creatures.

Finally we turn to 28:24–26. In the plan of Ezekiel's book (→25:1–17), the oracles against Gentile nations lead from prophecies of judgment against Israel to prophecies of restoration and indeed of eschatological fulfillment. Ezekiel 28:24–26 provides that outcome for the subgroup of six, thereby also anticipating it within the whole collection.

Ezekiel 28:24 begins the promise of salvation modestly: when her hostile near neighbors are squelched, "the house of Israel" will just so be saved from briers and thorns that have plagued her from the beginning of her time in the land. That it is "the house of Israel" that will thus find rest opens the discourse, however, to a grander and more eschatological promise.

Ezekiel is given a new messenger-word (28:25–26), a word that joins the chorus of promise voiced by his partly contemporaneous fellow prophets, Jeremiah and Second Isaiah. When the Lord has judged Israel's neighbors, he will gather all Israel, including the northern exiles, from the far places of their exile; Israel will reclaim the land promised to the patriarchs; and she will live there in permanent safety. Then at last Israel will know for certain and for good that *yhwh* is indeed their God.

Is this promise fulfilled? The church's theology has always seen it fulfilled in the creation of a new Israel by the death and resurrection of Israel's Christ. But the church is increasingly coming to realize that the great prophets' promises of salvation carry an "eschatological surplus," a burden that has not yet been fulfilled. The church must join the synagogue in waiting.

With the next chapter, we return to prophecies of judgment, against Judah's distant disaster, Egypt. Also the reader must wait for salvation until Egypt is attended to.

EZEKIEL 29:1–16

THE CROCODILE

These verses begin four chapters of prophecies against Egypt. She is the last of seven nations denounced in a collection (Ezek. 25–32) of oracles against Gentiles, which makes the hinge of Ezekiel's book (→25:1–17).

There are four chapters on Egypt after four on the other six nations together. Before taking up the oracles against Egypt one by one, we may ask: Why does Ezekiel give such special attention to the one nation? From the vehemence of Ezekiel's language and imagery, and from his and his editors' sheer persistence in attack, it is plain that he has a special animus against Egypt. On the other hand, Egypt is also given hope denied the other six: after suffering her punishment she will be restored—though not in a form she would have desired (29:13–16).

Israel remembered a long history with Egypt, not all of which was a story of oppression. Egypt had indeed been "the house of bondage." But Israel also remembered that she was in Egypt because Egypt had offered Jacob and his sons a place of refuge, as she had done to Abraham and his people before them—and the tradition continued with the family of Jesus finding safety in Egypt. Israel was enslaved by a pharaoh who had to be identified as the one who "knew not Joseph" (Exod. 1:8 KJV) precisely because there had been others who did remember Joseph and care for his people.

It is therefore not altogether surprising that during the Israelite monarchies' struggles with the Mesopotamian empires, their rulers invested hope in Egypt—a great power that was inevitably opposed to those in Mesopotamia, with whom for good and ill Israel had an ancient relation and whose forces were only a few hard marches away. In Ezekiel's time, Jehoiakim's and Zedekiah's rebellions against Babylon relied on Egyptian help and may indeed have been fomented by Egypt.

Such hopes were, to be sure, illusory. As Ezekiel will say at 29:6b–7, Egypt was a staff that when grasped broke and with its broken end stabbed Israel's hands[1] and that when leaned upon buckled to precipitate her fall. In Ezekiel's view, Egypt was a standing temptation for Israel: on the one hand, by offering military aid she tempted Israel to rely on her rather than on the Lord, a fatal sin in itself; and on the other hand, the aid was always too little and too late. Yet there was also that other side to his obsession with her.

As often in Ezekiel's book, 29:1–16 presents a primary prophecy to which thematically related passages are editorially attached. Whether the primary prophecy is 29:1–6b or continues though 29:9b is hard to say (I assume the former). The primary prophecy is dated; in our calendar the date resolves to the beginning of January 587, in the midst of the great siege of Jerusalem.

The word of the Lord comes to Ezekiel, addresses him as "you—son of a man," and tells him to prophesy against "Pharaoh king of Egypt."[2] As on other occasions, he is to address prophecy to this distant target by an *oth* (→3:22–5:4), ostentatiously turning his face toward it. The messenger-word begins as did the immediately previous oracle against Sidon, as a challenge to battle (29:3b; on the Lord as warrior, →28:20–26).

The indictment of the pharaoh is directly theological. He is depicted as a crocodile[3] "sprawling" in the channels of the Nile Delta. His crime is that he proclaims himself the source and proprietor of the Nile's life-giving power (29:3d); identification of the pharaoh's life force with that of the Nile and of both with such totems as the crocodile was indeed characteristic of Egyptian myth and cult. That all the little fish of the Nile cling to the great crocodile (29:4d) is Ezekiel's further pejorative—and zoologically improbable—image of the way in which Egyptian theology made the life of the people depend on the life of the pharaoh. Thus Egypt's king is guilty of the same delusion of divine kingship as the previously condemned king of Tyre (→28:1–19).

The Lord himself then enters the scenario he has portrayed: if Pharaoh is a crocodile, the Lord will go crocodile fishing (Greenberg 1997: 602). When he has caught him, he will neither keep him nor put him back, but will fling him and his dependent fish into the desert, there to die and be carrion. And then—readers of Ezekiel by now know it is coming—any surviving Egyptians will know that the Lord is the Lord.

A new indictment with "because" (29:6c–7) begins a new oracle. This is more in the standard form of oracles against Gentile nations than is the crocodile poem to which it is attached. Thus it proceeds from "because" to "therefore," leading to a

1. The standard English translations follow the Masoretic Text and speak awkwardly of "shoulders." But the Septuagint translated a Hebrew text that spoke more plausibly of "hands"; and Ezekiel is almost certainly dependent on Isa. 36:6, where what the broken reed does is pierce the hands.

2. "Pharaoh," the ancient title of Egypt's rulers, had by this time become almost a name.

3. The English translations agree in translating "dragon," following the Septuagint. The Hebrew word itself is of uncertain etymology and use. The Old Testament uses it and related words for everything from harmless snakes to sea monsters, so long as it is long, looks vaguely reptilian, and to the Israelite mind seems a bit uncanny. Zimmerli 1983: 110–11 successfully argues that in the present context the crocodile must be meant, since it is both the typical great water beast of the Nile Delta and prominent in Egyptian myth. Rashi makes this same point (Rosenberg 2000: 249).

messenger-word (29:8–9b). The word of Pharaoh's doom is here so short as to be almost perfunctory—there is nothing about crocodiles—but it is cut to fit Israel's memory of Egypt. Pharaoh is to see the death of both humans and animals, as once the pharaoh of the exodus saw the deaths of both. The outcome is again knowledge of the Lord.

Yet another new indictment (29:9c) begins another new prophecy, closely tied to the main prophecy by return to the image of Pharaoh as crocodile. The indictment is also the same, and what follows "therefore" is again the land's general desolation (29:10–12). But then there is an astonishing turn.

Egypt's doom is laid out chronologically and on the model of Israel's own punishment (29:10–12). When Egypt's land becomes desolate, this will have the same cause as does Judah's present desolation, the scattering of her leading people into exile, described in the very language Ezekiel uses of Israel's exile. As with Israel, the exile will not be forever. As Israel wandered forty years in the wilderness and as Ezekiel prophesied that Judah's exile would last forty years (4:6), so Egypt will be in a wilderness for forty years.

Finally, as Israel will be brought back, so Egypt will be gathered back to her homeland (29:13–16). Here the parallel breaks in significant fashion, for Egypt will be restored to no grand eschatological role. She will be stripped of her pretensions as a great power and returned to the status of a small state, in the original Egyptian center on the Upper Nile; thereby Israel will be saved from temptation to rely on her. Nevertheless, it is hard not to think that Ezekiel sees in Egypt's deprivation of great power a sort of salvation also for Egypt.

What are we to think about this paralleling of Israel and the—in Ezekiel's view—most dangerous of Gentile nations? Plainly, Ezekiel depends on what Christian theology has called analogy. In its more highly conceptualized form, the concept has been used to describe the epistemic status of statements about God: for example, when we say "God loves," we point to a reality in God—unknown in itself—that is the enabling model and purpose of what we know as love among creatures. Perhaps we may extend this to the relation between Israel—the nation in whom (and indeed *as* whom) the Lord dwells among nations—and the other nations. As the value of creatures depends upon and is somehow an image of God's value for himself—though we cannot specify that "somehow"—so the value of Egypt, or of Sidon or whomever, depends upon and is somehow an image of Israel's value for God and other communities. Thus Babylon may be "the most terrible of the nations" and Egypt the great temptation for Israel, but neither is valueless for Israel's Lord.

Finally, as to why Ezekiel sees analogy in the case of Egypt and not in that of, say, Edom, surely it is because Egypt's intimate and paradoxical relation to Israel casts the required light on the possibility of analogy. Theological analogy has been defined as a "likeness within a greater unlikeness." That very well fits the likeness that Ezekiel sees between Israel's doom and restoration and those of Egypt.

EZEKIEL 29:17–21

NEBUCHADNEZZAR'S
DUBIOUS CONSOLATION

Ezekiel 29:17–21 appears within a group of oracles against Egypt (Ezek. 25–32), but is clearly orphaned from some different context. The prophecies against Egypt are otherwise structured by a close succession of datings: the preceding date at 29:1 gives "the tenth year" of Jehoiachin's exile, and the following date at 30:20 gives "the eleventh year." Thus this prophecy from the "twenty-seventh year" is decidedly out of order. Indeed, if the book's array of dates is comprehensive—of which we cannot be sure—this must be Ezekiel's last prophecy, editorially imported back into this set of much earlier oracles solely on account of its reference to Egypt.

Moreover, the passage has its own attachment (29:21) that yet more obviously was once at home in some other context; Egypt appears in it only incidentally. It will be best to read the prophecy and its attached verse each strictly in its own terms.

The year given for the passage works out in our calendar to 571. In that year, the word of the Lord, without explanation in the present context, turns Ezekiel's attention back to the siege of Tyre. Ezekiel had prophesied immediate, total, and permanent disaster at the hand of Nebuchadnezzar (e.g., 26:19–21). But Nebuchadnezzar's siege had in fact lasted for thirteen years and ended with his frustrated withdrawal and with Tyre politically and economically reduced but intact (→26:1–21). The word of the Lord comes now to Ezekiel, addresses him in usual fashion as "you—son of a man," and gives him a new messenger-word involving Tyre.

The present word describes, unperturbed, what had in fact happened, and so the nonfulfillment of Ezekiel's prophecy. The Lord had sent Nebuchadnezzar against Tyre, and Nebuchadnezzar and his army had worn themselves out in labor to fulfill the commission (29:18)—though of course they did not know they had one. For their pains they had no reward; the booty of Tyre was denied them. In consequence, the Lord acknowledges that he owes Nebuchadnezzar and his troops.[1] And he announces that he will make it up to them by giving them Egypt instead (29:19–20).

Now—quite apart from the circumstance that this too did not in fact happen—this is one of the strangest and most offensive passages in Ezekiel to modern theological certainties. Does God give assignments that his agents cannot fulfill? If "the most terrible of nations," acting—unbeknownst to herself—as God's agent, fails to achieve his purpose, can God be said to owe them for the missed booty? We are at another of those points where the Old Testament leads us into theological places where modern prejudices do not want to go and where we are likely to resort quickly to vague remarks about "metaphor" or "anthropomorphism" (→28:20–26).

But can we elide all such language without finally abandoning the whole biblical narrative? On the other hand, if we abandon attempts to mitigate the offense and take what the passage says at face value, what then? Perhaps—I hesitantly suggest—we may discover that what is revealed in our passage is nothing less than the full earnestness of the Lord's commitment within his history with creation.

Humanity's usual construal of the intercourse of gods and mortals has been summarized in the maxim *do ut des* ("I give in order that you give"), said by either a god to a mortal or a mortal to a god. The arrangement is businesslike, and debts can pile up either way. Christian theology regularly deplores this notion; the faith's message of grace, of the final benefit that God does *not* owe us, breaks the pattern of *do ut des*. Or rather, it does insofar as *we* are concerned. It does not follow that God from his side does not regard himself as committed by our obedience to his historical commands and promises, even to recompensing us when we have labored for him in vain. And in our present passage, we see that he acknowledges such inner-historical obligation also to those of his created instruments who do not know him as the one who gives the commands by which they live.

Then there is the attached verse, 29:21. Can "that day"—which within this verse itself is clearly the eschatologically terrible day of 7:10–27 and of Amos 5:18–20—really be identified with Nebuchadnezzar's piratical expedition against Egypt? In all the prophets this absolute day is the day of the Lord's final triumph over all unrighteousness. Even if Nebuchadnezzar had brought Egypt to heel, would that have banished injustice and oppression from the world? In the New

---

1. Rashi has another explanation: "The sea rose and washed it away, because it was decreed that it and its booty be lost in the sea" (Rosenberg 2000: 254).

Testament the day is both the day of Christ's crucifixion and resurrection and the day of his final and glorious advent to bring the eternal kingdom of God.

I resisted the above identification through the writing of an entire draft of this commentary unit. Nevertheless, in the text as we have it, the pronominal reference is too plain finally to be resisted: what the phrase in present context does is attach Ezek. 29:21 to what precedes it. The Lord's great day of 29:21 is identified with Nebuchadnezzar's payday.

This initially implausible identification has, once acknowledged, a theologically drastic effect. Suddenly the story of Egypt's exile from power and restoration to peace is turned into eschatology: that is, into the story of Egypt's role at the end. And the few pronouncements that follow in the verse suddenly reveal their secret.

Had we encountered the verse by itself, we would surely have read the "horn" that "sprouts" for the house of Israel as a figure for the Messiah; and the eschatological sense given to Nebuchadnezzar's expedition allows—indeed forces—us to read it that way here. This is not the image's only appearance. Thus Ps. 132:17, read as messianic by both Judaism and the church, has: "I will make a horn to sprout for David; I have prepared a lamp for my anointed" (RSV). Thus the elimination of Israel's great temptation, Egypt, the Lord's faithfulness to Nebuchadnezzar and the advent of the Messiah all come together on the day.

One more item demands our attention. On that day Ezekiel's mouth will be opened and he will prophesy. There have been other references to Ezekiel's inability to speak until being released to prophesy, but it is not possible to be certain how often, when, for how long, or why Ezekiel's mouth was closed. But, since everything here refers to that day, the word's presence on the lips of his prophet, enabling all to know יהוה, belongs to the last day's salvation. If 29:17–21 was in fact the last prophecy of Ezekiel, then just as the world's judgment, Israel's redemption, and the coming of the great Son of David are to be united at the end, so the word of these things came together at Ezekiel's end.

EZEKIEL 30:1–19

THE DAY—FOR EGYPT

This passage continues the series of oracles against Egypt (Ezek. 29–32), that collectively make the conclusion of a collection of oracles against seven Gentile nations (Ezek. 25–32; →25:1–17).

The unit is undated. It shares language with an attachment (29:21) to the previous very late oracle and perhaps once somehow belonged with that verse. There is a usual opening: the word of the Lord comes to Ezekiel, addresses him as "you—son of a man," and tells him to prophesy. No addressee is specified, but the prophecy can have been addressed to Ezekiel's fellow exiles, since among them will have been those who had rested their hopes on Egypt. Four messenger-words follow (30:2c–5; 30:6–9; 30:10–12; 30:13–19), each identified by being introduced with "thus says the Lord."

What follows the first "thus says the Lord" is a call for an unidentified person or group to "wail."[1] They are to cry, "Alas for the day!" This "day" is certainly "the day" of 7:10–12 and of the long prophetic tradition of "the day of the Lord." An explanation of the cry follows (30:3). It picks up and compresses the eschatological rhetoric of →7:10–27: "For the day of the Lord is near—there will be a day—an end—of the nations."[2]

---

1. The verb is purely onomatopoeic, הֵילִילוּ (*hililu*), and has no meaning apart from its imitation of sounds made in grief.
2. The text translated is that of the Septuagint's translation of the Hebrew: ὅτι ἐγγὺς ἡ ἡμέρα τοῦ κυρίου ἡμέρα πέρας ἐθνῶν ἔσται. The Hebrew is obscure, and the text apparently read by the Greek translators fits much better with Ezekiel's usage in 7:10–27; so Eichrodt 1970: 414.

Ezekiel 30:2c–5 first invokes "the day" when all nations will come to an end of their might, when the Lord alone and forever will be victorious. But then these verses call for this day here and now, against Egypt and her immediate allies. Egypt's doom will be inflicted by warfare, with its attendant economic and political disasters—the "foundations are torn down." At first Ethiopia is paired with Egypt as her nearest considerable neighbor; then, in a flat prose passage (30:5) that contrasts with the elevated diction of the previous verses, sundry other allies are slated.

The second messenger-word (30:6–9) mostly elaborates the first. Egypt's desolation will be total and extend from the far north to the far south of that long and slender land. The "sword" appears again; it may be that readers are supposed to have the great sword poem of 21:8–17 in mind. And we are provided with Ezekiel's usual proclamation of the purpose of the Lord's acts: "They shall know that I am יהוה."

One verse (30:9), editorially tacked on to the end, is more arresting than the formulaic body of this messenger-word—at least for those who have been reading through Ezekiel's more lurid oracles of doom. It would appear that someone has noted the pairing of Egypt and Ethiopia in the previous oracle, has missed it here, and has added a verse to remedy the omission. The language of the added verse compels attention.

After a historically all-too-plausible narrative of ordinary military invasion and the havoc it brings, "that day" suddenly reappears with its full eschatological force. The best ordinary way for messages to be sent from the Nile Delta to Ethiopia was indeed partly by ship, but who are those "messengers"? Perhaps Ezekiel has ordinary officials in mind. But the Hebrew is מלאכים (malekim), regularly used for prophets and for the preternatural messengers of God we call "angels." Indeed, "*the* angel of the Lord," who is both other than and the same as the Lord (→introduction), is the מלאך יהוה (malek yhwh). Thus this addendum plunges us back into the atmosphere of the opening verses.

Then the third messenger-word (30:10–12)—at least in its present context—serves to identify how Egypt's doom will take place. Nebuchadnezzar will do it—and therewith we are back with history.

We continue the discussion begun in the previous unit, of the relation between the final end of the Lord's ways with his creation and endings that occur within history, between the nations' final defeat and such events as Nebuchadnezzar's sixth-century sacking of Egypt. If we take the Bible's eschatology with any seriousness, there are not many logical possibilities.

We may say that so long as history continues things will come to their ends and that eventually God will bring everything to its end. Undoubtedly, much Christian and Jewish piety has made this assumption. But the notion of so simply linear a succession of temporal events and the final event will not do: in the passage constituted by our three messenger-words, "the day" is *at once* the day of the absolute end and the day of Egypt's temporal fall. Scripture is shot through with similar phenomena.

We may make the move of most modern liberal theology and regard the eschatological end as the final but still inner-historical goal of human moral endeavor, with all the latter's endings and new beginnings. We may sophisticate the liberal picture and envision the end as the goal of an asymptotic convergence of God's final intention with our moral achievement. Or we may think of every moment in which we are brought to an end of our possibilities as *being* the end.

I am satisfied with none of these modern options. Perhaps we should take Ezekiel's—and other prophets'—own proclamation more directly as a pattern. There will indeed be a day that will without qualification be an end of what we know as history, a day when God will openly reign, without impediment of earthly powers. But because the same God who will bring all history to that end lives also within the history thus to be sublated, he is free and able to anticipate the great end within that history, as he chooses. Indeed, such anticipation is what we mean by "revelation." The great and indeed last such anticipation is, by Christian conviction, the cross from which Jesus says, "It is finished."

The final messenger-word (30:13–19) is a catalogue of the places in Egypt that the Lord will judge (30:19). It is notable for its rhetorical flair and for the unit's only reference to a reason for the Lord's judgment, the idolatry of the great cult center at Memphis (30:13).

The last messenger-word and the whole unit ends, as do many in Ezekiel, with "then they shall know that I am the Lord." In this case, the formula is given a very specific twist: it appears in strict three-beat parallel construction with "thus I will execute acts of judgment on Egypt" (30:19). The "acts of judgment" are thus here themselves the revelation of this God's identity.

We learn to know who God is from the history of his acts to establish righteousness; by Christian conviction these are summed up in the cross and resurrection of Israel's Christ. This means something also for our understanding of cross and resurrection; that the doom of Egypt—and the destruction of Jerusalem—can be included in the acts of righteousness epitomized in Christ's death and new life should warn us not to be glib or self-serving in speaking of Christ as a revelation of love. Perhaps we may say, as recent preaching has been eager to tell us, that he "loves unconditionally," but if this is taken to mean that he loves without judgment, it is false. It was because he loved Jerusalem and would never cease to love her that he sent Nebuchadnezzar to destroy her—moreover, the same may strangely be said about our passage's judgment of Egypt. And indeed, we must suppose that—with respect for the inscrutability of the Lord's judgments within the history of this age—it may be said also about the nations of those who may read these messenger-words, if they ignore the Lord's word to them.

EZEKIEL 30:20–26

LARVA DEI

With these verses we return to the set of dated oracles against Egypt. Their dates make the structure of the four chapters (Ezek. 29–32) directed against that nation, the last of seven Gentile nations denounced in Ezek. 25–32 (→29:1–16; →25:1–17).

The date specified works out in our calendar as the end of April 587, a few months before the walls of Jerusalem were breached (Zimmerli 1983: 137–38). There seem to have been those among the exiles who at that time still believed that God would use Egypt to rescue Jerusalem from Nebuchadnezzar; the present oracle was perhaps directed more against such hopes than against Egyptian wrongdoing as such. Indeed, we may summarize the whole passage here at the beginning: "I, the Lord, fight by the hand of Nebuchadnezzar and not by the hand of the Pharaoh" (on the Lord as warrior, →28:20–26).

The prophecy is given in the Lord's usual way with Ezekiel. The word of the Lord comes to him and addresses him as "you—son of a man." There is, however, no command to prophesy, since the Lord's first words (30:21) are information for Ezekiel himself. The Lord has broken Pharaoh's sword arm, nor will the break soon heal; therefore hopes invested in Pharaoh's might are misplaced.

After this private information, the Lord gives Ezekiel a messenger-word to deliver, beginning with the usual "thus says the Lord." No addressee is named for this message; its present context probably directs it against fans of Egypt among the exiles. The Lord will make the sword fall from Pharaoh's hand and strengthen the sword arm of Nebuchadnezzar, to "scatter" the Egyptians among the nations, as the exiles of Israel are scattered. We encounter again the Egyptian oracles' enigmatic paralleling of Egypt with Israel (→29:17–21; →30:1–19). And we encounter again the insistence that the Lord himself will determine the outcome of the armed clash—indeed that he is active in it, breaking Pharaoh's arms and providing his own sword to Nebuchadnezzar.

The relation between the private information to Ezekiel and the messenger-word proper poses a translation problem, with an associated historical problem. All else being equal, the verbs of 30:21 would be translated as NRSV does, with the English past tense (Zimmerli 1983: 137–38). The following messenger-word must surely be translated with English future tenses, as NRSV does. So when does this arm-breaking and strengthening happen?

If we were to encounter 30:20–21 by itself, we would certainly take it as a report to Ezekiel of something that the Lord has already done, shortly before the date specified. And a referent quickly presents itself: Pharaoh Hophra had in fact made an effort to relieve besieged Jerusalem, and after initial successes had given up and gone home.[1] If we read in this way, the point of the verse is "I, the Lord, did that to him. Some may have thought it was Nebuchadnezzar or adverse circumstances that undid Hophra, but it was I." But then the following messenger-word prophesies as a future event what surely seems to be exactly the same divine act: "I will strengthen the arms of the king of Babylon, but the arms of Pharaoh shall fall" (30:25).

This leaves two possibilities. We may exploit the possibility—open when circumstances are not equal—of translating the Hebrew verbs of 30:21 as present tense with future reference.[2] Then the whole of 30:20–26 is prophecy of future judgment. Or we may take 30:21 and the following messenger-word as having different referents: 30:21 reports what the Lord has done, and the messenger-word announces that he will do the same thing again. The text alone compels neither reading.

If the second reading is correct—if the information to Ezekiel is a report of recent history and the messenger-word is prophecy of future events—then also this text displays a historical anticipation of the eschatological future, such as that which occupied us in →30:1–19. If the first is correct and the whole passage is in the same future tense, there is no such theologically interesting suggestion.

In any case, the theologically most striking feature of this prophecy is its drastic identification of the Lord himself as the one who determines and indeed fights the battles waged by created armies. An actual pharaoh is or will be made militarily incapable; it is the Lord who breaks his arms. Nebuchadnezzar has been or will be victorious; the sword that wins victory is the Lord's own, put into Nebuchadnezzar's hand. Leaving aside at this point the question of God's involvement in violence (→7:10–27), how are we to understand the relation between God's act and creatures' act, when the event itself is but one?

1. Whether Hophra fought Nebuchadnezzar and lost or just went home again seems to be uncertain.

2. Zimmerli 1983: 138 notes this possibility in the present instance, but rejects it.

The question has been posed and debated throughout theological history. Traditional scholastic theology, Catholic and Protestant, has said that God is the "primary cause" of created events, which within creation have also created "secondary causes." Thus God is here the primary cause of Egypt's disaster, and Nebuchadnezzar the secondary cause. The doctrine is descriptively correct, but it is doubtful that it does much more than restate the problem. Through the latter part of the previous century, several movements attempted to place the scheme within a more substantive theory—in my judgment, without great success.

Thus some Christian members of philosophy departments have taken to doing what is in fact theology.[3] They are especially occupied with the question: How is an eternal God's agency within time possible? In my view they pose the question in a way that makes a faithful answer impossible, for they tend to use words like "eternal" or "agency" or "time" so uncritically within an Aristotelian frame that the notion of an eternal reality's agency in time becomes a simple oxymoron. If to be "eternal" is simply to be "not temporal," than an eternal entity[4] cannot do a temporal act, and there is little more to be said.

Some other recent movements have taken an opposite, drastically revisionary path. Process theology among liberal theologians[5] and open theism among evangelicals[6] have produced metaphysically more or less coherent accounts of primary divine agency and secondary temporal agency. But they have done so only by revising Christian language about God past all biblical recognition. A God who is one pole of a universal process is not the God of Ezekiel or any other prophet.

I have a diagnosis and suggestion. At least since the advent of modernity, Western thought has tended to see the universe as a *system*, a self-contained process determined by immanent regularities; much modern theology has—sometimes subliminally—accepted this vision. When the world is envisioned in this fashion, God is willy-nilly envisioned as a second something external to the world.[7] Then the question necessarily becomes: How does the eternal God *intervene* in the temporal system, without wrecking it? And the obvious answer is that he cannot: either it is simply closed to him, or his entry will compromise its constitutive laws.

But scripture does not envision the creation as a system at all, but rather—as Ezekiel and this commentary have all along construed the matter—as a *history*.

---

3. A sample can be found in Eleanore Stump and Michael J. Murray, *Philosophy of Religion: The Big Questions* (Malden: Blackwell, 1999).

4. As these thinkers construed reality, calling God an "entity" was proper.

5. For first acquaintance, see John B. Cobb Jr. and David Ray Griffin, *Process Theology: An Introductory Exposition* (Philadelphia: Westminster, 1976).

6. Clark Pinnock et al., *The Openness of God: A Biblical Challenge to the Traditional Understanding of God* (Downers Grove, IL: InterVarsity, 1994).

7. Or, à la Spinoza, as metaphysically identical with the temporal system, viewed according to the timeless structure of the system. This solves the problem by eliminating the God in question.

This vision poses quite a different question: How does God present himself as an actor in the drama of history? And to *that* question, one piece of theological history suggests at least the start of a—to my mind—faithful answer.

In ancient drama, the actors brought the gods and heroes into the theater by and as masks behind which the actors hid and through which they spoke; within the ceremony the masks were the *dramatis personae*. Martin Luther adduced this phenomenon, but reversed the relation of actors and masks. God brings the created heroes and villains of the temporal drama onto history's stage as masks that hide him—for were he to appear barefaced creation would perish. Thus Nebuchadnezzar and his like are *larva dei*, God's masks—as indeed are all creatures in one way or another. And we masks truly are the *personae*[8] of the drama; we are not puppets manipulated by someone distant from us. Yet behind us hides the Creator.

Calling the created carriers of history masks of God may at first sight seem to be a figure, not to be taken with ontological seriousness. But we should remember that the great metaphysical categories are always created by drafting ordinary language for heavy ontological duty.[9] To instance Scholasticism's language for our present matter, God is of course not a "cause" within any such cluster of cause and effect as quotidian language presumes; thus when the tradition calls him the primary cause of created events it drafts "cause" to serve in an alien discourse. And when Luther and I propose instead to draft "mask" for metaphysical duty, we perform the same move—but, just possibly, more appropriately.

---

8. *Personae* were in ancient Latin first the mask roles on the stage, the *dramatis personae*, then social roles in the general human drama, and from that use were taken into Christian theological discourse.

9. So, e.g., a "substance" was initially something that stands beneath something else, to hold it up.

EZEKIEL 31:1–18

THE GREAT TREE

Ezekiel 31:1–18 continues the series of oracles against Gentile nations (Ezek. 25–32; →25:1–17). The chapter is the third of four directed against Egypt, the last of seven nations accused and condemned. Ezekiel is obsessed with Egypt: he devotes one chapter (Ezek. 25) to four of the seven nations, three chapters (Ezek. 26–28) to Tyre and Sidon, and four long and complicated chapters (Ezek. 29–32) to Egypt alone (→29:1–16).

The chapter before us comprises an introduction and initial instruction to Ezekiel, at 31:1–2, followed by four clearly demarcated but—on the reading I adopt—logically related units: 31:3–9; 31:10–14; 31:15–17; 31:18. The passage—or perhaps only the first part of it—is dated; in our calendar the date works out to the end of June 587, two months after the date given for the just previous passage. Thus the oracle was delivered during the crisis of the siege of Jerusalem, but from the passage itself we would never know it, so single-mindedly does Ezekiel attend to his chief villain.

There is the usual opening: the word of the Lord comes to Ezekiel and addresses him as "you—son of a man." He is to speak—as often, from a distance—to Pharaoh and his "hordes." The initial word to the Egyptians is a question: "Whom are you like in your greatness?" This could mean, "Who will make a good comparison to highlight your greatness?"[1] Or the question could be rhetorical, equivalent to "your greatness is incomparable." Which it is depends on how we read the ex-

---

1. Rashi interprets the sentence as a question and gives it the sense: "Who do you think you are?" (Rosenberg 2000: 263).

tended figure into which Ezekiel launches with 31:3—how to do that, however, is just the problem.

A single image, of an empire as a great tree, persists through the chapter, developed with variations and internal messenger-words.[2] Thus the chapter is in general much like the earlier depictions of the pharaoh as a crocodile (29:3–12) or of Tyre as a great ship (27:4–36). Unfortunately, this observation does not fully determine the genre of the piece, since that turns out to depend on a textual question.

Since the oracle is explicitly directed against Egypt, we expect the tree to be Egypt. But the Masoretic Text, backed in this case by all the ancient versions, reads "consider *assur* [אשור]"; thus NRSV has "consider Assyria." If this is the right text, the figural narrative is not directly about Egypt at all, but is instead about Assyria and tells the story of that empire's fall some seventy years before. A commenting final verse (31:18) then makes the collapse of Assyria into an object lesson for Egypt.

Scholars, however, propose to rescue identification of the tree as Egypt. The appearance of *assur* in the Hebrew text can be explained as the result of scribal error of a sort that sometimes occurs: the skipping of an initial letter. There is a word, *tassur* (תאשור), that if it lost its initial letter would result in *assur*, and *tassur* is the Hebrew word for "sycamore," which seems to fit a story about a tree. If this emendation provides the true text, then we should render 31:3 with something like "see—a sycamore—indeed a very cedar of Lebanon!" This gets rid of the reference to Assyria and so allows the tree to be Egypt after all, and the passage to be prophecy of Egypt's future downfall. The past tense of the figural narrative must then be taken as a trope, a sort of prophetic anticipation. The critical consensus is in favor of the emendation (Zimmerli 1983: 141–42).

I am not, however, convinced by the proposal. If such a scribal error occurred, it spread remarkably early in the history of the text, since the Septuagint and the other ancient versions all translated a text with *assur*. And calling the same tree both a sycamore and a cedar poses its own problem. Since I follow NRSV except for good reason, I will read the text in the first way noted above and thus suppose that the body of the prophecy tells the true story of what happened to Assyria and finishes with a switch rather like with which Nathan shocked David (2 Sam. 12:7): "The story, including the descent that concludes it, applies to you, Pharaoh, as well as to Assyria—who, after all, was greater than are you" (Ezek. 31:18).

Assyria had been a preternaturally great tree, with her top in the clouds and her roots in the plentiful waters of the great deep (31:4), using the important word תהום (*tehom*). She was planted in God's garden of nation trees, where the other nations both sheltered in her shade (31:6c) and envied her (31:9). Indeed she was a blessing to the general creation (31:6). All this was the work of the Lord

---

2. The Targum suppresses all this, replacing it with a free composition of its own (Levey 1990: 89–90). Is this because of the mythic features, which I will shortly adduce?

(31:9a) and in itself was good. The Lord has no intrinsic objection to empire, even pagan empire.

Then a messenger-word (31:10–14)—meant to be overheard by the Egyptians—tells of the judgment that the Lord wreaked on the tree. Assyria became proud of her beauty and power, as if these were her own; again we see how nations who do not know the Lord are nevertheless bound to his standards and prerogatives. Therefore the Lord gave her over to Babylon, "the most terrible of the nations." She was cut down and her branches were scattered; the birds and animals still inhabit her, but now as brushwood (31:12b–13). The nations have fled (31:12d).

At its end, this messenger-word's discourse widens to something like an apocalyptic theology of history: if Assyria has been handed over to death, she but joins earlier nations, for she and they are alike mortal and like all mortals must go down to the grave (31:14b). There is bite to this eschatology, for nations, despite all the evidence, generally suppose themselves immortal. Americans can conceive and fear a period of American decline or defeat, but cannot conceive a world from which the United States has simply disappeared. But there are no immortal nations, says the Lord: if creation itself lasts so long, the United States—and Britain and France and China—will some day be one with Assyria and Babylon.

The image of a political power as a great tree is not unique to Ezekiel. It appears, for example, in Nebuchadnezzar's dream as interpreted by Daniel (Dan. 4:10–12), where the parallel extends to such details as the nesting birds and sheltered animals. The image has its home in cosmological myth, such as is found in many cultures:[3] there is a great world tree, rooted in a primeval realm below the world we see and reaching upward to the heavens beyond the world we see, thereby providing the structure and stability of the total universe, the unity of all things "seen and unseen."

To be sure Ezekiel does not speak of Assyria as the world tree itself; he uses the imagery of the myth to describe a created power. Nevertheless, his use of the image remains embedded in the myth—far more so than does Daniel's. The Assyria tree spans the "three-story universe"[4] of all myth. It grows in God's garden, indeed in Eden (31:9b). The source of its vigor is the ambiguous *tehom*, the primeval water banned beneath earth, that simultaneously is the source of earth's life-giving waters (as in 31:4) and threatens creation with return to chaos (as God once threatened to allow; Gen. 6). The word translated "death" at Ezek. 31:14, *moth* (מות), can be translated with the impersonal noun, but is also the personal name of the Canaanite god of the underworld—to which the Lord will send Assyria and Egypt. There is too heavy a carryover of the cosmological myth to be read as mere imagery detached from its source.[5]

---

3. For a quick list, see Eichrodt 1970: 425. For the sake of my ancestors, I would like to add the Norse Yggdrasill.

4. This is Rudolf Bultmann's notorious phrase for a decisive feature of myth.

5. Rashi demythologizes all this (Rosenberg 2000: 266–67).

Thus Ezekiel does not portray Assyria as a purely human construction; rather, he apprehends her as somehow ontologically prior to the power of her empirical kings and priests. She was a sort of local world tree. And the pride for which she was judged was therefore no ordinary human arrogance—perhaps we may say that Assyria thought she *was* the world tree (31:14).

A second messenger-word (31:15–17) says nothing further about Assyria's fault and evokes only the judgment visited on her. Accordingly the figures shift: the language becomes less protological, less drawn from myth, and more eschatological, indeed apocalyptic. The order of waters below and above is turned over, darkness descends (31:15), the nations quake, the great oppressor goes down to Sheol, and the nations she oppressed are delighted by her appearance there (31:16). We recognize the style—and much of the matter—of the book of Revelation. I will here refrain from comment on the notion of Sheol, as Ezekiel depicts the universal grave more fully in →32:17–32.

In dealing with political power such as Assyria's or Egypt's, Ezekiel is driven to the language of the old myths and begins also to construct the scenarios of apocalyptic. What moderns think of as empirical considerations and analyses can fully account neither for Assyria nor for her downfall—nor for outsized historical phenomena generally. Empires and tyrants and deliverers must be nourished and threatened by waters more potent than those that flow in ordinary channels. Both their beneficence and the mighty temptations to which they are subject are uncanny. "Principalities and powers" (Eph. 3:10 RSV) must lurk behind them.

There is truth here that moderns would do well to acknowledge. Our social sciences produce their—occasionally interesting—results only by abstracting from the reality of their matter, that is, from human history. Historians tell stories—at the height of their ambition one universal story. It is of course now common in academic departments for historians to shrink from the task and become sociologists or psychologists or political scientists of some past moment, abstracting that moment from historical reality exactly as do other social scientists.

Perhaps history telling has in fact ceased to be possible, and so-called historians should migrate to appropriate other departments. But if storytelling is now impossible, so is Christianity and its theology, because the object of Christian faith and theology *is* a story, of Israel and her Christ, and because that story claims to be final truth. If, on the other hand, storytelling is possible, we will inevitably tell of nations and movements and outsized historical actors as somehow more-than-individual personalities, for only personal actors and their interplay have stories. As we tell of Assyria or Rome or Hitler or Churchill we will merely by doing so evoke principalities and powers, realities outside the abstracted purview of the social sciences.

God, and not merely Nebuchadnezzar, undid Assyria and will undo Egypt. That is Ezekiel's message. Precisely when the event is so envisioned, Assyria and Egypt and the rest appear in their proper unearthly power and horror.

EZEKIEL 32:1–16

THE CROCODILE
LARGER THAN LIFE

Ezekiel 32 is the last of four chapters devoted to oracles against Egypt, and Egypt is the last of seven Gentile nations condemned in Ezek. 25–32 (→25:1–17).

Two sets of markers move us to take 32:1–16 as a unit. Ezekiel 32:1 dates a prophecy and 32:17 dates another. Ezekiel 32:2 mandates a funeral lament, a *kinah*, and 32:16 says that what precedes it has been one. If the canonical text did not thus bracket this piece of text, we might not know how to proceed, since the stretch of text displays little formal or material coherence in itself.

The prophecy is dated, but the ancient versions and the Masoretic Text differ on the date, locating the prophecy in 586 or 585 respectively (Zimmerli 1983: 158). Either date falls very shortly after the fall of Jerusalem. As with previous oracles against Egypt, we would not have known this portentous context from the text itself, so intent is Ezekiel on the coming downfall of Egypt (→29:1–16).

In the usual form of revelations to Ezekiel, the word of the Lord comes to him, addresses him as "you—son of a man," and gives him an assignment. As on other occasions, he is to raise a *kinah* ("funeral lament"), this time for the anticipated death of the pharaoh and his horde; and at the end (32:16) someone insists that 32:2b–15 has in fact been such a composition.

Already commentators are in trouble, for what in the present text appears between 32:2a and 32:16 is not in fact a *kinah* or anything formally like one.

At most the few lines at 32:2b–d could once have belonged to a *kinah*;[1] and if these lines were indeed once so intended, they are now but a fragment of a lost or deleted composition. Even 32:16 perhaps protests too much—"this really was one!"—suggesting that an ancient editor may have seen a problem and perhaps exhorted the reader to read the previous text as a word with the *burden* of a *kinah* (a real *kinah* is the lament for Tyre in →27:1–36).

Instead of the announced funeral lament, the passage brings two messenger-words (32:3–10; 32:11–15), each marked by the standard opening line, "Thus says the Lord." To compound incoherence yet a little, the first of these picks up the image of the pharaoh as crocodile, as this is introduced by the possible *kinah* fragment, but the second takes no notice of it.

This state of affairs has naturally occasioned attempts to reconstruct the unruly history of editings and interpolations that must have produced such a construction; but here as generally I have little trust in efforts of the sort. For our purposes it suffices simply to recognize the state of things. Nor will I try to force coherence on the existing text where none presents itself, but will take matters as they come.

Finally in this catalogue of impediments to reading, the little *kinah* fragment is itself a problem. The Masoretic Text of the first line is grammatically anomalous and as it stands not certainly translatable (Zimmerli 1983: 154, 158–59). Worse, neither the Masoretic Text of this line nor the proposed emendations show the connection between the initial image of the pharaoh as "lion" and the succeeding and dominating image of the pharaoh as "crocodile." For lack of reason not to, I will abide by NRSV's adversative construction: "You consider yourself . . . but you are. . . ."[2] The second beast is a crocodile and not, as in NRSV, a "dragon" (→29:1–16). And lacking most of the *kinah*, we cannot tell why the pharaoh's self-conception as a lion is rebuked or why calling him a crocodile is supposed to be more accurate.

The only thing really clear about the possible *kinah* fragment is that it takes up again the image from 29:1–16 of the pharaoh as a great crocodile in the channels of the Nile Delta, in Ezekiel's time the seat of Egyptian power. It bends the image in an empirical and negative direction: this crocodile pollutes its waters. Where an original *kinah* may once have gone with that, we do not know.

Be the foregoing as it may, the present text makes its real start at 32:3, with the first messenger-word, in which the Lord declares personal war on Egypt (32:4–10). And the Lord's involvement in battle is to be personal indeed: the rhetoric hammers the "I" at the beginning of each strophe, and Nebuchadnezzar's warriors drop out of the picture.

1. A *kinah* can be recognized by its "limping" meter: it moves in couplets, of which the first line has three beats and the second two.
2. Rashi glosses to somewhat similar effect: "You should have lain in the midst of your rivers . . . , and not gone out to the dry land; but you were haughty in your heart, and you compared yourself to a young lion" (Rosenberg 2000: 271).

Perhaps this is why the messenger-word's depiction of the crocodile and its destruction is more embedded in mythic background than is the use of the image in 29:1–16. When the Lord shows himself without the mask of his created agents, he unmasks also the realities he combats.

One did not hunt ordinary crocodiles with nets—thus in the crocodile hunt of 29:1–16 God uses a hook. But the Babylonian founder-god Marduk did subdue the watery chaos monster, Tiamat, with a net. Cast on land as carrion, a dead crocodile is a big corpse to be sure, but does not fill the dry land with its body or the watercourses with its blood—and no such hyperbole appeared in Ezek. 29. Marduk, however, did in the myth make the dry land and the watercourses by filling the space destined for human cultivation with the sorted-out solids and liquids of the ambiguous chaos that was Tiamat's body.[3]

Thus when Ezekiel here tells of Egypt as a doomed historical power, he alludes to old myth: Egypt's violence is the threat of returning chaos, as represented by Tiamat, and Egypt's fall will be like a primeval creative victory to make order out of chaos. Ezekiel does not attempt to account for outsized historical emergents like Egypt or Babylon in the abstractly empirical fashion of much ancient wisdom or of modern social science—and neither perhaps should we. To speak truly of powerful nations and their fates, or of history's heroes and villains, we in normal speech tell stories of personalities not discernible by methods that abstract from goals and purposes, and the purposes we invoke are carried by powers not quite identical with the empirically identifiable agents. We are right to speak so: as God's action in history is not empirically identifiable as such, neither are his agents and opponents. Stalin's terror, for example, was something "larger than life" in the ordered world, and we depart from reality if we do not speak of it so (similar phenomena appear in →31:1–18).[4]

Very much as in 31:1–18, the Lord's proclamation of Egypt's end segues into proclamation of a final end of history. Indeed, which does the prophecy finally envisage: a historical judgment of Egypt as known in this age, or God's final destruction of worldly power and the chaos that lurks behind it? It is a fundamental structure of Ezekiel's prophecy that the question allows of no unambiguous answer. Almost all the prophecies shimmer with both possibilities; in some the one is more obvious, in some the other.

The turn to eschatology does shift the rhetoric slightly, moving from the language of mythic beginnings to the language of apocalyptic, here—as in →31:1–18—to

3. That the messenger-word alludes to Tiamat might be taken to fight against the identification of the beast as a crocodile, for Tiamat was not one; and Eichrodt 1970: 432–33 makes that argument. But nor was she a dragon; and the dragons of legend were not watery or messengers of chaos. Crocodiles, on the other hand, are amphibians who inhabit ambiguously dry and wet places, and that suffices for the allusion.

4. It is noteworthy that the Targum eliminates both the crocodile-Tiamat imagery and the apocalyptic scenario next to be discussed, with rationalizing replacements and interpolations at every step (Levey 1990: 91–92). The Targum does not like myth or any but the most sober apocalyptic, perhaps in opposition to movements within Judaism that went overboard.

what will be a standard apocalyptic scenario: the lights of heaven will be put out and the peoples of earth cast into terror (32:7–10; see, e.g., Acts 2:20–21; →31:1–18).

The second messenger-word (32:11–15) eschews myth and apocalyptic for more usual prophetic proclamation and, moreover, does not connect to the crocodile image. As occurs elsewhere in Ezekiel's book, this probably was once a separate prophecy editorially attached to a dominating passage on account of some perceived relation or similarity; here that is probably shared emphasis on the Lord's personal combat with Egypt. The afflictions the Lord will visit on Egypt distantly mirror the plagues of the exodus story; the memory of the exodus shapes understanding of the present crises and indeed of the coming end.

Ezekiel 32:16 is then the aforementioned reidentification of the whole passage as a funeral lament. What remains to be said of it is again unsatisfactory: in the ancient world women are indeed the official mourners, but there were surely resonances here we miss because we lack the *kinah* to which this verse presumably refers.

Most of this commentary unit has been spent on matters preliminary to this commentary's theological concerns. This is an extreme example of a phenomenon mentioned in the introduction: as we advance through the book, more and more matters can and must be dealt with by reference to earlier discussion. If the present passage stood alone, it would raise enough theological matters for several commentary units; and if expositors assigned the passage follow the references, they will find more than sufficient matter.

EZEKIEL 32:17–32

DESCENDIT AD INFERNA

Ezekiel 32 is the last of four chapters devoted to oracles against Egypt, and Egypt is the last of seven Gentile nations condemned in Ezek. 25–32 (→25:1–17).

The present prophecy—at least the first and model part—is dated shortly after Jerusalem's fall,[1] as were the two dated prophecies just previous to it. As with them, you would not know of this terrible historical context from the prophecy itself, so obsessed with Egypt is Ezekiel (→29:1–16).

Following the date, there is the usual introduction: the word of the Lord comes to Ezekiel, addresses him as "you—son of a man," and commissions him. This time his commission is to "wail" for and to Egypt. If we have been reading through Ezekiel, we have encountered mandates of lamentation before (the classic instance is the lamentation over Tyre in →27:1–36). We may expect the present instruction to be like those other commands. But they mandate a specific literary genre, a *kinah* ("funeral lament"), whereas the verb here translated "wail" seems to mandate no specific form (Eichrodt 1970: 438). Since what follows is not in fact a *kinah*, this is a good thing for readers and commentators; we do not have the mismatch between mandate and actual text that we had with the similar →32:1–16.[2]

The first few lines following the commission are indeed a sort of howling that Ezekiel is to aim at Egypt herself. He is once again instructed to speak to a far distant target; the efficacy attributed to the Lord's word in the mouth of a prophet

---

1. In the Masoretic Text the passage is dated incompletely; the Septuagint has a complete date, which NRSV adopts. The divergence does not affect my point.
2. Undoubtedly, the succession of two passages with a mandate to lament followed by a few lines of lamentation and then something else signals some relation between them. But what?

does not—at least in Ezekiel's case—depend on its being heard. Ezekiel 32:18b–19 displays the efficacy itself in drastic fashion: by wailing to Egypt about her descent to the "world below," Ezekiel is actually to send her there (32:2); his "Go down!" (32:19) will accomplish the consignment. And Egypt should not be surprised to find herself descending to the dead: she is no more "beautiful," no more to be desired among the living, than are nations already there (32:19).

The bulk of the passage is then a hypnotically repetitious evocation of the scene in Sheol—a naming of nations there and a description of their situation. It is in the third person except for one sentence (32:28). This sentence again condemns Egypt in the second person, picking up the opening and so rounding off a neat rhetorical construction. It therefore seems likely that 32:28 is the conclusion of an original unit that named Assyria, Elam, and Meshech-Tubal as nations in Sheol and that this composition then provided the model for attachments at 32:29; 32:30; and 32:31–32.

"Sheol," "the pit," "the world below" are all names for the one great grave of which, in ancient cosmology generally, all particular graves are parts and manifestations. Israel shared the supposition of a cosmic grave; and from 32:20–32 we learn how at least some Israelites of Ezekiel's time further conceived it.

Israel did not regard the world of the dead, or any part of it, as a good place to be—when petitioners in the Psalms mention that world it is only to plead for postponement of arrival there, or for rescue from a situation so dire that Sheol offers the only analogy. For the dead are in the grave, and what is put into a grave is not a living person. There is only dust before a living human is made of it; and when God takes life away there is only dust again (Gen. 3:19).

Yet the thought of the dead as sheerly not existing cannot be fully carried through—and no ancient people, including Israel, quite managed it. The difficulty is not a special feature of ancient thinking. It is as impossible now as ever to think[3] one's own sheer nonbeing; and so—except perhaps by a remarkable feat of solipsism—it is also not finally possible to think of others who once lived as now merely nonexistent. The images by which I try to think my own nonbeing inevitably fail: when I envision my own habitation of a void, or of utter darkness, or of whatever other negativity, I am still positing myself as the inhabitant.[4] Thus no religion or mythology has been able to conceive the dead as simply nonexistent, at least not for themselves. In Sheol, Egypt will somehow know where she is and even be "consoled" because her doom is no worse than that of other great nations (32:31).

Accordingly, humankind has often posited an entire world of the dead, of those who have this strange negative mode of reality. In the Lord's depiction of this world to Ezekiel, it even has a moral topography.

---

3. One can of course assert it; thinking it is another matter.

4. For my further reflection on this, see Robert W. Jenson, *On Thinking the Human* (Grand Rapids, Eerdmans, 2003), 1–15.

The situations of Assyria, Elam, and Meshech-Tubal—and then of Edom and the Phoenicians—are depicted with such rigorously parallel rhetoric that we can take the depictions as one. These nations lie "with the uncircumcised," also in Sheol they are outside the covenant of the true God. It seems, moreover, that Egyptian nobles and priests were in fact circumcised and counted this as a mark of their status, so that being dispatched to the uncircumcised was a disgrace also in some Egyptians' own terms (Greenberg 1997: 661–62). Moreover, they lie among those who have been "killed by the sword." Here the phrase does not evoke a warrior's inevitable way to die, but punishment inflicted by the Lord on those who "spread terror in the land of the living"—for this expression, the Targum substitutes "exercised tyrannical dominion over the land of Israel," thereby catching at least part of the point (Levey 1990: 93; Rashi glosses to similar effect in Rosenberg 2000: 278).

It is to this circle of those religiously and morally disgraced by their acts among the living that Egypt is dispatched. Do Egypt and the rest know they are disgraced? It seems that somehow they do.

Sheol as here depicted offers only one contrast to the situation of Assyria and her like: that of "the fallen[5] warriors of long ago" (32:27),[6] the "mighty chiefs" (32:21) of legend. These lie in honor, with the accoutrements of noble burial, with their swords and shields upon them (32:27). Thus it is not for warlike prowess as such that Egypt and others lie in disgrace. It is, however, notable that to find such heroes, Ezekiel has to turn to "long ago."[7]

It is a final striking feature of this moral topography of the underworld that while the uncircumcised are assigned their place, there is no mention of the circumcised. Ezekiel's picture of Sheol offers no account of Israel's own dead. This observation leads to consideration of what Gerhard von Rad famously called "a strange theological lacuna" in Israel's thinking.

For much of its history, Israel did not know what to think about the relation between the Lord and the dead. If the Lord was almighty, a human creature's death had somehow to be in his hands; he could say, "There is no god beside me. I kill and I make alive" (Deut. 32:39). In our passage, he has just sentenced all Egypt to death and in earlier passages has promised to execute the verdict in person. Nevertheless, the Lord is not like the Canaanite Moth,[8] who waits eagerly in Sheol to receive his subjects, nor does the Lord accommodate a pantheon in which a subsidiary god could rule such a realm. The Lord's purpose for his creatures is life and not death (Ezek. 33:11).

---

5. Both Eichrodt 1970: 436 and Zimmerli 1983: 168 emend the Masoretic Text's *nophelim* ("fallen") to *nephilim* ("giants"), referring to Gen. 6:4. The emendation is easy, since it effects only the Masoretic vowel pointing. Should it be right, it would make little difference to my point, though it would add another bit of myth.

6. NRSV follows the versions in reading "of long ago." The Masoretic Text has "uncircumcised" again, which lacks point in this line.

7. Ezekiel even turns once again to myth, should the warriors "of long ago" be giants.

8. Moth is the Canaanite equivalent of Greek Hades, Persephone's horrid groom.

Therefore Israel sometimes said, without qualification, that the Lord and the dead have nothing more to do with one another.[9] Psalm 88 is drastic: Those who "lie in the grave" are simply forgotten by God, are "cut off" from him, and consequently can no longer praise him. According to Israel's doctrine of creation, which locates our existence solely in our relation to God, this should have meant that the dead—whether circumcised or uncircumcised—have no existence of any sort. But Israel could not quite think that. Necromancy was forbidden, but just so thought of as possible; the shade of Samuel could even emerge to prophesy (1 Sam. 28).

The lacuna was theologically tolerable so long as the individual Israelite, who must descend to Sheol, could nevertheless think of death as overcome in the life of his descendants and in the continued life of the nation. So long as there was hope for the nation and for the family, death had not won. But when in Ezekiel's time "the whole house of Israel" could be seen as a valley full of dry bones (37:1–14), there had to be theological movement, for the Lord cannot be defeated by death and remain the Lord. As Jesus said against the Sadducees, who persisted in the old view, "He is God not of the dead, but of the living" (Mark 12:27 and parallels).

"Immortality of the soul" could not in Israel meet the case, for again: "You are dust, and to dust you shall return" (Gen. 3:19). If "the Adam" had not sinned and so had not returned to dust, this would not have been due to anything immortal in the pair, but solely to God's will to sustain them in life. Once death had actually entered the picture, the only way for the particular God of Israel to overcome the death of individuals, the only immortality consistent with "you are dust," is resurrection of the body made from that dust. The logic of the whole Old Testament thus drives to the Lord's final question to Ezekiel, "Son of a man, can these bones live?" (Ezek. 37:3; →37:1–14).

In the meantime, the question of the being of the dead persists, for there are many dead and the general resurrection is not yet. Thinking only of the blessed dead, are they "at rest"? "With the Lord"? And if so where is that? Or are they in "soul sleep"? Or are they already in the kingdom? Heaven is prominent in both Testaments, but not as a place to which the dying go. What is the—in an unpleasing but common scholarly phrase—"intermediate state"? Even Paul, facing the possibility of dying before the Lord's final advent, was not sure what to expect and seems indeed to have been alarmed by the possibility of being temporarily "found naked," that is, without a body (2 Cor. 5:1–5). Perhaps no definitive construal of the time between death and resurrection is possible, so that a certain pluralism of views must be expected. But there is one restriction on how we may conceive the present situation of dead believers: it must be possible now to address them and to pray together with them, as all classical liturgies assume.[10]

9. Greenberg 1997: 669–70 notes the sheer absence of gods from Israel's depiction of the underworld.

10. Including Protestant liturgies whose eucharistic prayers maintain connection with the ancient tradition: "Therefore with angels and archangels, and with all the company of heaven."

Finally, the church confesses a quite different descent *ad inferna* than that of Egypt: "He ... died, and was buried. He descended to the world below [*descendit ad inferna*].[11] And on the third day. ..." To be sure, since the descent first entered the creed, its import too has been disputed. Was Jesus's descent a victorious mission to liberate Old Testament saints from Sheol? Or was it a continuation of his vicarious suffering, a suffering of the final punishment due to sin? Both have been taught.

Or was it something stranger: God the Son's moment of utter solidarity with the dead, a solidarity that was a necessary part of the work of salvation? Was it perhaps a descent of which such descents as that of Egypt were but a prefiguration? Was there indeed a moment when the second person in God was as forgotten and silenced as the shades in Ps. 88, or even was the only actual such negated person? The perhaps greatest, and certainly most creative, twentieth-century Roman Catholic theologian, Hans Urs von Balthasar, made this possibility a center of his thinking and devoted to it a book that will continue a classic.[12]

There remains for this commentary unit only a more mundane question: Why are Assyria, Elam, and Meshech-Tubal chosen to represent those disgraced in Sheol by their violence on earth? Assyria, the destroyer of the northern Israelite kingdom and energetic oppressor also of Judah, is an obvious candidate. Elam was a notoriously militaristic nation in southwestern Iran that had intermittently conquered parts of Mesopotamia and only recently been quelled by Nebuchadnezzar; seen from Ezekiel's location in Babylon, she was a paradigmatic spreader of terror. Meshech-Tubal probably represent the many warrior groups who raided the Fertile Crescent from Asia Minor, the recurring nightmare (Zimmerli 1983: 175) of the nations there. It was—perhaps we may say—blatantly "unjust" warfare that earned these nations their disgrace.

As for Edom (32:29) and the Phoenicians (32:30), they seem to have been added because someone thought they could not be left out, if those were to be listed who belonged in the bad part of Sheol (→25:1–17; →28:20–26).

11. Neither the old translation "hell," given the word's current meaning, nor the new "the dead" works. The *inferna* are the *place* of the dead.

12. Hans Urs von Balthasar, *Mysterium Paschale: The Mystery of Easter*, trans. Aidan Nichols (Grand Rapids: Eerdmans, 1993). I reference the English version instead of the German original publication, since it is better, incorporating material not in the German. Von Balthasar himself thought the book too hastily done, but the theological public has overruled him.

EZEKIEL 33:1–20

I HAVE NO PLEASURE IN THE DEATH OF THE WICKED

These verses make a clear unit. They begin with the regular introduction: the word of the Lord comes to Ezekiel, addresses him as "you—son of a man," and gives him a mission. He is to speak to the people on the themes of repentance and of the true nature of God's righteousness. The passage begins the third part of Ezekiel's book, after a first part that contains mostly prophecies of judgment directed against Israel and a second part devoted to prophecies against Gentile nations (→25:1–17).

As in some other cases, my comments can be short because so much of the theological import of this unit is dealt with in other commentary units. Readers who read it together with the cross-referenced passages and comments will, however, find our passage among the two or three most theologically rich in Ezekiel's book.

The prophet is addressed and instructed four times within what is clearly a thematic unit, dividing the text into four subunits: 33:2–6; 33:7–9; 33:10–11; 33:12–20. The first two clearly go together, as—despite a mildly puzzling shift of addressee—do the next two, so that we have two main units; whether these were or were not given on the same occasion makes little difference to our purpose. Ezekiel 33:2–6 and 33:12–20 are addressed to Ezekiel's own "people," who are undoubtedly the exiles; 33:10–11 is addressed to "the house of Israel," who may be the exiles together with those remaining in the land. Since this shift occurs between the two subunits of what now seems to be one discourse (33:10–20), there is undoubtedly some textual history behind our present text, but as usual I am skeptical about discerning what that was.

An obtrusive point about our passage is that much of it is duplicated or nearly duplicated elsewhere in the book: 33:7–9 at 3:16–21, and 33:10–20 at 18:21–32. This has of course provoked attempts to determine whether the earlier passages are taken from the later or vice versa, and why this was done. For our purposes, we need not settle this, but in →3:16–21 I allowed myself to guess that the present passages are the originals.

Be all that as it may, it is clear what 33:1–20 is doing at its present location in the book. It prepares the way for the promises of restoration that will be the burden of the book's third part, by opening to a despairing people the possibility of repentance, of a new start. The key to the whole complex is at 33:10: the people see that it is because of their sins that they "waste away," and they see no escape, since their past disobedience will always be there, prohibiting any hope of restoration. In this situation, they ask, "How . . . can we live?" Yet even as they acknowledge their sin, they compound it by complaining that the Lord is unfair in so—as they think—binding their fate to past transgressions (33:17–20). The attribution of unfairness to God so horrifies the Targum that it cannot quote it even from the mouths of the rebellious and substitutes "the good ways of the Lord have not been explained to us" (Levey 1990: 95).

The Lord's teaching by way of Ezekiel is that the supposed impasse does not obtain; the future is open. It is a chief theological message of Ezekiel's book: "I have no pleasure in the death of the wicked, but that the wicked turn from their ways and live" (33:11). Since this is the case, for the people not to turn from their ways would be tantamount to insisting on dying when there is no need (→18:1–32). Ezekiel is to teach the people the true principle of the Lord's righteousness: those who repent will not die for their past transgressions—though this appears here as its negative corollary (33:12–16). Through our whole passage, the offer of repentance seems sometimes addressed to the people as a community and sometimes to individuals; in my view we should not try to sort this out (contrary to Zimmerli 1983: 187).

The two discourses have, to be sure, each their own function. The scope of the first appears at 33:7–9, where the Lord speaks to Ezekiel himself, appointing him a "sentinel"[1] for the house of Israel: he is to alert sinners to the consequences of their ways. The Lord had made this appointment before, as part of Ezekiel's original commissioning (→3:16–21). But whereas Ezekiel's appointment was there given in expectation that Israel would not heed the sentinel, so that the account of the appointment serves to introduce the long series of prophecies that are mostly words of judgment, here the sentinel's office is to be exercised in the situation after the judgments have come to pass and all seems lost and in which Ezekiel's

---

1. The Targum substitutes "teacher"; the rabbi is the one who warns the people (Levey 1990: 94).

mission will be to open the future by proclaiming the possibility of a new start and to bring the Lord's promises for the new life (→18:1–32).

Ezekiel's reappointment as sentinel is preceded by the speech to the people (33:2–6) that was initially mandated (33:1), whose intent is to prepare the people for Ezekiel's new office. This speech, in form a partial allegory like several other passages in Ezekiel, makes a fundamental statement of the relation between God, the nations, and the prophets. On account of unrighteousness—as we learn from the following verses—"the sword" threatens every "land," and every land needs to post sentinels to warn of its coming. Moreover, it is the Lord himself who brings the sword when it comes (33:2b). In the figure of a sentinel we are to see the prophet, whose task it is to warn of the Lord's coming. It is then up to the people to take warning.

The Lord in this parable is at once the enemy at the gates and the one who— since he will immediately proceed to appoint Ezekiel as such a sentinel—appoints prophets to warn of the enemy. Indeed, if the prophet succeeds in his task, the Lord's sword will be warded off. We are again in a theological depth that Ezekiel so regularly opens. The Lord's rule of history is often in fact a terrifying rule of the sword—Ezekiel's allegory is drawn from his and our daily experience. And that same Lord in his incarnate reality commands us to pray, "Deliver us from the time of trial," and pronounces peacemakers blessed. The disaster of much modern theology is that it has attempted to smooth out this mystery, which surely will not be alleviated until the end comes that Ezekiel will prophesy in the upcoming chapters. Neither a message of the "unconditionally loving God" nor a message of strict retributive divine justice can be faithful to scripture.

EZEKIEL 33:21–22

SILENCE

This passage poses a literary problem that perhaps defies decisive solution. The two verses make a clear unit, and since this bit of canonical text is neither linguistically obscure nor apparently corrupt, we must try to read it. But the passage is of a sort that delivers no information without some context, and this is not provided at its present location, for the passage displays neither material nor formal connection to what precedes or follows it. Perhaps, therefore, we are permitted a modest reconstruction of a former context.

A possibility immediately presents itself and is regularly noted by commentators (e.g., Zimmerli 1983: 191): 33:21–22 plainly seems to report the occurrence of the event prophesied at 24:26–27 (→24:15–27). In the present layout of the book, this relation is obscured by the editorial construction that places Ezek. 25–32, the prophecies against enemy nations, between the prophecies of Israel's doom and the prophecies of her restoration (→25:1–17).

In Ezek. 24 we read of the death of Ezekiel's wife and of the prophetic sign then laid on Ezekiel, that he is to abstain from all outward expression of his grief; and we find a prophecy given Ezekiel, of a similar repression that will afflict the exiles when they hear of Jerusalem's fall. Then there is a mysterious prediction that the news of the fall will release Ezekiel from a period of silence.

It is not as clear to me as to some others what sequence of events results if we take Ezek. 24 and our present two verses together. Perhaps it may suffice to suppose that the death of Ezekiel's wife, the silencing of normal expression laid on Ezekiel, and the burst of prophecy that interrupted it had been succeeded by an imposition of the hand of the Lord to reduce Ezekiel to silence also as a prophet—a silence that was itself perhaps a sign—from which news of the catastrophe released him to renewed prophetic speech.

The problem just discussed is related to another, which we need only mention. It is difficult to work out the relation between the date at the beginning of our passage and the known date of the fall of Jerusalem. But whether the Masoretic Text's dating of our passage is correct—which it seems likely not to be—or what are the maximum and minimum times it would have taken for the news to travel to Babylonia are interesting questions but need not detain us here (see Zimmerli 1983: 192–93).

If the proposed context and consequent construal of our passage are correct, three theologically interesting questions arise. Why does Ezekiel attribute his enforced silence to the imposition of the hand of the Lord, every other mention of which introduces the giving of a vision? The phenomenon so puzzles the Targum that it substitutes "a prophecy from before the Lord" for "the hand of the Lord" (Levey 1990: 95). We may further ask: What is the point of the silencing? And finally: Why does the arrival of the news of Jerusalem's fall release Ezekiel to prophesy, an event that in every other case is attributed to the coming of the word of God?

To the first question. Ezekiel's usage must reflect some experienced likeness between the onset of vision and the imposition of silence. And perhaps we may, even at our great remove from Ezekiel's experience, discern something of what that likeness was.

The beginning of an address in language, even so sovereign a beginning as the coming of the word to a prophet, is intrinsically conversational and has this character also when no response ensues. An address in language appeals to the personhood of the hearer, even in the extreme case of Ezekiel, whose personhood is hidden by the event of prophecy. But if what is *seen* is similarly sovereign, as it surely is when the seeing is "visions of God" (1:1), the normal conditions of seeing must be reversed, for when we look about we are established as a subject in control of what is seen. Therefore a seeing that is a revelation from God cannot be accommodated in the regular structure of a seeing: the seer's control of his seeing ceases, his status as subject is challenged.

We cannot know what event or experience imposed prophetic silence on Ezekiel. But perhaps he tells us how it felt: like the onset of vision, it halted his life. From that we learn something about prophecy: for the prophet, the activity of prophesying simply *is* the reality of his subjectivity. And from that we learn something about the word that came to the prophets, as it comes also to us: Christ inhabits the heart of believers more intimately and decisively than does their own subjectivity. As Martin Luther said, "In faith itself, Christ is present."[1]

To the second question. If, again, the above construal of our text is correct, then Ezekiel's time of imposed silence occupied some or all of the time between the

---

1. On this, see a foundational work of contemporary Luther study: Tuomo Mannermaa, *Christ Present in Faith: Luther's View of Justification*, ed. Kirsi Stjerna (Minneapolis: Fortress, 2005).

revelation that the final siege of Jerusalem had begun and the normally transmitted news of her actual fall. During such waiting, what more is there to say? Even for God to say through his prophet? And if a nonverbal sign, an *oth* (→3:22–5:4), substitutes for speech, the sign may well be the sign of silence.

Silence is not in itself congenital to the biblical God, for he is the God whose second identity is precisely the Word—he is, we may say, an inherently communicative God. If at some times during his history with us, he is reduced to silence—as perhaps he was during the time between the Word's death on the cross and the Word's resurrection—we are in the presence of a final mystery of what it costs God to be our God.[2]

To the third question. Prophetic speech, as I said in the introduction and in other commentary units, does not merely predict what is to come, it brings it to pass. It is an utterance of that same word by which all things exist. Thus there is an order: prophetic speech, then event. If that order is followed here, the refugee who brings the news of Jerusalem's fall is for the moment the prophet, and Ezekiel's renewed prophecy is the event liberated by the prophecy. Prophecy can, it appears, sometimes be the simple reporting of a fact.

2. On this possibility, see the amazing book of Hans Urs von Balthasar, *Mysterium Paschale: The Mystery of Easter*, trans. Aidan Nichols (Grand Rapids: Eerdmans, 1993).

EZEKIEL 33:23–33

CHEAP GRACE

Ezekiel 33:23–33 begins with Ezekiel's standard introduction to the coming of verbal prophecy: the word of the Lord comes to Ezekiel, addresses him as "you—son of a man," and gives him instructions. In the text as we have it, the introduction covers two units (33:24–29; 33:30–33) of very different formal character, which have probably been brought together because they have similar themes. Both must come from a time not long after Jerusalem's destruction.

Ezekiel 33 is the first chapter of the book's third and last main part, which brings together Ezekiel's prophecies of restoration, given after fulfillment of the prophecies of judgment collected in the book's first main part (→25:1–17). But Ezekiel or some other compiler of the items assembled early in this last part seems to have found it hard to break with old habits. Through Ezek. 33–35 we find him working up to straightforward promises of blessing but then delaying for matters that he thinks must first be dealt with. The present passage takes up two disastrous and inwardly connected attitudes still found among the people.

The first unit (33:24–29) begins with the Lord's report to Ezekiel of a theological opinion found among those who remain in the land—in isolated reoccupied towns, in the Judean rough country, and perhaps in guerilla strongholds and hideaways (33:27). In their deprivation they appeal to a central point of Israel's faith: the Lord started with one man, Abraham, and against all likelihood made from him the great nation to whom he gave the land of Israel. The people left in the land have—surely by the special grace of God—survived the catastrophe and can provide the Lord an analogue to Abraham. As the Lord once made Israel of the one Abraham, surely he may now begin again with this remnant, to make of it a new Israel and give it the land.

It was a pious and theologically plausible argument.[1] It had only two flaws. One is the self-satisfaction embodied in that "we," which does not appear to include the exiles. But it is the other flaw that the prophecy emphasizes and on which we will dwell: the survivors' lives are not those of a purified remnant.

A messenger-word from the Lord—doubly emphasized as such (33:25, 27)—marshals yet again Ezekiel's standard roster of transgressions. There are "abominations" among these people, practices that render those who do them unfit to worship the Lord:[2] even minimal laws of ritual purity are not kept[3] and idols are still in use (33:25). And there is ordinary crime (33:26); those mentioned are those that then as now are typical of a society in which civil order has broken down, as it had in a Judea with no recognized government. The prophet then threatens with the Lord's standard weapons of judgment: the sword, unbound nature, and pestilence (33:27). Thus even after the destruction of Jerusalem, there is room for more catastrophe: the countryside remnant can also be undone (33:28). And when even the hideouts and missed-out areas have been devastated, then surely any survivors of the survivors will understand that "I am יהוה," that the Lord intends his commands seriously and has the power to enforce them.

It is always dangerous to derive generally applicable patterns from Old Testament particulars. Thus, for a central case, when oppressed groups have seen themselves modeled by Israel's slavery in Egypt and have seen their future modeled by the exodus, the results have been sometimes glorious[4] but at other times disastrous: the first "liberation theology" was that of the Boers, who were indeed oppressed by the British and undertook an actual trek through the wilderness to claim unoccupied lands as their promised land—a claim that quickly devolved into the justification for apartheid when Zulus began moving into those same lands. But in the present case, we may perhaps allow ourselves the generalization, for the error of the survivors is indeed the very same heresy[5] as one that regularly plagues the church.

The survivors whose error Ezekiel rebukes are not the old natural syncretists, nor yet hardened rebels against moral or religious teaching. Their appeal to the election of Abraham shows that they know something of the Deuteronomistic theology (von Rad 1962–66: 1.71–77, 223–26) of election and covenant promoted by Josiah's reform. Their appeal is to grace. But they see no necessary connection between relying on the promises of the covenant and taking up the covenant's offer of a specific righteousness.

---

1. For an exilic prophet's positive use of the appeal to Abraham, see Isa. 51:1–3.

2. Rashi glosses with "homosexual acts," plausibly in this context (Rosenberg 2000: 290).

3. It is likely that "abominations" in 33:26 are sexual. See Lev. 18:22–30 and 20:13—from Ezekiel's own theological tradition. See further Greenberg 1997: 685.

4. As in the case of the theology created by black slaves in America.

5. Antinomianism is not, to be sure, a heresy in the proper technical sense, since it has not been condemned by any ecumenically authoritative *magisterium*. Here, we simply need a label for a truly disastrous theological opinion.

This heresy has been labeled "antinomianism"; its principle is that grace and "commandments and ordinances" do not inwardly call for each other—though this is rarely stated in so many words. In scripture, grace is the new possibility of a holy life; antinomianism turns grace into an excuse from holy living. A common variant is the notion that while a holy life is indeed wanted, one can deduce the content of such a life from the message of grace itself; in practice this allows us to construe the good as what we anyway desire. The Lord's savage query remains in force: Shall those who excuse themselves from the righteousness of my covenant possess its blessing? Shall, for example, adultery become a virtuous act because adulterers call on grace to trump the law?

In the second unit (33:30–33) the Lord addresses Ezekiel himself and targets Israel obliquely. Ezekiel's prophecies against Jerusalem have been promptly and spectacularly fulfilled, and it seems that he has thus become a celebrity (33:30). It belonged to the office of a prophet to bring the people's queries to the Lord. Among the exiles it has now become the popular thing to do: bring a query to Ezekiel and see what happens (33:30–31). The Lord has no objection to the practice itself. The accusation is that if the Lord does provide an answer, this has no consequences, since the inquirers' hearts are not in their queries (33:31).

Thus the liturgy in Ezekiel's house, and the theological and ethical content of the queries and responses, is for these exiles something to be enjoyed for their own sake, as a virtuoso performance (33:32). Their pleasure is merely esthetic and intellectual, not the pleasure that faith takes in worship and God's teaching. This declension is something that always can happen, and we will come back to it. First, however, we must follow the leap our text makes at the end.

When "it"[6] happens, the exiles will learn that discourse with the Lord is not an entertainment—that a prophet has actually been among them, that it was really with the Lord that they spoke in Ezekiel's house (33:33). We are told nothing about what "it" is, and this evocation of mystery belongs to the point: After the end of everything—which the fall of Jerusalem certainly was for the exiles—what indeed comes next? There would seem to be only two possibilities: "bread and circuses," perhaps of the theological sort enjoyed by Ezekiel's audiences; or an eschatological "it," an act of God beyond all comparisons.

We have encountered this unspecified "it" once before, in →7:10–27. There it rhetorically alternates with "the day" and "an end," with the day of the Lord's final victory and the end of all that is not his will. Israel will finally learn with whom she has been speaking through all her history.

In the meantime, Ezekiel must reckon with being regarded as a performer. Perhaps, indeed, the Lord worries that he might acquiesce in the role. Perhaps I may a second time indulge in a generalization: it is indeed always easy for those

---

6. NRSV's "this" posits an antecedent that is not there. "When it happens" should be the translation.

who must speak for God to his people to hearken too much to the real pleasures—even if sometimes masochistic—of the game, and it is easy for the people to settle back in the same spirit. Theology is in fact a high intellectual exercise, and worship the center of all art; and both should indeed be enjoyed also for themselves. The temptation is to "do" and hear theology without investing our lives in its truth, to move with the liturgy without fearing the event in which we are participating.

The title of this commentary unit comes from a once immensely popular small book by Dietrich Bonhoeffer, one of the essential books of the previous century's Christian history.[7] One cannot, to be sure, obtain God's grace by paying for it. But if our reliance on grace costs us nothing, grace is cheapened, in both of the above senses.

7. Dietrich Bonhoeffer, *The Cost of Discipleship*, trans. R. H. Fuller (New York: Macmillan, 1953).

EZEKIEL 34:1–31

THE GOOD SHEPHERD

This chapter is long, and its conceptual coherence is not apparent at first glance. At second glance, however, we may discover that though once independent texts may have been used in the canonical text's construction, the result is so artfully knit a composition that we cannot divide it for comment—convenient though that would otherwise be.

Dating is a problem. The prophet explicitly presumes the completion of Israel's exile. But two initial component messenger-words (34:2–6; 34:7–10) proclaim the imminent rescue of Israel from the misrule of her princes, who after 586 are of course no longer ruling, well or badly. Perhaps the best solution is provided by the interpretation of "the shepherds" proposed below: that the phrase denotes Israelite monarchy as a single phenomenon. After the catastrophe, the monarchy also seems for a time and in some quarters to have been thought of as a continuing reality—whose termination the Lord here announces. I will therefore, with hesitation, assign the composition to a time shortly after Jerusalem's destruction.[1]

The title assigned this commentary unit is an obvious choice. Our passage is a key part of a discourse that runs through scripture and concludes with John 10:1–18, where Jesus identifies himself as the Good Shepherd, that is, the shepherd envisaged by the metaphor itself. Israel shared with much of the ancient world the image of a nation as a flock and of its ruler—divine or human—as a shepherd (for examples, see Zimmerli 1983: 213). In the Old

---

1. Greenberg's alternative proposal (1997: 694–95) deserves to be reported: Jehoiachin and Zedekiah, with their surviving nobles, are still thought of as Israel's princes by some, whom the prophets denounce.

Testament, Jeremiah seems to have been the first to turn the theme *against* the princes; and indeed Jer. 23:1–6 probably provided a model for Ezekiel's longer and richer construction.

The whole composition is introduced in Ezekiel's regular fashion: the word of the Lord comes to Ezekiel, addresses him as "you—son of a man," and commands him to prophesy. It is concluded with an appropriate version of Ezekiel's regular concluding formula, "then they shall know," and with a final—and lovely—statement of the salvation promised by the whole composition. In between, the text is divided by repetitions of the formula that announces messenger-words, which now for the first time in the book are mostly messages of salvation.

At 34:11 Ezekiel finally comes to an unadulterated promise of salvation, to what the Reformation tradition calls "gospel," and so to what the book's final main part (Ezek. 33–48) was editorially created to accommodate. We have to say "finally," for there have been thirty-two chapters that mostly prophesied somebody's doom, and even in Ezek. 33 we have still seen Ezekiel or an editor twice come to the brink of saving promise but then draw back to attend to a judgment that must first be made. Indeed, also in the present chapter Ezekiel cannot bring himself to proclaim the Lord's coming as the true shepherd without first denouncing the existing—or perhaps no longer existing!—shepherds.

First, then, the judgment of Israel's "shepherds" (34:1–10). In view of the word chosen for the one who will replace them, who will be a "prince" (34:24),[2] these must be Israel's monarchical rulers, as the metaphor's tradition would in any case lead us to expect. Since these are the princes simply "of Israel," they are the princes of both kingdoms (Zimmerli 1983: 214). And the unqualified plural "the shepherds" suggests that no particular king or pair of kings is intended, but rather Israelite monarchy as a historical phenomenon. The shepherds are here not judged for religious abominations, as more usually in Ezekiel, but for the simple injustice that more occupied earlier prophets (Eichrodt 1970: 473).

The accusation against the monarchy (34:2–6) is made with a rhetorically rich development of the flock and shepherd image, but is materially very simple. Shepherds necessarily live at least in part from the products of the flock,[3] but the calling for which they receive these privileges is to live *for* the flock, which the princes of Israel have not done. They have instead done exactly what the Lord predicted when Israel begged Samuel to replace divine rule through charismatics with kings like those of "all the nations": they have exploited the people for their own indulgence and ambition (1 Sam. 8:5–18). In consequence, the sheep are scattered, the prey of predators (Ezek. 34:5–6). Since these are the Lord's sheep (34:6), the

2. נשׂיא (*nasi*), conventionally translated "prince," does not, as recent English usage might suggest, denote a subordinate member of a royal household, but is a more specifically Israelite title for the monarch—or other great leader—as against the generally ancient Near Eastern title *melek* (מלך), conventionally translated "king"; see Zimmerli 1983: 218.

3. Since Israelite shepherds were not permitted to slaughter for food, the wicked shepherds' taking of meat from the flock was not only selfish but illegal; see Greenberg 1997: 696.

princes must expect the Lord's intervention. A specially announced messenger-word introduces the sentence: termination of the monarchy (34:10).

Two theologically rather weighty observations seem called for. First, the very thing that elsewhere in Ezekiel appears as the judgment of the Lord, Israel's scattering by Assyria and Babylon, appears here as the consequence of misrule by her princes, which the Lord now denounces and says he will punish. Or again, the Lord now blames Israel's exile on her princes, promises to rescue her, and calls the day on which Israel went into exile "a day of clouds and thick darkness" (34:12), that is, the prophetic tradition's "day of the Lord," the day of his own triumph (→7:10–27). The Lord thus shows up on both sides of the great catastrophe.

We have encountered this antinomy in earlier passages; here it appears with a starkness before which we must acknowledge that it escapes conceptual resolution. We can only say that the history in which the righteous Lord implicates himself by involving himself with unrighteous creatures must just so be filled with moral and theological antinomies. At the climax of the Lord's shepherding of Israel, the Lord God the Son will cry to the Lord God the Father, "Why have you forsaken me?" Perhaps we may then further ask why God's acts in history are so conflicted, why he continues to bother with us. To that, Ezekiel and Jesus have an answer: we are his lost sheep.

Second, we may observe that 34:2–6 provides something like a theology and estimate of politics. Rulers are there to care for those they rule. Their position in the nation is a particular opportunity to exercise righteousness, that is, in Israel's understanding, to make their specific contribution to a community ordered for mutual love. And we must expect them to reject the opportunity—Jesus's predecessors in shepherding were, he says, "thieves and bandits" (John 10:8). The last lines of Ezek. 34:2–10 then hint at the full-blooded promise that will immediately follow in a new messenger-word.

Ezekiel 34:11–16 is a word of gospel that corresponds to the foregoing judgment. It reaches its climax with the eschatologically drastic promise: "I myself will be the shepherd of my sheep" (34:15). The Lord will personally do what Israel's rulers were supposed to do and did not and what Jesus in a parable (Matt. 18:12 and parallels) describes as his own mission: the Lord will search for the lost sheep and bring them back. Indeed, the Lord will make a new exodus with them: bringing them from the places of their captivity, leading them into the land, and caring for them there.

The image of a renewed exodus has appeared before in Ezekiel (20:33–38), but to very different effect. There the tale was of the judgments that Israel brought on herself in the wilderness; here it is of the loving care that the Lord will lavish on his sheep in a new journey to and settlement in the land. Indeed, the blessings promised to Israel in her renewed occupation of the land clearly surpass what is possible in the world as we know it; and the promises will become even more explicitly eschatological in the concluding unit of the chapter (34:25–29).

There is, to be sure, one negative that this promise of a new exodus has in common with the earlier one: two incorporated messenger-words (34:17–19; 34:20–22) announce that during the journey there will be judgment "between sheep and sheep." Those who in fact arrive in the newly promised land will be a purified remnant, as were those who survived the original desert wanderings.

It is the standard of this judgment that arrests our attention; perhaps it suggests something like a theology of economics, to pair with the theology of politics suggested earlier. To the bad sheep the Lord says, "Is it not enough for you to feed on the good pasture, but you must tread down with your feet the rest of your pasture?" (34:18). The bad economic actors are not those who simply live well, but those who do so without regard for conditions that enable others to live well; the pasture itself is apparently to be cropped with enjoyment. In the economics of this passage, the supposition is plenty and not scarcity: my prosperity need not be purchased by your poverty. To create a zero-sum economic system requires, it seems, disregard on the part of the prosperous—which of course, like political misrule, is the all too likely event.

As the promise of a divinely shepherded new exodus followed judgment on previous shepherding, so now a promise follows proclamation of the judgment internal to the new exodus (34:23–24)—note the neat compositional nesting. And here a problem appears, indeed two linked problems, for we now do not read that the Lord will himself be Israel's Good Shepherd, but that he will establish "David" in that role.

In Jer. 23:5, the eschatological Good Shepherd is a "branch" of the house of David, that is, one of his descendants—and Matthew will be at pains to establish Jesus's Davidic lineage (Matt. 1:1–17). But here the future shepherd is David himself. Does Ezekiel announce David's resurrection, since he did, after all, expect resurrection of "the whole house of Israel" (Ezek. 37:11)? That is probably not the intent of the text. But how then can it refer to a future heir of David simply as David, rather than as his "branch"? In view of the dependence of our passage on that in Jeremiah, the removal of a standard prophetic trope—in the immediate connection see Isa. 11:1 or Jer. 33:15—can hardly be accidental.[4]

Does not Ezekiel contradict himself? He has made much of how great it will be when the Lord himself takes over from the earthly shepherds. But suddenly David—after all, the ancestral paradigm of those shepherds—is to be the eschatological shepherd. Ezekiel 34:24 does provide a description of the resulting situation—the Lord rules in his heaven and David is prince among the people—and that was perhaps enough for purposes of the composition. But noting this does not solve the theological problem.[5]

4. Rashi seems to identify the king as the Messiah (Rosenberg 2000: 299).
5. Historical-critical operations can of course abolish this problem as it does so many. But it can do so, here as so often elsewhere, only by abolishing the text that was to be explained. It is to Eichrodt's great credit that he recognizes that "he who is to come is much more intimately

Here, in my view, is one of the places where we must allow ourselves some of the conceptual play that is both the delight and temptation of theology. As it happens, the same classic doctrine provides an answer to both of our questions.

First the major problem and its remarkably available resolution. For our whole passage to make straightforward sense, the Good Shepherd must be at once God and a descendent of David. And that, of course, is exactly what classical Christology says of Jesus the Christ. In the traditional formulation: the hypostasis of God the Son is the hypostasis also of the human Davidic Messiah, Jesus. In more contemporary language: "God the Son is Jesus the Christ" is an identity statement. By either formulation of the rule: you cannot refer to God the Son without thereby referring to the man Jesus, and you cannot refer to the man Jesus without thereby referring to God the Son. There is just one identifiable person there (on this Christology, →1:25–28b).

A development of this claim within classical Christology then provides the conceptual framework within which we may understand the text's calling a descendent of David simply "David." In the jargon of traditional theology this development is called "the communication of attributes": if God the Son and Jesus are the same person, then what is true of the one must somehow be true of the other, divine and human attributes must somehow be mutually "communicated."[6] One of the things true of God the Son is that he transcends the divisions of time; therefore Jesus must somehow transcend them and so indeed be able to sum up in himself the whole Davidic history, appearing as himself the paradigm of Davidic rule.

It will be objected that these last paragraphs impose an alien Christian meaning on Ezekiel, who cannot have had Jesus or these conceptual moves in mind. But our reading is alien to the text actually before us only if the Christian doctrines adduced are not true. Those who suppose that the church's doctrine of Christ is true will hold that, whatever may or may not have been in the minds of Ezekiel or his editors,[7] the christological relations just traced are the structure by which the canonical text makes precisely its own—if you like, "original"—sense. This holds also for the previously noted description of the situation at 34:24. The verse is a variant of "I . . . will be your God, and you shall be my people" (Lev. 26:12), the great covenant promise: here the one side is as it is in the paradigm version: "I, the LORD, will be their God." But the people's side is now: "My servant David

---

associated with Yahweh, and more definitely taken into his divine being than any previous ruler" (1970: 478).

6. Resolution of that "somehow" has been disputed throughout the history of Christianity, and I will not attempt it here. Also the symmetry of the relation has been disputed; suffering is predicated of Jesus and so should apparently be predicated of God the Son; it however took the church centuries to acknowledge this. Finally she did and laid it down: "One of the Trinity suffered for us." And to this day, the scope of that proposition is disputed.

7. To what extent "authorial intent" should in general be determinative for interpretation or indeed whether such a thing is ascertainable at all have been much disputed questions. Within Christian theology, the debate is complicated by the further question: Who, after all, is finally the author of canonical texts? Whose authorial intent is to be discerned?

shall be prince among them" (Ezek. 34:24). The demanded insight is that the Lord and this prince are the one eschatological shepherd.

One unit of the composition (34:25–29) remains before the conclusion. Here we see nature itself transformed by the rule of the eschatological Good Shepherd—shepherds, after all, live with nature. Such marvels as are here promised did not appear in Ezekiel's day, nor were they seen as the exiles returned. If they are to happen at all, they await the day when David's shepherding will be universal and open for all to see, so that "creation itself will be set free from its bondage to decay and will obtain the freedom of the glory of the children of God" (Rom. 8:21).

Finally the construction is rounded off and concluded by a version of Ezekiel's regular finishing formula. Here the formula is completed by another and beautiful variant of the covenant promise: what the people will hear and learn when the Lord who is David takes over as shepherd is, "You are my sheep, the sheep of my pasture, and I am your God" (Ezek. 34:31).

EZEKIEL 35:1–36:15

THE MOUNTAINS OF EDOM
AND ISRAEL

Ezekiel 35:1–36:15 makes a single, if lengthy, unit for comment. Ezekiel 35:1 is Ezekiel's standard introduction for prophecy other than vision: the word of the Lord comes to him, addresses him as "you—son of a man," and instructs him. At 36:16 another such introduction is followed by a clearly structured unit. The verses between are, to be sure, divided by a second address to Ezekiel at 36:1; and we might therefore follow the chapter division and take 35:1–15 and 36:1–15 separately were they not joined by interior reference at 36:5–7. This embedded messenger-word instances the judgment of Edom as the reason for the prophecies of blessing in 36:1–15, but does not itself report that judgment. Such a report is, however, needed to make the prophecy of blessing intelligible in the form it here takes; prefixing 35:1–15 provides for that, and 36:5–7 makes the connection. This sort of linkage between the two passages of course creates a whole that exists in the book and hardly in antecedent proclamation.

Ezekiel 36:1–15 brings exuberant promises of salvation, addressed to the hill country just west of the Jordan, the original heartland of the nation: when the exiles return it will become an Eden, with prosperous towns and a numerous and preternaturally happy population (36:8–11). An earlier prophecy (→6:1–14) was addressed to those same hills, but to opposite effect. It is on account of this prophecy of salvation that the whole complex of our passage appears here in the concluding group of chapters (Ezek. 33–48) devoted to Israel's coming restoration.

The blessing is still backhanded: it is not motivated by Israel's repentance—if indeed there has been any—or even directly by the Lord's love of Israel, but by the insult Edom has offered to the Lord himself: contempt for a people who are the Lord's people and encroachments on a land that is his land (35:10–14; 36:5).[1] As appears throughout 35:1–15, the Lord will punish Edom by events precisely designed to refute her insults and by inflicting the very same aggression against her emblematic mountain that she is inflicting on Israel's heights—blood for blood (35:6). Indeed, we might easily get the impression that the promise of blessing to Israel is in the argument of the larger passage merely the reverse of the judgment against Edom: for Edom to be thoroughly confounded and her insults to the Lord refuted, Israel must be restored.

The date has to be deduced from content. To establish one term, Edom is not merely, as in 25:12–14, rejoicing in Judah's defeat, but is now encroaching on her territory. To establish the other, Edom is still free to do this (Zimmerli 1983: 234). Therefore we must think of a time some years after 586 but before Persia's provision for Judah's integrity within the empire.[2]

There are further divisions within the text. Within 35:1–15, these are marked by variations of the general formula for oracles against foreign nations (→25:1–17): "Because you did . . . , therefore. . . ." Within 36:1–15, we find a sort of mirror of this pattern: the protasis of such new beginnings is still the transgression of Edom, but the apodosis is the blessing to Israel. This mirroring again binds the two passages together. The nesting of the smaller units doubtless betrays a history of interpolations, but these—so far as I can see—need not detain us.

The theology of these rhetorical structures is arresting. Because Israel is the Lord's even when he undoes her, he cannot allow her to be bloodied by outsiders to their relation (35:5–6): the Lord indeed made wicked Babylon his instrument, but he did not send Edom. And because the land is the Lord's, it must be inhabited by his people or not at all (35:10).[3] Thus Edom's insults and aggressions are directly against the Lord; it is his *kabod*, his "glory" (→1:4–24), that is at stake. According to the Targum's gloss, the land that Edom has violated is "the abode of His Shekinah" (Levey 1990: 100), the place chosen by God for his dwelling in the world.

Accordingly, both units hammer home the Lord's personal involvement, with an insistent and sometimes grammatically emphasized first-person singular: I, the Lord will undo Edom, and I, the Lord, will bless Israel. This immediate involvement of the Lord in created history, including his taking a direct part in its

---

1. Also legally; see Lev. 25:23.

2. Indeed, one account of the Persian decree allowing the Jews to return says that it included a command for the Edomites to evacuate the villages they had seized; see Greenberg 1997: 723.

3. The position of modern Israel is an urgent question here, but one that goes beyond the limits of a commentary.

violence (→7:10–27), is a theme we have met repeatedly in Ezekiel. The Lord's special annoyance with Edom appears also in 25:12–14, where the formula for Edom's doom (25:14) differs ominously from that used for the other bad neighbors condemned in the chapter.

The precise way in which the Lord's glory is thus linked to Israel is—so far as I am aware—unique in religious history. The gods of the ancient world—as indeed of religion generally—are so very much the projection[4] of their adherents' values and fears that had the Lord been like, for example, Babylonian Marduk, the fall of Jerusalem and the exile of the princes and priesthood would have been the end of his *kabod* and so of him. The Lord transcends such challenges to his deity. Yet neither is the Lord like the neutral God imagined by the Western Enlightenment, with no stake in the fate of any particular nation.[5] Thus the Lord remains God after the events of 586, yet because he is the particular God יהוה, of the particular people Israel, he is not unaffected by them. He will continue to fight for his people also when his own judgments have undone them—even if that means that finally he suffers their undoing and his faithfulness to them in his own body on a cross.

The instructions for the oracle against Edom begin by mandating a prophetic gesture, an *oth* (→3:22–5:4) of a type familiar to those who have been reading through Ezekiel: the prophet is to aim his words at their distant target by a threatening geographical gesture, setting his face "against" Moab's highlands.[6] The introduction to a messenger-word follows; this seems in the present text to cover the whole chapter, despite the recurrence of "thus says the Lord" at 35:14. The very first lines carry the substance of the judgment: the Lord himself will be "against" Edom, to make it a "desolation and a waste," corresponding to the desolation of Israel, in which Edom rejoiced and exploited (35:12). From here on, I will take up our passage's subunits in order, commenting on a few special and interesting features of each.

I begin with 35:5–9. Edom has contemned Israel because she has "cherished an ancient enmity" (35:5). In Israel's memory, the enmity was indeed ancient, exemplified by an event on Israel's way from the wilderness into Palestine (Num. 20:14–21). Moses sends messengers to ask peaceful passage for "your brother Israel," pleading both the Lord's act to bring Israel from Egypt—which Moses presumes Edom will acknowledge!—and her sufferings on the way. Edom flatly refuses and threatens war. Why?

Perhaps precisely because of that appeal on behalf of "your brother Israel." In the Numbers account, this reference is not a mere piece of diplomatic language,

---

4. As a general analyst of religious phenomena, Ludwig Feuerbach got some things very right—which is not to approve the uses recently made of his theory. See Ludwig Feuerbach, *The Essence of Religion*, trans. Alexander Loos (Amherst: Prometheus, 2004).

5. Except, perhaps, as the nation-states that carried the Enlightenment appropriated him.

6. Seir is not the name of a particular peak, but a term for the hilly territory south of the Dead Sea, on both sides of the Jordan.

for in the long ethnographic memory of the ancient world, Israel and Edom were in fact brothers. "Edom" is the ethnographic name for Esau (Gen. 32:3; 36:1), the son of Isaac and barely older brother of that Jacob who himself became "Israel." As Edom would remember it, Jacob/Israel had taken Esau/Edom's right as Isaac's firstborn son by bribery and deceit, by these morally dubious means becoming heir of the promise to Abraham (25:30–33; 27:1–33). Thus Israel's appeal to brother Edom was not likely to be well received. In Edom's view, it should have been Edom that the Lord was leading to a promised land.

In this connection, readers may wish to follow up a recent and major exegetical-systematic enterprise. As the Old Testament narrates the generational descent of the promise to Abraham, being a father's first and beloved son—as Esau/Edom was—is not a safe position to occupy. The paradigmatic case is the almost sacrifice of Isaac (Gen. 22). In Judaism and recently in Christian theology this last event even has its own name, "the Akedah," "the binding," to signify its unique role in God's history with Israel: it is only after Isaac is bound for sacrifice, and so in fact given up to death, that the Lord binds himself by oath to his promise to Abraham (22:16). Jewish scholar Jon Levenson analyzes the dangerous situation of scripture's beloved sons with a fresh eye for textual phenomena and with conceptual daring in *The Death and Resurrection of the Beloved Son*, a title that suggests how far into Christian theology this Jewish thinker ventures.[7]

A second notable feature of 35:5 is its characterization of the fall of Jerusalem. To see this, however, we have to correct NRSV at several points. First, its "at the time of their final punishment" is a periphrastic smoothing of a rugged text, which in the process effaces the point. The word translated "punishment" (עָוֹן, *awon*)[8] is far more comprehensive than this translation suggests: in accord with Israel's general understanding of moral reality, it denotes a unitary moral disaster that comprehends in one reality sin, guilt, and punishment. Perhaps something like "ruin"—or even "damnation"—is as close as we can get in English. Next, the restricting possessive "their" has no basis in the Masoretic Text or the ancient versions. Finally, use of the adjective "final" obscures a feature of the text that must not be hidden. The Hebrew word intended to be represented is a noun, "an end," which those reading through Ezekiel will have encountered before: this is the absolute "an end" of →7:1–9. Thus what is here evoked is sheer eschatological termination, as ruin.

Ezekiel speaks of this end as in the past, so that he seems to speak from within some new order of things, after sin-guilt-punishment has had its final day. Again we encounter that simultaneity of *the* end with an inner-historical end that appears

7. Levenson goes on to argue that while the practice of firstborn sacrifice ceased, the conception that the beloved firstborn is intrinsically devoted to the Lord continued and underlies theology and practice in both Judaism and Christianity. The whole book is important, but I cannot follow it further here.

8. In this passage, the word is idiosyncratically translated "punishment" by RSV and NRSV. KJV has "iniquity," and the Septuagint has ἀδικία.

so often in Ezekiel: almost in principle in Ezek. 7 and in more or less the same way as here in, for example, the oracle against Egypt at 30:1–19.

The subunit ends with a version of Ezekiel's great outcome formula: "Then you/ they shall know that I am *yhwh*." This time the subject is in the second-person plural: the addressees of the judgment—any remaining inhabitants of Mt. Seir— shall know whom they had been mocking and who has undone them. We may ask: What good will that do anyone then? But we will ask that only because we moderns tend no more to reckon with God's glory than did Edom.

Ezekiel 35:10–15 is then notable for the clarity with which two phenomena appear on which I have already commented. The one: the Lord here simply identifies words directed "against the mountains of Israel" with "words against me" (35:12–14). The other: he inflicts a particularly biting reversal of Edom's sin into her punishment: as she rejoiced to see Israel's desolation, so "the whole earth" will rejoice to see hers. An eschatological tone infiltrates this repetition of the outcome formula: it is now "they," that is, the inhabitants of "the whole earth," who will learn who יהוה is. But when the whole earth knows that, the kingdom will have come.

Ezekiel 36:1–7 carries to the extreme the backhanded character of the complex's prophecy of blessing. It is a catena of messenger-words addressed to the desolate mountains of Israel. The pattern of oracles against enemy nations is reiterated: because "the enemy" has said and done such and such, therefore "thus says the Lord." But although the words are directed to Israel's mountains, nothing is said for or against them. The mountains of Israel are told only that because Edom—and indeed "the rest of the nations"—has made them "a source of plunder and an object of derision" Edom and the nations "shall themselves suffer insults." So far as these verses tell us, and indeed so far as their strange logic will allow, the only recompense to Israel's mountains will be the punishment of their despisers.

In 36:8–15 we finally get what the whole complex has been aiming at. The first verses say it all: the mountains of Israel will become a preternatural orchard like Eden (Gen. 2:9); and there will be multitudes to live from this bounty, for the people of Israel are coming home at last and for good. The promised paradisial degree of prosperity and happiness is of course inconceivable as the world now turns; once again the final kingdom of God and a renewed Israelite possession of her hill country coalesce in the word the Lord gives Ezekiel. To evoke the absolute character of the promised blessing, Ezekiel again recruits the language of myth, here of the world tree that nourishes all things from the underworld waters—as he does more explicitly in →31:1–18. The Targum glosses all this as the coming final *revelation* of God (Levey 1990: 100).

Two general theological problems are raised by the tenor of our passage and must at least be mentioned. The first is posed especially by the immediately foregoing observations: Is the promise for this age simply absorbed into the final promise, so that within history as know it we have nothing more to expect of the promise?[9] Or is there an actual deficit outstanding also in this age, so that the Jewish cry "Next year in Jerusalem!" remains a proper response to biblical promise? Both answers now have partisans within Christian theology—and I state my decision for the second.[10]

The second concerns the "motivation" of God's creating works and has divided the theological spirits through history: Does God do good for his creatures for their sake or for his own? Following the apparent logic of the first possibility, the more pusillanimous sorts of modernity have construed a god with no purposes of his own that might clash with ours, a god we posit to assist with what we in any case want to be and do. Following the apparent logic of the second, we conjure up the falsely so-called God of the Old Testament, against whom human dignity demands that we revolt.

In my judgment, the problem is resolvable, and no one has come closer to doing so than Jonathan Edwards (→26:1–21). Edwards taught that since God is the good itself, he must necessarily have himself as his object in all his acts. But since the *triune* God's very self is communication, if there are creatures, his act on his own behalf is just so his communication of himself—and so of supreme value—to the creatures to whom he turns.[11]

---

9. This view is not necessarily linked to supersessionism.

10. As one will do in reading the prophets, we again verge on the question: What of modern Israel? And this time, with a special bite, for Israel's homeland high country is now known as the West Bank. Again I will avoid the question.

11. For my fuller presentation of Edwards on this matter, see Robert W. Jenson, *America's Theologian: A Recommendation of Jonathan Edwards* (New York: Oxford University Press, 1988), 38–43.

EZEKIEL 36:16–38

WHAT THEN?

The passage has a clear structure. It begins with the usual introduction to a verbal prophecy: the word comes to Ezekiel and addresses him as "you—son of a man." What first follows is, as in some other passages, an address to Ezekiel himself, here a characterization of Israel's past, in her land and in exile. Then, because that history has been what it has been, Ezekiel is given a messenger-word to the exiles (36:22–32) that makes it clear with the first sentence and with the last: it is not on account of their worth that the Lord is about to restore them. Nevertheless, he will do it. As often happens in Ezekiel, other messenger-words have been editorially attached to this primary word at 36:33 and 36:37 because of their materially similar depictions of restoration.

The main prophecy was probably given toward the end of the time of exile, for there is a problem behind it that would be most likely to emerge when exilic prophets' promises of restoration were "about" (36:22) to be fulfilled. I may conveniently state it here at the beginning: Suppose Israel is indeed returned to her land, what then? Will not her dismal history of faithlessness and consequent disaster simply pick up where it left off?[1] She is, after all, a "rebellious house" almost by definition (→1:28c–3:15), and there are no good signs in her more recent centuries, at least as the Lord here characterizes them.

The Lord sums up Israel's history between settlement and exile in one sentence: "When the house of Israel lived on their own soil, they defiled it" (36:17). The defilements are of two sorts, which by now will be familiar—perhaps overfamiliar—to

---

1. Jeremiah also saw the problem. On the prophets of the exile in this context, see Zimmerli 1983: 248–49.

readers of Ezekiel: Israel has spilled blood unjustly, and she has indulged in idolatry (36:18; →22:1–16). We must pause for a point of translation, since it will later become important. The word NRSV here translates "soil" is *adamah* (אדמה), but in the story of the creation of "the Adam" (*haadam*), NRSV translates *adamah* with "ground" (Gen. 2:7), thereby concealing that it is the same Hebrew word in both passages.

We need to spend some time with the notion that Israel by her actions had defiled the land, for it is not obvious how something like a national territory can be made ritually unclean. Persons, actual cult sites, the particular ground on which blood was spilled, and all such things could be polluted, but the whole land of Israel and Judah? How can Israel have achieved this? And to answer that, we need to ask a prior question that this commentary has so far elided: What, indeed, does it mean to defile something?[2]

A place to start with the latter question can be the underlying analogy—or what moderns will call an analogy—with physical cleanliness and uncleanliness. As in most societies one should not, for the sake of the company, sit down at a party meal with mud on one's hands, so one should not attend a communal sacrifice in a state unfitting in the particular cultic community. Are dirty hands at dinner an offense against hygiene, manners, or the integrity of the fellowship? In intact societies, these are not separate questions. Just so, participating at the temple after, for example, dealing with a corpse, without intervening cleansing, is an offense at once against hygiene, manners, and the integrity of the fellowship—and this fellowship includes God, so that the pollution disrupts the community at its heart. Thus the Lord can propose to purify polluted and polluting Israel by *washing* her (36:25)—and indeed Israel's old ritual law specified washing with "purifying water" to cleanse from corpse pollution (Num. 19:13–20).

But in this context what counts as dirt? It is whatever offends—for rational reasons or by historical accident—the fellowship of Israel with the Lord and within herself; it is whatever as a matter of fact is simply foreign to this common life. Perhaps we may say: the clean in Israel is what *feels right* to the sensibility of Israel as a gathered fellowship, and the unclean is what is *repellent* for it. This can extend to what may seem arbitrary to outsiders. Thus the accustomed fish of the Sea of Galilee—as earlier the fish of the Nile—had proper skeletons and fins and scales; sea animals with little discernible inner structure and no scales were alien to the world of Israel, and so were not to be put on the communal table. And such a rule will persist, or indeed be reinforced, also when outsiders find such food delicious. For reasons lost in time, Israel could not offer pigs to the Lord; and since all meals are in some degree sacrifices, neither could she eat them.

The center of any ancient community's life—the "party" at which it gathered—was its cult. To defile someone or something was to make them unfit for

---

2. For the general distinction of clean and unclean in Israel, use the indices to Johannes Pedersen, *Israel: Its Life and Culture* (London: Oxford University Press, 1926).

participation or use in the cult—which is to say, in the life of the community. In Israel's case, this could happen from two quite opposite directions.

I remarked in the introduction that converse with the book of Ezekiel was considered by the rabbis greatly to "pollute the hands." That is, preoccupation with Ezekiel takes one so deeply into the mystery of God as to render the person temporarily unfit for ordinary human fellowship, even for the community's ordinary fellowship with God. Such pollution by extraordinary converse with God is obviously not what figures in our passage.

What does figure is the Lord's opposite, the realm of death. This was felt—and "felt" is the right word—as a sort of ontological filth, something beyond the bounds of accepted reality; thus this is, for example, a very different sensibility from that of Egypt, for which the gods and the dead were one. Death's realm of unbeing nevertheless often intrudes into reality. And when we are dirtied by contact with intruding death, we will require washing before returning to the community. Even those prohibited sea animals, as somehow imperfect fish, carry in that deficit of being a remote shadow of death's realm of unbeing, and someone who eats one will need cleansing.

Finally, polluting acts are reflexive. The dirt on my hands pollutes me before it pollutes the dinner party—though were it not for the sensibility of the community giving the party, neither would it pollute me. The Lord likens Israel to a menstruating woman: she is herself polluted—quite innocently, like those who attend to a relative's burial—by dying flows of the blood of life, and so will in turn pollute the community until she is purified.

Such apprehensions are not merely primitive or otherwise outmoded. No society is without a common sense of what is canny and uncanny or proper and improper; and a society that loses its hold on such distinctions will not endure. Moreover, since the heart of any culture is some relation—even pure negation—to some god or other, neither can a society endure without some sense of specifically cultic cleanliness and uncleanliness. Most Westerners, for example, might still feel that presenting a pornographic play in a church building, even one that no longer housed divine service, would somehow pollute it;[3] when we will have altogether lost such feelings, something of our civilization will have ceased.

Thus a place of execution—such as that of Jesus—was necessarily located outside the city gates, outside the boundaries of the living community; and even there the dead bodies could not be allowed to remain over the Sabbath (John 19:31). One could create an entire doctrine of atonement by describing the cross and resurrection as a culminating pollution and a final ritual of cleansing.

It should now be clear why arbitrary or otherwise unjust bloodshed, since it is the deliberate invocation of death and idolatry, the very essence of incompatibility with the community of the Lord, pollutes. But—to return to the other part of our question—how can a whole land be polluted?

---

3. A feeling shared in reverse by blasphemers who delight in creating such events.

A first clue is provided by the text's use of the word *adamah* for the land of Israel.[4] It was from the dust of *haadamah* ("the ground") that the Lord created *haadam* ("the Adam") (Gen. 2:7), and the play on words is intended: humankind and the ground from which it is taken belong together. Thus when humankind sinned that ground became a field of "thorns and thistles" (3:17–18). The pollution of Israel's land by Israel's sin is a local application of the universal event—or perhaps the Genesis story is a generalization of Israel's.[5]

A second clue is provided by the Targum. According to it, the whole land of Israel—not just the temple or even Jerusalem—is "the abode" of the Shekinah, of God, as he abides with Israel (Levey 1990: 100–101). Our passage presumes something like the Targum's construal and presumes also that the land remains the Lord's home also when Israel is exiled from it. Thus the land of Israel is effectively a single cult site for the worship of the Lord; and as injustice and idolatry have made the Jerusalem temple unfit for the Lord's dwelling (→8:1–11:25), so they have polluted the land of Israel.

We next hear that exile has not helped matters between the Lord and his people (36:20–21), for the mere presence of the exiles in other nations has undone the Lord's honor. Their presence has led the world to think: these are the Lord's people and the land of Israel is his land; if he could not maintain the one in the other, he must be an unreliable God indeed. Here we encounter yet again the antimony of the Lord's involvement in history, in which he regularly appears on both sides of its conflicts, for it was of course יהוה himself who had scattered them. Christian theology proposes—as noted in other commentary units—that this antinomy will be resolved when and only when the Lord gives Israel over to death on the cross and suffers that abandonment in a body that is his own.

In any case, the Lord now faces the problem stated at the beginning. For the sake of his "holy name" among the nations, he will restore Israel. But when they are again on the land, why will they not again pollute it? The Lord will take three steps to prevent this (36:25–27).

First, he will cleanse them from their existing pollution. He will wash Israel and so prepare them for a fresh start. But how is an entire nation to be thus baptized? It is impossible for Christian theology not to think of John the Baptist's call to all the people of Jerusalem and Judah and of the baptism of all who come into the church that claims to be a new Israel.[6] What sort of sacramental event, if any, Ezekiel himself may have anticipated, we do not know—though perhaps the baptism was to be in the supernaturally life-giving water flowing from the eschatological temple (47:1–12), whose building and rules are the subject of Ezekiel's final huge vision (Ezek. 40–48).

---

4. *Arets* is often used elsewhere; I am here concerned with this particular text.
5. As in general, the creation story is a retrojection of the exodus story.
6. Not necessarily exclusively. The claim is not in itself supersessionist.

The decisive act: the Israelites now have a "heart of stone"; the Lord will replace this with a "heart of flesh." The possessives and verbs are in the plural: it is no longer a single corporate entity called "Israel" who is the object of the Lord's action; for Israel to be transformed, the Israelites must be transformed (so also Eichrodt 1970: 500–501). We encountered this amazing and utterly eschatological promise before (→11:14–21).

The final cause of Israel's transformation will be the indwelling of the Lord's own Spirit, of his own *ruach* (→1:28c–3:15). The pronouns and verbs are again in the plural; it is all the Israelites whom the Spirit will enter.

In the Old Testament, the notion that God will put his own *ruach* "within" all those who belong to him is unique to Ezekiel and appears also in the great passage next to be considered. The closest parallel outside Ezekiel is the phenomenon of the Spirit's role in prophecy itself. In his role as an archetypical prophet, David said, "The spirit of the LORD speaks *through* me" (2 Sam. 23:2, emphasis added); in the case of Ezekiel, the Spirit "entered into" him to prepare him for the word (Ezek. 2:2); and a postexilic prophet proclaimed: "The Spirit of the Lord GOD is upon me . . . to bring good news to the oppressed" (Isa. 61:1).[7]

Joel finally joins the promise of the Spirit's universal indwelling of God's people with this conception of prophecy, in a passage that became central in Christian theology: "I will pour out my spirit on all flesh; your sons and your daughters shall prophesy" (Joel 2:28–29). From her beginning, the church has seen her own existence as a fulfillment of this promise (Acts 2:14–21).

Nevertheless, an indwelling of the Spirit *himself* in the baptized has always been hard for theology to accommodate: Would not the personal presence of God's Spirit within us overwhelm our small personhood? Moved by this worry, Western theology came to a fateful consensus during the twelfth century: what the Spirit gives cannot be his own personal inward presence; the biblical "gifts of the Spirit" are detached from the Spirit's person and made to be "created" gifts[8] that he infuses in us (Jenson 1997–99: 1.148–49). This consensus underlies many unfortunate developments in Western theology: not least its conception of scripture itself, as inspired by a Spirit who from outside the biblical writers "suggests" or even "dictates" what they are to say. The distinction between "created" and "uncreated" undoubtedly has its uses, but it cannot be used to tell us what the Creator can or cannot do. And there was no need for the worry behind this unfortunate theologoumenon, for since God's Spirit is the spirit of the Creator, his presence within us can only enhance our created personhood.

7. The earliest prophecy was always attributed to the Spirit. For reasons not altogether clear, this conception nearly disappears in the self-understanding of eighth- and seventh-century prophecy. After the exile, it again became central; Zechariah can say, as something self-understood, that the Lord sent all previous prophecy "by his spirit" (Zech. 7:12).

8. That is, virtues of the same ontological sort as our natural virtues, and so presumably compatible with them.

The descriptions of Israel's restored and transformed habitation in her land, both in the main messenger-word and in those attached to it, need not long detain us. They reprise those of the previous passage (→35:1–36:15) and indeed repeat themselves. Just as there were only so many varieties of doom that could be invoked in Ezek. 1–32, so there are only so many pictures of restoration and prosperity that can be depicted in Ezek. 33–36—though with the promise of resurrection in 37:1–14 we will indeed come to something radically new, as we will with the vision of an eschatological temple in Ezek. 40–48.

I may therefore end this commentary unit with the effective conclusion of our passage's message: "And you shall be my people, and I will be your God" (36:28). When Israel is washed clean and the people have new hearts because they are indwelt by the Spirit—and when they have given up all claims to deserve the Lord's mercy (36:31)—then this great formula of the covenant (e.g., Lev. 26:12) will at last be a simple description. Jews and Christians alike still await that day; and the church also claims to corroborate its coming by anticipating it in her sacraments and communal life.

EZEKIEL 37:1–14

CAN THESE BONES LIVE?

Ezekiel 37:1–14 is undoubtedly the most famous passage in Ezekiel's book: besides inspiring a popular song, it is prominent in both Jewish and Christian iconography and has been endlessly debated in Jewish and Christian exegesis and speculation (Zimmerli 1983: 263–65). I will declare my own enthusiasm immediately: the vision of Israel as dry bones and the promise of the bones' resurrection are from a certain Christian point of view the effective culmination of Ezekiel's prophecy and book, and indeed of the Old Testament.

For it has come to this: Israel as a whole and as such (37:11) is—as Ezekiel so often threatened—well and truly dead, a strewing of remains no longer even skeletal, so definitely of the past that the bones have separated and preserve no personal identities—no one can even point and say, "Alas, poor . . . I knew him well." The word of Gen. 2:17 has finally been fulfilled: the clash between God's will for his human creatures, by which alone they live, and their refusal to follow that will, has been worked out in the history of Israel and has come to its inevitable conclusion.

Is then what the Lord here shows Ezekiel what it appears to be, the irreversible end of Israel's history with the Lord? And that is, of the bearer of the Lord's history with all humanity? Can Israel rise again? Indeed, can humanity, dependent for its specific being on the Lord's presence in history, live as what it was created to be? The Lord puts the question to Ezekiel: "Son of a man, what do you think? Can the dead live again?"

Ezekiel has no answer; this knowledge is beyond a son of a man. But Ezekiel does know that the Lord is the giver of life; our passage is pervaded by reminiscence of the Lord's first vivification of humankind (Gen. 2:7). And he knows that therefore the Lord can answer the question yes or no as he chooses. So he throws the question back.[1]

For answer he receives an implicit yes: a command to prophesy life to the dead. Even in the nonbeing of death the bones can hear him, because the word given the prophet is the same word that gives being and life in the first place, that addresses precisely "things that are not" (1 Cor. 1:28). Thus Ezekiel is to do nothing less than speak the dead back to life (Ezek. 37:4–6): we arrive at the extreme possibility of the prophets' general assignment "to pluck up and to pull down, . . . to build and to plant" (Jer. 1:9–10). In the vision, Ezekiel speaks as commanded and the dead are raised (Ezek. 37:7–10).

We must break off such anticipations and return to more usual introductory matters. As to the date, the vision must have been given sometime between the fall of Jerusalem and the return from exile; but greater precision is unlikely to be achieved. The verses are plainly a unit, beginning with the announcement of a vision and concluding with a variant of Ezekiel's frequent conclusion: "Then you shall know. . . ." The passage has a complicated but usually clear structure.

As always to introduce a vision, the passage begins with "the hand of the Lord came upon me." Ezekiel is brought "in the spirit" (→8:1–18) to a valley full of bones and made to survey it (37:1–2). A dialogue that we have already recounted follows between him and the Lord (37:3–4). This concludes with the mandate of a messenger-word enjoining the bones to live again; this is to begin with "thus says the Lord," just as though it were a usual prophecy (37:5–6).

Ezekiel's prophesying to the bones and their consequent return to life are then narrated in two stages, corresponding to the two stages of the Lord's vivification of humanity as described at Gen. 2:7: first the body (Ezek. 37:7–8), then the "breath of life" (37:9–10).[2] The account of the second stage begins with the mandate of a specific messenger-word (37:9), marking this as the decisive step. We must remember that all this is within the vision and that to this point Ezekiel has not been told whose bones these are.

Then the Lord interprets the vision to Ezekiel (37:11). We are not told that the vision has ended, but it seems clear that it has. First the Lord identifies the bones as Israel's. Then he tells why he sent the vision: the remnant of Israel regards themselves as dead and indeed is chanting their own death dirge (37:11). Properly to display this chant we must translate with attention to the versification and word order:[3] "Dried up—our bones / perished—our hope / cut off—we ourselves."[4]

---

1. The Targum paraphrases "O Lord God, before You it is revealed," which makes the point exactly (Levey 1990: 102–3).

2. Which is not the "soul" in either the biblical or the modern senses.

3. The Hebrew is in irregularly rhyming two-emphasis lines—it is not a *kinah* funeral chant—with a decidedly ominous rhyming sound. It is truly unfortunate that NRSV does not print this as verse.

4. The last of these lines is נגזרנו לנו. On its grammar, see Greenberg 1997: 746.

"Therefore" Ezekiel is to bring a messenger-word, to an Israel that knows herself as over and done with (37:12–14). In it, the Lord says to Israel that she can and will live again. The language is bluntly physical: "I am going to open your graves, and bring you up from your graves, O my people" (37:12).

It is the scope of the promise of resurrection—both within the vision and in the messenger-word to Israel—that has occasioned centuries of exegetical argument. But before moving to the great issue, there are two matters to which we must attend.

In the vision, it is the breath of life as in Gen. 2:7 that comes into the restored bodies so that they live. This breath seems here to be an impersonal cosmic phenomena, arriving as the universally proverbial "four winds" (Ezek. 37:9). But in the following messenger-word to Israel, it is the Lord's own *ruach* (→1:28c–3:15) that the Lord will put "within" the Israelites to bring them to life. The change is important, and we will return to it.

The first line of the dirge is 37:11 and connects to the vision—or rather, the vision connects to it. The second describes Israel's situation: she has no future. In view of the situation and the eschatological tone of the whole passage, we are justified in a more specific identification of the lost hope: it is what was promised to Abraham, that Israel would be a special nation. The last line is decisive for interpretation of the promised resurrection: to be "cut off" is to be in the grave, cut off from life, cut off indeed from being. So, for example, at Isa. 53:8–9 of the Suffering Servant: "He was cut off from the land of the living. . . . They made his grave with the wicked" (for additional references, see Greenberg 1997: 745–46).

So—in what sense is resurrection promised? To deal with this question, we are forced to the sort of identification of alternative interpretations and of argument against them that in this commentary I have mostly avoided.

An initial phenomenon in the text must be our starting consideration: the promised resurrection is paired with the exiles' return to the land of Israel, either as identical with it or as its necessary condition (37:12). So a first step must be: Is this return itself to occur within history as we now know it?

If a this-worldly return is intended, there are two possibilities. We may read the vision and promise of resurrection as a powerful metaphor for national return and renewal (so Eichrodt 1970: 509–10) of the sort sometimes possible in this age. Or we may think they predict risings from the dead that are to occur before or during a this-worldly return of the exiles to Judah. The former reading was common in modern academic scholarship and some rabbinic exegesis; the second appeared in other rabbinic exegesis (for examples, see Greenberg 1997: 750).[5]

Interpretation of the promised resurrection as metaphor or simile can, in my opinion, be quickly eliminated as a category mistake. Within the vision, for what is the envisioned resurrection supposed to be a metaphor? Or between the vision

---

5. I rather enjoy this one, attributed to Rabbi Eliezer: "The dead that Ezekiel revived got up on their feet, sang a hymn, and died" (Babylonian Talmud, tractate *Sanhedrin* 92b).

and its interpretation, how is a vision of events a metaphor for them? In Ezekiel's other visions he sees events as stylized drama, for which the interpretation, if any, specifies the normally seen equivalent; here that equivalent is explicitly the future opening of Israel's graves. Thus if resurrection is metaphor it must be that in both vision and interpretation, again leaving nothing for which it can be metaphor.

However such questions are to be resolved, the promised return itself can be construed as simply an event of this age only by sheer determination to do so. It is plainly the same event as the return delineated in the previous chapter, whose features blatantly transcend what is possible within history as it now runs (→36:16–38). Moreover and decisively, the promised resurrection is identified, besides with a return to Judah, with an ineluctably eschatological event: when the Lord opens Israel's graves, he will put his own Spirit within the Israelites as their breath of life (37:13–14). That is, the Israelites will be raised to live God's own life.

We confront the same phenomenon as often in Ezekiel: a penultimate act of God and the ultimate act of God are seen together. Do Ezekiel's message and text here intend an imminent historical journey of his exilic community to reclaim the land of Israel? Yes, apparently. Do Ezekiel's message and text here intend a final act of God to transform the whole condition of Israel's existence? Yes, apparently.

Insofar as Ezekiel foretold events expected immediately to follow the exiles' return, his prophecy was not fulfilled. The new Persian Empire indeed gave permission for Babylon's captives to return home, and many did. But Jewish exiles' arrival did not transform the land of Israel into Eden. Judging from the writings of the postexilic prophets, neither was there any remarkable outpouring of the Spirit—at least not until the event the church calls Pentecost. And no resurrections are recorded—except, as Christians will think, a single one centuries later.

Again we are left with two possibilities. We may conclude that the Lord speaking by Ezekiel made a promise he could not or would not keep. Or we may read that promise according to its eschatological—and so also christological and ecclesiological—references. Christian theology must choose the second.

If then there is to be an eschatological resurrection of Israel, how are we to conceive it? Clearly, our passage intends a resurrection of the people as a single reality. It speaks, however, of graves and their occupants in the plural, and there is a reason for this: at such an end as, for example, →7:1–9 describes, the only Israel available to be raised will be the ensemble of dead Israelites. At the absolute end, the distinction between national resurrection and individual resurrections must be moot. Therefore we may conclude that this passage indeed envisions something like what later Judaism and Christianity conceive as a "resurrection of the dead."

Thus a full version of the question the Lord put to Ezekiel would be: When the Lord comes to the end of his ways with his people—to an eschatological assembly at Zion and a universal gift of his own life-giving Spirit—will he raise the diachronic whole of his people into this new life? It is this question that effectively concludes the dooms and promises given through Ezekiel. Christian faith and theology begin with the conviction that Jesus's resurrection is God's own answer (Jenson 1997–99: 1.4–5). The Lord spoke by Ezekiel, and in Christ's resurrection he has acted on what he said (37:14).

There remains only a subordinate question: Who will be included in the Israel that will rise at the end? Gentile Christians, baptized into the body of Christ, cling to Paul's image: by incorporation into Christ we have been grafted into Israel herself (Rom. 11:17). Will there be a resurrection also of those who are neither of the original tree nor grafted-in branches? And if so, a resurrection to what? Ezekiel's vision does not reach so far.

EZEKIEL 37:15–28

ONE HOLY . . .

At 37:15 we have the formula for the granting of a verbal prophecy, and at 38:1 we have another such. The verses thus bracketed make a plausible editorial unit of a sort we encounter elsewhere in Ezekiel—a main prophecy with editorial attachments— and we will treat them together. The passage makes an unrestricted promise of salvation, of the sort for which these final chapters are reserved (→25:1–17) and will therefore have been given after the destruction of Jerusalem. In my opinion, more precise dating is impossible.

The word of the Lord comes to Ezekiel, addresses him as always with "you—son of a man" and mandates an *oth*, a prophetic sign (37:16–17; →3:22–5:4). Then Ezekiel is given a messenger-word for the exiles, interpreting the sign (37:18–19). To the unit made by these four verses, 37:20 attaches another messenger-word (37:21–22) that picks up and elaborates the theme of the first. Finally, two further passages have been attached, the first (37:23) probably written as an intended supplement to the second messenger-word, the other (37:24–28) a sort of compendium of aspects of eschatological salvation, presumably put here because of the shared promise of the one Davidic king.

For the *oth*, Ezekiel is to take two sticks,[1] and write on one that it stands for the southern kingdom of Judah, and on the other that it stands for the northern

---

1. עֵץ is used for pieces of wood of various sorts. For this passage commentators have proposed "staff," "wooden tablet," and other possibilities. Since there seems to be no way to know for sure what sort of wooden thing was intended, the English versions' "stick" is a good choice. In any case, the two "sticks" must each have had a flat side, so that when held together they could be seen as one.

kingdom, here named after its dominating tribe, Joseph.[2] Then the Lord tells Ezekiel to put the two sticks together and hold them in one hand, so that they appear as one.

The following interpreting messenger-word is brief and simple: the Lord is about to do in fact what Ezekiel just did in mime, put Judah and Joseph together. The messenger-word contributes only one emphasis beyond what is already plain in the *oth*: it is indeed the Lord himself who—as so often in Ezekiel—will thus take geopolitical matters personally in hand.

In our prophet's discourse, as indeed in most of scripture, the Lord's involvement in his history with Israel and other nations is always direct and personal. Acknowledging this or failing to acknowledge it affects every step of biblical exegesis and indeed every construction of theology. In my conviction, it must be a maxim of all Christian theology: if there is a clash between abstract notions of what is appropriate to God and scripture's story of the Lord's active presence in time, it is the former that must be rethought.

Achieving and obeying that maxim has been a long and slow effort through the history of theology, and indeed has been resisted at every step, in the name of whatever is at the moment thought to be appropriate to God. At the time of this writing, the effort and the resistance circle around the notion of divine impassibility: How are we conceptually to accommodate the descriptions, appearing through the whole of scripture, of God being *affected* by temporal events and reacting to them? The temptation to resolve the problem by explaining scripture's language away seems to be as strong as ever.

The question we must next ask is another that regularly arises when reading Ezekiel: In what sort of history is the prophesied event to occur? Before experience of the way the return to Judea actually worked out, reestablishing a unified and sovereign Israelite state within the history of this age remained something for which one could reasonably hope. The exiles in Babylon were still a community, if a dispirited one; Assyria's scattering of the northern elites was not so far in the past that the exiles' descendents would not have known who they were; and much of the populace of both states had remained in place, even if religiously decadent and politically alienated.

But the second messenger-word (37:21–22) so develops the promise as to carry it beyond this-worldly possibility. It is made explicit that restoration of a unified kingdom will require a second exodus more wondrous than the first, in that the Lord must bring his people not from one nation but from many—a prophecy that readers of Ezekiel have encountered before at Ezek. 34. And even more plainly eschatological, the state reunified in its full territory will "never again" be undone.

The attached 37:23 then summarizes the measures the Lord will undertake to enable this "never again." Israel's historically proven unreliability posed an obvious

2. On the complicated and rather awkward manipulation of names in this passage, see Zimmerli 1983: 273–74.

problem for the perdurance of any restored Israel. The reality of this danger and the measures with which the Lord will avert it were laid out in →36:16–38.

The particular blessing now promised by the *oth* and the two messenger-words is rescue from division. Israel had been politically divided through most of her history in Syria-Palestine; nevertheless, in Israel's self-conception the entity that the Lord had called into being and to which he had made his promises was the one nation descended from Jacob/Israel. If this nation was to be monarchical, it had therefore to have a single monarch; and much of the glory that surrounded the memory of David and Solomon was that they had ruled the territory of all twelve tribes. Thus Ezekiel here explicitly names only the tribes by which the two monarchies were known, since it was their separation that was to be overcome, but is also careful to mention "all the house of Israel associated" with each.

The theology is straightforward. If Israel is the people of the one Lord, there cannot be two Israels. Indeed, in strict logic, a divided Israel could not be Israel at all. If Israel is to be restored to life, as promised in the previous verses of this chapter, she must before all be restored to unity.

Unity thus belongs to the very being of the Lord's people; and this conviction was carried from Israel directly into the theology of the church, and there maintained with respect both to canonical Israel and to herself. To celebrate canonical Israel's special presence in the kingdom, the Revelation both evokes a single Jewish multitude and pedantically lists all twelve tribes, with strict equality of representation (Rev. 7:5–8). And of herself the church first of all confesses that she is "one," even before confessing that she is "holy, catholic, and apostolic." As with Israel, a divided church could not in strict logic be church at all; we may be glad that the Lord's history with us does not always follow strict logic.

Moreover, the unity not just of God's particular people but of *all* humankind is a chief goal of Israel's and the church's divine missions. Israel's role in God's history is that "in days to come the mountain of the LORD's house shall be established as the highest of the mountains, and shall be raised up above the hills. Peoples shall stream to it" (Mic. 4:1). And the Second Vatican Council said nothing unique to Roman Catholicism when it taught that the church is an anticipation and agent, "a sacrament, as it were" (*uti sacramentum*), of the unity of all humanity.[3]

Returning to the text, the last attachment, 37:24–28, contains some of the most elevated promises of eschatological salvation in Ezekiel's book—mostly, to be sure, taken over from prophecies earlier in the book. The Lord's "servant David" will be Israel's one shepherd, as promised in →34:1–31. Both the nation's new possession of the land and the rule of this David will not be phenomena of this temporally fragile age, but will endure "forever."[4] Is it then the Messiah who is

3. Norman P. Tanner, ed., *Decrees of the Ecumenical Councils* (Washington, DC: Georgetown University Press, 1990), 2.849.

4. Both here and with the new covenant next adduced, the Hebrew is עולם (*olam*). The word evokes the "highest climax of the promise"; see Zimmerli 1983: 276.

promised here? That is, the anointed prince who will for good and all fulfill the role of David's house? In my judgment, only theological prejudice will deny it.

The Lord will make a new covenant with reestablished Israel, a "covenant of peace" (ברית שלום, *berith shalom*). This too was earlier promised, at Ezek. 34. Faith in the Lord's covenant with Israel is foundational in Ezekiel's theology, but the notion itself does not often appear in his discourse; here however it is central.

A "covenant" (*berith*) is a pact between two parties, granted unilaterally by one of them but binding on the actions of both (Jenni and Westermann 1997: 256–66). Scholarship discovers two covenants in the Old Testament's account of the Lord's life with Israel: the covenant with desert wanderers made at Sinai and the covenant with the monarchical dynasty of a settled nation (Jenson 1997–99: 1.66–71). In each its way, these covenants bound the Lord to cherish Israel as his "treasured possession" (סגלה, *segolah*; Exod. 19:5) and Israel to obey the Lord's "commands and ordinances."

The covenant now promised has the same content as the old covenants, here summarized as "peace," but like the newly promised possession of the land, it is to transcend created time, it is to be "everlasting." Its central fact will be a new and itself everlasting temple—to the form and estate of which Ezekiel's long concluding vision (Ezek. 40–48) will be devoted.

As in that final vision, this temple will be the Lord's "dwelling place" amid his people. The word so translated is *mishkan*. As noted the introduction, it is from the conception of the sanctuary as a *mishkan* that the rabbis derived the notion of the Shekinah, the Lord's indwelling of his people, that is both an entity distinguished from the Lord by the invariable genitive construction and yet is the same Lord as is the Lord. Thus the Targum paraphrases 37:27: "I will make My Shekinah dwell among them" (Levey 1990: 104). Because this presence of God amidst his people will—again—be "forevermore," the great formula of the covenant, that the Lord will be Israel's God and they will be his people, will finally be fulfilled.

EZEKIEL 38:1–39:20

GOG

Ezekiel 38–39 is introduced by a coming of the word, and 40:1 announces a new vision. The long passage thus marked out is divided into four parts by addresses to Ezekiel as "you—son of a man," commanding him to prophesy (38:2; 38:14; 39:1; 39:17). Each of the first two parts comprises more than one messenger-word; the third does not. The fourth presents a problem, for 39:21–29, including a new messenger-word beginning at 39:25, is attached to this fourth word, but says nothing about Gog or his attack and is materially a summary and conclusion of Ezek. 34–37. Thus these verses' position after Ezek. 34–37 and just before the concluding vision in Ezek. 40–48 is more important for their interpretation than is their tenuous relation to 38:1–39:20.

Ezekiel 38:1–39:20 still comprises a lot of text and shows signs of major additions to an original complex, but because as it stands it tells a continuous and in its own fashion simple story[1] of Gog and his destruction, I will take these verses together, in a long commentary unit. Since within the story of Gog the final reestablishment of Israel in her land appears as an achieved and eternal fact, the prophecies are probably to be dated together with those in Ezek. 36–37: some time after the destruction of Jerusalem but before the prospective return began to look too much like a merely this-worldly and partial arrangement.

With Ezek. 38–39, Ezekiel takes almost complete leave of what is conceivable within history as it now runs. Until this point in his book, Ezekiel's evocations of coming doom or blessing have usually had a simultaneous double reference: to

---

1. Eichrodt 1970: 521 has his usual difficulty in acknowledging the narrative coherence of an editorial composition.

events conceivable in this age and to events conceivable only as or indeed after "the end" as it is depicted in →7:1–9. With Ezek. 38, the this-worldly reference almost entirely disappears. Indeed, the departure from what modernity calls history is explicit: the final restoration of Israel in her own land, variously promised from Ezek. 34 on, figures here as indeed the end of God's historical ways with Israel (38:8, 11–12), to be *followed* by the Lord's summons to Gog. We will have to ask: How can even prophecy speak of something that follows the end of everything?

The language of nations and battles does remain; this language tenuously maintains the tie to history that I earlier noted as essential to prophesy (→1:1–3). But as the names of nations now appear, their reference to known entities is opaque or disturbed. And in the great battle, human combatants on the Lord's side have vanished altogether: he tells of no instrument like Nebuchadnezzar, and the people of Israel appear only after the victory, to dispose of the enemy dead. The passage is perhaps not quite a formal apocalypse (→1:1–3) but in the content of its narrative and in its style and diction it could just as well be, which makes its proclamation outside a vision all the more radical.

The word comes to Ezekiel, addresses him with the invariable "you—son of a man," and commands him to aim a message of doom at far distant Gog, by a bodily gesture (38:1–2; →6:1–14). So far so familiar to readers of Ezekiel. But immediately the discourse turns uncanny, even by Ezekiel's standards.

Gog and his horde are "from the remotest parts of the north" (38:6, 15). Figures from "the north" seem to have been as a semimythic permanent threat in certain prophetic traditions (Zimmerli 1983: 299–300). Gog emerges from this threat's remotest lair.

And who is Gog? Presumably Ezekiel did not simply invent him for this prophecy, but the name's only other appearance (1 Chr. 5:4) before Ezekiel's book itself made the name current in later Judaism and in Christianity[2] is in a context irrelevant to our question. Both in our text and in scholarship, Gog remains ominously unidentified.[3]

We do hear that Gog is from "the land of Magog" and is "prince of Meshech and Tubal." The latter two, listed without further identification as trading partners of Tyre at 27:13, are among the paradigmatically disgraced inhabitants of Sheol in 32:17–32, and there seem to represent sheer violence from—again—the north. Thus their naming here only contributes to the atmosphere of threatening mystery surrounding Gog's appearance. And Magog is probably no more than a linguistic construction for "land of Gog" (Zimmerli 1983: 301) and so an empty identification.

Gog's horde is equally shadowy. Magog, Gomer, Togarmah, Tubal, and Meshech appear in Genesis's ethnographic table among Japheth's descendants, who are

2. For a rich selection of texts, see R. H. Charles, *The Revelation of St. John*, International Critical Commentary (Edinburgh: Clark, 1920), 2.188–89.

3. For scholars' desperate attempts to trace down some earlier reference for this name, see Zimmerli 1983: 300–302. Zimmerli finds all proposals unsatisfactory, as do I.

"the coastland peoples" (Gen. 10:2–5), a tradition on which Ezekiel seems to have depended (Ezek. 39:6). The coasts in question must be those of the Black or Caspian Seas, which were for the peoples of the Fertile Crescent a legendary and uncanny region. And the Persia, Ethiopia, and Put that we know were of course not in fact north of Israel at all.[4] Taken all in all, Ezekiel's description of the horde does not seem to be ethnographically intended, but rather evokes sheer violence, by allusion to mysterious or notoriously destructive peoples.

We turn more directly to the narrative, taking up the messenger-words in order. In the first messenger-word (38:3–9), addressed to Gog directly, the Lord announces that he is against Gog and that he himself (→37:15–28) will forcibly bring him and his horde from their mysterious redoubt to play their imposed role. A specific reason for the Lord's enmity to Gog is not given: there is no "because you have," as elsewhere in oracles against enemy nations. Nor is the Lord's specific intention with him and his army stated. Gog and his horde appear simply as occasions of divine wrath.

The Lord commands Gog to keep ready for his summons. Gog will, to be sure, have to wait "many days" for this call, but it will certainly come, "in the latter years," that is, when the entire this-worldly succession of years is over.

The second messenger-word (38:10–13), again addressed to Gog, tells how the Lord's summons will be made (Rashi in Rosenberg 2000: 327): "Evil thoughts will come into [Gog's] mind." Gog will be deluded into seeing the now permanent peace of Israel as defenselessness and so as an invitation to violence. And the merchants of the world—doubtless the same merchants who appear in Rev. 18—will be equally deluded, seeing Gog's illusory plunder as an opportunity for profit (Ezek. 38:14).

A third messenger-word (38:14–16), the first in our passage's second main part, is still addressed to Gog and is for the most part a rhetorically evoked repetition of the first. It does, however, add the motive and outcome of the Lord's summons: what happens to Gog will reveal the Lord universally and finally, by displaying before all the world his holiness, that is, his utter singularity and inescapability.[5] Again the finality of the coming event is driven home; the Lord proclaims that "in the latter days . . . the nations" will simply "know" him (38:16). When the world knows the Lord in person, nothing more will be outstanding.

The fourth messenger-word (38:17–23) begins as an address to Gog, in the form of a rhetorical question, but later refers to him in the third person—both phenomena betray a probably complicated textual history that we need not and probably could not reconstruct. Successive messenger-words have been gradually filling in the context of Gog's coming; now we learn that it was foretold by all

4. Before, of course, Persia became a world empire.
5. Rudolf Otto's *The Idea of the Holy* (London: Oxford University Press, 1936) remains the classic analysis of this universal religious phenomenon. Holiness is, in the famous phrase, the *myterium fascinosum et tremendum* ("the captivating and overwhelming mystery").

"the prophets of Israel."[6] There is a parallel in the New Testament, referred in the introduction: "All the prophets, . . . from Samuel and those after him" predicted the time of Christ (Acts 3:24). In both cases, the claim—that all the prophets spoke of Gog or that all spoke of Christ—can be true only if the coming of Gog, or of the Christ, concludes and wraps up all the previous history, particularly including the words of the prophets who announced and moved it. This, of course, is exactly how the church has from her beginning read the Old Testament.

That the coming of Gog is indeed a second end of this world appears when this messenger-word describes what will happen on Gog's arrival. The Lord will unleash all the cosmic fireworks with which apocalyptic prophecy describes the final destruction of evil power—for a particularly relevant display of these, see Matt. 27:51–52. Indeed, it appears that Gog has been summoned precisely to occasion the catastrophe. In it Gog and his host will perish, at least in part because they will turn their swords against one another (Ezek. 38:21), seized by the divine panic that in ancient tradition went before Israel in her holy wars.[7]

A fifth messenger-word (39:1–16) occupies the whole of the passage's third main part and is editorially constructed from four pieces that probably were once independent. A primary prophecy (39:1–6) again summons Gog to his doom. It emphasizes that "the mountains of Israel" are the chosen site of evil's eschatological destruction and begins a description of the aftermath of the battle, which will occupy much of the remaining text. Here—and in 39:17–20—it is mandated that the bodies of Gog and his horde be left unburied for scavengers and so denied even entry into Sheol, the universal grave (→32:17–32). Thus Gog and his horde, the summation of history's violence, will not exist even as shades in the underworld, but will simply cease. Ezekiel 39:11–16 will contradict this; we must shortly consider the nature of apparently incompatible eschatological descriptions.

The first attached piece, 39:7–8, does two things. It gives a negative background of the Lord's determination to make the nations know his holiness: the judgments he has brought on Israel have had the collateral effect of giving him a bad name among the nations of Israel's captivity.[8] And decisively for interpretation of the whole complex, the day of Gog's destruction is identified as the "the day" of Ezekiel's other prophecy (→7:10–27). Perhaps there has been among the exiles some skepticism on account of the day's delay; we are here assured that the great day will be when, and only when, a final attempt by evil's power is summoned and eliminated.

Ezekiel 39:9–10 provides metaphor for the size of Gog's army and the completeness of its destruction. Ezekiel 39:11–16 describes Israel's burying of the corpses of

6. Rashi makes Ezekiel himself be one of these prophets (Rosenberg 2000: 331).

7. On Israel's holy wars, see Gerhard von Rad, *Holy War in Ancient Israel*, trans. Marva J. Dawn (Grand Rapids: Eerdmans, 1991). For a parallel prophetic use of this tradition, see Zech. 14:13.

8. Rashi says: "Inasmuch as it is said of them, 'these are the people of the Lord . . . and he is unable to save them'" (Rosenberg 2000: 335).

Gog's host, in order to purify the Lord's land polluted by them (see Num. 35:33 and →36:16–38).[9] The work will begin as a general labor of the peaceful people of Israel and will be completed by official commissions (39:14–15). Scholarly efforts to locate the "Valley of the Travelers" on the map of Israel have been—to say the least—inconclusive (Zimmerli 1983: 317).[10]

Description of the burial of Gog's horde seems to contradict 39:1–6 as well as the very next attachment (39:17–20), in both of which the Lord mandates that the corpses are to be left for disposal by scavengers. Perhaps in a previous state as separate texts, these passages indeed projected merely different visions, but the editing that produced the canonical text has let both stand in immediate juxtaposition. How are we to understand this?

We need to ask: What would constitute a contradiction in such apocalyptic discourse as that of these chapters? Very little in it obeys accustomed rules: thus we may observe that the seemingly this-worldly burial efforts laid down in 39:13–16 are so minutely and pedantically insisted upon—we must even be told of a bureaucracy for Gog disposal—that in their fashion they are as strange as the rest of the complex, approaching indeed the style of apocalypse. Do such pictures need to fit together to be in some appropriate sense consistent?

Finally, 39:17–20 is again introduced by an address to "you—son of a man" and a command to prophesy. This fourth main part of our passage includes just one messenger-word, whether or not we detach 39:21–29. The Lord's summons to the scavenger birds and beasts, assembling them to devour Gog's fallen, grimly expands the judgment of 39:4. Two vital points emerge. It is finally explicit that Gog and his horde are indeed but a cipher for "the mighty" in general, for "the princes of the earth" (39:18) and their violence. And the scavenger's feast is now called a "sacrificial feast."

The slaughter of "the day of the Lord" was seen as sacrificial also by earlier prophecy, suggesting that the phrase had in part a cultic background (→7:10–27). It may be that the victory of the Creator over the forces of chaos was celebrated in the temple on a fixed day. If such a connection indeed obtains, we should read the coming and destruction of Gog even more cosmically than we have so far done. At the beginning the Lord chose an ordered creation instead of chaos; in response to humankind's rebellion he allowed chaos's near return in the great flood; and in the prophecy of Ezekiel and other prophets it appears as a background threat. The day now prophesied will see the Lord's final evocation and elimination of this shadow.

How shall we appropriate the story we have just surveyed? Let us label it an "eschatological scenario"; it is not formally an apocalypse, and we need a more inclusive category. Scripture is full of such scenarios, from one-verse narratives like

9. Rashi says: "Wayfarers who see a human bone sill construct a marker . . . , in order that wayfarers and those who prepare ritually pure food should stay away from it" (Rosenberg 2000: 338).
10. Nor indeed is it sure that "travelers" is the right translation.

that in Mic. 4:2, of all nations gathering at Mt. Zion to be made righteous by the law, or the longer proclamation of eschatological landscaping in Zech. 14:1–11, through, for a New Testament example, 1 Thess. 4:15–17 to the whole book of Revelation. Hardly any two of these scenarios can be fitted together.

There is a logical twist behind this phenomenon. To state the promise finally made by the prophets, and made immediate by the preaching and life of Jesus, one must narrate the termination of all narrative—just as Gen. 1:1–2 must narrate the inauguration of all narrative. We therefore cannot expect that what we think of as normal rules of narrative succession will be followed. In particular we must not expect that one (in its way) true eschatological scenario will fit together with another (in its way) true eschatological scenario. We have rather to ask what is promised to us by any and all of them—and if this is modernity talking, so be it. I elsewhere propose that we are promised a final implosion of God's personal and active love, to include all the past loves of his people, and so those people themselves (Jenson 1997–99: 2.309–69). Negatively, as in our passage: violence will become absolutely past, not accommodated even in Sheol and its form of being past.

When in the great Christian apocalypse the warfare of the "Logos of God" against "the beast" reaches its climax, Ezekiel is reprised. An angel summons the scavenger birds to a sacrificial "supper of God," where they will eat the flesh of "the mighty" (Rev. 19:11–21). And just as in Ezekiel, *after* a first peace of the saints, Gog and Magog[11] appear as evil's last spasm. It seems to be an ineradicable theme in biblical eschatology that God will first bring his history with his people to fulfillment *before* settling finally with evil. Gog and Magog appear with a horde "as numerous as the sands of the sea," to attack the "beloved city" and be destroyed directly by God (20:4–9). The only significant variation from Ezekiel is explicit identification of the Lord who wars against Gog: he is the incarnate Logos.

Eschatological narrative is thus a mix of metaphysics and fancy and is none the worse for it. That Christ will triumph and evil be abolished and that all things have their present being from that future is Christian theology's rigorously intended ontological first axiom. But narrating that triumph demands visionary poets.

---

11. Later Judaism and early Christianity took both Gog and Magog as personal names and may have been right in this. The Hebrew is indeterminate; KJV reproduces it literally: "Gog, the land of Magog." The Septuagint does not identify Gog by way of Magog, and for the rest is ambiguous.

EZEKIEL 39:21–29

LAW AND GOSPEL

To place these verses within the book, we need to be aware that the preceding oracle against Gog comprises several parts, divided by divine addresses to Ezekiel as "you—son of a man," and that some of these parts include more than one messenger-word. In the text as we have it, 39:21–29 seems to belong to this oracle's final part: no new beginning is formally marked at 39:21 (or at 39:23, if one prefers to locate the break there), so that 39:21–24 apparently continues a first messenger-word within that part and 39:25–29 seems to be a second messenger-word in the same part. The problem is: neither set of verses has anything to do with Gog; nor is it easy to think of a good reason of any sort why they should have been attached to the oracle against him.[1]

Materially, and if we read 39:21–24 and 39:25–29 for themselves, things are much clearer: separated from the Gog oracle, the verses make a narratively and conceptually coherent whole that, moreover, conclude and neatly summarize the promises of blessing collected in Ezek. 34–37. Indeed, we may surmise that at some earlier stage of our book's editing, 39:21–29 continued directly from Ezek. 34–37 and that this continuity was later broken by interpolation of the oracle against Gog. If this is what happened, the lack of any beginning or introduction for 39:21–24 is explained. If this is not what happened, so that some other textual history produced the present situation, there is in my judgment no telling what this was.

In any case of the historical possibilities, the presently most important thing about our verses is their general position in the book: after Ezek. 34–37 and

1. Zimmerli 1983: 319–22 takes quite a different view of these verses.

immediately before the great concluding vision in Ezek. 40–48. In this position, they serve to sum up Ezekiel's promises of blessing and to prepare the beginning of a very different discourse. For reasons that will become apparent at the end, we will take the two subunits in order.

Ezekiel 39:21–24 begins with a theme sentence: "I will display my glory among the nations." In general Old Testament usage, personal "glory" is the "weight" that persons have in community, their impact on others. In Ezekiel's tradition, the experience of divine weight melds with experience of the Lord's theophanies as light phenomena, as lightning and illumination, so that God's glory is the weight of his brilliance (→1:25–28b).

The exile of the Lord's chosen people had hidden the Lord's glory also from the Gentiles: How can this יהוה be God if he cannot protect his people from defeat and captivity? What the Lord must show, for the nations to see his deity, is that also the disaster to Israel was his own work, that he himself "hid [his] face"[2] from them, that Israel went into captivity because they had "dealt treacherously" with him by offending his holiness and by transgressing his will. When the Lord does what he is now about to do, the exile will be revealed as a manifestation of the Lord's glory and not as its failure.

Moreover, "from that day forward," from the day when the Lord openly demonstrates his deity, also the house of Israel will acknowledge "that I am יהוה, their God" (→introduction). Here this outcome of the Lord's act is stated with special intensity, for the event that will compel this knowledge is the revelation of God's deity itself: Israel—like the nations—will know God precisely as God. But for Israel to know this is to acknowledge her own faithlessness, to acknowledge that her disaster was divine justice.

The Lord will demonstrate his glory on "that day." This is surely the great and terrible day of →7:10–17, the day when the Lord will at last defeat forever all history's violence, even if Israel herself should be among it perpetrators. Thus an ambiguity present in many of Ezekiel's prophecies, between prophecy of events conceivable in this age and those conceivable only in a transformed world, is absent here. The prophesied display of God's glory is clearly eschatological: it will be the final victory, and what follows will be universal acquaintance with God.

If we ask what precisely the Lord will do to display his deity and refute suspicion of his weakness, we are brought to 39:25–29. This messenger-word begins with "therefore": according to the preceding verses the Lord must show his glory, and "therefore" he will do what follows. Against all probability he will now "restore the fortunes of Jacob" (39:25). Putting the argument rather bluntly: if the Lord shows that he has the power to do such a thing, then all must grant that Israel's disaster cannot have been caused by the Lord's weakness. We encounter yet again the inner motive of all the Lord's dealings with faithless Israel, according to Ezekiel's

2. Throughout our passage, the Targum replaces "hid my face from them" with "removed My Shekinah"—a paraphrase that is much to the point (Levey 1990: 109).

prophecy: just because יהוה is יהוה, he must be "jealous" for that name, and so identified is the name with Israel that his concern for it must rescue her.[3]

The most remarkable part of Jacob's restoration is that the Israelites themselves will be changed: they will "forget" their faithlessness (39:26); that is, within Israel's understanding of human existence, they will leave it behind them. With 39:26–27, the Lord seems to attribute this transformation simply to the exiles' return to the land and their security there; but the secret will come out at the end of the passage, the Lord will pour out his very own Spirit (→36:16–38).

The conclusion of it all: Israel will know that the Lord is the Lord precisely in the conjunction of exile and return (39:28), in the historical union of his justice and his mercy. And when that has been worked out, the Lord will "never again" hide his face from them (39:29).

Christian theology, especially in the traditions coming from the Reformation, has often spoken of the difference and unity of "law and gospel" as two modes of God's address to us. The law, in this technical language, is the sort of thing that dominates Ezek. 1–32: the proclamation of God's moral will and of the judgment that those who rebel against it must bring upon themselves. This word is reprised in 39:21–24. On the other hand, the gospel is the sort of thing that dominates Ezek. 33–48: the promise that God will nevertheless bring his people to the perfection for which he chose them. And this word is reprised in 39:25–29.

There has, moreover, been an ongoing dispute, particularly between branches of the Reformation, about the relation of these two words from God.[4] The general structure of the book of Ezekiel and the sequence of our passage—first 39:21–24, then 39:25–29—seem remarkably to reflect the Lutheran view: God by his prophets and other preachers first smites us with the law, in order thereupon to bless us with the gospel. There is a motto followed by much Lutheran preaching: "First law, then gospel." Yet if we look to the interior structures of our present law passage and of our present gospel passage, these seem rather to reflect the Reformed view: law and gospel go back and forth within each, the law can be a form of the gospel and the gospel a form of the law.

Perhaps the present summary of Ezekiel's prophesying—at least as we have read it—can suggest a resolution of the old dispute. Law and gospel are indeed one, but their unity is not a general convertibility, as Reformed theology has tended to present the matter. They are indeed distinct, but their difference is not an abstract feature of reality, as some Lutheran theology has construed reality. Both Reformed and Lutheran have, in my judgment, thought too little in terms of God's history with us. God moves us from law to gospel, and joins them in so doing. Law and gospel are not rubrics that God follows: they are what he does as he speaks; and his speech is one coherent discourse.

---

3. The Targum is, as always, nervous about mercy not triggered by repentance. Wherever our text seems to proclaim it, the Targum inserts "when they repented" (Levey 1990: 109).

4. See Gerhard O. Forde, *The Law-Gospel Debate: An Interpretation of Its Historical Development* (Minneapolis: Augsburg, 1968).

EZEKIEL 40:1–42:20

THE PLAN OF GOD'S HOUSE

Ezekiel 40–48—our book's final chapters—records a single if much interpolated vision. Thus Ezekiel's book begins and ends with major visionary events. Gregory the Great notes this and Ezekiel's insistent dating of both and takes occasion to reiterate (→1:1–3) an ancient—and sound—principle of premodern exegesis: "About to speak mysteries, [the prophet] begins with a historical notice, in order to fix the reception of revelation in time" (1986–90: 2.47).

The vision is announced, as are all of Ezekiel's visions, with "the hand of the Lord was upon me." Its end is marked by none of Ezekiel's usual formulas; rather an abruptly interrupting interpolation at 48:30–35 ends the book.

I obviously cannot accommodate so much text in one commentary unit, but must break the account of the vision into a series of units. Ezekiel 40–42 is devoted to the plan of an envisioned eschatological temple and makes an obvious if frustrating unit.

Indeed, Gregory the Great found the temple plan so frustrating as to defy literal appropriation. Calculating measurements as they appeared in the Latin text before him, and by his understanding of the measures, he found the measurements were not coherent: for example, gates were wider than the walls they pierced. "It is not possible to work out the construction of this complex according to the letter of the text [*iuxta litteram*]." Therefore, he concludes, Ezekiel describes a spiritual edifice, and his descriptions are to be interpreted allegorically (1986–90: 2.50–54). With this, Gregory adduces a principle frequently invoked by patristic exegetes: texts that "according to the letter" are incoherent or offensive are not to be explained into harmlessness; rather they are to be taken as a challenge to seek deeper meaning. In his ten long homilies on Ezek. 40, Gregory thus reads

Ezekiel's entire description of the envisioned temple as a doctrine of the church: of its hierarchy, its foundation, its virtues, and so on. Nor indeed is this figurative reading as arbitrary as moderns may assume—where, after all, is the vision of a perfected temple fulfilled?

The date (40:1) is for the whole vision, though we may doubt that it fits some of the interpolations. Given the vision's concluding place both in Ezekiel's prophesying and in the book (→25:1–17), it is not surprising that Ezekiel or an editor wanted to secure the date by counting both from the initial deportation as usual and from the destruction of Jerusalem. These work out in our calendar to a date in April 573 (Zimmerli 1983: 345).

The vision begins immediately, with no preliminaries or complications like those that precede the paired visions at Ezek. 8–11. Nor is there any ambiguity about the agent of visionary transportation, as there was there: the Lord himself begins the vision by summarily placing Ezekiel in the land of Israel and on Jerusalem's Temple Mount.

This previously modest hill has become a "superlatively high" ("very" is too weak) mountain, a reference to prophetic tradition that readers are expected to catch.[1] To cite Isaiah: "In days to come the mountain of the LORD's house shall be established as the highest of the mountains . . . ; all the nations shall stream to it . . . , and say, 'Come, let us go up to . . . the house of the God of Jacob; that he may teach us his ways. . . .' [There the LORD] shall judge between the nations . . . ; nation shall not lift up sword against nation" (Isa. 2:2–4). Ezekiel's concluding vision is of precisely those "days to come."

Ezekiel sees Isaiah's "house of the God of Jacob" triumphant on its world mountain and monumental as a city in itself. In its eastern gateway a heavenly guide—not God himself, as in Ezek. 8–11—awaits him.[2] The guide has a measuring line for longer distances and a measuring stick for shorter ones: the stick is 6 long cubits (40:5) in length (roughly 10.5 feet);[3] we are not told the length of the line. The guide instructs Ezekiel to pay close attention to what he is about

1. Rashi notes the reference to Isaiah (Rosenberg 2000: 343) and construes as I will. Gregory the Great also notes the reference to Isaiah; but true to his reading of the whole vision construes it "spiritually," of the basis on which the church stands, "the Mediator of God and man, the man Christ Jesus." Like a mountain, this man is "of the earth," but he also "transcends earth, because while [he] . . . has matter from below he from the heights is pre-eminent in power" (1986–90: 2.54).

2. Gregory 1986–90: 2.66 interprets this "man" as the Christ. I cannot resist displaying the ingenuity and rigor of Gregory's exegetical reasoning, once the need of allegory is granted, by a longer citation: "The same one is signified by the man and is figured by the mountain. . . . And it is right that the Lord is signified both by the man and by the mountain, for the self-same Lord both orders and judges all things in the holy church, and bears up that very church."

3. The cubit was a standard unit of measurement in the ancient Middle East, usually thought to equal 18 inches, the supposed distance from elbow to fingertip. The long cubit equaled a normal cubit plus the supposed width of the hand, which would make 21 or 22 inches. Both in Israel and elsewhere, this longer unit of measurement seems to have been archaic, its use being maintained in ceremonial contexts. All cubits noted in this vision are long cubits.

to see, in order to report it to "the house of Israel" when he emerges from vision (40:2–4).

The guide goes through the eastern gate and then from feature to feature of the temple complex, measuring as he goes, with Ezekiel in train. Ezekiel's visionary tour of the old temple (Ezek. 8–11) was of a busy sanctuary, crowded among other things with idolaters and apostate priests; this tour is of a temple so pristine that there is nothing to observe but its architecture and—later—the glory of the Lord. As we go through the chapters we will encounter more of this character of the vision: what Ezekiel now sees is the antithesis of what he saw before.

Reading through three chapters of measurements and sometimes obdurately obscure architectural references is tedious enough; commenting on each item in turn would undo any ordinary attention span. Blessedly, it would also be beside the point of this commentary: it is rather the sheer insistence on material details that speaks theologically. The size and general plan of the envisioned temple are clear enough, and noting them will suffice for our purpose. I gather that information here for convenience, before proceeding to other reflections.

From a little distance the temple looks like a city because it is enclosed by a wall with imposing gatehouses and visibly mounts up from all sides toward a central structure. The enclosure is square; on the outside it measures 500 cubits (just under 300 yards) in each dimension (42:15–20). The wall itself, at only 6 cubits high by 6 cubits thick, is apparently built to deter unauthorized entry but not armed attack—this is, after all, the temple to which the nations will come in peace. It is pierced by elaborately developed gatehouses on the south, east, and north.[4] These are ceremonial entrances for processions and pilgrims, but may also serve to screen those who would enter,[5] above all, no doubt, for ceremonial purity.

Within this wall is a second wall, so that the temple close is divided into outer and inner courts.[6] This wall too has elaborately constructed entrances, on the same three sides. The inner court is 100 cubits (175 feet) on each side (40:47). It is the scene of the sacrifices and is reserved for the priests. The temple close is not flat: moving through any of its outer entrances to the temple itself, one would mount successive flights of stairs.

Entering the inner court through the eastern entrance and going straight ahead, one would first encounter the altar of burnt sacrifice and then the entrance of the temple proper. This building occupies the place where western entrances to the

---

4. True to his spiritual reading of the temple as the church, Gregory 1986–90: 2.380–82 interprets the gates as the preachers of the word, the outer gates those of the Old Testament, the inner gates those of the New. Nor, when one stops to think about it, is this out of the way; entry into the church indeed "comes by hearing."

5. Those entering the temple courts would traverse a heavily constructed passage some 90 feet long. The recesses are apparently guard stations, accommodating three guards on each side of the passage.

6. Throughout, Rashi conflates Ezekiel's plan with that of the actual Second Temple, as tradition tells him of the latter, which results in such things as identification of Ezekiel's outer court with "the Women's Court" (Rosenberg 2000: 345 and ad loc).

inner court would have been. It consists of three rooms opening off one another from east to west. An entrance hall leads into a chamber for priests ministering to the divine presence—misleadingly called "the nave" by NRSV[7]—which measures 20 cubits (35 feet) wide and 40 cubits long (70 feet). In it, placed just before the entrance to the most holy place, is a wooden table "resembling an altar" (41:21–22); this must be the table for the "showbread," the immemorial[8] offering of bread placed each day before the Lord. Finally there is the most holy place, measuring 20 cubits (35 feet) square (40:48–41:4). What furniture, if any, is there, Ezekiel does not tell us, since—being neither a heavenly being nor the high priest—he may not enter (41:3–4).

We read of many other structures located within the enclosures—accommodations for priests on duty, rooms and spaces for various functions, known and unknown to us,[9] and so on. These need not concern us here.[10]

The eschatological temple, like Solomon's before it, thus follows the general pattern of ancient temples—the connection to this world and its religion is tenuously maintained by certain formal resemblances. Ancient temples were built to provide a housing for the divine presence, with perhaps an adjacent room for priests approaching it. The people gathered outside, accommodated in a colonnade or in courtyards as here or in no special way. Normally the divine presence in the inner chamber was mediated by an icon or totem of the god. As is always emphasized, the distinction of Jerusalem's temple was that its inner chamber contained no such thing,[11] only the wilderness ark for the documents of the covenant and an empty throne (→1:4–24). Whether the now envisioned temple contains such things, we are not told.

So—what is the point of all the measuring and description of details? Ezekiel is to report it to "the house of Israel" when he emerges from the vision. Why?

An initial orientation to the general import of the vision may help. For this, we may look ahead to the promise with which the vision—and Ezekiel's book and all his prophesying—end: "And the name of the city from that time on shall be, The Lord Is There" (48:35). It is the Lord's final and irrevocable presence among his people that the vision and in one way or another all its parts anticipate and that

7. The Hebrew is ההיכל, a word that can denote any grand space. Presumably, NRSV interprets as it does on account of a similarity between the spatial relation of this space to the most holy place and the spatial relation of nave to choir in a Christian church. But this is misleading, since the nave of a church is the assembly place of the people, which this room precisely is not.

8. The display of bread before the Lord antedated the temple; David was involved with it in a famous incident (1 Sam. 21:1–6).

9. Thus there is a large room between the temple proper and the outer west wall, called "the Binyan" (41:12), evidently on the assumption that readers will know what that is, which we do not.

10. For a complete and laborious discussion of the visionary floor plan, see Zimmerli 1983: 342–81. Eichrodt 1970: 537 provides a map.

11. That was anyway what reformers and the canonical prophets thought should be the case.

Ezekiel's report is to prepare among the exiles. The vision of the temple's plan is a vision of the accommodation prepared for that presence and for the people's life around it.

Ezekiel is instructed simply to report the facts of this accommodation, not to exhort Israel to build it or even to promise that they will be enabled to build it. The building will just be there; by his report to the exiles, Ezekiel is to prepare them for the gift.

Thus it appears that the Lord's eschatological presence will involve material accommodation—to be sure, of a sort appropriate to its provision by the Lord himself. If all the describing and measuring communicate anything, it is that the eschatological presence will not be a merely—in our modern sense—"inward" reality: the Lord's final dwelling with his people will bring a house with this wall of so many cubits and that set of windows making a sort of clerestory and those sacristies for changing out of vestments and so forth. We have read (36:16–38) that for Israel to be redeemed, she and all her members must be given a new heart that will be nothing less than inner participation in the Lord's own life. If it was not clear before the present vision, Israel's new heart will not be a merely spiritual entity, in the sense of immateriality. The new heart of the eschatological nation and her members will be the life lived in and around a presence with describable features.

The envisioned temple both is and is not like Solomon's. Its basic plan is clearly modeled on the old complex, yet there are eloquent differences. The walls and courts of Solomon's temple were part of the royal enclosure; this temple has its own free-standing walls and its own close. Thus the eschatological temple simply stands there alone; it no longer depends on any princely patron or military protection or civil benefactors. Indeed, its wall is "to make a separation between the holy and the common" (42:20).

Moreover, the envisioned temple is plotted with an abstract will to perfection that overrides such compromises as any earthly builder, Solomon included, must always make: to the contours of the site, the relation to other buildings, and so on. Here, on the contrary, we deal with strictly geometrical squares and rectangles. A line drawn through the middle of its most holy place and through the middle of the eastern entrances would divide the structures and grounds into two halves in perfect symmetry. There even seems to be a number system underlying the plan's dimensions: most measurements are multiples of fifty. Fifty was in turn an accepted approximation of seven times seven, seven being the number of completeness—it is probably not even accidental that the unit of visionary measurement, 6 cubits, is 7 normal cubits. Doubtless there were specific messages encoded in the play with numbers that we cannot now decipher; but we can detect something of the urge behind it.

Thus the plan of Ezekiel's eschatological temple is at once a rebuke of the old earthly temple and its fulfillment. Therein it embodies the great blessing and conceptual challenge of all Jewish and Christian eschatology: the "world to come" or "kingdom of heaven" will be at once the undoing of all earthly power and achievement and their perfecting. The final temple will be at once the absence of any temple, as at Rev. 21:16–23, and a formalist architect's impossible improvement on Solomon's, as here. The "new heaven and new earth" will replace the old ones and are that for which they long (Rom. 8:18–25). There is an ontological foundation for these identities in difference: the risen Lord is a new creature and is the very same person as the historical and crucified Jesus.

EZEKIEL 43:1–12

THE GLORY RETURNS

This passage, like the others we distinguish within Ezek. 40–48, is a segment of one long report of a concluding vision, which I divide out of practical necessity. The Lord has brought Ezekiel in vision to an eschatologically transformed land of Israel and to its temple; →40:1–42:20 records Ezekiel's tour of this temple's architecture, led by a heavenly guide. Since the record of this tour provides both the technical and theological contexts of everything that follows, readers should read the commentary units on Ezek. 40–42 before continuing here.

With 43:1, Ezekiel's temple tour takes a new turn. His guide leaves off measuring, takes Ezekiel to the eastern entrance in the outer wall, and momentarily retires from the narrative. From this station Ezekiel sees the event for which the envisioned temple has been prepared: the return of the glory of the Lord to a temple on Mount Zion. This eschatological event is thus the precise saving antithesis of the event envisioned in 10:1–22; 11:22–25, the departure of the glory.

When the glory has passed through the east entrance of the outer court, and in unspecified fashion into and through the inner court and into the temple proper, the Spirit brings the prophet into the inner court. From there he can see the glory within the temple, described with clear reference to Isaiah's call-vision (Isa. 6:1–4) and in general to the whole tradition shaping Ezekiel's own call-vision (Ezek. 1:4–28b). The parallel with Ezekiel's call-vision is close: his immediate reaction is told in the same words as then, "I fell on my face" (1:28), and just as at 2:2 it is the Spirit who picks him up again.

The Lord addresses Ezekiel from the most holy place, with the usual "you—son of a man." This speech from the temple is divided into two units by a second such address (43:10). Within a vision—here as in the call-vision at 1:28—the word of the Lord does not need to "come" to Ezekiel; the Lord simply speaks. Rashi glosses this passage in remarkably trinitarian fashion: "He spoke between Himself and His Glory, and the voice came to me" (Rosenberg 2000: 380).

Twice before, as Ezekiel emphasizes (43:3), he had heard and seen this rush of the Lord's glory: by Babylon's river Chebar when the Lord came to call him to prophesy (1:25–3:15), and in his vision of Jerusalem's former temple (Ezek. 8–11), when he witnessed the glory's departure from it and from Jerusalem. Ezekiel's specific concept of the divine *kabod* is at the heart of his doctrine of God (→1:25–28b).

Here we will only reemphasize the trinitarian character of the phenomenon: the glory of the Lord—like the angel of the Lord, or the name of the Lord, or the Word of the Lord—is a reality related *to* the Lord by constructions that in English we must render with the preposition "of," so that the glory is somehow other than the Lord whose glory he is, yet one who when he speaks and acts does so simply *as* the Lord. The glory of the Lord—and the angel and so on—are the Lord as himself a *persona* within a narrative of which he is simultaneously the author.

From the viewpoint to which Ezekiel has now brought us, the whole of his book and of his prophesying is plotted around the two visions of the glory in the temple. In the first (10:1–22; 11:22–25) the glory departs from the temple toward the east; now the glory returns from the east. The departure of the Lord's presence from the midst of his people is the heart and culmination of the doom that Israel's faithlessness has brought upon her and to which the first half of his book was devoted. The return of the presence is the heart and culmination of her redemption. All the prophecies of judgment by war and captivity depicted only the surface of the disaster: the Lord's separation from his people. And all the promises of prosperity and peace evoke only the surface of the final blessing: the Lord's permanent return.

The first part of the address from the temple is for Ezekiel himself. In it the Lord proclaims the new most holy place as the place of his throne and as the place where his feet are planted on the same earth as are the feet of his people. We do not know whether or not there is a cherubim throne in this final holy of holies. However that may be, the Lord is established in the new temple not for the temple's sake but in order to "reside" among the people of Israel (43:7). The verb translated "reside" (שָׁכַן, *shakan*) is the verbal root of the rabbinic word "Shekinah" (→introduction). The Targum in fact paraphrases 43:7 as "this is the place of the abode where My Shekinah dwells" (Levey 1990: 116). And the Shekinah's presence among the Lord's people is now "forever" (לְעוֹלָם).

This eternal presence of the Lord will be matched by an eternal faithfulness of Israel, characteristically stated in the negative: Israel and her kings will never again defile the Lord's name (43:7b). This new faithfulness is not a condition of the Lord's remaining, it is simply the other side of a new reality. We may ask what about the new reality is to prevent Israel's history of betrayal from beginning over again; an earlier passage, →36:16–38, takes up this seeming possibility and describes the Lord's measures against it.

Finally, this part of the Lord's speech specifies wherein Israel had polluted the Lord's name, doing so in a way appropriate to a vision of temple architecture. By locating her old temple as part of the palace, with only an interior wall between the temple's courts and those of the prince, Israel had exposed the Lord to the idolatry practiced in the palace and to a polluting nearby presence of dead kings. The word translated "corpses" by NRSV is usually so translated; if it is to be translated that way here, we must suppose that at least some kings were buried within the royal compound, thereby making it into a graveyard, a permanently polluted place (→5:5–17). The difficulty is that there is no record of royal burials within the palace compound (Zimmerli 1983: 417). But we might also translate the Hebrew (if we ignore the Masoretic vowel pointing) with something like "monuments to their dead kings." Either way, the arrogance of the kings has inflicted the presence of death on the royal courts and so on the incorporated temple. The eschatological temple as described in Ezek. 40–42 has no neighbors, notably not the palace; now we see the reason why. The Lord tells Ezekiel that it is to remain that way (43:9).

The second part of the address (43:10–12) renews the mandate that Ezekiel is to report what he has seen to "the house of Israel," with all the detail it had in his vision. Indeed, he is apparently to create a sort of blueprint of the temple, for them to trace. And in his report he is to include something we have yet to encounter, but shortly will: the Torah of the promised temple.

Christians have regularly translated *torah* with "law"; and indeed this is often appropriate. Moreover, the negative contexts in which "the law" often appears in St. Paul and in some Christian tradition are not—as is sometimes alleged—foreign to the Old Testament: it was, after all, Israel's failure to obey the Lord's "commandments and ordinances" that according to Ezekiel compelled the Lord to destroy her. Nevertheless, it here appears that Torah will be a living feature also in the life of an Israel that will have passed beyond the possibility of disobedience.

The Torah that will thus abide is the command to respect the holiness of the eschatological temple, on its high (40:2) mountain, the mountain to which all the nations will flock to learn righteousness (e.g., Mic. 4:1–2). The temple close and "the whole territory on the top of the mountain"—of which we will in the next chapters hear more—will be holy and not made common. Even when the Lord dwells forever among his people, his holiness, his utter distinction from any creature, will be maintained (→38:1–39:20; →39:21–29).

Since there will be no possibility of eschatological Israel's not honoring the Lord's holiness, the notion of *torah* loses its threatening aspect: there will be no more "do this, or else." This supports the translations of *torah* now often preferred also by Christian scholars, with "guidance" and similar affirmative terms. For the central case, are the Ten Commandments "law" in the alarming sense the term sometimes carries in Paul or Reformation theology? Or are they gracious paths to further holiness? The answer would not seem difficult: insofar as we are sinners, they are surely the first; in the kingdom they will be only the second; and in the time between they must be both.[1]

The exiles are to study the plan of the temple that will be given them and the ordinances that the voice from the temple will shortly communicate. It cannot be meant that when Ezekiel makes his report the exiles must undertake to obey these ordinances, since the temple and community to which they apply will not yet exist, nor is there any suggestion they are to set out to create them. Rather, the exiles are to steep themselves in the ontology and moral structure of the Lord's coming return, to prepare themselves for it.

Finally, the fruit of Ezekiel's report will in the interim be that the exiles will be "ashamed of their iniquities." In the plan and ordinances of the eschatological temple, they will see how badly they had erred in where and how they had built the old temple and in the way they had used it. It is a peculiarity of Ezekiel's discourse that *remembrance* of past sin is enjoined only in the context of promised salvation, and there regularly (Zimmerli 1983: 419). This no doubt reflects Ezekiel's temperament. But it is also theologically indicative: final salvation is also final judgment, in which we will indeed be reminded of the hay and straw in the lives we bring to the Lord and in remembering find them burned away (1 Cor. 3:15).

---

1. Christian theologians—and indeed entire denominations—have divided here. Some have insisted that the law always "kills"—like the more ideological in my own Lutheran denomination. Others have seen the law as pure delight—like the happy preachers of mainline liberalism. In theology, the middle way is not often the right one, but here it surely is.

EZEKIEL 43:13–17

THE ALTAR

Again—mostly for practicality's sake—we isolate for comment a set of verses from Ezekiel's long report of his concluding vision (Ezek. 40–48). Without the earlier parts of the report (→40:1–42:20; →43:1–12) our present passage is unintelligible.

The first thing we notice about 43:13–17 is that these verses have nothing directly to do with what immediately precedes them, the account of the Lord's entry into his eschatological temple. Architectural description of this temple was rounded off at the end of Ezek. 42, and the Shekinah has settled in the new and final most holy place (43:1–12). Then suddenly the measurements begin again, without logical connection or literary mediation to the foregoing and without anyone doing the measuring.

On the other hand, 43:13–17 is obviously connected to what follows in 43:18–27. There the Lord, speaking from the most holy place, begins to lay out the "ordinances" that shall obtain when this temple is used by a transformed Israel, starting with those for dedicating the altar of burnt offering. Presumably, someone—perhaps Ezekiel himself—has noticed that from Ezek. 40–42 the reader would know very little about this altar, apart from its location in the inner court just before the entrance to the temple proper (40:47), and has prefixed measurements more or less of the kind earlier provided for other features of the envisioned complex. I therefore take 43:13–17 together with 43:18–27.

For the same reasons as before, we can make short work of the measurements. It is again not the details that speak theologically[1] but rather the sheer insistence that the eschatological altar is a palpable structure. As for the measurements

1. Or if they do, we cannot understand them.

themselves, a general picture will satisfy our more urgent curiosity. The altar is 9 cubits (16 feet) high, measured from ground level, and is stepped.[2] The top, the actual hearth for burnt sacrifice, measures 12 cubits (a bit over 21 feet) on each side, providing the sizable space (roughly 460 square feet) needed to accommodate the offering by fire of an entire beast.

That there will be "ordinances" for the altar's dedicatory sacrifices (43:18–27) is not surprising. The Lord will provide the final temple; but when Israel occupies it, there will of course be appropriate initiatory rites, however eschatological. For this commentary, the chief import of these ordinances is that also in the eschatological worship of God's people the smoke of sacrifice will ascend before the Lord.[3] We need, however, to delay consideration of this central notion, to consider two features of the ordinances.

First, the instructions about how to offer the dedicatory sacrifices are directed to Ezekiel himself. He is to provide the animals and to perform the chief act of splashing the altar with their blood. It therefore seems that when the vision was given, the transformation of Israel and her entry into the eschatological temple were so imminently expected that the priest Ezekiel could himself expect to be part of the new priesthood.[4] The editors of Ezekiel's book will have known that this expectation was not fulfilled, and nevertheless let the text stand. Just so, the followers of Jesus initially expected his imminent return and do not appear to have been overly disconcerted by the failure of this expectation.

Second, the sacrifices, in the NRSV translation, are to "make atonement" (43:20) for the altar. How can an altar need atonement? Particularly when the obedience of Israel is assured, so that they cannot have defiled this altar?

To this question there may be a purely linguistic answer. The problem is provoked by the usual and in itself legitimate translation: "make atonement." The verb in question (כפר), however, appears in the Old Testament in contexts where other translations are appropriate; moreover, it does not seem possible to determine a basic meaning etymologically or by reference to one determining context. We will therefore adopt Jenni and Westermann's suggestion (1997: 633) that such things as altars need "atonement" not for what we would usually call sin or pollution but for the sheer unworthiness of creatures—sinful or not—to stand before the

2. In the literature, there is much speculation about the ziggurat shape that Ezekiel will have known in Babylon. In my judgment, no such model need be posited; an altar 16 feet high will have to be stepped.

3. There is some critical consensus (Zimmerli 1983: 432) that the origin of these rubrics is priestly rulings about how, on return from exile, one would go about consecrating a new altar of sacrifice, such a thing not having been done for centuries. The hypothesis is plausible, but it remains that in the canonical text this altar is to be in a temple that could not be built on the present earth, requiring as it does a transformation of the modest Temple Mount into the highest of the mountains.

4. The implausibility of this seems to have occasioned confusion in the text's later history. The Masoretic Text itself slips from "you" to "they"; and the Septuagint and other versions present various combinations of the pronouns.

Lord. Rashi's gloss is: "You shall 'wipe' it of its *ordinariness*" (Rosenberg 2000: 387, emphasis added). Ezekiel and other priests are to prepare the altar to serve that Lord whose holiness burns before it in the most holy place.

To return to the main line of our reflections, I have already noted that in the last future, as Ezekiel is shown it, the Lord's presence in the midst of his people will occupy a palpable structure built as an eschatological version of the old temple. Now the persistence also of sacrifices much like those offered in the old temple is added to this embodiment. What are we to make of all this? Even if a holy people's sacrifices are not for sin, how can sacrifices—those most blatant acts of human religion—continue at all? And how can the life of an eschatological people of God be so palpably embodied as the vision depicts it?

To the first question, we may perhaps take our clue from the unproblematic and unself-conscious way in which the ancient church regularly referred to the Eucharist as its specific "sacrifice"—and indeed from recent ecumenical agreement that Catholic continuation of this language, understood as it was in the ancient church, does not divide the Catholic Church from the churches who come from the Reformation.[5] When the ancient church thought of the Eucharist as a sacrifice, they did not mean—as in later times one was likely to suppose—that the Eucharist was an action intended to reconcile God to us, though some pagan sacrifices had indeed been so intended. When an actual regime of sacrifice was a fact of every-day life, as in old Israel or in the milieu of the ancient church, the acts so named were of such various forms and intentions that we can define the practice only in some such inclusive fashion as this: a sacrifice is a prayer made not with words only but also with visible and tangible gestures, with actions done using objects. Augustine set the terms of the Western church's sacramental doctrine when he defined a sacrament as "a visible word" (*In Johannem* 80.3) of God's message for us. The equivalent can be said of sacrifice: it is a visible word of our prayer, of our response to God's address.

In the case of Israel's animal sacrifices, the visible gesture is double. Except in the case of "whole burnt offering," it is first the surrender of the animal and its life to enable a meal of fellowship with the Lord. And it is the surrender of the animal's best bits—throughout most of history, the fatty parts—to the Lord, in the flame burning before him. The prayer could be of any legitimate sort; the gesture of offering embodied an implicit "Hear us, good Lord."

In Ezekiel's vision of the life of God's eschatological people, the embodiment of prayer in sacrifice continues. We see the same in the Christian apocalypse. The saints—and heavenly beings with the faces of the cherubim from Ezekiel's call-vision!—are depicted before the throne of God, eternally engaged in prayers of thanksgiving (Rev. 4–5). As has often been remarked, this assembly and the earliest church's eucharistic assemblies have the same general arrangement of

---

5. See Robert W. Jenson, *Unbaptized God: The Basic Flaw in Ecumenical Theology* (Minneapolis: Fortress, 1992), 34–44.

participants. We then see between the throne and the worshipers, where in the church the eucharistic altar would be, a Lamb, portrayed as a sacrificed animal (5:6). The assembly sings: "You are worthy" to open the scroll of history "for you were slain[6] and by your blood you ransomed some for God from every . . . nation" (5:9–10, my translation). We could set this liturgy neatly down in Ezekiel's inner court before the throne in the most holy place, except that at the place of the altar there would be the person of the crucified and risen Christ.

The ancient church rightly assumed that the Eucharist is a sacrifice. The throne, the people, and the sacrifice between them are the pattern of the life of God's people, in this age or the next. The Lord is there for his people; the people approach him; and in the presence of the Lamb we see how we dare do this, indeed, we see what Israel's sacrifices had always been, an embodied and confident "Lord, have mercy."

That the risen Christ is eternally the mediation of the Lord's people to his presence answers also the second question—though unpacking that answer has been the not yet finished work of the theological centuries. In Christian confession, the risen Christ is not a ghost or disembodied spirit. Therefore what is promised also to his disciples is not the immortality of a disembodied soul, but the "resurrection of the body." In the kingdom, Christ will be present to us and will be our mediator with the Father precisely as the fully embodied person he is: we will *see* him and seeing him see the Father (John 6:46).

To be sure, also in this respect scripture's eschatological scenarios—as we earlier (→38:1–39:20) called them—cannot simply be fitted together. "Resurrection of the body" is not, in scripture or tradition, resuscitation—Lazarus was resuscitated and later died. Nor, at least according to Paul, will the resurrection body be an organism such as each of us now knows as his/her body: this "organic body"[7] is "sown" and dies, and a "spiritual body"[8] appears in its place (1 Cor. 15:44). It is not altogether clear what Paul means by "spiritual body" (and perhaps not to him either), but the phrase anyway describes something other and more than an organism.

It will be seen that accommodating the biblical notion of bodily resurrection will require some drastic revisions of our inherited and assumed metaphysics. In particular, we will need to consider anew what we mean or should mean by "the body of. . . ." But that is for discourse of a different genre (Jenson 1997–99: 2.211–15). For now it may be sufficient to say that Christ and we will be available to one another, and so to the Father, in the same way we are now mutually available in the eucharistic gathering of Christ's visible and tangible "body and blood."

6. NRSV's "slaughtered" and "saints" are plausible glosses, but hardly translations.

7. Σῶμα ψυχικόν is a formed object animated by a "soul," by a specific principal of action. The versions' "physical" or "natural" do not quite catch it.

8. Σῶμα πνευματικόν is a formed object animated by the Spirit.

EZEKIEL 44:1–3

THE LOCKED GATE
AND THE PRINCE

Like all passages in Ezek. 40–48, 44:1–3 belongs to the report of one long vision and can be understood only if some of what has gone before is in the reader's mind (→40:1–42:20).

Ezekiel 44:1–3 makes a clear unit for comment, despite the brevity of the passage. With 44:1, Ezekiel's guided tour of the eschatological temple resumes and brings him to a stopping place, where he learns about another feature of this temple; 44:4 begins another episode, in which he receives a long divine discourse on wholly different matters.

The guide brings Ezekiel to the east gate of the compound's outer wall; there the doors are shut. The Lord tells him why: because the God of Israel passed through this gate to occupy his temple it is eternally his gate and no one else may use it—indeed, we may add a gloss to the effect that no one else could now survive using it.

Here we see again how the holiness of the Lord, how his utter difference from all creatures (→1:25–28b) is maintained even as he dwells intimately with his people. In the eschatological temple the east gate is the Lord's, and even the most passionate procession of perfected pilgrims or triumphal march of the eschatological prince will have to go around to one of the side doors. We see also the eschatological finality of the Lord's new dwelling in this temple: his gate will *remain* shut, it will not be needed again.

But then 44:3 brings a needed qualification: when "the prince" participates in a sacrificial meal, he may enter the gate's "vestibule," to eat his portion there.

This room is the innermost part of the passage through the outer gatehouse and opens into the outer court; the locked doors themselves are behind it to the east. To eat his meal, the prince is to enter the vestibule from the court, not from the outside, and is to return the same way. Thus he may enter the gatehouse, but not pass through the gates.

Why does the prince have this privilege? NRSV's translation supposes it goes with his rank; but this depends on a speculative resolution of a recalcitrant piece of text. The Hebrew baffles the experts, and in this case the versions are no help, being apparently based on the same recalcitrant Hebrew text that the Masoretes had. Simply laying out English equivalents of the Hebrew words in order, we have "for the prince—(a) prince—he. . . ." Even given Hebrew's freedom in sentence construction, this sequence of nouns and an explicit pronoun is remarkably indeterminate (for the possibilities, see Zimmerli 1983: 438). With no claim to authority, I lean to a rendering like "as for the prince, he. . . ."

If then we do not follow NRSV's ascription of the prince's privilege to his rank, to what shall we ascribe it? This question leads to another, which is the real question about our passage: Who is this prince? There are two possibilities.[1] He may be just whoever happens to be prince at any time. This supposes that also in eschatological Israel there will be a succession of monarchs.[2] Or he may be the prince promised at the end of the Good Shepherd passage (Ezek. 34), that is, the Christ.

How shall we decide? The new Israel and her temple, as Ezekiel is shown them, are indeed tied to old Israel and her temple by many analogies (→40:1–42:20). But surely continuation of a line of monarchs in the perfected Israel of the latter days stretches analogy too far. In my judgment, it is the alternative possibility that the text rather plainly presumes: it is because this prince is the Messiah that he communes with the Lord from his own holy place.

The picture of a prince worshiping the God of Israel, from the vestibule of God's way to his people's place of assembly, gave premodern exegetes a splendid occasion for christological extrapolations, that we may call "allegorical" if we choose. Modern exegetes have of course regarded these as absurd (e.g., Zimmerli 1983: 441), but if the passage is, as I have argued, christological in its own terms, judgment should be less hasty. Origen's reading is at the very least interesting: Who is this prince? "It is the Savior who eats this bread, who guards the door of the Father, who nourishes himself with spiritual food, saying 'my food is to do the will of him who sent me'" (1989: 440).

---

1. Rashi understandably but quite implausibly makes him be the high priest (Rosenberg 2000: 389).

2. NRSV's translation probably depends on the translators' choice of this interpretation.

EZEKIEL 44:4–31

PURITY FOR THE TEMPLE

Ezekiel 40–48 is a single—if much interpolated—long report of Ezekiel's concluding vision; thus the successive sections that we take for comment can be understood only if we each time have something of the previous narrative in mind (→40:1–42:20).

Ezekiel 44:4–46:18 is clearly intended as a unit: 44:4–5 tells of an episode in Ezekiel's tour of the envisioned temple, and 46:19 tells of the next. The complex thus marked comprises a set of messenger-words for Ezekiel to bring to Israel, each beginning with "thus says the Lord" (44:6–8; 44:9–45:8; 45:9–17; 45:18–25; 46:1–15; 46:16–18). The series thus displays a structure we often encounter in Ezekiel. In such complex texts, there is a primary messenger-word, often provided with its historical or theological context. In the present instance, 44:6–8 is the primary messenger-word; and its context is the scene narrated by 44:4–5, with the Lord's renewed address to Ezekiel as "you—son of a man." Then the primary messenger-word and its context serve to anchor one or more editorially attached additional messenger-words. In the present case, there are five of these, of which the first, 44:9–45:8, is most closely related to 44:6–8.

Clearly we have to divide this long unit for comment. I will consider 44:4–5 and the first two messenger-words in this commentary unit, except for the last part (45:1–8) of the second, which I will reserve for the next commentary unit.

The guide brings Ezekiel back into the inner court—avoiding the east gate (→44:1–3)—and to a place where Ezekiel had been at an earlier stop (43:4–6), just outside the entrance of the temple proper. There Ezekiel experiences something like a reprise of the former occasion: he again sees the blazing glory of the Lord, again falls on his face, again is addressed from the temple with "you—son of a man," and again is commanded to report to Israel when he emerges from the vision.

It is hard not to think that 44:4–5 was directly modeled on the earlier text—which in turn is modeled on the call-vision—and was composed and inserted here to prepare a place in the book for the messenger-words that follow. The mandate to Ezekiel does, however, differ from the earlier mandate: this time, Ezekiel is not to report a vision but to carry oral messages, of legal character, "the ordinances of the temple of the LORD." Indeed, the mandated texts are in the exact style of the so-called Holiness Code in Leviticus (Lev. 17–26). The theme of this collection of laws is stated in a famous passage: "You [Israel] shall be holy, for I the LORD your God am holy" (19:2); thus the Holiness Code brings rules for maintaining the people's fitness to approach the holy God.

The formal oddity of the present messages as messenger-words is thus that holiness rules are cast by prefixing "thus says the Lord" (Zimmerli 1983: 452–53). Messenger-words are properly threats of doom or promises of blessing; here we find instead, for example, regulations about where priests should change their clothes. What is the function of this hybrid form?

The beginning of the primary messenger-word provides a clue. When Ezekiel delivers the mandated messages, it will be to an Israel characterized by the Lord's epithet for the nation to whom he first sent Ezekiel, the "rebellious house" (→1:25–28b; →1:28c–3:15). Ezekiel's mission will be to an exilic community that in the Lord's view remains much as it was when he first sent Ezekiel to preach repentance, an Israel not yet transformed by or ready for the Lord's imminent and final act of sanctification (→36:16–38).

Proclamation of holiness rules is thus to prepare the exiles for the coming salvation. In the case of the present rules for the coming temple, they are to give the exiles a vision of what will be and, by stark contrast with what had happened in the old temple, to rebuke them and call for repentance.

Thus the primary messenger-word begins in Ezekiel's best threatening fashion: "O house of Israel, let there be an end to all your abominations!" (44:6). The abomination then specified, however, is not injustice or idolatry or sexual perversion but violation of a rule about who could do what in the temple. In the old and now destroyed temple, "foreigners" (44:7) had at some time been substituted (44:8)[1] for those responsible to offer sacrifice. It is not now clear who such interlopers can have been or what specifically they had been allowed to do (Zimmerli 1983: 453–54); what matters is that they were uncircumcised and yet in some way served the sacrifices, which was enough to profane the temple. Nor does the Lord shrink from the strongest possible conclusion from this pollution: "You have broken my covenant." These persons

---

1. "Foreigners" does not appear in either the Hebrew or the Septuagint of 44:8, both of which might best be translated more vaguely, "You have set others to attend to my holy things." NRSV's insertion is an explanation, deduced from 44:7. No great harm is done. But why do NRSV's translators allow themselves these unnecessary explanatory translations?

were "uncircumcised" both in their flesh *and* in their hearts, which reminds us of Paul's judgment at Rom. 2:28–29.

Moderns may be tempted to regard the exclusion of the uncircumcised from Israel's sacrificial life as exclusivism, which in our prejudice is a very bad thing. But we should consider the result of simply turning to the apparent alternative, inclusivism. In the kingdom, there will indeed be no need to close the gates to those outside, since there will be no aspiration or energy there. But in the meantime, it is modernity's utopian delusion that we can achieve such a blessed state of openness without waiting for God's final act of transformation. The great scourges of late modernity have been movements like Marxism or National Socialism, which suppose that a "classless society" or "pure nation" can be achieved by our action in this age. Pending the end, a community with no boundary would be no community at all, which is why Marxism and the rest are after all driven to impose arbitrary limits enforced by sheer power. As for Israel or the church, a simply inclusive Israel or church would quickly cease to be an identifiable community.

The first of the attached messenger-words (44:9–31) considers those who, instead of the "foreigners," should properly be ministers in the temple. These are the levitical priests, who appear here in two groups: those simply called "the Levites" (44:10–14) and "the levitical priests, the sons[2] of Zadok" (44:15–31 RSV).

Who exactly were the so-called Levites, and what was their role at various times in Israel's history? Are the Levites and the tribe of Levi the same? If not, what happened to the tribe of Levi? This may be said with some confidence: between Israel's settlement in Syria-Palestine and Josiah's centralizing reforms, the Levites were priests and/or preachers in the towns and countryside; then Josiah's centralization brought them to Jerusalem as a class of temple priests.

As for the "levitical priests" who are "sons of Zadok," it seems that by Ezekiel's time all priests could be called "levitical." The differentium is then the connection to Zadok, who was a priest of the ark at Jerusalem in David's time and belonged to David's inner circle (1 Kgs. 1:26–45; 2:35). The "sons of Zadok" were thus the group of priests at Jerusalem who claimed to minister in succession from David's chief priest.

At the beginning of 44:10–14, it is laid down: in the new temple the Levites shall do much of what the interlopers had illegitimately done. This is a punishment, for the Levites are restricted to services that NRSV characterizes as "chores" (44:14).[3] They are not to carry out actual sacrifice; and we will later learn (44:16–17) that this includes exclusion from the inner court and everything done there. They are to stand guard in the gates, be responsible for those steps in offering sacrifice that could be done in the outer court, and carry out like functions. According to Ezekiel, their sin was that before Josiah's reform, their

2. The Hebrew word is indeed "sons" (as in RSV and KJV), not "descendents" (NRSV). For better or worse, the Jerusalem priests were in fact all male; nor is it clear that "sons" must here refer to lineage; "the sons of Zadok" may simple mean "the Zadokites"

3. This is another of NRSV's explanatory translations, this time perhaps a good one.

activity at the countryside sanctuaries had included serving the Canaanite gods who there often shared worship with יהוה (44:10–12; →6:1–14).[4]

The core priestly service is now to be done only by the Zadokite priests—one of whom, it may be worth remembering, was Ezekiel—who had remained faithful "when the people of Israel went astray" (44:15). How we are to reconcile this praise with what Ezekiel saw in his visionary tour of the old temple (Ezek. 8–11) is far from clear.[5] However that may be, it is the Zadokites who may enter the inner court to offer "the fat and the blood" on the great altar and may enter the chamber next the most holy place (44:15–17).

There follows a set of regulations about the Zadokite priests' liturgical vestments (44:17–19) and other requirements for service close to the Holy One (44:20–31; →38:1–39:20; →39:21–29; →36:16–38). In the present context it is important to remember that while sin indeed defiles, the concepts of sin and defilement are not identical; a meritorious act, like attending to the corpse of a family member, can also defile (44:25–27).

Why are the priests so hedged about with rules about things to be done and not done? Our text gives the answer: because they are to "teach [the] people the difference between the holy and the common" (44:23). The "common," that is, the quotidian and unremarkable, is not as such defiled or defiling. But the holy is precisely the utterly uncommon, and mixing the holy and the common is therefore indeed a profanation. Instruction about observing the difference between the holy and the everyday will inevitably have a sacramental side: the difference will be visibly embodied by such things as excluding gateways and strange clothing worn on their other side or by a priesthood obligated to redoubled avoidance of pollution (44:20–27) and entirely dependent on gifts (44:28–30). Moderns will be inclined to ask questions such as, Why could not the priests' vestments just as well have been of wool and not linen? With the earlier discussion of pollution, we must answer: they could have been, in a community with another history and a consequent other sensibility.

Two further questions nevertheless arise. What are such temporal things as the punishment of erring Levites or Israel's contingent ceremonial attachment to linen doing in the description of life in an eschatological temple? Indeed, what role can the whole distinction of the holy from the common have in the life of an eschatological Israel?

The first question is the more easily dealt with. If the recitation of holiness rules is to function as rebuke and promise to the exiles, the double reference

---

4. Ezekiel's description of the Levites' sin is vague as to time and place. And indeed, Gerhard von Rad's classic studies on Deuteronomy (*Studies in Deuteronomy*, trans. David Stalker [London: SCM, 1961]) cast the country Levites as the preachers of Josiah's reform. Convicting or acquitting the Levites is not, to be sure, within our present brief; Ezekiel charged the Levites with idolatry at the countryside sanctuaries, and that must suffice.

5. As Eichrodt remarks, this exculpation of the Jerusalem priesthood "has little connection with historical fact" (1970: 565).

characteristic of Ezekiel's earlier prophecies of doom or salvation must reemerge, after being more or less hidden from Ezek. 38 on: the prophecy of a reformed priesthood must refer at once to a reformation in some conceivable continuity with the old priesthood and its sins and to a new reality beyond anything conceivable in this age (→40:1–42:20).

The remaining question is perhaps more dangerous to the line of interpretation taken in this and the closely preceding commentary units. In modern Christian theology it has often been supposed that the coming of Christ overcomes the ancient distinction between the holy and the common and that practices in the church that presume the distinction are a relapse from Christian freedom. And there must be something to such "low-church" protest, for Jesus indeed once said that the only true defilement is done by what comes from within the person and that such outward things as eating with unwashed hands cannot do it (Mark 7:5–23). Yet we should not be too hasty in drawing conceptually abstract conclusions from Jesus's saying. For this is the same Jesus who very much in Ezekiel's style denounced the presence of everyday activities in the temple—even in an outer court—and violently dispersed them.

Puritan movements throughout the church's history have protested against vestments and clerical rank and all such externalities. But a strange thing regularly happens: having gotten rid of the old outward things, such movements quickly develop new ones. The impulse to embody a line between holy and common, to make it visible and tangible, seems to be ineradicable. Perhaps this is because backsliding from the purity of Jesus's maxim is ineradicable. But perhaps it is because the maxim is not ahistorical in its import and requires new consideration in new situations such as the church.

EZEKIEL 45:1–8

THE HOLY DISTRICT

Ezekiel 45:1–8, like all units in Ezek. 40–48, belongs—with greater or less cogency—to a continuing report of the great vision that concludes the work; thus it can be understood only if at least some of what has gone before is in the reader's mind (→40:1–42:20).

Formally, 45:1–8 belongs to a messenger-word that began at 44:9 (→44:4–31). I take these verses in a separate unit for two reasons: to lighten the burden on the previous commentary unit, even if only a trifle, and, more importantly, because 45:1–8 has little material relation to 44:4–31 and even less to the new messenger-word that begins at 45:9, but is entirely of a piece with the long passage (47:13–48:35) that concludes the vision and all Ezekiel's prophesying—indeed 45:1–8 gives every sign of having been composed as an extract from 47:13 and 48:8–14.

The opening sentence of this passage announces its subject and therewith that also of 47:13–48:35: provision of regulations for the final and permanent occupation and division of the promised land. Ezekiel's book concludes with an account of Israel's eschatological entry into the land, parallel to—if very different from—the accounts of the twelve tribes' original settlement, the fullest of which is in Josh. 13–21.

What then is Ezek. 45:1–8 doing in its present detached and seemingly premature location? We can never, of course, be sure of the personal intention of ancient editors, and even when we can make a good guess it should not dominate interpretation. But here guessing may be helpful. Someone has thought that the holiness regulations for the priests' lives that occupy 44:15–31, since they included provision for the priests' maintenance, should also include provision for their dwelling, in a properly holy place (45:1).

Moreover, it has plausibly been proposed that insertion of these verses had a second purpose, of resolving a perceived contradiction. Ezekiel 44:28 says explicitly that the Zadokite priests are to own no land in Israel, but to live from the temple offerings, whereas 48:10–14 specifies an area 25,000 cubits by 10,000 cubits as their "allotment," just as the tribes have. In our present passage the word "allotment" disappears; the stipulated territory is described as itself an offering to the temple (Zimmerli 1983: 468–69).

Most of what is to be said about Israel's eschatological reoccupation of the land must await the longer and fuller passage. We can, however, conveniently now take up some things about that part of the land designated as the "holy district."

To begin, we can, as we did with the temple and the temple close, note the little we need to know of the plan's features. The holy district is a rectangle: 25,000 cubits from west to east and 20,000 cubits from north to south (about 8.33 miles by 6.5 miles). A rectangle adjoining to the south is set aside for the city and its environs (45:6). Together, these make another of the squares with which Ezek. 40–42 was obsessed.

The holy district itself is divided into two parts, each 25,000 cubits by 10,000 cubits. The one is occupied by the temple and its close, and by housing and fields for the Zadokite priests; the other accommodates the more numerous Levites. The temple close is as before (42:15–19) 500 cubits (just under 900 feet) square. Here we find it set off even from the rest of the holy district by a belt of open land, 50 cubits (88 feet) wide.[1]

If we have read the opening scenes of the vision, we will surely be struck by the similarity between the sensibility here displayed in the description of the holy district's plan and that displayed in the earlier picture of the temple's plan. There are of course differences: Ezek. 40–42 is narrative, whereas our present verses are regulations; in Ezek. 40–42 the figures are ascertained by measuring a complex envisioned as complete, whereas here they are legislated for the future. But the sensibility is the same: just as the divine layout of the temple and its close took no account of the facts on any ground conceivable in this age, so this edict outdoes the most arbitrary and mathematically obsessed practitioners of earthly land-use planning. Where—and especially around Jerusalem—could you actually lay out these rectangles?

The reason for the abstraction is plain: planning for the eschatological holy district and its neighborhood need not concern itself with antecedent topography, since the holy district creates its own incommensurably perfect topography. The old temple had its precincts; and the eschatological temple will be like it in this. But the new precincts will be such a geometrically exact layout as no zoning of this age could encompass (→40:1–42:20).

1. This may seem like an inconsiderable green belt, until we consider the close quarters of premodern cities.

"Alongside"—not around and assuredly not overlapping—the holy district there is an area set aside for the city and its environs (45:6): thus there will be no spatial or structural enclosure of the temple or its appurtenances by the city's structures and life. Moreover, that the city has its own district will also serve to shield the holy district from the palace located within the city. Indeed, this land plan is designed to spare the city and—as we will later see—the tribes from the prince's use of eminent domain or confiscation for taxes, by giving the prince his own estate and restricting him to it (45:8).

In discussion of Ezekiel's initial tour of the eschatological temple (→40:1–42:20), I noted how this temple would stand and live on its own; now this point is hammered home. In eschatological Israel as laid out in these stipulations, there appears in fact something remarkably like the modern distinction of church, civil society, and state—and indeed, achieving this distinction in lived common life may be more an eschatological hope than a possible achievement of this age. Or rather, perhaps, the secret hidden in the eschatological ground plan for Israel's temple, city, and royal demesne is a final harmony of worship, civil/economic interchange, and righteousness that is so clear and guaranteed as no longer to be an object of concern.

EZEKIEL 45:9–25

THE PRINCE AND THE OFFERINGS

Ezekiel 45:9–25 comprises the second (45:9–17) and third (45:18–25) of five messenger-words attached to an initial messenger-word at 44:6–8 (→44:4–31). I take these two messenger-words together because they deal with the same matter; indeed, the ending of the first (45:17) formally states the concern also of the second. Finally, these verses, like all subunits in Ezek. 40–48, belong to a continuing report of the single great vision that concludes the work (→40:1–42:20).

Ezekiel 45:9–17 begins in the proper form of a messenger-word. Ezekiel, bringing the Lord's message, is to rebuke the "princes[1] of Israel"—that is, kings of Israel and Judah—for unjust rule. At the time when Ezekiel would return from his vision and deliver this message, demanding repentance for royal abuse of power, he could hardly address ruling Israelite monarchs, since there were none. As sometimes elsewhere in Ezekiel, the judgment is rather of the whole monarchical system as it functioned through history (→34:1–31).

The princely sin initially named at 45:9 is abuse either of what we would now call eminent domain or of confiscation for nonpayment of taxes; in either case the result is expansion of royal property at the expense of the ancient tribal holdings. This rebuke of the "princes" provides the attachment to the previous messenger-word, which ended (45:8) with the promise of respite from just this sort of oppression.

Indeed, 45:9c seems mostly intended to provide this attachment, since once that is attended to the prophecy drops the subject of land seizures, to take up a

---

1. The translation of נשיא with "princes" may be misleading, since English usage suggests lesser members of a royal house. The Hebrew word simply denotes great rulers.

different form of governmental malpractice: inflation of the measures of trade and exchange (45:10–12). And even this does not turn out to be the real concern, which is proper management of the offerings to the temple. Honest standard measures are here demanded because offerings to the temple are stipulated in their terms: "one-sixth of an ephah" can be much or little, depending on the official ephah. If our passage's opening denunciation of the princes still determines the rhetoric here, it appears that monarchs had in former days manipulated the measures in order to reduce their obligations to the temple.

At 45:13 the text abruptly abandons the normal style of messenger-words to simply lay down regulations for offerings to the temple and for who shall be responsible for what in dealing with them (45:13–17). We have encountered this hybrid form before—ritual rules as the content of messenger-words (→44:4–31)—and so I summarize: when Ezekiel emerges from vision and proclaims these laws to Israel, he will do it to call Israel to repentance, by contrasting what will be with what has been; and thereby he will prepare her for the coming salvation.

Ezekiel 45:13–17 stipulates provisions for the temple's sacrificial routine. The text is not transparent to the rites to which it refers.[2] The chief concern, however, is clear enough: it is to fix the responsibility of the prince. The people are to bring the prince the mandated portions of the yield of field and pasture, and from them and his own resources the prince is to make precise and honest provision for the regular offerings.

The second messenger-word, 45:18–25, makes similar stipulations for offerings at certain festivals. This passage also presents some problems.

Who is addressed? "You" in 45:18–20 is singular—whereas in 45:21 it is plural. We might suppose that in 45:18–20 the prophet himself is addressed, except that the mandate does not limit the yearly recurrence of the stipulated festivals. Probably we should refer "you" to the prince, the only other individual in purview, despite the anonymity of "you" itself and despite concentration of the verses' attention on the role of the priests; at least in the canonical text, 45:18–20 is one messenger-word with 45:21–25, and 45:21–25 is explicitly about the prince's responsibilities.

What are the festivals in question? The Passover is named, but the identity of the three others—referred to at 45:18, 20, 25—is not as clear as one might wish. If, as seems likely, the rite described at 45:18–19 is for the great Day of Atonement, its dating here clashes with the date stipulated at Lev. 16:29. And what is Ezek. 45:20 about, which stipulates an asymmetrical repeat of the ritual seven—not six—months after the first (Zimmerli 1983: 482–83)? Finally, 45:25, with its brief mention of "the festival," seems to refer to old Israel's once-dominant

2. For the possibilities and for a valiant attempt to sort out the textual history behind the confusion, see Zimmerli 1983: 475–79. The Targum interpolates freely in order to explain the quantities in question, which do not cohere with those stipulated elsewhere in Mosaic law (Levey 1990: 122).

harvest festival—known in Ezekiel's time as the Feast of Booths (Deut. 16)—but in a remarkably offhand fashion.

These verses' treatment of the great festivals differs from that found elsewhere in the Old Testament, in two ways. One we can dispose of quickly. In the historical-critical literature, discrepancies between the ritual order here presumed and legislated and that found in the Pentateuch—some of which was just noted—provoke interesting and difficult investigations about priority, possible motives for changes, and the like. For our purposes, however, we need go no further with such questions than to note their existence (Zimmerli 1983: 481–86).

More puzzling for us, our passage's great concern in all its legislating is the need to "purify" the temple and the use to that end of the blood of a "sin offering" (חַטָּאת; see Jenni and Westermann 1997: 406–11). But in other accounts of Passover and the harvest festival, atonement is not central; this emphasis is unique to Ezekiel. And why in any case is he so emphatic that the temple of an eschatologically established Israel be purified? From defilement by what sins? Indeed, why a Day of Atonement at all?

We encountered this problem at the first appearance of holiness laws within Ezek. 40–48 (→43:13–27). It seems obvious that in the cases of an altar or a building we cannot take the notion of a *sin* offering too literally. As I noted in the earlier commentary unit, in Israel's construal of reality, even a human person need not be actually defiled to require purification if he is to survive before the holy God; mere uncleansed creatureliness suffices. Still, this observation carries us only part of the way.

We may make a start on the rest of the way by noting that the double reference characteristic of Ezekiel's earlier prophecies reappears in these verses—if only to vanish again. Ezekiel's usual prophecies of doom or blessing simultaneously envisioned both an event conceivable in this age and one conceivable only eschatologically. The this-worldly side nearly disappeared in the oracle against Gog (→38:1–39:20) and in much of Ezek. 44–48. But it necessarily returns with messenger-words on such subjects as are here addressed, for these regulations for sacrifice and festival could very well be initiated and enforced in a community of the present age. Will then the Israel established by a final return need periodically to purify her temple? Yes, insofar as that Israel is the same community as the old Israel. No, insofar as she is confirmed in her radical otherness (for the duality of Ezekiel's eschatology and its import, →40:1–42:20).

Consideration of the phenomena just instanced leads to the main interesting question posed by our passage: Who is this prince whose responsibilities are here laid down? The princely line that cheated on the offerings is finished: the prince cannot within Ezekiel's purview be a reformed successor to Zedekiah (→34:1–31). Thus, reference to what is possible within the history of this age becomes shadowy again. This leaves one possibility: whatever picture Ezekiel may have had in his own mind, the prince of an eschatological Israel, responsible for her offerings in the perfect temple, can only be that prince whom tradition came to call the "Messiah," the "Christ."

Thus, in my judgment, we may with full loyalty to the text as it stands read "Christ" for "the prince." When we do that, we learn something vital about the reign of Christ: he now and eschatologically continues to mediate our creaturely presence before the holy God. He now and in all eternity provides the sacrifice that enables us to survive life with and in the holy God. And from the Gospels and the book of Hebrews we further learn that this sacrifice is himself.

EZEKIEL 46:1–18

THE PRINCE AND THE PEOPLE

Like all subunits in Ezek. 40–48, these verses in their canonical location belong to the continuing report of a single great vision; thus they can be understood only if at least some of what has gone before is in the reader's mind (→40:1–42:20).

Ezekiel 46:1–15 and 46:16–18 are the last two of five messenger-words attached to an initial messenger-word at 44:6–8, a prophecy given to Ezekiel during an episode of his visionary tour of the final temple, where he again encounters the divine glory (44:4–5). Thus they conclude a long and rather awkward construction interior to the report of the vision, stretching from 44:4 through 46:18 (→44:4–31). The end of the complex and of our current passage is obvious, since with 46:19 the guide resumes Ezekiel's tour.

Ezekiel 46:1–18 shares a theme with the two previous messenger-words: concentration on the role of "the prince" in restored Israel and, in that context, rubrics for sacrifice in the temple. Whether 46:1–15 and 46:16–18 were once independent prophecies editorially attached here because of common concerns or were always related to the previous passages, we cannot say. The relation is anyway so close (especially in regard to the prince within an eschatologically perfected Israel), that I will concentrate on aspects of the prince's role not emphasized in →45:9–25.

Both of our messenger-words are about the relation of the prince to "the people of the land"; it seems that in this case these are those we might now simply call "the people."[1] Ezekiel 46:1–15 deals with the prince's relation to them in worship, 46:16–18 with their relation with respect to the reoccupied and transformed

---

1. This phrase had a complicated history. In 12:17–20 it referred to rural magnates. After the return from exile, it came to designate those who had remained behind in the countryside and

land. We should remember that in Israel these were not fully distinct spheres, since the land belongs to the Lord.

In part, 46:1–15 simply carries on from 45:13–25, with rules for offerings and sacrifices and for the prince's responsibility with respect to them, now providing rubrics for the Sabbath (46:4–5), for the festivals at the new moon (46:6–7), and for the daily morning sacrifice (46:13–15). Interpolated verses (46:11–12) provide additional rules for the great festivals and the minimums necessary for unscheduled offerings from the prince (→45:9–25).

This is perhaps the place to consider a phenomenon that has caused puzzlement since early rabbinic times: Ezekiel's laws for temple ritual vary significantly from or even contradict legislation that the Old Testament elsewhere gives Mosaic authority.[2] One way of dealing with this is historical-critical: the variations provide clues to the development of "Mosaic" law in Israel's history. This is an interesting enterprise, but not ours. What is significant for our concern is that Ezekiel nowhere claims Mosaic authority for the legislation the vision provides him and that he is to propound when he emerges; he claims instead the Lord's direct communication to him as a prophet. In effect he acts as a new Moses. Again we encounter the duality of his eschatology and perhaps of all eschatology: the laws of the end have the form of those given by Moses and yet are free from them in their immediacy to God. Jesus will say, "You have heard that it was said, . . . but I say . . ." (Matt. 5:21–44), fulfilling eschatological immediacy in his own person.

What is specific to Ezek. 46:1–15 is its regulation of liturgical relations between prince and people. On the Sabbaths and at the new moons, and for some other occasions, the east gate into the inner court is opened. This gate is directly in line with the east gate into the outer court, which is itself permanently shut because the glory returned through it (→44:1–3). The prince, as administrator of the sacrifices, is allowed to go through the gatehouse leading to the inner court, as far as he can go without actually stepping out into the priestly reserve. There he takes a station from which he can see the act of sacrifice. When the sacrifice is accomplished, he retreats the way he came. The people assemble just outside the gate, perhaps where a few can see through it. Only one liturgical action is specified for either prince or people during the sacrifice, and it is the same for both: prostration before the Lord present in the most holy place. Whatever power relations may otherwise obtain between prince and people, before the most holy place both must fall on their faces.

As to processions, prince and people enter the outer court through the north or south gate[3] and leave by the opposite one—we do not know what significance

---

clashed with the returnees. Here it seems to simply denote the general population, without praise or denigration.

2. So, e.g., Ezek. 44:22 vs. Lev. 21:7; Ezek. 45:18–20 vs. the established calendar system; Ezek. 46:7 vs. Num. 29:3–4; or indeed the appearance in the present verses of festivals at the new moon.

3. There is no west gate, and the east gate is sealed.

this mandate of straight-ahead movement may have had. What we can appropriate is that again the prince joins the people, now in obedience to this inconvenient law.

On the supposition that the prince is here that king of Israel called the Messiah (→45:9–25) what do we now hear about him? Previous christological passages in Ezekiel have displayed the mediator between the Lord and the people as a second identity of the Lord himself, coming to and abiding among his people. Here, however, the Messiah appears from the side of the people. He indeed mediates between us and the Lord, but precisely in and by his membership in and solidarity with us. In classical terminology: on account of the "sharing of attributes" (*communicatio idiomatum*) between the eternal Son and the man Jesus, the work of the Son is done precisely in and by the man; this man does the divine things he does because he simply is the eternal Son. The one who provides himself as a sacrifice to unite us with holiness and preserve us in it is Jesus of Nazareth, born of a woman and under the same Torah that rules all God's people (Gal. 4:4).

The second of our two messenger-words, Ezek. 46:16–18, regulates the prince's disposal of the perfectly rectangular and ideologically located royal demesne stipulated in 45:7–8. He may grant portions of it outright to his sons, since it will then remain intact within the dynasty. But if in feudal fashion he grants territories to magnates, such grants terminate at the year of Jubilee, when all properties are to be restored to their original, God-determined owners (Lev. 25:10). And above all he is not to infringe on the people's holdings. In eschatological Israel's transformed land, prince and people alike will hold precisely what the Lord allots, no more and no less.

Two phenomena call for comment. One perhaps presents a problem for our christological identification of the prince: Who are these "sons"? If the prince is the David (Ezek. 34:23–24) of an eschatologically perfected Israel, presumably he has no successors.

I noted before (→45:9–25) that merely by their mixed genre the messenger-words within 44:6–46:18 bring back the double reference characteristic of Ezekiel's earlier prophecies: to events conceivable in this age and simultaneously to events conceivable only in a new creation. With mention of the prince's descendents, the first reference reappears in rather blunt fashion. Obviously, Ezekiel's expectation for the prince is here partly shaped by what would obtain if the exiles simply returned and set up a polity again—though abstraction from what is conceivable in this age rules also here, since permanent division of the royal holdings among several sons would over two or three generations assuredly lead to civil war. Does this phenomenon disallow my christological reading of this part of the vision? I think not—but may be wrong.

As for the import of the passage as such, we encounter again that sheer indifference to any conceivable facts on the ground of this age that shaped specifications for the temple (→40:1–42:20) and the layout of the special districts (→45:1–8).

The actual preexilic holdings of the monarch were scattered all over Judea, which is the normal way of historically accumulated landholdings, and particularly those of a sovereign. In restored Israel, however, neither is this-worldly history reckoned with nor is any such history to recur and disturb the eschatologically perfect geometry of transformed Israel.

EZEKIEL 46:19–24

THE HOLY AND THE COMMON

With 46:19, the guide resumes Ezekiel's tour of the envisioned temple and at 46:21 carries on with it again. We can take the two episodes together, since very little happens during either and since most theological questions that appear in these passages were handled earlier.

The tour and the episodes on its way make the narrative structure of the vision that concludes Ezekiel's book; here this structure appears at its plainest, after long passages that partially obscure it. These verses have the whole vision as its context and so cannot be fully understood in isolation from it (→40:1–42:20).

In 46:19–20 the guide takes Ezekiel from the entrance of the temple proper, where he had again encountered the glory (44:4–6), and brings him to where he can see the northwest corner of the inner court—there is some circumlocution about Ezekiel's own location, the reason for which is not apparent. In that corner there is what can only be called a holy kitchen, where the priests' portions of the offerings are cooked.

The whole burnt offering is missing from the list of sacrifices at 46:20,[1] since after the fire there is in this case nothing left to make a sacramental meal. The dominant sense of whole burnt offering is sheer return to the Lord of the gift of life, the life of the beast and of those who live from its life.[2] But with other types

---

1. On Israel's sacrificial order, see conveniently and with little speculation, von Rad 1962–66: 1.250–62.

2. In comment on another passage, Gregory the Great takes the two forms of sacrifice as figures of two forms of human dedication to God: "There are those in the great multitude of the faithful who altogether relinquish everything belonging to the world. . . . And there are others who take care for their own household, who think of their children and look out for

of offerings the sense of meal communion with the Lord dominates, precisely in the case of atonement or guilt offerings, whose purpose after all is the restoration of fellowship. The fat bits[3] are given to the Lord by burning on the altar; and from the rest the worshipers make a festal meal to eat "before the Lord" (44:3) and with each other.

Some of the meat and of the accompanying offerings of flour and oil are brought with the fat and blood into the inner court, for the priests' part of the fellowship meal. Once in the inner court, these gifts are themselves holy and cannot be taken out again. They must be cooked and eaten there in the inner court, in order not to "make the people holy," that is, blur the difference between those feasting in the inner court and those feasting in the outer court.

Then in 46:21–24, Ezekiel is shown around the outer court, where he sees kitchens in all four corners, there of course being many more laity than priests. These are for the Levites to prepare feasts from the greater part of the offerings, for those who provided them. Even the prince, readers of Ezekiel will remember, must take his meal with the Lord in the outer court, if indeed in a special place (44:3).

In both of our linked passages, the concern of the regulations is to preserve the distinction between the common and the holy, between the everyday and the utter exceptionality of the Lord and of what is separated from the everyday to be his. That priests and laity eat separately to preserve the distinction of the holy from the common is not mere clericalism:[4] the assumption is rather that the priests are shielded by their office and can deal with holy things within a margin of safety. For Israel's primal sense of the danger even in innocent but unshielded contact with holiness, see, for example, the story of Uzzah and the ark in 2 Sam. 6:6–7 (for further discussion of the relation of the holy,[5] the common, and the polluted, →44:4–31).

One suspects that in the old temple, practice with respect to cooking and such matters may have been decidedly more lax. And such stories as that of Samuel's sacrificial hospitality at Bethel (1 Sam. 16:2–5) suggest great freedom in Israel's native practice. In the eschatological temple, however, there will be no intentional or unintentional mixings of the holy and the common—which is part of what makes this temple eschatological, perfection in the matter being impossible in any now conceivable order of things.

---

their inheritance, who nevertheless, mindful of eternal judgment, exercise mercy to the poor (etc.)" (1986–90: 2.452). The figure is in fact faithful to at least one aspect of the meaning of the two modes of sacrifice.

3. One should remember that in most times and places the fat, as the storehouse of energy, is the treasured part.

4. In the actual practice of the old temple, which these rubrics both trace and contradict, there was undoubtedly plenty of clericalism, as indeed there would be in the Second Temple, which returning exiles in fact built and inhabited.

5. Sometimes in Ezekiel the "most holy" and the "holy" are distinguished, sometimes not.

But why will there be a difference between the holy and the common in the eschatologically perfected life of God's people? It is because in the kingdom—precisely within an intimacy of God and creature that in Christian theology can even be called "deification"—the distinction of Creator and creature will finally be established beyond all blurring by our rebellion. Critics of Athanasius's classic teaching that "God became man in order that we might become God" often suppose that this suggests a violation of the difference between God and creature; the opposite is the case.

EZEKIEL 47:1–12

THE RIVER OF THE WATER OF LIFE

As so often in Ezekiel, our present passage shows signs of editorial interpolations, but none seem to raise theological questions (on the general narrative, →40:1–42:20).

There is one editorial intervention of which we must take note. Ezekiel 47:1–12 is the last record of an episode on Ezekiel's tour through the eschatological temple. Since neither this episode nor the remainder of the book provides a conclusion of the tour appropriate to its beginning (40:1), it appears that an original ending of the tour may be missing from the canonical text; I will discuss the import of this for our present passage in this commentary unit and its import for the following passage in the next.

In this episode of his tour, Ezekiel is first brought to the door of the temple proper, where he sees water coming from beneath its threshold and flowing east; we are to suppose that the spring is under the most holy place. Since the altar blocks a straight path east from the threshold's center, a stream emerging from the center would have to deviate from geometrical perfection to go around the altar; to avoid this the stream emerges from the south side of the threshold and so can flow on a straight line past the altar. How the stream passes through the temple's courts and the wall between them is not said.

Ezekiel is then taken from the temple compound by the north gates (→44:1–3) and around to the east side of the temple's outer wall; there he sees the stream emerging into the open. And so rigidly geometric is the stream's eastern orientation that, its path having been initially offset to the south, it exits the temple close with the same offset, emerging along the south side of the eastern gatehouse. If the circumstance that the stream's offset is to the south rather than to the north once had significance, it is lost to us.

The stream then continues due and rigidly east (47:8) across the landscape, taking no notice of such this-worldly facts as existing valleys or streams. The guide measures precisely equal intervals at which Ezekiel is instructed to ford the stream, to demonstrate how regularly it grows in volume (47:3–5). Finally it empties into the Dead Sea. Thus the path and development of this watercourse manifest the same transcendence of any impediments in the topology of this age as did the layout for the envisioned temple and its close (→40:1–42:20) or the land-use plan for the special district in the new Israel (→45:1–8).

Ezekiel's classic prophecies of doom or blessing (Ezek. 4–36) normally had a double reference: to coming events conceivable within history and geography as we now experience them and simultaneously to events conceivable only in an eschatologically transformed history and world. But in later passages, such as the vision of the dry bones (37:1–14) or the oracle against Gog (38:1–39:20) the first reference recedes, and in some segments of Ezekiel's temple tour he sees even more strictly eschatological states of affairs, almost wholly abstracted from what is possible in this age.

The present passage is decidedly of the latter sort. To the this-worldly impossibilities already noted, we may add a spring emerging from the precise top of "the highest of the mountains," a stream that without further sources of water increases in volume as it flows, and the need for the Mount of Olives to disappear or split open, to enable the stream's straight path to the east.

Yet more telling is of course the explicitly eschatological potency of this stream. In the Judean wilderness—in which John the Baptist would preach and Jesus be baptized—Genesis's paradise is restored and outdone: along the stream's banks flourish not one tree of life but whole groves of them. And when the stream enters the Dead Sea this is transformed into a sea both full of life and prodigal in its support of life.[1] Every mythic paradise is paradisial chiefly because like this one it is well watered; thus central to the Genesis account of "the garden" is a river that flows "out of Eden" to water it and then divides into four branches to water the earth (Gen. 2:10–14) (for the biblical use of myth in eschatological discourse, →28:1–19).

The Christian apocalypse, the book of Revelation, reprises and interprets also this part[2] of Ezekiel. John sees a river "flowing from the throne of God and of the Lamb.... On either side of the river is the tree of life..., producing its fruit each month; and the leaves of the tree are for the healing of the nations" (Rev. 22:1–2). Just as in Ezekiel, the source of the river is the throne of God, but now this is identified as the throne of God "and" of the crucified and risen Christ. The distinction between the throne of God in the heavens and the throne of the

---

1. Someone has noted that plentiful salt also belongs to a paradise, particularly one with a fishery, and has set aside precincts of the old sea to that end (47:11).

2. An earlier major instance is Revelation's reprise of Ezek. 38:1–39:29.

Shekinah in the temple has been overcome—which is part of why there is no need of a separate temple in the new Jerusalem (21:22). And the river's identity is explicitly revealed: it is "the river of the water of life."

Flowing freshwater is for obvious reasons a universally encountered sacramental sign of life: we die of dehydration more quickly than of any other deprivation except of breath. If we know that sin is a pollution that renders us unfit for God and one another, washing with water will be a further sacramental sign; and if we further know that fitness for God and fitness for life are the same, we will see also this sign as life giving. It is perhaps not altogether fanciful to see Jesus's baptism in the Judean wilderness, and our baptism into him, as a fulfillment of the promised transformation of the Jordan wilderness by a river of life.

Life flows from God's throne. From where else should it flow? If God were not, or indeed if most of human religion's proposed gods were God, there could be no such river: death would have won, or rather it would be the antecedent ground of all things.

When we come to 47:13, we will find a sudden and unprepared "thus says the Lord" introducing instructions for returning Israel's division of the land. These occupy a long section that both is utterly unrelated to the vision of the stream and ends the book awkwardly. There is no concluding narration of Ezekiel's tour of the eschatological temple, nor indeed is there any other narrative conclusion of the whole vision. The tour simply breaks off with our present passage. Since the episodes on Ezekiel's tour structure the account of the vision and since no final such episode or other closure of this structure appears, we must suppose that what might have been the book's narrative conclusion has been lost or editorially suppressed. The result is that the canonical account of Ezekiel's vision is rather like Luke's account of the Christian mission in lacking closure—and perhaps for a similar reason: the story is expected to continue.

Indeed, the canonical Ezekiel's lack of a proper ending makes a decisive point about its content:[3] whatever story may be told about the final goal of God's way with us, it must not be told as the achievement of a thereafter static perfection. Had Ezekiel or his editors wrapped everything up neatly, they would have belied the story they had been telling about God, for the heaven of popular apprehension, where nothing more ever happens, is not a place into which the biblical God would or indeed could bring his people. Rather, whatever blessing we may in a particular context invoke to speak of the kingdom, we must imagine a sort of spiral of the granting and pursuit of that blessing.

That is why throughout Christian history love has been the favored blessing by which to characterize the life of the kingdom, for love is the gift and goal that, once given and achieved, is both a completed work and each time a new beginning. Jonathan Edwards, having in biblical fashion equated knowledge and love, put it so: "It seems to be quite a wrong notion of the happiness of heaven that it

3. Precisely if it is only the Spirit who makes it.

is in that manner unchangeable that it admits not of new joys."[4] On the contrary, "the saints will be progressive in knowledge [of God] . . . to all eternity."[5]

4. Jonathan Edwards, *Miscellanies 853–1152*, Works of Jonathan Edwards 20 (New Haven: Yale University Press, 2002), no. 472.
    5. Ibid., no. 435.

EZEKIEL 47:13–48:29

THEOLOGICAL GEOGRAPHY

Ezekiel 47:13–48:29 begins with the formula that introduces a messenger-word, "Thus says the Lord." The occasion on which Ezekiel was given the prophecy is not described; nor is our passage otherwise connected to the preceding episode of Ezekiel's tour of the eschatological temple (→40:1–42:20). Indeed, 47:13 breaks unmediated into the narrative of the tour and deprives it of an appropriate conclusion (→46:19–24; →47:1–12). We are not given even such minimal placement of our verses as would have been provided by the usual introduction or by a report of God's usual address to the prophet, as "you—son of a man." At its end the passage is bounded by a formula often used by Ezekiel to conclude messenger-words: "says the Lord God."

What appears between the two formulas bears the marks of a complicated textual history, most of which, in my judgment, cannot be reconstructed. The passage is obviously put together from items of various genres: some lines are in the second person, some in the third; there are mandates, regulations, descriptions, and lists. But a genre that is not represented is the very one that its introduction and conclusion stipulate—the prophetic messenger-word.

In this hybrid structure—which we have encountered before in Ezekiel, at 44:4–31 and elsewhere—what the prophet is given to speak to Israel when he emerges from the vision is an assemblage of rules and regulations, instead of the prophecies of judgment or blessing that messenger-words normally bring. We cannot know whether the editor who encompassed these various materials within the formulas of a messenger-word intended by so doing to give them the force of prophecy, but that is the consequence in the resultant text. Thus the regulations here assembled do not in context command that Israel should work harder to divide the land in accord with the Lord's will, as much of the material would in isolation suggest,[1] but rather promise that the land will in fact be so divided and implicitly judge Israel for having previously arranged matters differently.

Taking all the various bits together, what we have before us is a map of a transformed land of Israel, to be proclaimed to the exiles as preparation for them to occupy it. For our purposes, the chief point about this map is that the projection—to borrow a technical term of mapmakers—is theological. In the nature of the case, a map of the land to which exiles are to *return* must pay some attention to the previous geography. But the political and physical geography of old Israel does not finally control the mapping presented here and is freely overridden whenever theological considerations suggest it.

This land is defined (47:15–20) as the territory that the Lord "swore to give . . . to your fathers" (47:14 RSV). The very existence of the land as a particular land with ascertainable boundaries is presumed to be determined by a promise once made by the Lord. Nor is Israel's renewed occupancy of that land thought to rest on conquest or even on her new relation to the Lord, but on that same unilateral promise. Thus, in stark contrast with the account of Israel's original occupation presented in the book of Joshua, we now read nothing about battles or political-religious struggles: the returning Israelite tribes are simply to proceed in and take their allotted places. Nor are we told how the exiles of the northern tribes, scattered over much of the ancient East, are to be gathered. The Lord himself will bring all Israel into a patrimony unilaterally created by his promises and now transformed by them, and that is that.

Moreover, the land to be occupied is not identical with the territory that old Israel ever encompassed or even wanted to encompass. What determines the map is not history but what God promised, as the promise was remembered in the tradition that Ezekiel relies on (Zimmerli 1983: 531–32).

On the north, the boundary laid out by 47:15–17 includes much of Lebanon, which even in David and Solomon's time was simply another country and remained that way. On the west (47:20), the Mediterranean is the only boundary, despite Judah having never subdued Philistia.

On the other hand, territory east of the Jordan that was in fact settled by Israelite tribes is not included in Israel as now eschatologically mapped (47:18), since Transjordan was not included in the remembered promise. Thus according to the story in Num. 32,[2] when Gad and Reuben asked permission to settle in Gilead east of Jordan, because its land was suited to their cattle-based economy and its

---

1. The view that "the house of Israel . . . will be given the task of doing better what it had already done at the beginning when it first settled the land" (Zimmerli 1983: 527) is, in my judgment, exactly what our passage is not. We have here a neat instance of historical critics' penchant for exegeting what an individual text may have been before it was brought together with others as scripture, instead of exegeting the scripture.

2. It matters little whether the Pentateuch's account of Israel's early history is historical or partly legendary—in modernity's sense of these terms.

inhabitants were already subservient, Moses granted their request on condition that their warriors accompany the rest of Israel across the Jordan, since only on the other side was "the land that the LORD has given" to be found. On our map of theologically defined Israel, Gad, Reuben, and the half-tribe of Manasseh are uprooted from Gilead and arbitrarily located west of Jordan (Ezek. 48:1, 6).

Finally on this line, Gentiles living as Israelites are to share in the tribal allotments (47:22–23).[3] In a returned and perfected Israel, who belongs to the land will not be determined merely by ethnicity but by adherence to the Lord. The Targum glosses the text "the proselytes who have converted among you" (Levey 1990: 126).

The promise to the fathers also determines the political structure of the restored nation: she appears here not as the kingdoms of Ephraim and Judah, as elsewhere in Ezekiel, but as "the twelve tribes of Israel" (47:13).[4] As a political or military reality, the tribal system had by Ezekiel's time become a memory; and indeed some of the tribes had for some time existed only as names, and not only on account of the depredations of Assyria and Babylon. But it was to "the fathers" that the promise had been made, and therefore a perfected Israel must despite all this-worldly history consist of entities identified by the traditional patronyms.

Continuing through our passage, we come to the interior map of eschatological Israel (48:1–29). The tribal allotments and a special zone[5] encompassing the temple close, Jerusalem, and the royal demesne are arrayed as thirteen strips stacked north to south and divided by straight boundary lines running west to east from the Mediterranean to the Jordan or the two seas. The tribal allotments are ordered around the special zone: Judah and Benjamin, the tribes of Judea, flank it north and south, and the other tribes are arrayed north from Judah (48:1–7) and south from Benjamin (48:23–29). To put the special zone in the north-south middle of this array, several tribes—including Benjamin itself—have had to be moved from their historical locations north of Jerusalem to fill in the space south of Jerusalem. Rashi comments: "How is it possible that Jerusalem should be in [this] place? Was not Jerusalem on the northern border of Judah. . . ? And here it is in the middle of the tribes! This division is not like Joshua's division, for this one is like the rows of a vineyard, and all the portions are equal" (Rosenberg 2000: 425). Precisely; and it need hardly be pointed out that such a neat ordering of ethnic and political units is not found or indeed conceivable in any nation of this age.

3. The children "begotten" of Israelite women by Gentile men had counted as Israelites—as children born of Jewish mothers and Gentile fathers still do. Now, however, the alien men themselves are included in the Lord's congregation. On the history, see Zimmerli 1983: 532.

4. Much twentieth-century scholarship held that Israel had once been an amphictyony, that is, a group of tribes bound together by shared sanctuaries and that occasionally rallied for mutual action by charismatic war chiefs (von Rad 1962–66: 1.16–17). This is now disputed. But in Israel's memory there had been a time to which the term roughly applies, and that suffices for our purpose.

5. Unknown in the traditional mapping of Israel (Josh. 13, 15–19).

Like the tribal allotments, the special zone reaches west to east from the Mediterranean to the Jordan and the Dead Sea (Zimmerli 1983: 535 provides a sketch map). Its special character is created by the presence of the temple "in the middle of it" (48:8). As this zone is the center of the whole land, so it has its own center in the holy area "set apart for the LORD"; and this area is in turn marked by the presence of the temple, again "in the middle of it" (48:10). The map of the special zone was anticipated at →45:1–8.

The properly holy area is a rectangle of 25,000 cubits (8.33 miles) from west to east and 20,000 cubits (6.5 miles) from north to south. Adjoining this holy portion on the south is a rectangle 25,000 cubits by 5,000 cubits, accommodating the city of Jerusalem at its center and lands to east and west to support the urban population (48:18). The holy portion and the civic portion together make yet another square—a figure beloved in the layout of the temple and its compound (→40:1–42:20). Precisely conjoined to this square on its west and east sides are the two parts of the prince's demesne, one reaching to the Mediterranean and the other to the Jordan and the Dead Sea.

Ezekiel 47:13–48:29, together with 45:1–8, thus presents the vision of a political community ordered around the worship of the Lord that occurs "in the middle of it." Nevertheless, it is not a theocracy as modernity tends to use the word pejoratively: the priests do not displace the prince. Yet it is also a decidedly limited monarchy: the prince—who here does not appear as Messiah as he does at 34:24 and 37:25—and his establishment are checked by their separation from the temple. And it is of course very little democratic: priests and prince each dispense their sort of justice without elected bodies or general consultation.[6]

The political geography of eschatological Israel, with its ordering center in worship and its division of spheres, thus mirrors the great political problem: of mutual order around a "common good." Christian theology has generally supposed that this problem is not solvable within the limits of this present world—as has indeed been repeatedly demonstrated through the millennia, when theocracies, monarchies, and democracies alike have self-destructed.

St. Augustine provided a diagnosis of the impasse and therewith set the terms for Western theology's general understanding of politics.[7] Every community subsists, he argued, by common love of some good, a good for the enjoyment of which persons and groups are willing to band together and to establish laws enabling life within the mutual commitment. The difficulty is that an intrinsically common good, a universal good, would just so be God, and that gathering around God is precisely what fallen humanity refuses to do. The polities of this world, therefore, rely on substitutes. Each is united by common allegiance to some finite good, to a particular that it treats as if it were universal. But despite such shared fictions,

6. Roland de Vaux, *Ancient Israel: Its Life and Institutions*, trans. John McHugh (London: Darton, Longman & Todd, 1961).

7. On the following from Augustine and on the problem itself, see Jenson 1997–99: 2.76–98. The chief though not only source of my exposition there is of course *The City of God*.

particular individuals or factions can compete for possession of any particular good. Thus precisely what unites a community of this world is also a standing temptation to disunity; in Augustine's great example, if it was love of glory that bound together the heroes of the Roman Republic, it was individuals' love of their own glory, in competition with others, that eventually tore the republic apart. If love of a common good is the supreme political virtue, the love of seizing this good for oneself—in Augustine's splendid phrase, the *libido dominandi*—is the supreme political vice that sooner or later undoes every polity of this world.

We have been led by Ezekiel to envision the fulfillment of God's ways with us in several ways. One way is that with which he here concludes his work: at the end and after it, there will be a political community of perfect mutual love—glorious with the Lord's own glory, of which the supply is infinite.

EZEKIEL 48:30–35

י ה ו ה ה /THERE

The immediately preceding map of eschatological Israel (47:13–48:29) intruded unmediated on Ezekiel's visionary tour of the eschatological temple (40:1–47:12), even depriving it of a dramatically appropriate conclusion. In somewhat similar fashion 48:30–35 is without mediation or introduction pasted onto the map, despite that passage's formal conclusion with "says the Lord." It is hard to avoid the impression that some rather abrupt editors have shaped the last chapters of our book.

Ezekiel 48:30–35 is, moreover, obviously written by someone other than the author of the previous verses—a circumstance of the sort that I have often passed over but that requires notice here. To make this judgment about authorship, we do not need to depend on precarious judgments about emphases or style; it suffices to notice that Levi is here listed as one of the twelve tribes, whereas in all the foregoing the Levites were with theological emphasis placed outside the system of tribes, and that place is then made for Levi by listing Joseph instead of his two sons Manasseh and Ephraim as heretofore.

The visionary tour of the temple and even the just previous mapping of eschatological Israel were impressive and theologically weighty; whereas except for its last two words the present short passage is not. Only those final words, and the passage's unmediated position in the book, provide between them matter for theological reflection—but then it is matter enough to make a fitting end for Ezekiel's book and for this commentary.

Perhaps I may be incautious enough to propose a motive for the attachment: the "someone" mentioned above has noticed that in Ezekiel's prophecies of restoration and transformation, the land to which the exiles are to return is splendidly celebrated, as is the temple in the sanctifying midst of it, but that Jerusalem, which was, after all, the chief target of Ezekiel's prophecies of doom, receives but perfunctory attention in his prophecies of restoration (Zimmerli 1983: 547). Our six verses are perhaps an attempt to balance the picture.

At the beginning of the book (→1:1–3), an editorial intervention created a theologically interesting situation: two modes of prophecy were in the resultant and canonical text so bluntly juxtaposed as to compel us to consider their difference and identity. Here we find an equally abrupt juxtaposition that likewise provokes thought—and indeed will be the key to our reading.

There was in Israel a theology of the temple, cultivated by priestly scholars like Ezekiel himself—of which indeed the book before us is a chief document. And there was a theology of Zion, of the Lord's city, presumably cultivated in less clerical circles. We may see this theology in Isa. 51, a chapter from the other great prophet of the exile (the so-called Second Isaiah), which shares the central themes of Ezekiel's eschatology, but puts the city where Ezekiel has the temple; or indeed we may see it in the present passage's demotion of the Levites from being an order made special by its relation to the temple to being just another of the tribes. These theologies could and did compete: Which is the place chosen by the Lord for his presence? The city, which, to be sure, has a temple? Or the temple with or without a city?

The consequence of the unmediated way in which these verses about a final Jerusalem are attached to the vision of a land ordered around a final temple is to bring the two theologies bluntly together without space for conceptual compromise. Just as the canonical text of Ezek. 1:1–3 compelled us to reflect on the difference between seeing and hearing and then on how as prophecy they could be one, so in the canonical text of Ezek. 48 the Lord's residence in the temple and his residence in the city—which in the rest of Ezekiel is not itself a holy space—appear neither as alternatives nor as matter for conceptual reconciliation.

The city is mapped as yet another square, like the temple close in Ezek. 40–42 and like the special zone in the previous passage: whoever drew this city outline shares at least so much of the eschatological sensibility of the great vision. And the temporal specification in the last line should be translated by the KJV's "from that day" and not by NRSV's vague "from that time on." The phrase *miyom* ("from day"; מיום) certainly refers to the terrible last "day" (*yom*) of →7:10–27. It is after final judgment that there will be this geometrically and tribally perfect and strangely renamed city.

In the usual rendering, Jerusalem's new name will be "The LORD is There" (יהוה שמה). To feel the force of this phrase-name we must, however, reproduce the Hebrew ability to do without the copula, for in this case it produces the powerful construction: "יהוה/There." This is not a proposition[1] but a name within a proposition. And since the unmediated juxtaposition of the two

---

1. It is indeed a Hebrew sentence, but not a proposition.

theologies short-circuits the difference between hope for the Lord's presence in the city and hope for the Lord's presence in the temple, it is the import of the name itself that grasps us: this God, יהוה, the God of Israel and her scripture, has a "there." Indeed, we might almost say that he is identified with his "there."

Here is a chief reason for all the geometry in Ezek. 40–48: in the present text's measurements of the eschatological city, in the mapping of the envisioned final temple (→40:1–42:20), and in the theological division of the land (48:1–29). Stipulating a "there," or even that in some context there is such a thing as a "there," requires some system of coordinates, however arbitrary or visionary.

We must recognize how religiously anomalous this is. The gods of the religions have no "there"; they are either remote from such identifications, as was the abstracted divinity of high pre-Christian Greek theology, or are at so many locations as to cleave to none, as in the polytheism that always underlies normal religion. Whereas, to repeat an earlier citation from a contemporary Jewish thinker, the God of Israel "has an address."[2]

Thus this concluding two-word grammatical construct—whoever may have drafted it and for whatever reason—carries in its canonical context much of the weight of Ezekiel's whole affirmative message: the God of Israel has been and will again and finally be *there* with his people. Ezekiel has told the story: in judgment, the Lord removed himself from his place among them; in mercy he showed himself available (→1:25–28) on the banks of Babylonian Chebar, to be there even for his exiles; and at the end he will be so sheerly *there*, so strictly and with such concentration present to his people that he cannot again be hidden by sin or the uproar of nations.

When the New Testament, and particularly Paul to the Corinthians (1 Cor. 10–11), speaks of "body" in theological context, it is this very availability that it posits. The loaf and cup on the altar are the body of Christ in that they are where the risen Christ is visibly and tangibly available "in the middle of" (Ezek. 48:8–11) the gathered congregation. The congregation itself is the body of Christ in that it is the place where the risen Christ is so present in the middle of the world as to be available to the nations.[3] Thus a central Christian affirmation is that the promise hidden in Ezekiel's concluding phrase-name for Jerusalem, "יהוה/There," is fulfilled in Christ's risen reality.

Moreover, Christ's resurrection makes a promise in its turn: if the risen Christ is embodied for us, we too are embodied for him. This is the other great burden of Ezekiel's message, carried, at a pivot of the biblical story, by the vision of the defunct people of God and the promise of their resurrection (37:1–14). If God is "יהוה/There" with us, a chief blessing thus bestowed is that we will necessarily

---

2. Michael Wyschograd, "Incarnation," *Pro ecclesia* 3 (1993): 220.

3. For further discussion of the use of "body" within theology, see Jenson 1997–99: 1.201–6; 2.212–16.

be likewise there for him, must be embodied and available to him: that there will be a "resurrection of the body."

The last book of the Christian Bible reprises this last part of Ezekiel (Rev. 21:9–21). John sees a holy Jerusalem coming down from God, after all the judgments that fill his book and Ezekiel's are concluded. It has the twelve gates of Ezekiel's city, still dedicated to the tribes of Israel. John even sees an angel with a measuring stick, taken from earlier parts of Ezekiel's vision. And Ezekiel's name for the city has become its metaphysical description, for the city simply *is* God's "There" and so—with imagery taken from the vision of a postexilic prophet (Isa. 60)—shines with that deity that God himself is. Therefore it needs no separate temple. And amazingly, the saints are to dwell in it, to inhabit the place that God is for himself.

The fulfillment envisioned by John the Seer is the final fulfillment of "יהוה / There," future even to its fulfillment in Eucharist and church. Yet this is not another fulfillment than that accomplished in the risen Christ, for precisely he himself with his Father will be the final city's most holy place (Rev. 21:22–23). Thus Christ's embodied mediation of God to his creation is eternal. A Christian theological commentary on the book of Ezekiel may well end as does the Revelation itself: "Amen. Come, Lord Jesus,"[4] both now and at the last.

---

4. Some readers may note that my other venture into biblical scholarship (*Song of Songs*, Interpretation [Louisville: John Knox, 2005]) ends with this same citation. This is neither a personal quirk nor coincidence; Ezekiel and the Song of Songs both "most pollute the hands."

BIBLIOGRAPHY

Works listed are directly used and useful for interpreting the text. Works mentioned in more remote connections are documented in the footnotes.

Christman, Angela Rusell, *What Did Ezekiel See? Christian Exegesis of Ezekiel's Vision of the Chariot from Irenaeus to Gregory the Great.* Leiden: Brill, 2005.

Eichrodt, Walther. *Ezekiel.* Translated by Cosslett Quin. Old Testament Library. Philadelphia: Westminster, 1970.

Greenberg, Moshe. *Ezekiel 1–20.* Anchor Bible 22. Garden City: Doubleday, 1983.

———. *Ezekiel 21–37.* Anchor Bible 22A. New York: Doubleday, 1997.

Gregory the Great. *Grégoire le Grand: Homélies sur Ézéchiel.* Edited by Charles Morel. 2 vols. Sources Chrétiennes 327 and 360. Paris: Cerf, 1986–90.

Jenni, Ernst, and Claus Westermann. *Theological Lexicon of the Old Testament.* 3 vols. Translated by Mark E. Bibble. Peabody, Mass.: Hendrickson, 1997.

Jenson, Robert W. *Systematic Theology.* 3 vols. New York: Oxford University Press, 1997–99.

Lapsley, Jacqueline. *Can These Bones Live? The Problem of the Moral Self in the Book of Ezekiel.* New York: de Gruyter, 2000.

Levey, Samson H. *The Targum of Ezekiel.* Aramaic Bible 13. Collegeville: Liturgical Press, 1990.

Odell, Margaret. *Ezekiel.* Macon, Ga.: Smyth & Helwys, 2005.

Origen. *Origène: Homélies sur Ézéchiel.* Edited by Marcel Borret. Sources Chrétiennes 352. Paris: Cerf, 1989.

von Rad, Gerhard. *Old Testament Theology.* Translated by D. M. G. Stalker. New York: Harper & Row, 1962–66.

Rosenberg, A. J. *Ezekiel: Translation of Text, Rashi, and Other Commentaries.* New York: Judaica Press, 2000.

Zimmerli, Walther. *Ezekiel,* vol. 1. Translated by Ronald E. Clements. Hermeneia. Philadelphia: Fortress, 1979.

———. *Ezekiel,* vol. 2. Translated by James D. Martin. Hermeneia. Philadelphia: Fortress, 1983.

SUBJECT INDEX

abominations, 36n1, 65, 70, 80, 82, 103, 126–31, 133–34, 155, 208, 260, 316
abortion, 127, 178
Abraham, 98, 122, 135, 260, 261, 272
Adam, 53, 159, 220, 276
adonai, 29
Akedah, 272
Akiba, Rabbi, 17
Alexander, 22
Alexandria, 91
allegory, 108, 126–31, 132–34, 150, 189–93, 255, 300n2, 314
altar, 80, 309–10
American Civil War, 195
Ammonites, 171, 174–76, 207, 208
Amorites, 127
Amos, 74, 75
amulets, 113
analogy, 229, 276
angel of the Lord, 234, 306
angels, 83–84, 89
animal sacrifices, 58, 129
animism, 130
anthropomorphism, 201, 224, 231
antinomianism, 62, 130, 260n5, 261
Antioch, 91
anti-Semitism, 208
apartheid, 260
apocalyptic literature, 32, 47, 79, 242, 247, 291
apocalyptic prophecy, 85–87, 198
apostasy, 85
Aramaic, 24
Aristotle, 76, 107, 128, 190n1, 238

Ash Wednesday, 84
Assyria, 20–21, 190–92, 241–43, 249–50, 252, 287
Astarte, 60, 65, 66, 80n3, 81, 129–30, 191, 196
Athanasius, 333
atonement, 195, 277, 310, 332
auguries, 171, 175
Augustine, 57, 114, 115, 156, 311, 341–42
authorial intent, 267n7
autonomy, 146, 178

Baal, 60, 66
Babylon, 21–22, 36–37, 74, 75, 121, 152, 171, 175, 191, 192
Balaam, 94
Balthasar, Hans Urs von, 169, 252
baptism, 99, 278, 336
Barth, Karl, 86, 87, 109, 115, 117, 157, 159, 214
Baruch Apocalypse, 85
beast, 295
beauty, 168–69
Benjamin (tribe), 340
berith, 139
biblical scholarship, 108
blessing, 273, 336
    of Judah, 172–73
blessings and curses, 94
bloodshed, 177–79, 200–201, 277
bodily resurrection, 312, 346
body of Christ, 345
Boers, 260
bondage, of Ezekiel, 55, 57
Bonhoeffer, Dietrich, 262
branch, 266

branch to the nose, 81
breach, repair of, 112
bread, from multiple grains, 56
breath of life, 282, 283
bride, Jerusalem as, 126, 128–29
Brunner, Emil, 109n5
Bultmann, Rudolf, 94, 109, 125, 213n8, 221n7, 242n4
burning bush, 66
Byassee, Jason, 24n19

call-vision, 46, 305, 316
Canaanites, 127, 130, 133, 161, 208n1
cannibalism, 61
canonical text, 22–23, 102, 267n7
cedar, 138, 142, 241
chaos, 214, 242, 246, 294
cheap grace, 262
Chebar, 37, 42, 48, 54, 79, 90, 306
cherubim, 37–38, 88–90, 97
Chesterton, G. K., 82
children, and iniquity of fathers, 145–48
child sacrifice, 130, 158, 196
Christian doctrine, 25
"christological plain sense", 24
Christology, 91, 156, 267
church
  as new Israel, 209, 226, 278
  as prophetic community, 49, 105
  as temple, 300, 301n1
  unity of, 288
church fathers, 32, 42
circumcision, 58
civil society, 322
cleanliness and uncleanliness, 276–78
cleansing, 89
clericalism, 332
common good, 341–42
communication of attributes, 267, 329
community, and individual, 145–48
conquest, 339
conversation, history as, 95
cooking pot, 93, 198–201
corpses, in the temple, 307
Council of Chalcedon, 43n7
covenant, 68, 99, 119, 128, 134–35, 139, 261, 289
  Davidic, 91, 289
  in the desert, 91, 289
  formula of, 280, 289
  promise of, 97, 268
covenant of creation, 121
covenant of peace, 289

creation, 33, 57, 222, 251, 278n5
  as history, 239
  order of, 294
  as system, 238–39
Creator-creature distinction, 333
creeping things, 80
crime, 177–78, 260
critical theory, 24
crocodile, 228–29, 241, 245–46
cross, 163, 225
cubit, 300n3
cult, 276–77
cult sites, 64
cup of the wine of wrath, 195
curse, prophecy as, 93–94
cut off, 283
Cyrus, 206

damnation, 214
Daniel, 86, 242
Daniel (legend), 121, 122
David, capture of Jerusalem, 127
Davidic dynasty, 98, 266–67
Day of Atonement, 324–25
day of the Lord, 73, 74–75, 107, 112–13, 125, 166, 178, 185–86, 231–32, 233–35, 262, 265, 293–94, 297
dead, 249–52
Dead Sea, 335
death, 51, 61, 147, 242, 277
  of Ezekiel's wife, 202–3, 256
debate, 144
Deborah, 113
deification, 333
democracy, 341
demythologizing, 213–14, 221n7
deus absconditus, 163
Deuteronomistic theology, 261
dialectical theology, 109
disgrace, 134, 250
divination, 113–14, 171
divine impassibility, 287. See also God, as affectless
double predestination, 156
do ut des, 231
dragon, 228n2, 245, 246n3
drama, 239
dramatic coherence, 166
dramatis personae, 239
dreams, 33
dross, 181–82
dry bones, 153, 281–82, 335
dwelling place, 289

eagles, 137–38, 141–43
earth and heaven, 90
Eastern theology, 44, 91
eating a book, 47
Ebeling, Gerhard, 94
economics, 266
economic Trinity, 143n4
Eden, 242, 269, 273, 335
editors, of Ezekiel, 23
Edom, 207, 208, 252, 269–73
Edwards, Jonathan, 212–13, 274, 337
Egypt, 21, 74, 80, 138, 139, 152, 191, 260
    oracles against, 207, 227–52
    as temptation for Israel, 191, 228, 229, 232
Eichrodt, Walthar, 80n3, 102n2, 124, 132n1,
        152n4, 168, 196n2, 198–99, 246n3, 250n5,
        266n5, 290n1, 318n4
Elam, 249–50, 252
elders, 116–19
election, 25, 127–28, 155–56, 261
Eliezer, Rabbi, 283n5
empires, 243
end, 2, 25, 62, 75, 98, 125, 186
    of Israel, 69–72
enemies, of God, 225
enemy nations. See Gentile nations
Enlightenment, 271
Esau, 272
eschatological glory, 297
eschatological Israel, 284, 325, 329–30, 339–41,
        343
eschatological Jerusalem. See new Jerusalem
eschatological justice, 52
eschatological promises, 98–99
eschatological surplus, 226
eschatological temple, 299–304, 307–8, 309, 313,
        315–18, 327, 331–33, 334–36, 343
eschatological wilderness, 162
eschatology, 71, 75–76, 108–9, 142–43, 162, 232,
        242, 246, 295
eschaton, 125
eternal life, 113
eternity, and time, 103, 110, 238–39
Ethiopia, 234, 292
Eucharist, 195, 311–12, 346
everlasting covenant, 134–35, 289
evil, 75, 86, 115, 158
exalting, of humbled, 172
exile, 21–22, 179
    return from, 96–98, 186
exiles, 36, 260, 287
exodus, 155, 156–57, 162, 191, 247, 260, 278n5

exposing unwanted children, 127
Ezekiel
    as accuser of Jerusalem, 177
    commissioning of, 19, 46–49
    lack of proper ending to book, 336
    as new Moses, 328
    as performer, 262
    silence of, 55, 204–5, 232, 257–58
    style, 19
    wife of, 202–3, 256

fairness, 148–49, 254
false prophets, 106, 107, 111–15
family, 196–97
famine, 120
Feast of Booths, 325
fellowship, 276, 332
feminist theologies, 41, 61n8
fertility religion, 80–82, 130, 133, 179
festivals, 324–25, 328
Feuerbach, Ludwig, 271n4
figural exegesis, 23–24, 176
final judgment, 134, 162, 246, 308
final temple. See eschatological temple
financial crimes, 179
fire, 88–89, 165
1 and 2 Enoch, 85
firstborn, 272n7
flood, 70, 75, 294
foreigners, 316–17
form criticism, 28n30, 117, 124, 199n1
4 Ezra, 85
four winds, 283
fruits of the Spirit, 62
Fuchs, Ernst, 94
fulfillment, of prophecy, 106–8
funeral lament. See kinah
future, openness of, 94, 254

galgal, 89
general revelation, 121
generations, folly across, 145–48
genre, 117–18
Gentile nations, 120–21, 196n2, 206–8, 218, 223
Gentiles, and tribal allotments, 340
giants, 250n5
Gideon, 191–92
gifts of the Spirit, 279
Gilead, 339–40
glory, 41–44, 90, 169, 224, 270–71, 331
    among the nations, 297
    leaves temple, 89–90

glory of the Lord, 39–40, 42, 306, 315, 342
God. *See also* Lord
  as affectless, 128, 130, 287
  attributes of, 63
  "gaining glory", 224
  as hidden, 163
  and history, 72, 76–77, 103, 119, 126, 143, 189,
    201, 225, 238–39, 278, 298
  internal conflict of, 188
  as just, 123
  as primary cause, 238
  war with Jerusalem, 165
Gog, 290–95, 296, 335
Gogarten, Friedrich, 109n5
Gomer, 291
Good Shepherd, 263, 268, 314
gospel, 37, 38, 265, 298
gospels, 264
grace, 53, 261–62
grave, 249–51
great tree, Egypt as, 241
Greek thought, 63, 107, 128, 130, 190n1
Greenberg, Moshe, 130n7, 220n6, 251n9, 263n1
Gregory the Great, 23n17, 24, 32, 43, 299–300,
    301n4, 331n2
ground, 276, 278
guilt offerings, 332

Hades, 250n5
hair, 56, 57, 61
Hamutal, 151
hand of the Lord, 28, 32, 50
Hauerwas, Stanley, 76n6, 192
hearing, 35
heart, 111, 112, 114
heart of flesh, 98, 279
heart of stone, 98, 279
heaven, 33, 37, 39, 251
heaven and earth, 38
heavenly throne, 90
Hebrew, 26
Heidegger, Martin, 82n8
Hermann, Siegfried, 19n6
high places, 64–65
hill sanctuaries, 64–65
Hiram, 210, 218n1
historical-critical methods, 22–23, 86, 102, 198–99,
    226n5, 328
historical Jesus, 86
history, 48–49, 94–95. *See also* God, and history
  as apocalyptic, 86–87, 242
  as reactive, 106
  and stories, 243

Hittites, 127
holiness, 161, 292, 293, 307–8, 313
Holiness Code, 179, 316
holiness laws, 316–18, 320, 325
holy and common, 318–19, 332–33
Holy Spirit, 18
Hophra, 237
house of bondage, 227
house of David, 138, 152
house of Israel, 102, 162, 225, 300–301, 302, 307
  resurrection of, 266–67
human dung, 56, 61
humbling, of exalted, 172
hypostasis, 43

idolatry, 36, 81–82, 83, 116–19, 159, 179, 183,
    277, 307
idols, 65–66
images, 130
imagination, 111n1
immanent Trinity, 143n4
immortality of the soul, 71–72, 251
incarnation, 39, 40, 49, 91, 142, 159, 195, 199
individual, and community, 52, 145–48
indwelling of Spirit, 279
inferna, 252
"inhabitants of Jerusalem", 125
iniquity, 117
injustice, 133
inner court, 80, 301–2, 309, 312, 315, 328, 331,
    332
inspiration, 23, 176
intermediate state, 251
interpolation, 102–3
inwardness, 111, 112
Irenaeus, 42n4
Isaac, 272
Isaiah, 182, 300n1
Israel. *See also* rebellious house, Israel as
  blinding and deafening of, 100
  election of, 155–56
  and Lord's glory, 271
  new faithfulness, 306
  as personal name, 68
  recreation of, 99
  resurrection of, 281–84
  as single diachronic entity, 47
  slavery in Egypt, 260
  unfaithfulness, 66, 155, 193, 206, 275
  unity of, 288
  as whoring bride, 190–91
  in wilderness, 191
Israel (modern state), 274n10

Jacob/Israel, 272, 288
Japheth, 291
Jebusites, 127
Jehoahaz, 21, 151
Jehoiachin, 21, 138, 207, 263n1
Jehoiakim, 21, 74, 80, 93, 191, 201
Jenni, Ernst, 310
Jeremiah, 21, 74, 201, 225, 264, 275n1
Jerusalem, 170
    as bloody city, 177–79, 200–201
    as bride, 126, 128–29
    exalted status, 60
    faithlessness, 125, 126, 131, 132, 134
    fall of, 21, 55–56, 59–61, 112, 123, 166, 185,
        260, 272
    false hopes for, 122
    God's departure from, 88–89
    idolatries of, 83
    restoration of, 344–46
    sins of, 126
    as a pot, 182, 198–201
    in vision, 79–80
    as whoring bride, 190–93
Jesus
    ascension of, 142
    baptism of, 336
    crucifixion of, 123, 140, 188, 219
    descent of, 252
    as fulfillment of promises, 108–9
    glory of, 142–43
    as Good Shepherd, 262, 265–68
    humility of, 142–43, 180
    as new Israel, 99
    as prince, 314, 326
    resurrection of, 123, 131, 188, 285
    sacrifice of, 326
    suffering of, 195, 267n6
Jesus of Nazareth, 43
Jesus Seminar, 85n4
Jewish revolt, 22
Job, 120, 122
John the Baptist, 278, 335
Joseph, 227
Joseph (dominating tribe), 287
Josiah, 21, 65, 74, 80, 151, 188, 261, 317, 318n4
Jubilee, 329
Judah (southern kingdom), 20, 21
    as sister to Samaria, 195, 196n2
Judah (tribe), 340
judgment, 66, 74, 75, 81, 85, 104, 134, 179
    after destruction of Jerusalem, 260
    and love, 183–84, 235
    in new exodus, 266

judicial proceeding, 177
justice, 52–53, 123
just war, 178, 225

kabod, 41, 43, 67, 169, 224, 270–71
Kant, Immanuel, 146
kerygma, 105
killing, 178
kinah, 150–52, 213, 215–16, 220, 244–47, 248
kingdom of God/heaven, 71, 109, 232, 273, 303–4,
    336
knowledge, and love, 337
Korah, 89

lament, 150–52, 161
Lamentations, 21
land, 69–70, 185–86, 320–21, 328, 329, 339
    defiling of, 275–76
last judgment, 212
late modernity, 317
    on blessings and curses, 94
    on history, 48, 76–77
    on idolatry, 82
    on individualism, 148
law, 117–18, 123, 179, 307–8
law and gospel, 125, 298
Lebanon, 339
Levenson, Jon, 158, 272
Levi, 343
Levites, 317–18, 321, 343
lewdness, 196
liberal theology, 86, 146, 224, 235, 238
liberation, 66
liberation theology, 187, 260
life, 147, 177
lifeblood, 61n8, 178, 179
light theophanies, 42
lion, pharaoh as, 245
lioness and cubs, 151
"little temple", 97
liver, of sacrificed animal, 171
loathsome animals, 80
Logos, 35, 44, 50, 295
Lord, 29. *See also* God
    departure from Jerusalem, 88–89
    faithfulness of, 135
    fairness of, 148–49, 254
    jealousy of, 61, 62–63, 66, 298
    as king, 161
    presence beyond temple, 97
    universal lordship of, 121, 146, 206
    as warrior, 224

Lot, 122
love, 128, 183–84, 235
Lubac, Henri de, 23n18
Lutheranism, 91, 298, 308n1
Luther, Martin, 35, 77, 115, 141, 159, 163, 239, 257

magic, 113–15
Magog, 291, 295
Maimonides, 18
Manasseh, 343
mapping of Israel, 339–41, 343
Marduk, 246, 271
mark on forehead, 84
marriage ceremonies, 128
Marxism, 187, 317
mashal, 107, 138, 140, 145, 164, 199
mask, 141–42, 239
Masoretes, 26
Masoretic text, 56, 81n6, 182, 245
meal communion, 332
Medes, 176
mediator, 42
Memphis, 235
Merkabah, 39, 90, 140, 154
Meshech-Tubal, 249–50, 252, 291
Mesopotamia, 20
messenger-word, 28
Messiah, 152–53, 232, 326, 329
metaphor, 41n2, 201, 231
  resurrection as, 283–84
mishkan, 289
Mishnah, 25n26
Moab, 207, 208, 271
model, of Jerusalem, 56, 59
modernity, 38, 65, 176, 178
  on autonomy, 146
  on disinterest of God, 63
  on god with no purposes, 274
  on history, 48, 76–77, 86, 291
  theology of, 108–9
  on universe as system, 238
  utopian delusion of, 317
modern theology, on justice, 255
Molech, 130, 196
Moloch, 121
Moltmann, Jürgen, 188n5
monarchy, 264–65, 323, 341
  reunification of, 287–88
monotheism, 219
Mosaic law, development of, 328
Moses, 66, 85

most holy place, 36, 67, 79, 80–81, 89–90, 302n7,
  303, 306, 309, 328, 334
Moth, 250
mountain, 143
mountains of Israel, 64, 273, 293
Mount of Olives, 335
mourning, 46
Mowinckel, Sigmund, 74n3
mystery, 292n5
mystery of iniquity, 53, 115
myth, 213n8, 220–22, 242, 247

name of the Lord, 27, 40, 306
narrative succession, 295
National Socialism, 86, 317
nations, 121–22, 291
  blessing of, 135
natural law, 121
nature and grace, 217
navel of cosmos, 60
Nebuchadnezzar, 21, 60, 66, 74, 103, 138, 139, 142,
  152, 168, 171, 173, 175
  attack against Egypt, 231, 234, 236–39, 243
  defeat of Tyre, 211–13, 230–31
  as instrument of Lord, 206
necromancy, 251
Negeb, 165
neo-Protestantism, 109
new covenant, 135, 288n4, 289
new creation, 71, 99, 131
new exodus, 162, 265–66, 287
new heart, 97, 98, 303
new heaven and new earth, 303
new Israel, 143, 226
new Jerusalem, 89, 346
new moons, 328
Nicene Creed, 43n6, 142
Nicodemus, 99
Nile, 228, 234, 245
Nineveh, 177
Noah, 120–21, 122
nonbeing, 249
nonsupersessionism, 109
north, 291
northern kingdom, 20, 85, 97, 287
Noth, Martin, 19n6
nouvelle théologie, 217n3

obedience, and commission, 47
offerings to the temple, 324
Oholah and Oholibah, 190–92, 195, 197
Old Testament, 25

one and the many, 193
ontotheology, 82n8
open theism, 238
oracles, against enemy nations, 207, 270
ordinances, 309–11. *See also* statutes and ordinances
Origen, 24, 35, 113, 127n1, 128, 176, 314
oth, 57–58, 59, 61, 64, 100, 101–2, 104, 119, 124,
    164, 170, 200, 202, 258, 271, 286–87
Otto, Rudolf, 292n5
outer court, 301n1, 305, 314, 317, 319, 328, 332

pacifism, 225
paganism, 81–82, 219, 221
Pannenberg, Wolfhart, 87n8
parables, of Jesus, 138–39
parousia, delay of, 109
Passover, 195, 324
peace, 112–13, 192, 289
Pedersen, Johannes, 98n5
Pelatiah, 94
Pentecost, 284
people, 327–29
permission, 38, 157
Persia, 22, 176, 284, 292
personal names, 67
perversity, 85
pestilence, 120
phalluses, 130
Pharaoh, 228–29, 237, 240–41, 245
Pharaoh Neco, 21, 138, 151
Philistia, 207, 208, 339
Phoenicia, 252
physical transportation, 48, 79, 92
picture word, 124, 181
pity, 128
plagues, 247
plain meaning, 176
plants, 138, 141–43
platforms, 129
Plato, 72, 107, 128, 190n1
Plotinus, 190n1
poetry, 167–68, 171, 194–95, 199–200
"policy advisors", 92–93
politics, 187, 242, 265–66, 341–42
pollution, 56, 61, 65–66, 179, 194, 196, 200,
    276–78, 307
polytheism, 117
poor, 187, 225
postmodernity, 178
pot. *See* cooking pot
prayer, 311
predestination, 119, 128, 156

preferential option for poor, 187, 225
premodern exegesis, 23–24, 176, 199, 314
premodern theology, 108–9
pride, 133
priesthood, reform of, 316–19
priestly tradition, 42n3, 70, 99
prince, 264, 313–14, 324–26, 327, 329, 341
    of Tyre, 218–19
principalities and powers, 243
process theology, 238
promise, 38, 97–99, 108–9, 273–74, 339
prophecy, 199
    composed after the fact, 102
    fulfillment of, 106–8
    speech, and event, 258
prophets, 18–19
    commissioning of, 46
    and eschatology, 162
    as interceders, 85, 112
    and repentance, 183
prosperity, 266, 273
prostitution, 129, 191
pseudonymity, 102
purification, 179, 276, 325
Puritan movements, 319
Put, 292

queen of Sheba, 129, 138

Rabbah, 170, 175–76
rabbinic Judaism, 24, 25n26, 39, 60, 209, 283
rabbis, 22
Rad, Gerhard von, 250, 318n4
Rashi, 24, 28, 211n4, 219n3, 228n2, 231n1, 240n1,
    242n5, 245n2, 250, 260, 266n4, 292, 293n6,
    293n8, 294n9, 300n1, 301n6, 306, 311, 314n1,
    340
rebellious house, Israel as, 47, 55, 100, 101, 139,
    149, 154, 186, 199, 275, 316
refining, 182–83
Reformation, 298, 311
Reformed, 91, 298
register of Israel, 113
religion, 117
religious experence, 161
remembering, 66, 308
remnant, 56, 66, 180, 183, 260
repentance, 66, 112, 148–49, 165, 183, 253-54,
    270, 298n3, 324
restoration, 97, 134, 207, 225–26, 254, 259, 270,
    275, 280, 287, 298
resurrection, 44, 71, 251, 281–85, 312, 346

retributive divine justice, 255
revelation, 32
Revelation (book), 83
riddle, 138–40, 141
righteousness, 51–52, 120–23
river of the water of life, 334–36
Roman Catholicism, 288, 311
Roman Empire, 22
ruach, 48, 279, 283
Rubenstein, Richard L., 77n7
rule of faith, 105
rust, 201

Sabbath, 157, 328
sacramental ordination, 46
sacraments, 57–58, 114–15, 280, 311
sacrifice, 310–12, 328, 331
salvation, 134–36, 264, 286, 308
Samaria, 133–34, 190–93, 195, 196n2
Samson, 138
Sartre, Jean-Paul, 67n5
scattering, of people, 180
Schleiermacher, Friedrich, 109
Scholasticism, 239
Schweitzer, Albert, 86
scroll, 46
secondary causes, 238
second exodus. *See* new exodus
Second Isaiah, 186, 195, 206, 225, 344
Second Temple, 22, 186, 301n6, 332n4
Second Vatican Council, 217n3, 288
seeing, 35, 257
Seir, 271n6, 273
self-exaltation, 219
sentinel, 51, 116, 254–55
Septuagint, 26, 56, 81n6, 228nn1–2, 295n11
sexual immorality, 133, 179, 196
sexuality, 82, 192–93, 196-97
shamanistic flights, 79
Shekinah, 27, 90, 289, 306, 309, 336
Sheol, 214, 243, 249–52, 291, 293
shepherds, 263–68
Shiloh, 172–73n12
ship, Tyre as, 215–16, 220, 241
Shoah, 77, 208–9
showbread, 302
Sidon, 207, 223–26, 228
signs, 56–57, 59, 64, 258
silence, 205, 257–58
silver, 181–82
sin, 159
sin offering, 325

skepticism, about prophecy, 106–8, 111
smelting pot, 181–82
social justice, 93, 187
Sodom, 122, 133–34
Solomon
    dedicatory prayer, 39–40
    splendor of, 129
    temple, 302–3
Son
    and theophanies of Old Testament, 43
    as Word and image of God, 34, 43
Song of Songs, 63, 129n4, 192
son of a man, 28–29, 51
sons of Zadok, 317
soul, 67–68, 98
southern kingdom. *See* Judah (southern kingdom)
sower, parable of, 138–39
Spinoza, Baruch, 238n7
spiritual body, 312
Stalin, Joseph, 246
starvation, 56
statutes and ordinances, 60, 61–62, 146, 157, 307–8
Stephen, 127, 154
sticks, 286–87
stories, 243
storm, 36–37, 213
stumbling block, 51, 53
suffering, 52
suffering servant, 142, 283
supernature, 217
supersessionism, 209, 274n9, 278n6
superstition, 114
sword, 65, 164, 165, 167, 168, 170, 171, 174, 234, 255
sword-razor, 56, 61
sycamore, 241
syncretism, 65
Syria-Palestine, 20–21, 74, 190, 210–11, 288

Tabor, 44–45
Tammuz, 80
Targum, 24, 33, 39, 46–47, 71, 81n6, 113, 130, 148n4, 152nn3–5, 158, 171–72, 180n3, 192n7, 200n2, 208, 216n1, 241n2, 246n4, 250, 254n1, 270, 273, 278, 282n1, 289, 297n2, 298n3, 306, 324n2, 340
Tel-abib, 48
temple, 39–40
    destruction of, 22, 204
    as exile's love, 203
    pollution of, 84
    return of glory to, 305
    theology of, 344

temple prostitution, 80n4, 126, 130
Ten Commandments, 60, 118, 145, 147, 179, 307
teraphim, 171
Tertullian, 142n1
Testament of the Twelve Patriarchs, 85
theocracy, 341
theodicy, 123
theological exegesis, 23
theophanies, and Son, 43
throne, 37–40, 41, 88–90, 97, 312, 366
"thus says the Lord", 57
Tiamat, 246
time, 76, 178, 238–39
Togarmah, 291
Torah, 22, 60, 307
Torah/prophecy and sacrifice, 115
totems, 138
tour, of idolatry, 83
Toynbee, Arnold, 48n1
transfiguration, 44–45
Transjordan, 339
transportation. *See* physical transportation
tree, 142–43
tribal allotments, 340–41
Trinity, 25, 33–34, 42–43, 50, 142, 143, 184, 189, 199, 207, 306
true prophecy, 113
twelve tribes of Israel, 340
two diverging roads, 170
Tyre, 207, 210–14, 215–17, 218–22, 223, 230–31, 241, 291

uncircumcised, 250, 317
United States, 242
unrighteousness, 255
Uriah, 127
Urim and Thummim, 171n6

valley, 54–55
Valley of the Travelers, 294
vaticinia ex eventu, 102–3
vendetta, 178n1
vengeance, 178n1, 200
vine and branch, 124–25, 151–53
violence, 75–77, 104n1, 192, 225, 295
vision, 32, 33–34, 257

wailing, 233
wall of Jerusalem, fragility of, 112
war, 74–75, 120, 295
watery chaos, 213–14, 246
weight, 42, 297
Westermann, Claus, 310
Western theology, 44, 91, 201, 311
Western tradition, 48–49
wheels, 38
whole burnt offering, 331
whoring, 129–31, 191
wicked, death of, 254
wickedness, 51, 93, 104
wife, of Ezekiel, 202–3, 256
wild beasts, 120
wilderness, 120, 162, 191, 335
wilderness generation, 157
will of God and human will, 101, 119
wisdom literature, 124
woe, 46
women prophets, 113–14
word and sacrament, 114–15
word event, 94
word of God, 25, 27, 50, 207, 212, 258, 306
and vision of God, 33–34
words, 57
world-mountain, 143
world to come, 303
World War I, 86
World War II, 86, 209
wrath of God, 61, 62–63, 71, 183, 188

yhwh, 29

Zadokite priest, 317, 318, 321
Zedekiah, 21, 93, 102, 138, 139, 140, 151–52, 171–72, 175–76, 191, 201, 263n1
Zephaniah, 74, 75, 186n3
Zeus, 219
Zimmerli, Walther, 23, 80n3, 122n1, 152n3, 176n3, 198–99, 228n2, 237n2, 250n5, 291n3
Zion, 344
Zulus, 260

SCRIPTURE INDEX

Acts

2:9–11 22
2:14–18 105
2:14–21 279
2:16–18 49, 205
2:20–21 247
3:24 24, 293
7 127
19:28 129

Amos

1:1 35
5:18–20 74, 231
7:14 18n4

1 Chronicles

5:4 291
11:4 127
28:18 39n5

2 Chronicles

9:29 32

Colossians

1:15 34

1 Corinthians

1:28 282
3:12–15 163
3:15 308
10–11 345

13:12 34
15:44 312

2 Corinthians

5:1–5 251
5:17 99

Daniel

2:27 18n3
4:10–12 242
7:1–14 86
7:10 84
7:13 28n31
10:7 32, 33n8

Deuteronomy

5 66
5:4 162
7:6–8 156
10:18 187
12:5–11 40
16 324–25
22:24 196
26:5–9 127, 155
26:8 162
30:15–20 157
30:19 51
32:39 250
33:26 37

Ephesians

3:3–9 159

3:10 243
5:31–32 193

Exodus

1:8 227
7:3–5 119
14:4 224
14:17–18 224
15:3 76
15:8–12 48
15:20 113
19:1–23:19 158
19:5 289
19:6 162
19:9 34
20:1–17 118
20:5 117, 145
20:11-17 60
22:18 114
22:29 157, 158
23:27 168
28:17–20 220n6
28:30 171n6
3:6 66
3:14 29n35
3:15 67
33:20 34, 42
34:14 61
34:19–20 158
40:34 27

Ezekiel

1–24 206
1–32 280, 298
1:1 20nn7–8, 31, 32, 257
1:1–3 26, 31, 37, 38, 47, 48, 77, 79, 83, 198, 204, 212, 291, 299, 344
1:1–21 96
1:1–24 39
1:1–28 26
1:2 20
1:2–3 31, 32
1:4 31, 32, 33, 88
1:4–24 17, 41, 42, 54, 97, 140, 270, 302
1:4–26 90
1:4–28 154, 305
1:4–3:15 50
1:8–17 90
1:13 88
1:15 38, 39
1:22 38
1:25–28 26, 27, 28, 34, 39, 67, 89, 140, 169, 224, 267, 297, 313, 316, 345
1:25–3:15 306
1:26 41
1:26–28 79
1:28 41, 305
1:28–3:15 52, 92, 275, 279, 283, 316
2:1 46
2:1–10 55
2:2 279, 305
2:8–3:3 46
3:12–15 46
3:15 26, 31, 205
3:16 50
3:16–21 50, 54, 103, 116, 254
3:20 51
3:22 50
3:22–5:4 59, 64, 100, 104, 119, 124, 170, 202, 223, 228, 258, 271, 286
3:22–5:17 54
3:23 54
3:25 56
3:26–27 205
3:27 54
4–36 335
4:1–5:4 137

4:3 57
4:6 229
5:2–4 56
5:5 54, 56, 122
5:5–17 56, 58, 59, 62, 84, 101, 137, 147, 157, 179, 307
5:8 60
5:9 61
5:13–17 61
5:17 54
6 64
6:1–14 163, 269, 291, 317–18
6:8 66
6:9 66
6:11 64, 65
7 64, 69, 83
7–8 196
7:1–2 69
7:1–9 73, 98, 99, 125, 174, 178, 272, 284, 291
7:2–4 69, 70, 73
7:2–7 172
7:3–4 70
7:4 69
7:5 69
7:5–9 69, 70, 73
7:7 71
7:9 69
7:10–11 75
7:10–12 233
7:10–17 71, 186, 297
7:10–27 69, 107, 112, 113, 125, 166, 172, 178, 186, 231, 233, 238, 262, 265, 271, 293, 294, 344
7:14 75
7:24 75
7:27 69, 75
8 60
8:1 69, 79
8:1–18 83, 84, 88, 92, 96, 154, 282
8:1–11:25 278
8:3 48, 79, 84
8:4 79, 89
8:5–10:22 83
8:5–17 79
8:6 80
8–10 78
8–11 78, 92, 300, 301, 306, 318
9 79
9–10 78

9:1–11 88, 109
9:3 79, 84
9:9 88
9:10 84
10:1 89, 90
10:1–22 79, 84, 305, 306
10:2 89n1
10:2–7 79
10:3–5 89
10:4–5 89
10:13 89
10:18–19 90
10:20–22 90
10:21 90
11 116
11:1 78
11:1–13 96
11:1–21 78
11:1–22 92
11:2 92n1
11:3 144, 199, 200
11:6 93, 97
11:14 92
11:14–16 93
11:14–21 111n1, 279
11:17–20 97
11:22–25 78, 83, 84, 90, 305, 306
11:25 79
12:1–16 100, 119
12:3 102
12:3–5 100
12:4–6 102
12:8–9 101
12:10 102
12:10–20 101
12:12 102, 168
12:12–13 102
12:12–14 102
12:14–15 103
12:16 103
12:17–20 100, 2
12:21–22 107
12:21–25 106, 111
12:22 144
12:24 171
12:26–28 106, 111
13 116
13:1–16 112, 115
13:1–23 106, 111, 112
13:2 111
13:3 112

13:4–5 112
13:5 112
13:6 112
13:9 113, 118
13:10 112
13:12–20 120
13:17 111, 113
13:17–23 112, 115
13:19 114
13:22–23 114
14:1 111
14:1–11 116
14:3 116
14:4 117
14:4–5 118
14:5 118
14:6 118
14:8 118, 119
14:12 116
14:12–20 122, 123
14:13 121
14:21 122
14:22–23 123
15 181
15–17 137, 150
15:1–8 164
15:2–5 124
15:6 125
15:6–8 124–25
15:7 125
15:8 125
16 126, 155n1, 189
16:1–14 130
16:1–43 80n4, 132, 133, 134,
    141, 151, 152, 161, 168, 179,
    191, 196
16:3 127
16:4–8 127
16:5 128
16:8 128
16:9–13 128
16:14 129
16:15 129
16:16 129n6
16:17 130
16:25 129
16:26–29 131
16:31 129
16:31–34 131
16:35–43 131
16:44 126, 132

16:44–63 80n4, 132, 137, 139,
    141, 151, 179, 191, 196
16:45–46 133
16:47 133
16:48–52 134
16:49–50 133
16:51–52 134
16:52 132
16:53 134
16:53–58 134
16:54 134
16:58 134
16:59–63 134
16:62–63 135
17 137, 150
17:1 138
17:1–10 137
17:1–21 140, 141, 164, 183
17:2–8 138
17:2–10 139
17:7 138
17:7–8 137
17:9–10 138
17:11–15 139
17:11–21 137, 141
17:12 139
17:13–18 139
17:19 140
17:21 137
17:22 141
17:22–24 137, 141, 187
17:24 143
18 150, 165
18:1–32 144, 254, 255
18:2 144
18:2–18 147
18:4 146
18:4–9 146
18:6 65, 147
18:6–8 146
18:10–11 146
18:10–13 146
18:14–18 146
18:15–17 146
18:19 144, 147
18:19–20 147
18:20 52
18:21–24 148
18:21–32 254
18:23 148, 188
18:25 144
18:29 148, 149

18:30–32 149
18:32 148
19:1–9 150
19:2–9 151
19:9 151
19:10 150
19:10–14 150, 151
19:12 152
19:14 150–51, 152
20:1–31 160, 161
20:3–4 155
20:5 155, 156, 157
20:5–6 190
20:5–8 155
20:5–29 155
20:5–31 189
20:7 156
20:8 156
20:8–13 155
20:9 156
20:10–12 157
20:11 157
20:13 157
20:13–31 155
20:15–16 157
20:21–22 157
20:23–24 157
20:25 52, 154, 157
20:26 157, 158
20:28 157
20:28–29 159
20:30–31 159
20:31 155
20:32 154, 160
20:33 183
20:33–38 265
20:34–38 162
20:37–38 162
20:39 162
20:39–44 161
20:41 161
20:42 162
20:43 163
20:44 163
20:45–21:7 164n1
20:45–21:32 164
20:45–48 164
20:45–49 164
20:49 164, 165
21:1–5 164, 165
21:2–22:16 60
21:6 166

21:6–7 164
21:7 165, 166
21:8–9 167
21:8–11 168
21:8–13 167
21:8–17 167, 176, 213, 234
21:8–27 175
21:9–11 175
21:10 167
21:12 168
21:13 167
21:14 168
21:14–17 167
21:15 168
21:17 167, 168
21:18–19 170
21:18–27 170n1
21:20 170
21:20–23 170
21:21–23 171, 175
21:22 171n5
21:23 171, 173
21:24–27 170, 171
21:25 172
21:26 172
21:27 172
21:28 175–76
21:28–29 175
21:28–32 174, 175
21:29 175
21:30 175, 176
22 180, 185, 187
22:1–16 276
22:1–31 196
22:3 177
22:3–4 178
22:3–5 177
22:4 178
22:6–8 179
22:6–12 177, 178, 179
22:9–11 179
22:12 178, 179
22:13–16 177, 179–80
22:14 179
22:15 179
22:16 180
22:17–22 181
22:18 181, 182
22:19–20 182
22:19–22 181
22:21 182
22:21–22 183

22:23–31 185, 186
22:24 185
22:25–29 186
22:30–31 187
23 99, 189
23:1–27 189, 194, 196, 197
23:5–10 190
23:7 192
23:11–21 190
23:19–20 191
23:22 190
23:22–27 191, 193
23:24 193
23:28–31 194
23:28–49 194, 189
23:32 195
23:32–34 194
23:35 195
23:36–45 195
23:44–45 195
23:46–49 196, 197
23:48 196
23:49 196
24 256
24:1 199
24:3 200
24:3–5 199
24:6 200, 201
24:6–8 200
24:6–14 200
24:7 200–201
24:8 201
24:9 200
24:9–10 201
24:10 201
24:11 201
24:12 200
24:13 201
24:14 201
24:15–27 256
24:16–17 202
24:19 203
24:21 203
24:21–24 203
24:22–23 204
24:24 31n1, 204, 267–68
24:25–26 204
24:26–27 256
25–27 204
25–32 174, 206, 207, 210, 215,
    218, 223, 227, 230, , 233,
    236, 240, 244, 248

25:1–17 97, 210, 215, 223, 225,
    227, 233, 236, 240, 244, 248,
    252, 253, 256, 259, 270,
    286, 300
25:3 208
25:4–5 206, 208
25:8 208
25:12 208
25:12–14 270
25:14 208, 271
25:15 208
26:1–6 210
26:1–21 215, 223, 230, 274
26:1–28:19 207, 218
26:3–5 211
26:4 211
26:5 212
26:5–6 211
26:7 211
26:7–14 210, 211, 213
26:8–15 211
26:14 212
26:15–18 210, 213
26:19–21 210, 213, 230
26:20 214
26:21 214
27:1–36 220, 245, 248
27:2 215
27:3 215, 216n2
27:3–9 216
27:4 216n2
27:4–36 241
27:9–11 215
27:11 215
27:12–25 216
27:13 291
27:25–36 216
27:29–36 216
27:32–36 215, 216
28:1–10 218
28:1–19 218, 228, 335
28:2 219
28:3 121
28:9 219
28:11–19 218, 220
28:12–15 220
28:13 220, 221
28:14 220, 221
28:15 220, 221
28:15–19 221
28:16 220
28:17 221

28:18 221
28:19 221
28:20–23 207, 223
28:20–26 218, 228, 231, 236,
    252
28:21 224
28:22 224
28:23 224
28:24 225
28:24–26 225
28:25–26 225
29 246
29–32 207, 233, 236, 240
29:1 230
29:1–16 228, 236, 240, 244,
    245, 246, 248
29:3 228
29:3–12 241
29:4 228
29:6–7 227, 228
29:8–9 228–29
29:9 228, 229
29:10–12 229
29:13–16 227, 229
29:17–21 212, 230, 232, 237
29:18 231
29:19–20 231
29:21 230, 231, 232, 233
30:1–19 237, 273
30:2–5 233
30:3 233
30:5 234
30:6–9 233, 234
30:9 234
30:10–12 233, 234
30:13 235
30:13–19 233, 235
30:19 235
30:20 230
30:20–21 237
30:20–26 237
30:21 236, 237
30:25 237
31:1–2 240
31:1–18 240, 246, 247, 273
31:3 241
31:3–9 240
31:4 241, 242
31:6 241
31:9 241–42
31:10–14 240, 242
31:12–13 242

31:14 242, 243
31:15 243
31:15–17 240, 243
31:16 243
31:18 240, 241
32 244, 248
32:1–16 248
32:2 244, 245, 249
32:2–15 244
32:3 245
32:3–10 245
32:4–10 245
32:7–10 247
32:11–15 245, 247
32:16 244, 245, 247
32:17 244
32:17–32 214, 243, 291, 293
32:18–19 249
32:19 249
32:20–32 249
32:21 250
32:27 250
32:28 249
32:29 249, 252
32:30 249, 252
32:31 195, 249
32:31–32 249
33 264
33–35 259
33–36 280
33–48 206, 264, 270, 298
33:1 255
33:1–20 254
33:2 255
33:2–6 253, 255
33:7–9 50, 253, 254
33:10 254
33:10–11 253
33:10–20 254
33:11 17, 148, 221, 250, 254
33:12–16 254
33:12–20 253
33:17–20 254
33:21–22 204, 256
33:22 204
33:23–33 259
33:24–29 259
33:25 260
33:26 260
33:27 259–60
33:28 260
33:30 261

33:30–33 259, 261
33:31 261
33:32 261
33:33 261
34 287, 291, 314
34–37 290, 296
34:1–10 264
34:1–31 288, 323, 325
34:2–6 263, 264, 265
34:2–10 265
34:5–6 264
34:6 264
34:7–10 263
34:10 265
34:11 264
34:11–16 265
34:12 265
34:15 265
34:17–19 266
34:18 266
34:20–22 266
34:23–24 266
34:24 264, 266, 267, 341
34:25–29 265, 268
34:31 268
34:32–24 329
35:1 269
35:1–15 269, 270
35:1–36:15 208, 269, 280
35:5 271, 272
35:5–6 270
35:5–9 271
35:6 270
35:10 270
35:10–14 270
35:10–15 273
35:12 271
35:12–14 273
35:14 271
36–37 290
36:1 269
36:1–7 273
36:1–15 269, 270
36:5 270
36:5–7 269
36:8–11 269
36:8–15 273
36:16–38 284, 288, 293–94,
    298, 303, 306–7, 316, 318
36:17 275
36:18 276
36:20–21 278

36:22 275
36:22–32 275
36:25 276
36:25–27 278
36:28 280
36:31 280
36:33 275
36:37 275
37 186
37:1–2 282
37:1–14 251, 280, 281, 345
37:3 153, 251
37:3–4 282
37:4–6 282
37:5–6 282
37:7–8 282
37:7–10 282
37:9 282, 283
37:9–10 282
37:11 266, 281, 282, 283
37:12 283
37:12–14 283
37:13–14 284
37:14 285
37:15 286
37:15–28 292
37:16–17 286
37:18–19 286
37:21–22 286, 287
37:23 286, 287
37:24–28 286, 288
37:25 341
37:27 289
38 291
38–39 290
38:1–2 291
38:1–39:20 290, 307, 312, 318, 325, 335
38:1–39:29 335n2
38:2 290
38:3–9 292
38:6 291
38:8 291
38:10–13 292
38:11–12 291
38:14 290, 292
38:14–16 292
38:15 291
38:16 292
38:17–23 292
38:21 293
39:1 290

39:1–6 294
39:1–16 293
39:4 294
39:6 292
39:7–8 293
39:9–10 293
39:11–16 293
39:13–16 294
39:14–15 294
39:17 290
39:17–20 293
39:18 294
39:21 296
39:21–24 296, 297, 298
39:21–29 294, 296, 307, 318
39:23 296
39:25 290, 297
39:25–29 296, 297, 298
39:26 298
39:28 298
40 24n22, 299
40–42 305, 307, 309, 321, 344
40–48 84, 278, 280, 289, 290, 296–97, 299, 305, 309, 313, 315, 320, 323, 325, 327, 345
40:1 300, 334
40:1–3 48
40:1–42:20 313, 305, 309, 314, 315, 319, 320, 321, 322, 325, 327, 329, 331, 334, 335, 338, 341, 345
40:1–47:12 343
40:2 307
40:2–4 300–301
40:5 300
40:47 301, 309
40:48–41:4 302
41:3–4 302
41:12 302n9
41:21–22 302
42 309
42:15–20 301
42:20 303
43:1 305
43:1–5 90
43:1–12 309
43:3 306
43:4–6 315
43:7 306
43:9 307
43:10 305
43:10–12 307

43:13–17 309
43:13–27 325
43:18–27 309, 310
43:20 310
44:1 313
44:1–3 313, 315, 328, 334
4:3 313, 332
44:4 313, 327
44:4–5 315, 316
44:4–6 331
44:4–31 320, 323, 324, 327, 332, 338
44:4–46:19 315
44:6 316
44:6–8 315, 323
44:6–46:18 329
44:7 316
44:8 316
44:9 320
44:9–31 317
44:9–45:8 315
44:10–12 317–18
44:10–14 317
44:14 317
44:15 318
44:15–17 318
44:15–31 317
44:16–17 317
44:17–19 318
44:20–27 318
44:20–31 318
44:22 328n2
44:23 318
44:25–27 318
44:28–30 318
45:1 320–21
45:1–8 315, 320, 329, 335, 341
45:6 321, 322
45:7–8 329
45:8 322, 323
45:9 320, 323
45:9–17 315, 323
45:9–25 323, 327, 328, 329
45:10–12 323–24
45:13 324
45:13–17 324
45:13–25 328
45:15–31 320
45:17 323
45:18 324
45:18–19 324
45:18–20 328n2

45:18–25 315, 324
45:20 324
45:21 324
45:21–25 324
45:25 324
45:28–25 323
46:1–15 315, 327, 328
46:4–5 328
46:6–7 328
46:11–12 328
46:13–15 328
46:16–18 315, 327, 327, 329
46:18 327
46:19 315, 331
46:19–20 331
46:19–24 338
46:20 331
46:21 331
46:21–24 332
47:1–12 278, 334, 338
47:3–5 335
47:8 335
47:11 335n1
47:13 320, 336, 338, 340
47:13–48:29 338, 341, 343
47:14 339
47:15–17 339
47:15–20 339
47:18 339
47:20 339
47:22–23 340
48 344
48:1 340
48:1–7 340
48:1–29 340, 345
48:6 340
48:8 341
48:8–11 345
48:8–14 320
48:10 341
48:10–14 321
48:18 341
45:18–20 324
48:23–29 340
48:30–35 299, 343
48:35 302

Galatians

4:4 329
5:22 62

Genesis

1 128, 213
1:1 213n7
1:1–2 295
1:1–2:3 57
1:2 213–14
1:2–3 213
1:14–15 221
2–3 220
2:7 276, 278, 281, 283
2:9 273
2:10–14 335
2:17 51, 281
3:17–18 278
3:19 249, 251
4:10 200
6 242
6–8 213
6:4 250n5
6:7 75, 77
6:13 70
6:17 75
9:14–15 178
9:20–23 120–21
10:2–5 291–92
12:3 98
15:18 135
16:7–12 27
17:2 135
17:5–7 135
18:22–23 122
19 133
22 272
22:9–18 27
25:30–33 272
27:1–33 272
31:19 171
32:3 272
36:1 272
49:10 172

Habakkuk

2:4 85

Hebrews

1:1 222
1:3 34
11:1 212

Hosea

1–6 130
1:2 130
3:1–3 203
8:5–6 133

Isaiah

1:24–25 181
2:2 98
2:2–4 300
6 37
6:1–4 305
6:1–5 89
6:1–10 46
6:8 177
6:9–10 100, 139
8:3 113
9:7 98, 113
11:9 143
13:6–9 74
20 57
32:1 153
36:6 228n1
37:19 160–61
40–66 186
40:8 212
43:8 100
44:28 206–7
51 344
51:1–3 260n1
51:17 195
52 142
52:7 113
53:8–9 283
57:5 158
60 346
61:1 279

Jeremiah

1:9–10 18, 282
2:2 155, 190
5:21 100
5:31 31
6:14 112–13
7:4 133
7:31 158
8:11 112–13
14:14 31
20 55
23:1–6 264
23:5 266

25:15–17 195
25:27–28 195
27 31
27:3 210n1
27–28 57
28:7–9 19n5
29:26 55
30:29–30 145n2
33:15 266
38:6–11 201
46:10 74

Job

4:13 33

Joel

2:28 33
2:28–29 279

John

1:1 212
1:1–14 34, 50
1:13 29
1:14 27
2:21 22n15
3:3–5 99
6:46 312
6:65 119
8:33 130
8:58 212
10:1–18 263
10:8 265
14:9 34
19:31 277

Joshua

13 340n5
13–21 320
15–19 340n5

Judges

4:4 113
7:2–7 192
13:2–23 27
14:12–19 138
17 65
17:5 171n7

1 Kings

1:26–45 317
2:35 317

3:2–5:5 27
5:1 210
8:13 39
8:30 40
10:1 138
10:1–5 129
20:13 207
20:28 207
22:22–23 158

2 Kings

25:1 198
25:4 102
25:7 152

Leviticus

16:29 324
17–26 179, 316
17:3 118
17:10 118
17:16 118
18:5 157
18:22–30 260n3
19:2 316
19:4 118
20:13 260n3
21:7 328n2
25:23 270n1
26:12 99, 267, 280

Luke

1:46–55 168
1:52 172
14:8–11 172

Malachi

3:3 181

Mark

2:15–17 172
4:3–10 138
7:5–23 319
9:2–8 44
10:25–27 135
12:27 251

Matthew

1:1–17 266
5:21–44 328
6:9–13 49

7:27 112
11:24 134
18:12 265
20–23 195
20:16 172
23:37 201
27:51–52 293

Micah

3:9–12 85
4:1 288
4:1–2 307
4:1–4 135
4:2 294–95

Nahum

3:1 177

Numbers

14:12–15 85
14:22–23 157
16:35 89
19:13–20 276
20:14–21 271
22 94
22–24 207
32 339
35:33 293–94
35:33–34 61n7

2 Peter

3:9 108

Philippians

2:12–13 101

Proverbs

7 196

Psalms

11:4 37, 40
18:8–14 37
88 251, 252
95:1–3 161
96–100 75
96:10–13 161
106 127
119:35 157
119:103 47

132:17 232
137:1–4 36

Revelation

4–5 311
4:1 33, 83
4:1–2 32
5:6 312
5:9–10 312
5:22 47
7:4–8 179–80
7:5–8 288
13:8 143
14:8 36n1
14:10 195
19:11–21 295
20:4–9 295
20:12 84
21:9–21 346
21:16–23 304
21:22 336
21:22–23 346
22:1–2 335–36

Romans

1:18 63
1:21 224
1:24–27 88
1:25 81
2:28–29 317
6:1–14 99
8:21 268
8:28–25 304
11:17 285
15:8 109

1 Samuel

8:5–7 160
8:5–18 264
16:2–5 332
16:6–13 155
16:14–23 158
21:1–6 302n8
28 251

2 Samuel

6:6–7 332
7:1–16 91

7:16 152
11:3–26 127
23:2 279

Song of Songs

8:6 63n9

1 Thessalonians

4:15–17 295

Zechariah

1:7 32
1:7–8 32n3
7:12 279n7
9:10 153
13:9 181
14:1–11 294–95
14:13 293n7

Zephaniah

1:2–4 75
1:4–9 74
1:14 74
3:3–4 187